THE ARCHAEOLOGY OF THE PAMPAS AND PATAGONIA

In this book, Gustavo G. Politis and Luis A. Borrero explore the archaeology and ethnography of the indigenous people who inhabited Argentina's Pampas and the Patagonia region from the end of the Pleistocene until the twentieth century. Offering a history of the nomadic foragers living in the harsh habitats of the South America's Southern Cone, they provide a detailed account of human adaptations to a range of environmental and social conditions. The authors show how the region's earliest inhabitants interacted with now-extinct animals as they explored and settled in the vast open prairies and steppes of the region until they occupied most of its available habitats. They also trace technological advances, including the development of pottery, the use of bows and arrows, and horticulture. Making new research and data available for the first time, Politis and Borrero's volume demonstrates how geographical variation in the Southern Cone generated diverse adaptation strategies.

GUSTAVO G. POLITIS is Researcher at the Consejo Nacional de Investigaciones Científicas y Técnicas (CONICET) of Argentina and Professor at the Universidad del Centro de la Provincia de Buenos Aires. A scholar of the archaeology and ethnoarchaeology of South American hunter-gatherers, he is the author of six books and recipient of a fellowship from the John Simon Guggenheim Foundation.

LUIS A. BORRERO is Researcher Emeritus at the National Council for Scientific and Technical Research and Professor Emeritus at the University of Buenos Aires, as well as International Member of the National Academy of Sciences of the United States. He is a specialist in vertebrate taphonomy and hunter-gatherer archaeology, particularly the peopling of South America.

CAMBRIDGE WORLD ARCHAEOLOGY

SERIES EDITOR

NORMAN YOFFEE, *University of Michigan*

GENERAL EDITORS

ADAM T. SMITH, *Cornell University*

NORMAN YOFFEE, *University of Michigan, Emeritus*

EDITORIAL BOARD

TOM DILLEHAY, *Vanderbilt University*

CORISANDE FENWICK, *University College London*

LINDSAY MONTGOMERY, *University of Toronto*

DMITRI NAKASSIS, *University of Colorado, Boulder*

FRANÇOIS RICHARD, *University of Chicago*

LIV NILSSON STUTZ, *Linnaeus University*

MIRIAM STARK, *University of Hawai'i*

DAVID WENGROW, *University College London*

ASTRID VAN OYEN, *Radboud University*

ALICE YAO, *University of Chicago*

The Cambridge World Archaeology series is addressed to students and professional archaeologists, and to academics in related disciplines. Most volumes present a survey of the archaeology of a region of the world, providing an up-to-date account of research and integrating recent findings with new concerns of interpretation. While the focus is on a specific region, broader cultural trends are discussed and the implications of regional findings for cross-cultural interpretations considered. The authors also bring anthropological and historical expertise to bear on archaeological problems and show how both new data and changing intellectual trends in archaeology shape inferences about the past. More recently, the series has expanded to include thematic volumes.

RECENT BOOKS IN THE SERIES

RICHARD BUSSMANN, *The Archaeology of Pharaonic Egypt: Society and Culture, 2700–1700 BC*

DOUGLAS B. BAMFORTH, *The Archaeology of the North American Great Plains*

RAPHAEL GREENBERG, *The Archaeology of the Bronze Age Levant*

KATINA T. LILLIOS, *The Archaeology of the Iberian Peninsula*

RICHARD BRADLEY, *The Prehistory of Britain and Ireland*

STEPHEN SHENNAN, *The First Farmers of Europe*

KOJI MIZOGUCHI, *The Archaeology of Japan*

ANTONIO SAGONA, *The Archaeology of the Caucasus*

D. T. POTTS, *The Archaeology of Elam*

ROBIN CONINGHAM and RUTH YOUNG, *The Archaeology of South Asia*

CLAUDIA SAGONA, *The Archaeology of Malta*

PETER MAGEE, *The Archaeology of Prehistoric Arabia*

FRANCES F. BERDAN, *Aztec Archaeology and Ethnohistory*

LUDMILA KORYAKOVA and ANDREJ EPIMAKHOV, *The Urals and Western Siberia in the Bronze and Iron Ages*

A. BERNARD KNAPP, *The Archaeology of Cyprus*

MIKE SMITH, *The Archaeology of Australia's Deserts*

LI LIU and XINGCAN CHEN, *The Archaeology of China*

STEPHEN D. HOUSTON and TAKESHI INOMATA, *The Classic Maya*

THE ARCHAEOLOGY OF THE PAMPAS AND PATAGONIA

GUSTAVO G. POLITIS
Universidad del Centro de la Provincia de Buenos Aires

LUIS A. BORRERO
Universidad de Buenos Aires

Shaftesbury Road, Cambridge CB2 8EA, United Kingdom

One Liberty Plaza, 20th Floor, New York, NY 10006, USA

477 Williamstown Road, Port Melbourne, VIC 3207, Australia

314–321, 3rd Floor, Plot 3, Splendor Forum, Jasola District Centre, New Delhi – 110025, India

103 Penang Road, #05-06/07, Visioncrest Commercial, Singapore 238467

Cambridge University Press is part of Cambridge University Press & Assessment, a department of the University of Cambridge.

We share the University's mission to contribute to society through the pursuit of education, learning and research at the highest international levels of excellence.

www.cambridge.org
Information on this title: www.cambridge.org/9780521768214

DOI: 10.1017/9780511993251

© Gustavo G. Politis and Luis A. Borrero 2024

This publication is in copyright. Subject to statutory exception and to the provisions of relevant collective licensing agreements, no reproduction of any part may take place without the written permission of Cambridge University Press & Assessment.

First published 2024

A catalogue record for this publication is available from the British Library.

Library of Congress Cataloging-in-Publication Data
NAMES: Politis, Gustavo, author. | Borrero, Luis Alberto, author.
TITLE: The archaeology of the Pampas and Patagonia / Gustavo G. Politis, Luis A. Borrero.
DESCRIPTION: Cambridge, United Kingdom ; New York, NY : Cambridge University Press, 2023. | SERIES: Cambridge world archaeology | Includes bibliographical references and index.
IDENTIFIERS: LCCN 2023019827 (print) | LCCN 2023019828 (ebook) | ISBN 9780521768214 (hardback) | ISBN 9780511993251 (epub)
SUBJECTS: LCSH: Prehistoric peoples–Argentina–Patagonia. | Prehistoric peoples–Argentina–Pampas | Indians of South America–Argentina–Patagonia. | Indians of South America–Argentina–Pampas. | Excavations (Archaeology)–Argentina–Patagonia. | Excavations (Archaeology)–Argentina–Patagonia.
CLASSIFICATION: LCC F2821.1.P29 P65 2023 (print) | LCC F2821.1.P29 (ebook) | DDC 982/.701–dc23/eng/20230512
LC record available at https://lccn.loc.gov/2023019827
LC ebook record available at https://lccn.loc.gov/2023019828

ISBN 978-0-521-76821-4 Hardback

Cambridge University Press & Assessment has no responsibility for the persistence or accuracy of URLs for external or third-party internet websites referred to in this publication and does not guarantee that any content on such websites is, or will remain, accurate or appropriate.

To Ingrid

To Fabiana

CONTENTS

Acknowledgments .... *page* xi

1   **Introduction** 1
     Present and Past Environments   4
     The Pampas and Patagonia as Geographical Units for
     Archaeological Analysis   10
     Supra-Regional Significance of the Archaeology of the Pampas
     and Patagonia   24

2   **Historical Background** 27
     The Early Years   27
     The First Shift: Toward a More Scientific Archaeology   43
     The Austrian-German Cultural-History School: A New Paradigm
     Arrives at the Pampas and Patagonia   52
     The Theoretical Alternatives in the 1960s   58
     The Decade of the 1980s: New Directions   63

3   **Resources: Prey, Plants, and Stones** 67
     Faunal and Floral Resources   68
     Lithic Raw Materials   78
     Lithic Raw Materials in the Pampas   81
     Lithic Procurement in Patagonia   96
     Other Stones in Patagonia   101
     Final Remarks   112

4   **The Early Peopling: The Late Pleistocene to Early Holocene** 115
     The Pampas   115
     Patagonia   132
     Final Remarks   151

5   **The Middle Holocene (~ 8200–4200 cal BP; ~ 7500–3800 BP)** 157
     The Pampas   158
     Patagonia   177
     Final Remarks   191

ix

6	The Late Holocene Diversification (~ 4200 cal BP to ~ 400 cal BP; ~ 3800 to ~ 400 BP)	194
	The Pampas	196
	Patagonia	215
	The Contact Period and the Colonial Times	235
7	Final Remarks	245
	The Early Peopling	246
	Demographic Dynamics along the Holocene	257
	The Late Holocene: Innovations, Diversification, and Intensification	265
	Lithic Resources, Territory, and Mobility	270
	Ethnicity and Territory	276
	Final Remarks	283

Select Bibliography 285

Full bibliography available at www.cambridge.org/politis borrerofullbibliography.

Index 311

ACKNOWLEDGMENTS

First of all, we have been lucky enough to be invited by Tom Dillehay and Norman Yoffee to publish this book in the prestigious World Archaeology series of Cambridge University Press. We are particularly grateful to both for being encouraging and patient throughout the long (too long) writing process. Otherwise, this book would never have been written.

The content of many chapters was discussed with Paula Barros, Juan Bautista Belardi, Mariano Bonomo, Karen Borrazzo, Manuel Carrera Aizpitarte, Nora V. Franco, Fabiana Martin, Gustavo Martínez, Diana Mazzanti, and Pablo Messineo, and many more friends and colleagues patiently answered specific questions. All of them significantly contributed to the final version.

Many friends and colleagues shared photos and figures with us to illustrate this book: Margarita Alvarado, Maria Clara Álvarez, Pablo Ambrústolo, Ramiro Barberena, Juan Bautista Belardi, Mónica Berón, Mariano Bonomo, Florencia Borella, Karen Borrazzo, Patricia Campan, Analía Castro Esnal, Nora Flegenheimer, Nora V. Franco, María A. Gutiérrez, Heidi Hammond, Fabiana Martin, César Méndez, Laura Miotti, Osvaldo L. Mondelo, Flavia Morello, Rafael Paunero, Luciano Prates, Omar Reyes, Martín Vázquez, Guadalupe Romero Villanueva, Atilio F. Zangrando, Leandro Zilio, and Mikel Zubimendi.

We also want to thank many people who have helped us in different matters for this book. Milagros Rios Malán organized and checked the bibliography and helped with the radiocarbon database, and Luciano Prates shared with us the database he compiled for the earliest period. S. Ivan Perez ran the database and generated the summed calibrated probability density (SCPD) curve.

Juan Manuel Capuano, Diego Gobbo, and Rocío Torino drew the maps and improved the illustrations. Cecilia Pallo prepared the Patagonian maps.

One of us (GP) was benefited by the intellectual atmosphere and the daily interaction with researchers and fellows of the Instituto de Investigaciones Arqueológicas y Paleontológicas del Cuaternario Pampeano (INCUAPA), of CONICET and the Universidad Nacional del Centro de la Provincia de

Buenos Aires, and those of the División Arqueología del Museo de la Plata, Universidad Nacional de La Plata, Argentina. The other (LAB) enjoyed the same benefits at the Instituto Multidisciplinario de Historia y Ciencias Humanas (IMHICIHU) from CONICET and at the Instituto de la Patagonia, Universidad de Magallanes, Chile.

The two of us are researchers at CONICET, the national research institution of Argentina, which has backed our work since our doctoral studies. We are extremely grateful to this institution for its constant support.

One of us (GP) made the final adjustment to the book while he was Scientific Fellow of the DFG Center for Advanced Studies "Words, Bones, Genes, Tools: Tracking Linguistic, Cultural and Biological Trajectories of the Human Past" at Tübingen University (Germany), directed by Katerina Harvati and Gerhard Jaeger, to whom I am grateful.

Finally, we want to recognize the work of countless archaeologists who have been investigating for more than 140 years in the Pampas and Patagonia. The results of their sustained research are what we summarize and discuss in this book, which is ultimately a tribute to all of them.

CHAPTER 1

INTRODUCTION

This book summarizes the current archaeological and ethnographic knowledge regarding the indigenous people who inhabited the South American Southern Cone since the end of the Pleistocene (Figure 1.1). This land, roughly between 32° and 56° S latitude, comprises the Pampas and Patagonia. Since the beginning of the European conquest in the sixteenth century, both regions have attracted the attention of conquerors and explorers even though there were no precious rocks or metals within them, nor were they inhabited by indigenous populations who could be easily exploited or subjugated to slavery or *encomiendas*. This is not to say that there were no fabulations – notably, the legend of the Ciudad de Los Césares, or Trapalanda, where supposedly fabulous riches could be found. This legend originated around the sixteenth century when stories after the inland trip by Francisco César, a captain from the Sebastian Gaboto expedition, began to circulate. Also, the castaways from the shipwreck of one of Francisco Camargo's expeditions fueled these legends. The sad reality was that no evidence existed about the fate of those castaways.

Except for the societies living in the Lower Paraná and Uruguay Rivers (Guaraní, Chaná, Timbú, etc.), all the others were nomadic foragers who hunted terrestrial mammals such as guanacos and Pampas deer and fished and collected mollusks on the Patagonian coast. Societies in Tierra del Fuego and the southern archipelagos hunted sea mammals, fished, and collected mollusks. Conversely, the Pampas and Patagonia have been a fascinating location not only for the study of past hunter-gatherers but also for theoretical reflection on the evolutionary scheme that anthropology and archaeology have used to define them. The Selk'nam and Yámana of Tierra del Fuego, considered to be "archetypically" "primitive" hunter-gatherers (Gamble 1992; Martinic 1995; Steward 1955; Vidal 1999), were seen in the dawn of anthropology as the prototype of primitive society.

Needless to say, nomadic foragers held little appeal for the economic ambition of European conquerors first and Hispanic-criollo people later.

Figure 1.1 Map showing the regions of the Southern Cone of South America.

Introduction 3

Only in the nineteenth century, with the industrial expansion of Europe and the subsequent need for raw material and new lands, were these vast territories effectively annexed to the national political control and introduced into the global market. The indigenous people who lived in these territories had a fascinating history of 14,000 years, which archaeology has uncovered mainly during the last decades. How did these people live? How did they explore and occupy new environments? What was the temporal and spatial variability of their basic foraging life throughout the millennia? How did some of these groups incorporate horticulture, and how did some adapt to live in the very harsh environment of the southern channels? How did they significantly change their mode of life since the Late Pleistocene times? This book aims to answer these questions.

The Pampas and Patagonia are among the main regions in South America. The former is an extensive grassland plain located in the eastern part of the South American Southern Cone, roughly between 32° and 39° S, comprising over 700,000 km² (Figure 1.1). Although several limits have been proposed based on different criteria, in this book we will consider the Pampas as the extended plains that border the Atlantic coast and the La Plata and Uruguay Rivers to the east; the Basaltic Plateau, the Salado-Desaguadero Rivers, and the foothills of the Central Hills to the west; and the Colorado River (including its paleo delta) to the south; and that has a diffuse border with the Chaco-Santiagueña Plains, marked by the xerophytic forest (the Spinal phytogeographic province, sensu Cabrera 1971) to the north. In Uruguay and southeastern Brazil, these prairies are called Campos or Uruguayan Pampas; to the north, they border the Brazilian Planalto at approximately 28° S.

The Pampas, a Quechua word that means plains or flatness, is a gentle, widespread prairie developed on loess deposits. Forests were limited, and the great majority of the land was treeless. However, nowadays, patches of foreign trees can be seen here and there. The climate varies from dry-tempered to sub-humid, with warm summers and rainfall distributed throughout the year. This vast prairie is interrupted, in the southern sector, by two major hill systems, Tandilia and Ventania, and smaller hilly ranges (Choique Mahuida, Lihué Calel, Calencó), as well as by several isolated hills, low rocky plateaus (e.g., El Fresco Plateau), and ridges with scattered rugged rock outcrops (especially in the southwest). The Pampas have traditionally been divided into two sub-regions, based on the 600 isohyets (although it has been moved to the west in the last decades): Humid Pampa to the east (with average rainfalls that reach 1,200 mm in the northeast) and Dry Pampa to the west (with a rainfall average of 400 mm in the southwest). To the south, the Pampas border the Colorado River, beyond which extends semi-arid Northeast Patagonia.

Patagonia's name originates with the identification of the Aónikenk with the giant Patagon from Spanish chivalry tales (Duviols 1997; Vidal de Battini 1975). Patagonia and Tierra del Fuego extend over more than 1 million square kilometers in Chile and Argentina in the southern extreme of South America. This large territory comprises a variety of environments that go from the foot of the Andes through dissected basaltic plateaus to the coasts of the Atlantic. As we will see, there are many ways of dividing this area, none of which is perfect.

Despite the long tradition of archaeological research in these regions, the knowledge of its prehistoric past is still uneven, providing an incomplete perspective on the indigenous historical trajectories. Therefore, the coverage of this book, in some ways, reflects this unevenness. Although it is focused on the Argentine Pampas and the whole of Patagonia, including Argentina and Chile, there are some references to the Campos of Uruguay, which integrates the same macro-region. Some cultural processes (the Late Pleistocene occupation, the *cerritos* phenomenon, the expansion of the Guaraní Indians, etc.) were shared by both regions.

In order to follow the international consensus, we set the subdivision of the Holocene defined based on physical and chemical markers (Walker et al. 2018). These reflect abrupt climatic events at the onset of the Holocene at ~ 11.7 cal BP, and later at ~ 8.2 cal BP and ~ 4.2 cal BP. Therefore, we will use these dates for the limits between the Late Pleistocene and Early Holocene, as well as for the boundaries between the Early and Middle Holocene, and the Middle and Late Holocene. We will also use BP for uncalibrated radiocarbon years before present, cal. BP for calibrated radiocarbon years before present, and kyr for thousands of years. All radiocarbon dates in the text will be cited without the statistical error, laboratory code, and type of sample dated. This information is detailed in the Supplementary Tables 1–6, found online (www .cambridge.org/politisborrero_tables1-6).

PRESENT AND PAST ENVIRONMENTS

The primary environment of the Pampas grasslands is a plain with a temperate climate, without a marked dry season, and covered the entire year by a gramineous carpet (Daus 1968). This plain has a gentle slope toward the east-southeast, and its horizontality is interrupted only by the reliefs of the Ventania and Tandilia systems in the eastern Pampa, and the Mahuidas hills and El Fresco Plateau in the western Pampa. The palynological record indicates that grasslands and xerophytic shrubs have been the typical vegetation of the region since at least the Late Pleistocene and all along the Holocene (Mancini et al. 2005; Messineo et al. 2019; Tonello and Prieto 2010; Vilanova et al. 2006).

The Lower Paraná Delta constitutes a specific environment within the Pampean. This delta presents a high environmental heterogeneity represented by rich and abundant biota of both subtropical and temperate origin (Blanco and Méndez 2010; Bó and Malvárez 1999; Malvárez 1999). Its landscape is mainly characterized by islands produced by the accumulation of sediments

Introduction

Figure 1.2 View of the gallery forest in the Paraná River Delta.

supplied by major Paraná River tributaries (e.g., Bermejo, Paraguay, Pilcomayo). The lower Uruguay River contributes to the delta but has a more narrow alluvial plain and much fewer islands. The vegetation in the lower Paraná and Uruguay Rivers has been characterized as an "azonal" ecoregion. Biogeographically, it is an extension of the subtropical gallery forest (Figure 1.2), which penetrates within a template zone of the Pampean grasslands as a moderator effect of the climate produced by the rivers.

Toward the southern Pampa, there is an ecotonal environment (Abraham de Vázquez et al. 2000; Morello 1958) dominated by the so-called Arid Diagonal, characterized by warm and dry steppe arid climate, with a mean annual rainfall of 466 mm (Sánchez et al. 1998). The dominant vegetation belongs to the Caldén District, although vegetal communities of the Monte phytogeographic province can also be observed in the area (Morello 1958). Thus, this arid to semi-arid sandy area presents a shrub-steppe, an open vegetal formation composed of short xeric trees mixed with hardy and scarce herbaceous grasses (Martínez et al. 2009; Villamil and Scoffield 2003).

In Patagonia, the climate is influenced by the seasonally shifting Pacific westerlies, which produce strong summer winds in South Patagonia. Continental climates are characteristic of most of Patagonia, while in Tierra del Fuego and the western archipelagos, climates are moderated by the ocean masses (Tonello et al. 2009). Temperatures fluctuate between $-10°C$ and

Figure 1.3 South Ice Field is located between the fjords on the Pacific coast and the eastern Patagonian steppes.

32°C in the north, with very cold winters and hot summers. In the south, temperatures can reach −20°C or lower in winter, and summers are also cold, particularly because of the chilling effect of the wind (Papadakis 1974). The Andean range and two large continental ice fields constitute an effective barrier between the eastern steppes and the Pacific between 46° and 52° S (Figure 1.3). The result is a dramatic contrast between both sides of the Andes. An intricate maze of archipelagos with very high precipitation that reaches above 4,000 mm/year characterizes the west side. On the eastern steppes, precipitation diminishes to around 200 mm/year. As a result of the rainshadow effect produced by the Andes intercepting the humid air masses transported by the westerlies, a narrow belt of forests can be found at the foot of the eastern side of the mountains. In contrast, the western side, particularly the islands, was fully covered by forest during the Holocene (Figure 1.4). In the fjords, these forests are usually dominated by *Nothofagus*, *Weinmannia*, and conifers (Villagrán 1988). Extensive peat bogs cover many of the islands, particularly near Cape Horn. Some sectors were described as Magellanic tundra, a habitat with a very cold and humid climate that was not particularly attractive to humans. *Sphagnum magellanicum* dominates bogs, and sometimes they have attached patches of *Pilgerodendron uviferus* (Pisano 1973). South of

Introduction

Figure 1.4 View of Yalac Island, Refugio Channel, Chonos Archipelago, Chile. Photo courtesy Omar Reyes.

45° S coastal peatlands of *Donatia* and *Oreobolus* predominate (Luebert and Pliscoff 2006). Precipitation of up to 5,000 mm/year or more is recorded at some islands, which even present ice fields (Schimpf et al. 2011).

There is a long history of glacial advances and retreats in Patagonia that starts with the Greatest Patagonian Glaciation about 1 million years ago or before. This was the only glaciation that reached the coasts of the Atlantic Ocean, near the mouth of the Gallegos River (Coronato and Rabassa 2011). The succession of advances and retreats of the ice was studied in detail at several localities, particularly in the Chilean Lakes Region at ca. 41° S (Denton et al. 1999) and the Strait of Magellan at ca. 52° S (Sugden et al. 2005). Even when differences in timing were noted, the movement of ice masses was more or less in sync. At any rate, it was suggested that only in the southern extreme was there an influence from the Antarctic (McCulloch et al. 2005).

The Last Glacial Maximum (LGM) occurred sometime around 24,000–20,000 BP, during which the ice extended beyond the Andes. The retreat of the Pleistocene glaciers, which started sometime before 15,000 BP, was not a linear process, but punctuated with short, cold pulses around 11,000 BP in North Patagonia, perhaps correlated with the Younger Dryas (Ariztegui et al. 1997), and around 12,300 BP or before in South Patagonia and Tierra del Fuego in synchrony with the Antarctic Cold Reversal (Jouzel et al. 2001; McCulloch et al. 2005). It must be recalled that the human exploration and colonization of Fuego-Patagonia at large began sometime before 12,000 BP (Borrero and Franco 1997; Miotti 1996). What this means is that the process of initial human dispersal into Patagonia basically occurred under cold conditions. Nevertheless, the process of deglaciation was marked by a warmer trend, during which floral and faunal communities expanded from unknown Pleistocene refugia into locations near the Cordillera. As a result of all these recent changes, it was indicated that most near Andean environments are still unstable (Pisano 1975).

Palynological studies have a long tradition in Patagonia, starting with the work of Vaino Auer in the 1930s (Auer 1974). Several pollen columns were analyzed that cover the Holocene and the end of the Pleistocene (Heusser 2003; Mancini et al. 2012; Markgraf 1993; McCulloch et al. 2005; Villa-Martinez and Moreno 2007). Most of this research took place near the Andean range, where the most extensive peat bogs are located. A few localities away from the Andes were intensively interrogated. Among them, the Cardiel Lake (Ariztegui et al. 2009; Stine and Stine 1990) and the Potrok Aike Lake (Zolitschka et al. 2013) must be mentioned. The variation observed between both extra-Andean records is notable, and one conclusion is that local sequences are needed to assess the interaction between humans and climate.

The extent of glaciation during these later times was limited, with calving glaciers reaching the Pacific coast on the west, but is mostly confined to Andean valleys on the east. The latter formed proglacial lakes dammed by ice walls. Several of these lakes had high stands at the end of the Pleistocene, which was the time when humans were dispersing into Patagonia. However, there is also a variation, with some lakes showing high stands during the Holocene (Horta et al. 2011). Well-studied examples of proglacial lakes are those of the Consuelo or Tehuelche paleolake in Última Esperanza (García et al. 2014; Stern et al. 2011) or the Strait of Magellan west of the first narrow (McCulloch et al. 2005). Their importance to understanding the process of human colonization of South Patagonia rests on the fact that these paleolakes concentrated megafauna and large mammals that are well represented in the nearest paleontological sequences (Martin et al. 2013; Stern et al. 2011).

The postglacial warming period favored the expansion of prairies and forests in the west and steppes in the east. There was not much floristic variation during the Holocene (Mancini 1998), except during minor climatic punctuations, like the Medieval Climatic Anomaly (Stine and Stine 1990) or the Little Ice Age (Masiokas et al. 2008). However, at each of these events, there were fluctuations in the character and eastern limit of the forest. Environmental conditions in extra-Andean Fuego-Patagonia near the end of the Pleistocene were unstable, and foraging resources were not necessarily abundant (Clapperton 1993; Markgraf 1988; Pisano 1975). The environmental conditions were cold but not extreme, but probably adequate for human dispersal during transition times from their low

Figure 1.5 View of Perito Moreno Glacier, Argentina.

demography enclaves. During the Early Holocene, not only were more habitats available, but the flux of people from the north probably increased.

Tierra del Fuego is today separated from continental Patagonia by the Strait of Magellan, but in Late Pleistocene times, it was still part of the continent. After the successive late-glacial advances documented at the Strait of Magellan began, a large proglacial lake dammed by the ice was formed west of Primera Angostura. Land bridges existed around 13,100 BP and between 10,300 and 8300–7500 BP (McCulloch and Morello 2009). Ice and water barriers occurred before and after that time, respectively, constituting important obstacles for the dispersal of humans and animals. The Strait of Magellan opened only in the Early Holocene, around 9000–8000 BP, after the deglaciation and discharge of the west paleolake (McCulloch et al. 2005). In sum, at the end of the Pleistocene, the connection with Tierra del Fuego was interrupted several times, but circulation was intermittently possible (Coronato et al. 1999; McCulloch et al. 1997). The available early subsistence and technological evidence for Tierra del Fuego indicates a terrestrial crossing into the island.

The Holocene environment was characterized by the opening of the connection between the Pacific and the Atlantic through the Strait of Magellan, as well as its connection with the Otway and Skyring interior seas. As mentioned, at the beginning of the Holocene warmer conditions returned that prompted an expansion of the forests from the Andes (Moreno et al. 2012) (Figure 1.5). The sea level was rising up until ca. 6000 BP, and later progressively retreated, shaping the actual coastal landforms (Isla and Bujalesky 2008). The mentioned Holocene warm trend was shortly interrupted by Neoglacial advances that were confined to the Andes.

THE PAMPAS AND PATAGONIA AS GEOGRAPHICAL UNITS FOR ARCHAEOLOGICAL ANALYSIS

The Pampas

Until the beginning of the twentieth century, the discussion about the archaeological remains of the Pampas and Patagonia was centered, one way or another, on the topic of the antiquity of humans in both regions (Podgorny 1999a). For the most part, this debate in the Pampas region originated with Florentino Ameghino (1880–1881), with his postulation of the Pampean-Patagonian origin of humanity (see Chapter 2). At that time, Ameghino referred to a vaguely defined region he dubbed "El Plata" (hence the title of his famous book, *La antigüedad del hombre en el Plata*), which included the Pampas of Argentina and Uruguay. However, from the beginning of the twentieth century, an alternative was developed for the organization of past and present indigenous peoples: the combination of temporal and geographical division (Podgorny 1999a). Outes and Bruch (1910) introduced a new concept in the definition of the spatial units since they organized the archaeological material based on the European units: Paleolithic, Neolithic, and Bronze Age. However, the historical indigenous peoples were grouped within "geo-ethnical provinces" and thus described through various associated features. This new concept was later utilized by Torres (1917), who grouped cultural series for each physical region of the country (Podgorny 1999a). In a new edition and enhancement of the original work, Torres (1935) modified the 1917 map and defined the "four natural regions of the Argentine territory," including what we today define as the Pampas region and another as Patagonia.

During this period, the Pampas, along with the indigenous people who had lived within it, were considered to be an ecological and cultural unity with little internal variation. However, there are various precedents for the identification of differences within the region. One was set by Lothrop (1932), who proposed three different cultures in the delta of the Paraná River. Another was Howard and Willey (1948), who proposed several areas within this region, although they included some which at the time and now are considered to be beyond the Pampas region. A significant contribution was that of Madrazo (1973, 1979), who identified physiographic – and to him, cultural, too – differences within the region and proposed the existence of "aspects" and "foci." Although these two categories were imperfectly defined and were not very operational, they captured to some extent the intra-regional variation, which up until that point had barely been taken into consideration.

Introduction

Until the 1980s, the idea of the Pampas as a great, relatively homogeneous, cultural region was prevalent (e.g., Austral 1971; Menghin and Bórmida 1950). Likewise, in his synthesis of Argentine archaeology, Fernández (1982) referred to the Argentine territory's areas and expressed that, besides the southern Andean area (to him the best defined), the remainder of the territory "should no doubt be the object of more exact divisions in the future" (Fernández 1982).

In the 1980s, Politis (1984) formalized the region's internal differences and defined seven areas for the eastern sector, or the Humid Pampa subregion: North, Salado River Depression (Depresión del Río Salado), West, Tandilia, Ventania, Interserrana, and South. In physiographic and ecological terms, this proposal was based on the classic geographical research of Daus (1968, 1969) and contributions from geology (Rolleri 1975). Subsequently, and following similar criteria, the Dry Pampa subregion was also divided into four areas: Close Basins (Bajos sin Salida), Basaltic Plateau (Meseta Basáltica), Caldenar, and Salado-Chadileuvú-Curacó (Berón and Politis 1997). In both cases, the differentiation of areas was mainly based on ecological features, although the archaeological record was taken also into account. However, these differences were not attributed to cultural distinctions, and it was, in fact, proposed that the same societies could occupy different areas and leave diverse archaeological records depending on the exploited resources, the technology utilized, and the type of settlement (this was specifically discussed for the differences between the Interserrana and Tandilia areas). Consequently, it could be concluded that the areas defined by Politis first and by Berón and Politis later were based primarily on ecological criteria and secondarily on archaeological. Therefore, under these terms, the Pampas region is not assignable to a "cultural area" in the classical sense of the concept (Steward 1955), but archaeological features intervened in its definition (see discussion in Politis and Barros 2006).

Although there were some exceptions (e.g., Orquera 1987), most of the authors who have researched in the region considered these spatial units of analysis, which is reflected in the regional or areal synthesis (Berón 2006; Carrera Aizpitarte 2014; Martínez and Gutiérrez 2004; Martínez et al. 2015; Mazzanti 1993; Politis and Madrid 2001; Salemme 1987; among many others). In this way, by customary use and not by an explicit agreement, the proposed areas were transformed into operational and relatively consensual spatial units of analysis.

The area that encompasses the lower Paraná and Uruguay Rivers, located in Northeast Pampa, belongs to another tradition of investigation: the one of the Argentine Northeast or Littoral (Aparicio 1948; Caggiano 1984; Ceruti 2003; González 1977; González and Pérez 1966; Lafon 1971, 1972; Serrano 1972). In this sense, the synthesis of the Pampas and Patagonia's archaeology made by Orquera (1987) defined a sharp separation at the Salado River of the Buenos Aires province, noting the integration existing between the indigenous peoples

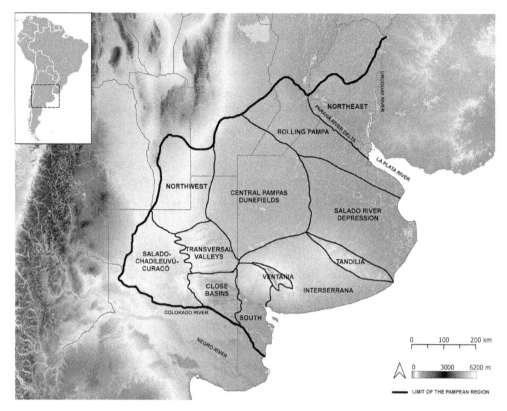

Figure 1.6 Map showing the areas of the Pampas region.

who lived to the north of this river during the Late Holocene and the cultural tradition of the Argentine Northwest.

In summary, considering the advances of the last years and the ecological and archaeological spatial variations, the Pampas region is susceptible to being divided into twelve areas (Figure 1.6).

1. *Northeast or Mesopotamic Pampa.* This includes the alluvial plains of the lower courses of the Paraná and Uruguay Rivers and the intermediate plains. The Lower Paraná River forms an extensive delta that is considered a complex estuarine delta influenced by the rising of the Paraná and Uruguay Rivers and the La Plata River's freshwater tides (Kandus et al. 2011). It covers over 17,000 km² and is formed over a Middle Holocene marine littoral complex that started to define its current morphology after the last transgressive event at ~ 6000 BP (Cavallotto et al. 2004, 2005; Codignotto 2004; Iriondo and Kröhling 2008).

Between the Paraná and Uruguay Rivers, to the south of ~ 32° S, there is a low grassland plain, as well as three rivers that cross it from north to south: Nogoyá, Gualeguay, and Gualeguaychú. This plain is bordered to the south by the tidal flat of the Paraná River Delta (Cavallotto et al. 2005) and contrasts

Introduction 13

with the undulated (which forms the so-called *cuchillas*) and forested (the Spinal District) relief that develops toward the north and constitutes the limit of the Pampas region.

2. *Rolling Pampa.* This is formed by rolling plains that are located to the west of the Paraná River, up to the Central Pampean Dunefields and the Salado River Depression areas and the transition toward the Chaco-Santiagueña Plains. This northern border is also the end of the grasslands and the beginning of the xerophytic forest (the Spinal District). This is a grassland plain with no outcropping of hard rocks. Toward the southeast, this area reaches the river and the estuary of La Plata River, and through the length of this riverside, a dense gallery forest of subtropical stock has developed, which goes toward the south and is known as the *tala* forests. These forests, formed mainly by *tala* (*Celtis tala*), *molle* (*Schinus longifolius*), and *coronillo* (*Scutia buxifolia*), extend parallel to the river and have developed over shell deposits (Cerro de la Gloria Member from the Las Escobas Formation, Fidalgo et al. 1973), a product of the regressive stages of the last Holocene marine ingression.

3. *Central Pampas Dunefield (CPD).* This area, previously called West (Politis 1984; Politis and Barros 2006), has recently been redefined by Messineo et al. (2018) based on geomorphological characteristics. The CPD is an eolian system of the central Pampean region formed by linear dunes of eolian origin, 100–130 km long and 2–3 km wide (Messineo et al. 2019; Zárate and Tripaldi 2012). The dune landscape produces an irregular relief, about 2–5 m high, where the depressions between the sand ridges commonly have numerous temporary or permanent shallow lakes. Through periods of drought, the number of lakes in the area decreased and the salinity of the water increased (Quiroz et al. 2003). However, a few permanent lake systems occurred in the area: Las Encadenadas (which comprises the Alsina, Cochicó, del Monte del Venado, La Paraguaya, and Epecuén lakes) and Hinojo-Las Tunas. Although most of these dunes are fixed nowadays, during dry periods in the Late Pleistocene and the Holocene, they lost grass coverage and became active dunes.

4. *Tandilia.* This area is formed by a discontinuous range of low hills, their foothills, and intermediate valleys. The hill system is an elongated range of 340 km in length with a maximum width of 60 km, which runs southeast by northwest, from Cabo Corrientes on the Atlantic coast to the last Quillalauquen hills in the northwestern end (Figure 1.7). This is a treeless environment where grasses and shrub communities of *currumamuel* (*Colletia paradoxa*) predominate (Cabrera 1971). This area is one of the main sources of toolstones, and these raw materials are found in almost all areas of the Pampas region (see Chapter 3).

5. *Ventania.* This system is a continuous mountain range approximately 180 km long in a southeast-northwest direction and 60 km wide in the central

Figure 1.7 View of Cerro Curicó, in the northwestern sector of the Tandilia Hill Range.

part, with heights of over 1,000 m (Figure 1.8). It is composed of Paleozoic sedimentary rocks, with a predominance of quartzite, and a lower proportion of granite and rhyolite of Precambrian age. It has also been one of the main sources of toolstones not only in the outcrops of the hills but also in secondary deposits transported by the creeks. Specific grass communities, adapted to higher and colder environments, predominate. On the banks of rivers and creeks that were born in the hill (e.g., Sauce Grande, Sauce Chico, Las Mostazas, Chasicó) some Humboldt's willow (*Salix humboldtiana*) forests have developed.

6. *South*. This area is formed by a flat land that extends from the southwestern foothills of Ventania up to the paleochannel system of the Colorado River. It borders the Atlantic seashore to the east, and to the west, it is transitional to the Close Basins. The Colorado River is one of its main features (Figure 1.9a). It flows northwest to southeast across the area and forms an alluvial plain that ends in an ancient delta (Spaletti and Isla 2003). Abundant recent channels, paleochannels, abandoned meanders, levees, and saltpans characterize this alluvial plain. The area is dominated by the Spinal phytogeographical province (Cabrera 1971, 1976).

Figure 1.8 Guanaco in the Ventania Hill Range. Photo courtesy Cristian Kaufmann.

7. *Interserrana*. This is a treeless plain with soft undulations, basically loess slopes that were deposited on the Plio-Pleistocene relief that extends between the hill systems of Tandilia and Ventania. To the south, it borders the Atlantic seashore, and to the north, the CPD. This area is limited by the south area at the southeast, the Napostá Grande creek being the approximate limit. The Gramineae of genera *Stipa*, *Piptochaetium*, *Poa*, *Hordeum*, and *Melita* dominate these grasslands. This zone's basins are drained by rivers or streams whose headwaters can be found in the hills (e.g., Quequén Grande River, Sauce Grande River), although other courses originate in the plains themselves (e.g., Claromecó basin). There are only small and isolated outcrops of hard rock (Lumb, Gonzáles Chaves, etc.)

Within the area, there is a zone with its own very strong distinguishing characteristics, which is the Atlantic seashore. It comprises a chain of mobile dunes of variable width that can reach 5 km and beaches with rounded cobble deposits. In some sectors, there are coasts of abrasions with pronounced

Figure 1.9 (a) Lower course of the Colorado River; (b) Salado-Chadileuvú-Curacó area; (c) Close Basins; (d) Transversal Valleys. Photos courtesy Manuel Carrera Aizpitarte.

ravines, while in others, the coast is lower with wide beaches that continue on the chain of dunes.

8. *The Salado River Depression*. This area is characterized by a large depression, with the main course, the Salado River, flowing northwest to southeast and emptying into the estuary of the La Plata River. It has been divided into two parts: the eastern one, lower (<30 masl) in which lakes are abundant and the drainage is deficient, and the western one, higher (>30 masl), with a greater slope and better drainage (although still deficient). The lowlands are covered by hydrophilic species (*Stipa formicarum* and *Stipa bavioensis*). On the border of the abundant lakes, there are dense communities of reed beds (*Scirpus ruparius*) accompanied by waxy leaf nightshade (*Solanum glaucum*) and *totora* (*Typha* sp.). Elongated forests of *tala*, *molle*, and *coronillo* extend along the shores of the estuary. Active dunes develop along the seashore in the southeastern strip.

9. *Salado-Chadileuvú-Curacó*. This area is heterogeneous and consists of several environments. To the west, it borders the Basaltic Plateau, and to the east, the Transversal Valleys and the Close Basins. To the south, it is limited by the Colorado River Valley. It is a flat area with an axis formed by the

Introduction   17

Salado-Chadileuvú-Curacó fluvial system, which flows northwest to southeast (Figure 1.9b). It is dominated by the Monte Province, made up of open xerophytic shrubs, mainly *jarilla*, although, in the eastern sector, *caldén* forests develop. The area has a great diversity of toolstones, among which stand out the siliceous chert from the El Fresco Plateau and the variety of cobbles that form the northern strip of the Patagonian Shingle Mantle.

10. *Close Basins.* This is an area formed by plateaus and a system of valleys (of 100–300 km in length) arranged in the shape of hand fans. The width among the plateaus is 15–20 km, and among the valleys is varies between 5 and 15 km. These geoforms are composed of dune cords, the lateral plain sectors that constitute the transversal valleys, and the chaining of very salty lakes on the borders of the dune cords (Figure 1.9c). The area is characterized by a semi-arid climate with 400 mm/year precipitation and by the presence of sandy and stony soils. It is predominated by the *caldén* forest with grasslands, low gramin-eous grasslands with shrubs, *jarilla* shrubland, and the halophilic vegetation (Carrera Aizpitarte 2014).

In this environment of plateaus and valleys, the Cerro de Los Viejos stands out: a granite massif with an elliptical shape of 1.5 km × 1 km that reaches 216 masl, making it the highest elevation of the zone. This geoform gives particular characteristics to this area's environment (Lucero et al. 2020; Piana 1981).

11. *Transversal Valleys.* This area corresponds to the topography of plateaus and transversal valleys, which run in an east-west direction (Figure 1.9d). Besides the Argentino-Utracan valley, which is the biggest, other valleys are also found in the area: Hucal, Maracó Grande, Chapalcó, Quehué, Nerecó, and Daza-Chillén. It stands as a structural plain with low isolated hills covered by a calcareous crust; some plateau relicts that have resisted the hydric activity that shaped the plains can also be observed (Carrera Aizpitarte 2014). The Spinal Province dominates it. However, in the east, grasslands are well developed. The area lacks toolstones, except for a few highly localized out-crops of good quality chert and quartzite such as Valle Daza and El Carancho lake (Berón and Curtoni 2002; see Chapter 3).

12. *Northwest.* This area is not well defined and coincides in part with the Caldenar area (Berón and Politis 1997) and with the Western Pampas Dunefields (Zárate and Tripaldi 2012: 403). The landscape is a very softly undulated uniform plain with a regional slope in a southwest-northeast direc-tion and a micro-relief comprised of small hills with depressions and dispersed salty lakes. It has an ecotonal biogeographic position between the Pampas, Spinal, and Monte phytogeographical provinces (Cabrera 1971, 1976). From east to west, this transitional area combines grassland from the Humid Pampa, *caldén* xerophytic forest from the Spinal District, and grassland and shrubs from Monte province (Heider and Demichelis 2015). In the northeast portion of the area, extended active dunes can be observed. There are a very few toolstone

outcrops, such as a particular type of chalcedony in the Loma de Los Pedernales (Heider and Demichelis 2015) and an isolated granite hill known as Lonco Vaca (Heider 2015).

Micro-regions have also been recognized within some of these areas, which have some ecological particularities and have served as spatial units of analysis for some research teams. Among these can be found: (1) a strip of land that runs north to south, more or less on the 62° meridian and between 33° and 39° S, which has been named "Pampean Ecotonal Humid-Dry Area" (Oliva 2006), and (2) a sector of the alluvial plains of the western shore of the Lower Paraná River, which has been named Bajíos Rivereños Meridionales (Southern Coastal Shoals) by Lafon (1971) and is currently in use by Acosta (2005), Loponte (2008), and collaborators. Last, in the west of the La Pampa province are the Basaltic Plateau, the Chicalcó Plains, and the lower course of the Atuel River, which in some syntheses has been included in the Pampas region (Berón and Politis 1997; Politis and Barros 2006) but which we will not address in this book because it is ecologically and culturally related to southern Cuyo (Aguerre 1987a; see below).

Patagonia

One way of segmenting Patagonia is the simple separation into North Patagonia, which would extend between 39° S, location of the Colorado River, and 50° S, the approximate latitude of the Santa Cruz River; South Patagonia, which goes from 50° S to the Strait of Magellan (~ 52° S); and the southwestern archipelagos that extend in a long arc from the island of Chiloé to Cape Horn, at 56° S.

Diversity of environments exist in Patagonia, with important differences in extension. Several subdivisions can be made based on primary productivity, availability of water, and other important variables for human adaptation. However, all this variability can be reduced to four basic environments: the steppes, the forested foothills, the Atlantic coast, and the southwestern archipelagos. These four environments present sufficient individuality to make them significant units to characterize the habitats of Patagonian hunter-gatherers.

Most of the archaeological information was obtained in the steppe, which for some specialists can be distinguished from the Monte of South Cuyo and Northeast Patagonia (Parodi 1945) (Figure 1.10). They basically constitute extensive plains with a limited cover of grass and shrubs, sometimes interrupted by low-altitude plateaus. Information from the other areas is slowly growing, particularly from the Atlantic coast. Only during the last few decades has the archaeological exploration of the forests and the western archipelagos begun to offer consistent results.

Introduction

Figure 1.10 View of Monte environment near Huenul Cave, Northwest Patagonia, Argentina. Photo courtesy Guadalupe Romero Villanueva.

The history of research in Patagonia also reflects an implicit assumption of widespread homogeneity (Vignati 1939), even when the existence of a huge variety of environments within which many significant subdivisions were possible was recognized. Importantly, studies were not coordinated across this vast and largely disconnected region, making it difficult to find agreement concerning the most relevant limits for culturally significant areas. As a result, the ghost of homogeneity is still flying over Patagonia.

The important synthesis made by Junius Bird for the *Handbook of South American Indians* recognized – extending a characterization by Cooper (1917) – what he called "two cultural areas ... now occupied by the canoe Indians ... and that of the foot Indians" (Bird 1946: 18). These areas corresponded to the obvious contrast between the steppes in the east and the southwestern archipelagos and planted a dichotomy that is still affecting our interpretation. More recently, Carlos Gradin (1980) presented units with clear physical limits as a framework for Patagonian archaeology. His way of segmenting the space was based on recognizing two transitional areas, one with the Andean lands in Northwest Patagonia and the other with the Pampas, and subsuming all the rest – including Tierra del Fuego and other islands – as the proper Patagonia land. These three areas were determined on the basis of cultural criteria, separating regions with substantial differences in human adaptation. In turn, Gradin's ample category "Patagonia" was subdivided into four units: North

Patagonia between the Negro and Chubut basins, Central Patagonia between the Chubut and Santa Cruz basins (in turn subdivided in two by the Deseado River), and South Patagonia between the Santa Cruz basin and the Strait of Magellan; he also identified Tierra del Fuego as another unit (Gradin 1980). This was a geographic characterization probably selected in order to facilitate the management of the existent information. The available evidence from each of the proposed units was variable, to the point that only very preliminary work was done in some cases.

Luis A. Orquera organized his discussion of Patagonian archaeology in "units of convenience," recognizing three major subdivisions within the steppes. He also distinguished the Lower Negro River Valley and North Patagonian Coast as an area that "displays a strong cultural individuality," the Limay and Negro Basins and North Tierra del Fuego (Orquera 1987: 337). He was justifiably more detailed in his analysis of the archipelagos, considering the Beagle Channel, the area where most of his research took place, the Western Magellan Strait, and the Magellan-Fuegian Channels and Islands as units with cultural individuality.

Having at our disposal a richer archaeological record, the pragmatic decision of changing the defining criteria was made. At this time, we opted to emphasize geographic but anthropologically relevant characteristics for the segmentation of the steppes. Accordingly, we organized the archaeological information from that vast area using the hydrological basins as our main focus since the limited availability of drinking water makes them powerful attractors for human populations (Pérez et al. 2016). This decision makes sense in a land where precipitations barely average 200 mm/year. The island of Tierra del Fuego and the southwestern archipelagos constitute additional areas in our discussion of Patagonian archaeology.

The Colorado Basin is considered the limit between the Pampas and Patagonia, a demarcation that responds more to political purposes and research traditions than to significant ecological differences. For example, the Grande River in the headwaters of this hydrographic system connects with northwest of the Province of Neuquén and South Cuyo. The latter is considered to be part of Patagonia on the basis of both cultural and environmental evidence (Borrero 2011).

The Neuquén-Limay-Negro Basin was a major waterway between the Andes and the Atlantic that, in historical times, was characterized by relatively high human demography. However, the archaeological evidence suggests relative autonomy between units using both extremes of the hydrographic system.

The Chubut Basin has offered substantial human occupations since the Middle Holocene. There is no evidence of Late Pleistocene occupations, but the important research area of Aisén, Chile, located between the headwaters of the Chubut and Deseado basins, is basic for our understanding of the process of human exploration of the western fringes of the steppes.

Introduction

The Deseado hydrographic system is not comparable in flow with the rest of the Patagonian rivers, but this was not necessarily the case in the past. This system originally drained Lago Buenos Aires-General Carrera, the second largest lake of South America, but the North Patagonian Ice Field's shrinking, in combination with terminal moraines and basaltic lava deposits, changed it all. Effectively, when the Baker River captured the drainage of both basins toward the Pacific Ocean, the hydrological landscape of that zone of Patagonia changed drastically (Isla et al. 2014).

It must be mentioned that the Deseado system is related to some of the most significant archaeological expressions of central Patagonia. The Deseado Massif, which constituted the most important node of early human occupation in Patagonia, is located south of this system. Also, near its headwaters is located the Pinturas River, where some of the more studied archaeological sequences of Patagonia were recorded. Cueva de las Manos is just one of those sites (Gradin et al. 1976). Also, high-altitude archaeological localities are found north and south of the Pueyrredón-General Carreras Lake (Aschero et al. 2005). Importantly, at the beginning of the deglaciation, "the Deseado and Pinturas rivers [had] a maximum discharge capacity of eroding their present canyons" (Isla et al. 2014: 6), which was followed by a Holocene diminution in the discharge of the river that may have affected human settlement.

The Santa Cruz basin is the most important hydrographic system of Patagonia, given its large flow and significance for hunter-gatherer populations. It was an important frontier for historical societies that were already using European horses, but before that time, it was less a limit than an attractor for human populations (Belardi et al. 1992). The crossing of the river was difficult but viable, as proved by the peopling of South Patagonia.

The Coyle basin is particularly rich given its complex net of branches, availability of lithic raw materials, and extensive wetlands at the lower Coyle. For these reasons, it attracted intense human activity that showed regular use of the basin without any major organizational changes through time (Belardi et al. 2006; Espinosa et al. 2020).

The Gallegos basin, with its southern affluents, Rubens, Penitentes, and Chico, encompasses the Pali Aike Volcanic Field (PAVF) (Figure 1.11). This field resulted from the contact between three tectonic plaques. Abundant volcanic formations resulted during three volcanic cycles: the Basal Lava Plateaus, 3.8 my old; the Older Cones and Lava Flows, with maares, cones, and tuff rings formed ca. 200,000 BP; and the Younger Cones and Lava Flows, restricted to a small area near the center of the volcanic field and formed during the Late Pleistocene (D'Orazio et al. 2000). Its importance derives from the fact that some of the older evidence for the human installation in Patagonia was found at this volcanic field. Near the Pacific Ocean, and not too far away from the headwaters of the Gallegos River, is located Última Esperanza, one of

Figure 1.11 View of the Chico River, Pali Aike Volcanic Field, Chile. Photo courtesy Fabiana Martin.

the few known nodes of early human occupation in Patagonia (Figure 1.12). It was recently claimed that the early occupations at Última Esperanza were connected with those at the PAVF through the Gallegos basin (Martin and Borrero 2017). An additional reason to highlight the significance of this hydrological system is that the south affluents connect with the more productive zones of the Strait of Magellan.

The classic subdivision of Tierra del Fuego between the northern plains and the southern mountains and forests makes sense in terms of human use of the environment. It is in the northern plains that the isthmus between Bahía Inútil and Bahía San Sebastián is located. This is where the Tres Arroyos site, the only Late Pleistocene evidence of human occupation on Tierra del Fuego, is located. That area was already a treeless habitat with a relatively rich fauna available (Massone 2004).

Finally, the western archipelagos, extending from Chiloé to the Beagle Channel – and responding to some of the already mentioned climatic and

Introduction 23

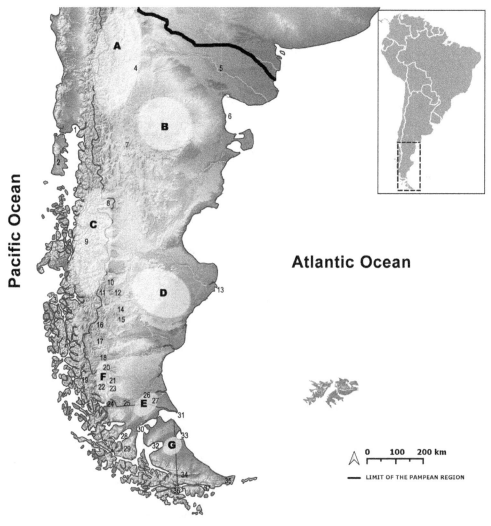

Figure 1.12 Map showing early occupational nodes in Patagonia and geographic features mentioned in the text. Nodes: (A) Northwest Patagonia; (B) Meseta Somuncurá; (C) Aisén; (D) Deseado Massif; (E) Pali Aike Volcanic Field; (F) Última Esperanza Sound; (G) Cerro de los Onas. Geographic features: (1) Seno Reloncaví; (2) Chiloé; (3) Guayaneco Archipelago; (4) Limay Basin; (5) Negro Basin; (6) San Matías Gulf; (7) Piedra Parada Valley; (8) Cisnes Valley; (9) Hudson volcano; (10) Lakes Cochrane/Posadas/Pueyrredón; (11) Perito Moreno Park; (12) Pampa del Asador, Cerro Pampa; (13) Oso Marino Bay; (14) Strobel Plateau; (15) Cardiel Lake; (16) Peninsula Maipú, San Martín Lake; (17) Viedma Lake; (18) Argentino Lake; (19) Reclus volcano; (20) Baguales Range; (21) Cancha Carrera; (22) Oriental Range; (23) Cordillera Chica; (24) Llanuras de Diana; (25) Zurdo Basin; (26) Gallegos River; (27) Chico River; (28) Otway Sound; (29) Brunswick Peninsula; (30) Strait of Magellan; (31) Cabo Vírgenes; (32) Bahía Inútil; (33) Bahía San Sebastián; (34) Fagnano Lake; (35) Península Mitre; (36) Hoste Island; (37) Picton Island.

phytogeographic characteristics – present a variety of peculiar habitats. The northern archipelagos even offer the possibility of important plant resources at Chiloé (Reyes et al. 2020). Except for a few islands, like Chiloé, where pudu populations exist, and Wellington, where living populations of huemul were reported (Curry 1991; Emperaire 1963), the southwestern archipelagos have practically no land vertebrates of any economic importance. In some places, like Madre de Dios (Jaillet et al. 2010), huemul remains were recovered at archaeological sites, perhaps suggesting their local presence. However, it is not always clear if they were acquired locally. The main subsistence resource in the Western archipelagos consists of birds, fish, mollusks, and marine mammals that concentrate on a narrow fringe of the Pacific Ocean (Reyes 2021).

SUPRA-REGIONAL SIGNIFICANCE OF THE ARCHAEOLOGY OF THE PAMPAS AND PATAGONIA

There are several reasons to defend the supra-regional significance of the archaeology of the Southern Cone of the continent. In practical terms, not only does this area, excepting Antarctica, reflect the geographical end of the colonization of the continental landmasses, but there are also interesting implications of the initial results obtained in that area.

Since the earliest archaeological explorations of the Pampas and Patagonia, important implications for the Americas, in general, were evident. Ameghino's efforts at the end of the nineteenth century trying to substantiate his thesis about the South American origin of humankind offers an extreme example (Ameghino 1880–1881). Needless to say, this thesis generated heated discussions with researchers from North America (Hrdlička 1912) and from Europe (see review in Orquera 1971). This debate, which will be summarized in Chapter 2, colored the archaeology of the first half of the twentieth century. In the end, Ameghino's thesis was proved inadequate to accommodate the available facts, and the idea of a late peopling was dominant for some time. It was necessary to wait for the results of Bird's excavations in Patagonia and Madrazo's discoveries of Fishtail projectile points at Cerro El Sombrero in the Pampas to reopen the possibility of Late Pleistocene human occupations in the Southern Cone.

Significantly, the results of the 1930s excavations of Junius Bird in South Patagonia produced archaeological evidence – basically Fishtail projectile points in association with extinct Pleistocene fauna (Bird 1938, 1946) – which was to play a crucial role in the debate concerning the antiquity of peopling of the Americas, a debate that is still developing. This evidence – particularly the similarity of Fishtail projectile points from the Pampas and Patagonia to Clovis points from the Great Plains – was many times used to substantiate a very fast model of peopling of the Americas, in which basically similar adaptations were described for the north and south of the continent (Morrow and Morrow 1999).

As mentioned, the contrast between the Pampas and Patagonia is not marked: gradual ecological changes can be observed, and, basically, the same fauna was available everywhere. Without any doubt, the guanaco (*Lama guanicoe*) was the key prey in both regions all along the Holocene. More relevant, no important barriers separate both regions, and evidence of intense ethnographic and archaeological interaction is well recorded. The presence of long-term hunter-gatherer adaptations since the end of the Pleistocene up to historical times is another important commonality as well as the adoption of horses very early during the first phase of the Spanish Conquest. The similarity of the geographic and ecological settings, basically open plains, suggested a common type of hunter-gatherer organizational adaptation strategy (Steward 1955) in comparison with other zones across the continent. As a result, for decades the archaeology of the North American Great Plains was taken as a model for the earliest occupations in the south of the continent. This way of thinking is not accepted today. This is not only on the basis of chronology (Chapter 4), but because there are important differences when we compare the earliest forager adaptations from the Pampas-Patagonia and the Great Plains. Fishtails have been a chronological marker for Late Pleistocene sites in South America, but important differences with the Clovis projectile points have been pointed out many times (Hermo and Terranova 2012; Politis 1991; Suárez 2014). Also, the importance of extinct fauna at the earliest recognized sites from the Northern Plains was not replicated in the Southern Cone, where at best it constitutes a complementary resource (see Chapter 4). The question of specialized versus generalist adaptations is at stake here, with the South American evidence for wide-spectrum diets contrasting with the presumed specialization on megafauna and large mammals in the Clovis sites. This difference is endorsed by the absence of kill sites in the southern archaeological record, which differs substantially from the North American Plains sites. Given that a large component of the southern archaeological record – in particular, in Patagonia – consists of caves, this can easily be a taphonomic artifact. However, this issue also highlights the under-utilization of caves by early foragers in the Great Plains, suggesting the possibility that we are dealing with important differences in human land use.

Site size suggests the existence of larger human groups in northern plains than in southern grasslands, while the varied quality of the usual local rocks selected to make projectile points in the Pampas and Patagonia differs from the careful selection of high-quality, usually exotic rocks in the Plains. Finally, lithic projectile points are less frequent and less diverse in the Pampas and Patagonia compared with the Plains. Part of the explanation could be the popularity of the bola stones, which in Pampas are abundant and probably reflect their effectiveness to hunt in open grasslands. Bola stones surely complemented spears, atlatl, and arrows in the hunting technology along the Holocene. When comparing both regions, it seems that the Plains had denser demography since the Late Pleistocene, although sampling biases cannot be ruled out, since there were much more intense surveys and excavations in the Plains than in the Pampas and Patagonia.

Summing up, a model of human colonization not necessarily centered on large mammal hunting can be defended for the Pampas and Patagonia. Beyond the demonstrated importance of medium-sized mammals in both regions, this opens the door to the potentiality of small-package lower-return resources, including plants, in early human adaptations and all along the Holocene. The analyses of plant remains at sites in the Pampas and Patagonia are only beginning (Belmar 2019; Belmar et al. 2017; Bernal et al. 2007; Brea et al. 2014; López et al. 2020; Mazzanti and Bonnat 2013; Paleo and Perez Meroni 2004), but the importance of plants as seasonally complementary resources is clear. Although bola stones were recorded in other regions of America, it was in the Pampas and Patagonia where they probably became the main hunting weapon. If we look at the earliest record and the Holocene developments of the different regions of South America, this is exactly what is shown, a situation that provides strong support to the existence of several divergent cultural trajectories in the continent.

CHAPTER 2

HISTORICAL BACKGROUND

In this chapter, the historical background of the archaeology in the Pampas and Patagonia is discussed and summarized. It encompasses a period of about 100 years, between the 1870s when the first archaeological investigations took place in the Pampas and Patagonia (Ameghino 1880–1881; Holmberg 1884; Moreno 1874; Moseley 1892; Zeballos and Pico 1878) and the late 1970s when there was a theoretical and methodological shift in the archaeology of both regions, which gave rise to modern research. The current regional models in the Pampas and Patagonia are a product of this last period's research, first with a processual orientation and then adding other theoretical approaches (evolutionary, processual-plus/neo-processualism, post-processualism, etc.). However, some of the data and ideas generated in this first 100 years of investigation are still present in contemporary debates, as shown in the following chapters of this book.

The Pampas and Patagonia were also the stages for some methodological development propelled by the influence of processual archaeology. We are mainly referring to the developments of taphonomy, zooarchaeology, experimental archaeology, and geoarchaeology, which had their momentum in the early 1980s and have maintained a continual flow of research since then. The contributions of these developments not only helped us to better interpret the archaeological record of both regions but also impacted hunter-gatherer research worldwide.

THE EARLY YEARS

Archaeology emerged in Argentina, and in the Pampas and Patagonia, at the end of the nineteenth century, when the country was dominated by the ideas of the so-called 1880s Generation (Madrazo 1985; Politis 1992). They strongly promoted European values (borrowed predominantly from France and England) instead of those followed by indigenous people, mestizos, and criollos. In this context, Florentino Ameghino, Samuel Lafone Quevedo, Juan B. Ambrosetti, and others, the first scholars interested in local archaeology, started their research (Fernández 1982; Podgorny 1997, 2021). The idea of "progress" at that time justified the colonization of the remaining indigenous territories and caused the extermination of many indigenous people. Actually, some pioneer researchers, such as Estanislao Zeballos, were instrumental in conquering and controlling the Indian territories.

The most important museums were created in Argentina at the end of the nineteenth century as part of a strategy to keep indigenous cultures in the past (e.g., Museo de La Plata and the nationalization of the Museo Bernardino Rivadavia in Buenos Aires). By exhibiting indigenous people's material culture and their physical remains, the western-influenced society broke the cultural continuity and managed to freeze a past that was full of vitality in the present (Podgorny and Lópes 2008). Among the key research questions in those times were discussions on the origin of humankind and the "American man" (see Ameghino 1880–1881 and review in Hrdlička 1912), the earth mounds of the Paraná River Delta (Lista 1878; Zeballos and Pico 1978), and the coexistence between people and Pleistocene mammals until recent times in the Cueva del Milodón (Hauthal 1899; Moreno 1899; Nordenskjöld 1996 [1900]). All of these themes were quite distant from the issues concerning indigenous communities and their situation at the time (Politis and Curtoni 2011).

The first information about the Pampas indigenous people comes from the conquerors and explorers who entered the La Plata River at the beginning of the sixteenth century. The expeditions of Sebastian Gaboto, Diego García de Moguer, Pero Lopes de Souza, and Pedro de Mendoza provided abundant descriptions of the several ethnic groups, such Querandíes, Guaraníes, Chaná, Timbúes, and Mbeguá, who inhabited the region. However, this information referred only to the riverside and the adjacent plains. In 1581, Juan de Garay crossed the Salado River to the south and reached the southeastern extreme of Tandilia, providing the first data about the indigenous people of these areas. Later, Jesuit missionaries (e.g., Cardiel 1933 [1748]; Falkner 1974 [1774]) and castaway Isaac Morris (2004 [1743]) also produced firsthand data on the Indians living in Tandilia and the Interserrana areas in the mid-eighteenth century. Although vague, the first published archaeological references from the Pampas are from the first half of the nineteenth century, and they correspond to the isolated findings of Guaraní corrugated and polychrome pottery in the Paraná River Delta (Muñiz 1825; Sastre 2010 [1856]).

European contact in Patagonia started at the beginning of the sixteenth century when Hernando de Magallanes stopped there during his trip around the world. The interaction between him and his crew with Patagonian natives on the coast of Santa Cruz was widely known. Frequent contact with sailors

Historical Background 29

and explorers occurred during the following centuries, all of it basically restricted to the coastal zone. During these initial contacts, the natives living near the coast were identified with the giant Patagon of Spanish chivalry tales, and were considered giants by the first European explorers (Duviols 1997). This identification exacerbated the phenotypic contrast with the shorter inhabitants of the archipelagos, commonly referred to as the "canoe people," and became a persisting simplification of a more complex reality. One of the many effects of using this dichotomy as a framework for archaeological research was the reduction of cultural variability to two recorded polar types.

With very few exceptions, such as the expedition by Antonio Viedma that probably reached the lakes near the Cordillera in the eighteenth century, or the expedition up the Santa Cruz River by Robert Fitz Roy, captain of the HMS *Beagle*, in the beginning of the nineteenth century (Fitz Roy 1839; Viedma 1980 [1783]), travels to the hinterland of Patagonia began near the end of the nineteenth century. That was also the time when archaeological research began in the region. Accordingly, the first excavations occurred not too far away from the ocean. Effectively, stratigraphic excavations took place at Elizabeth Island in the Strait of Magellan in 1876. At that time, members of the crew of HMS *Challenger*, an oceanographic expedition, were circling the globe, and they excavated, documented, and collected artifacts at an archaeological site on the island. Mr. Murray was in charge of the excavation of a shell midden that "found some stone arrow-heads and stone fishing-net sinkers" (Moseley 1892: 480), as well as marine mammal bones and mollusks. This was the first archaeological excavation in Patagonia, but it remained little known for decades, an isolated event that did not produce any impact beyond attracting other explorers to that island. Effectively, in 1882 Domenico Lovisato, a member of an Italian expedition led by Giacomo Bove, visited Elizabeth Island and also excavated. He probably tested the same site studied by Murray and others and published a description of several shell middens (Bove 1984; Lovisato 1884). The few materials recovered from the dig made by Murray were donated to the British Museum by Thomson and Moseley in 1877–1878 and were studied only at the beginning of the twenty-first century (Borrero and Franco 2001). Those artifacts, photographs, and drawings deposited at the British Museum were the basis for a recent study of the island that reexamined and dated the site around 2500 BP (Borrero et al. 2019). The already mentioned expeditions by Viedma and Fitz Roy covered uncharted terrain for Europeans. More limited entries, like that of the missionaries Titus Coan and William Arms in 1833–1834, started in Gregory Bay on the Strait of Magellan and probably reached the modern frontier between Chile and Argentina north of the Bay, not too far from the coast.

In the Pampas region, the first archaeological excavation was the pioneering work of Estanislao Zeballos and Pedro Pico (1878) at the end of the nineteenth century, who intensely excavated a site that they named "Túmulo de

Figure 2.1 (a) Sketch of the Túmulo de Campana (shaded), after Torres (1907); (b) the famous pottery appendage representing a bird head. It was excavated by Estanislao Zeballos and Pedro Pico in 1978 in the Túmulo de Campana. Currently at the archaeology collections, the Museo de La Plata.

Campana" ("Campana tumulus"). The site was located in the alluvial plain of the Paraná River, close to the present city of Campana, and was one of the first sites to be excavated and published with some scientific criteria (Aparicio 1948: 60). Zeballos was a prestigious young student of Exact Sciences at the University of Buenos Aires who founded the Sociedad Científica Argentina in 1872 (Podgorny and Lopes 2008: 134). By the time of the Túmulo de Campana excavation, he had already carried out, along with some other scholars of the time, various archaeological and geological expeditions in the region, among which stand out a trip to the Paraná Delta and a visit to the Cañada Rocha site, which had been recently discovered by Florentino Ameghino (Politis and Bonomo 2015). The approach followed was empiricist and essentially exploratory. The methodology used was simple excavation with shovels, with the help of local workers and enthusiastic neighbors who collaborated in removing the sediment. With this amount of handwork, Zeballos and Pico were able to excavate almost the entire mound (an ellipsis of 79 m × 52 m and about 2.5 m high) in about two weeks (Figure 2.1a).

Historical Background

It was an artificial mount, where 28 human skeletons were recovered, as well as faunal remains, bone instruments, and pottery with zoomorphic appendages representing bird heads, mammals, and mollusks. The authors were sure that this was "the first tumulus of the prehistoric man of Buenos Aires" (Zeballos and Pico 1878: 252) and concluded that it corresponded to a "prehistoric monument of the famous Guaraní race."

After the excavation, the Sociedad Científica created a commission to study the remains that had been found. However, due to various circumstances, these researchers never undertook the study of the materials, and the firsthand information remained only in the two short articles by Zeballos (1878) and Zeballos and Pico (1878). The site's findings remained forgotten and were only analyzed and published by Torres (1907) almost 30 years later. Torres also had access to Zeballos and Pico's unpublished documentation, and he incorporated the site into discussions at the time, particularly concerning the "mound builders" and the archaeology of the Pampas and Argentine Northeast regions. The figure of one of the modeled ceramics that represented a parrot's head ("Papagayo") coming from the site (Figure 2.1b) was reproduced by the British Museum's researcher Thomas Joyce (1913: 261) to illustrate the findings on the Central and East of South America in one of the first syntheses of the continent's archaeology. The same figure was also reproduced by Erland Nordenskjöld (1930: 27) to demonstrate the dispersion of the Arawak up to the La Plata River. This image stimulated hypotheses and models about the population dynamics of the South American lowland (Politis and Bonomo 2015). Based on great ethnographic, historical, and archaeological knowledge, Nordenskjöld produced a convincing model to explain the Arawak expansion in the Southern Lowlands. Except for a human skeleton, a few pottery fragments, and some bone artifacts that remain in the Museo de La Plata, the rest of the collection from the Zeballos and Pico excavation has been lost. The site is nowadays considered as the southernmost expansion of the archaeological entity known as Goya-Malabrigo (Politis and Bonomo 2012 and Chapter 6).

In the 1870s, Florentino Ameghino was starting his archaeological, paleontological, and geological investigations in the Rolling Pampa. One of the most important sites that he discovered very early in his career was Cañada Rocha on the margins of the homonymous creek (present Arroyo El Haras), a tributary of the Luján River (Ameghino 1880–1881). Almost the entirety of this site's collection was lost, except for a part of the pottery and some faunal remains. To him, Cañada Rocha was formed in the "Mesolithic epoch," when the great mammals of the Pleistocene were already extinct (Ameghino 1880–1881). The remaining collection has been studied with contemporary criteria by Salemme (1983, 1987) and also has been radiocarbon dated by Toledo (2011) and Buc and Loponte (2016) to be between ~ 550 and 450 BP, although the samples are heavily contaminated (see discussion in Politis et al. 2019 and Chapter 6).

Figure 2.2 (a) View of the Arroyo de Frías, approximately where Ameghino found the human skeletons; (b) possible location of Ameghino's excavation. Photo taken in 1970 by Luis A. Orquera.

Between 1870 and 1874, a very young Florentino Ameghino recovered archaeological materials at Arroyo de Frías, another affluent of the Luján River, including the skeletal remains of two individuals on the left bank of the creek (Politis et al. 2011) (Figure 2.2). The best-preserved skeleton, exhumed in 1870, was almost entirely articulated (Ameghino 1935: 865). Three years later, Ameghino unearthed more human remains, which he interpreted as belonging to the same skeleton recovered in 1870 (see discussion in Orquera 1971; Toledo 2016). However, H. Leboucq identified some of the bones as belonging to a second, taller, and more robust individual (Lehmann-

Historical Background

Nitsche 1907: 249–250; but see Ameghino 1935: 867). Two samples from this second individual were dated to 10,300 BP and 9520 BP (Politis et al. 2011a; see Table 2.1).

Ameghino's *La antigüedad del hombre en el Plata* was published in 1880 when he was only 26 years old and had caught up with the archaeological currents of the time. He proposed the great antiquity of the human peopling of the Pampas based on the putative association between lithic artifacts and bones of extinct mammals and the human-made marks in these bones. He placed these associations in strata assigned to the Tertiary (Miocene), comparable to the antiquity attributed to early humans by several contemporary European scholars (e.g., C. Vogt, P. Gervais, G. De Mortillet, A. de Quatrefages, etc.; see Ameghino [1880–1881]). The basic premise of his thesis on the South American origin of humankind is that humans descended not from any form of Old World monkey but from the ancient South American fossil primates, one of which – the *Homunculus patagonicus* – was named and described by him after the discovery of its bones in Tertiary deposits from South Patagonia.

Ameghino based his theory on a series of human skeletons, found by different people and in some cases in dubious circumstances (Hrdlička 1912; Lehmann-Nitsche 1907; Orquera 1971; Politis and Bonomo 2011; Politis et al. 2011a; Toledo 2009). One of them was Arroyo La Tigra's skeleton, also referred to as the "Miramar skeleton." Ameghino (1909a) attributed the latter to the Pliocene, despite an original Quaternary assignment by Santiago Roth and Robert Lehmann-Nitsche (1907: 335). Based on many allegedly primitive traits, Ameghino ascribed the remains to *Homo pampaeus*, an ancestral species of *Homo* created by him. Another human remain analyzed by him was the Arroyo Chocorí skeleton, found a few kilometers away from Arroyo La Tigra. Ameghino (1909a) included the Chocorí skeleton among the later representatives of the *Homo pampaeus*, and, against the geological position of the finding, considered it of a Late Pliocene age. Two human skeletons coming from Arroyo del Moro, also known by Malacara findings (Ameghino 1910a), were the base to define the extinct species of *Homo sinemento* and were interpreted as two female individuals buried directly in the Early Pliocene layers. Finally, three skulls with part of the postcranial skeleton were recovered first in the proximity of Necochea, while the remains of another three individuals were found later (Ameghino 1909a, b). They were interpreted as adult female individuals with pseudocircular deformations and assigned to *Homo pampaeus* (Ameghino 1911).

All these skeletons were recovered in different circumstances and in many cases by non-qualified men, are from modern humans, and, except those from Arroyo de Frías, were dated to the Middle Holocene (Table 2.1). There is no evidence of older ages and they show how Ameghino failed in his bioanthropological interpretation as well as in his chronological estimations. His main problems when analyzing the skulls were their wrong orientation (especially

Table 2.1 List of radiocarbon dates from Pampas human skeletons discussed by Ameghino

Site and catalog number	Ameghino's taxonomy	Lab. number	Date (in yrs BP)	References
Arroyo de Frías (MLP 5582)	–	CAMS-16598	10,300 ± 60	Politis et al. 2011
Arroyo de Frías (MLP 5582)	–	OxA-8545	9520 ± 75	Politis et al. 2011
Meseta del Chocorí (MACN-Pv s/no.)	–	AA90124	7623 ± 78	Politis and Bonomo 2011
		Beta	6320 ± 40	Toledo 2009
Arroyo La Tigra o Miramar (MLP 401)	*Homo pampaeus*	CAMS-16173	7270 ± 60	Politis et al. 2011
Necochea (MACN-Pv 5004)	*Homo pampaeus*	AA90125	7162 ± 74	Politis and Bonomo 2011
		Beta	6220 ± 40	Toledo et al. 2011
Necochea (MACN-Pv 5008)	*Homo pampaeus*	AA90122	7013 ± 67	Politis and Bonomo 2011
Arroyo Chocorí (MLP 400)		CAMS-16593	7010 ± 60	Politis et al. 2011
		Beta	6830 ± 40	Toledo 2009
Arroyo del Moro (MACN-Pv 5141)	*Homo sinemento*	AA90123	6885 ± 73	Politis and Bonomo 2011
		Beta	6220 ± 40	Toledo 2009
Arroyo El Siasgo	*Homo caputiniclinatus*	UGAMS 22952	3590 ± 25	Escoteguy et al. 2017
Fontezuelas (MZUC)	–	UCIAMS- 85299	1985 ± 15	Politis and Bonomo 2011
Puerto de Buenos Aires (MACN-Pv 5003)	*Diprothomo platensis*	UCR-3590/ CAMS-44656	230 ± 40	Politis and Bonomo 2011

Historical Background 35

the angle of the frontal bone) and not having taken into account the artificial deformation of some of them. Having greatly contributed to the paleontology and the geology of the Pampas, Ameghino's shortcomings in understanding human evolution drove him to a dead end.

In the Salado River Depression, Carlos Ameghino found an incomplete human skeleton known as Arroyo El Siasgo, which his brother Florentino Ameghino (1910b) attributed to a new species, *Homo caputinclinatus*. As usual, other contemporary researchers (e.g., Hrdlička 1912; see discussion in Orquera 1971) rejected this interpretation, positing that the skeleton was modern and that the skull was artificially deformed. A recent analysis concluded that the human remains belonged to a Late Holocene juvenile (between 12 and 15 years old), buried in a primary inhumation, and that its skull showed circular artificial deformation (Escoteguy et al. 2017; see Table 2.1).

Besides these skeletons, there were two emblematic findings that Ameghino interpreted to sustain his model, although neither of them was recovered by himself. The first was the "Port of Buenos Aires Calotte" (MACN.Pc 5003), known by the name of *Diprothomo*. It refers to the remains of an incomplete human calotte found in 1896 by the workers of the dry dock of the Buenos Aires Port. Ameghino (1909a) proposed that it was a "direct precursor of humanity" and that it was found at an early stage of human evolution in the early Pliocene. The calotte was dated in the late 1990s (Politis and Bonomo 2011) and gave a very recent age (Table 2.1), which can be explained in two ways: a significant redeposit in ancient strata or a fraud performed by the people who supposedly discovered the calotte (Hrdlička 1912; Politis and Bonomo 2011).

The second emblematic finding was the Fontezuelas human skeleton found by Santiago Roth, some 2 or 3 km from the Arrecifes River (Figure 2.3). It was attributed by Ameghino (1889) to the Late Pliocene, against Lehmann-Nitsche (1910), who placed it to the Late Pleistocene (Orquera 1971: 140). The most relevant characteristic of this finding was that a fragment of *Glyptodon* armor covered it, which could not be dated despite several attempts. The human skeleton gave a Late Holocene age (Politis and Bonomo 2011; Supplementary Table 3.1) and therefore the association with the glyptodont was secondary.

While Ameghino was discussing the origin of humankind, fascinating discoveries were taking place in South Patagonia at Cueva del Milodón, a very large cave at Last Hope Sound near the Pacific Ocean (Figure 2.4). This cave was discovered in 1895 by Herman Eberhard, who found a large piece of *Mylodon* skin on the surface. Explorers from different countries, notably Otto Nordenskjöld, Francisco P. Moreno, Erland Nordenskjöld, and Rodolfo Hauthal, were among the many who visited the site at the end of the nineteenth century. The latter two separately excavated the site in 1899 (Hauthal 1899; Nordenskjöld 1996 [1900]). The published report

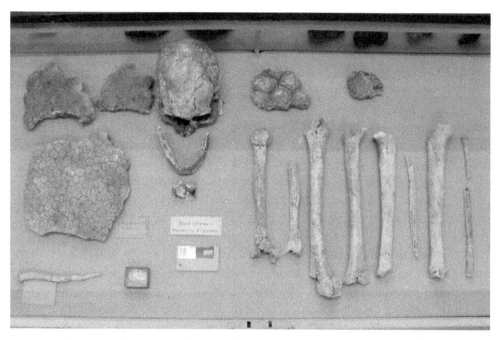

Figure 2.3 Original exhibition of the Fontezuelas skeleton (also named Pontimelo) at the Zoology Museum of the University of Copenhagen. The showcase is now in the storage room of the museum.

Figure 2.4 Cueva del Milodón, Ultima Esperanza, Magallanes, Chile.

Historical Background 37

of the excavation by Rodolfo Hauthal lacked stratigraphic information. The description by Roth and Lehmann-Nitsche of abundant and well-preserved animal remains was the main contribution of this excavation (Lehmann-Nitsche 1899; Roth 1899). These descriptions were detailed and accurate.

The excavation by Erland Nordenskjöld (1996 [1900]) was particularly important, given his careful stratigraphic observations. He recognized three main layers at Cueva del Milodón. His Layer A, on top of the sequence, was characterized by broken bones of extant species – mainly camelids and huemul – and some *Mytilus* valves. Layer B contained bones of the extinct American horse and camelids, while the presence of ground sloth was minimal. Finally, the faunal remains of his Layer C are dominated by ground sloth bones. In striking contrast with Lehmann-Nitsche (1902), he found no convincing evidence of an association between humans and ground sloths. He considered the possibility that humans were involved only in forming his Layer B, but the minimal human evidence found at the cave was confined to the top layer, in a deposit that was recently dated to around 2500 BP (Saxon 1979). It must also be emphasized that Nordenskjöld's work took advantage of what today we could call taphonomic insight, distinguishing bones with trampling marks or that had been abraded by sand (Martin 2013). The fact that Nordenskjöld's paper was originally published in Swedish (Nordenskjöld 1996 [1900]) conspired against its utilization by others. Only in the 1970s did an unpublished English translation begin to circulate, and finally, in 1996, a Spanish translation was available in print (Nordenskjöld 1996 [1900]). At the time, other studies of sloth remains were being published in Europe, basically with materials taken to England by Moreno (Moreno 1899; Smith-Woodward 1899, 1900). Since those materials were very well preserved, including dung, bones with soft tissues adhered, and a piece of skin of an extinct sloth, the fame of the cave attracted relic hunters who excavated to produce collections to be sold in Punta Arenas first and Europe after (Dabbene 2009; Emperaire and Laming 1954; Lehmann-Nitsche 1904; Martinic 1996; Mol et al. 2003). Some collections were sold to the Rothschild family and the British Museum (Natural History) in 1904 (Burleigh et al. 1977; Chatwin 1979: 275; A. Currant, pers. comm.), while others found their way to museums in Berlin or Zurich, among other institutions.

Given what was found on the surface of the cave at the time of its discovery, the site was on the covers of newspapers around the world. Accordingly, in contrast to the case of Elizabeth Island, these findings produced a huge impact. The remarkable discovery of well-preserved fragments of the skin of *Mylodon darwini*, a large extinct ground sloth, together with the rumor that it was still alive in Patagonia not only attracted wide attention but also prompted intense research. This situation reached a climax when the explorer Carlos Ameghino reported to his brother Florentino that perhaps there was a basis for the existence of living ground sloths (Vizcaino 2011). Apparently, the explorer Ramón Lista

Figure 2.5 Excavations at Cueva del Milodón in the zone where Hauthal defined a sloth corral. Photo courtesy Fabiana Martin.

observed an animal similar to a "pangolin" (*Manis* sp.), which was assumed to be a ground sloth. On that basis, Florentino Ameghino published a short note coining the name *Neomylodon listai* for what he considered a new species of sloth (Ameghino 1898). He also suggested that natives used the denomination *Jemisch* in Patagonia for the sloths. Of course, not all accepted that sloths were still roaming in Patagonia, and according to Lehmann-Nitsche (1902), *Jemisch* was used not for sloths as interpreted by Ameghino, but for either *Lutra felina* or *Felis onca*. At any rate, when the news about this discussion was known across Europe, several expeditions were mounted to hunt or capture sloths (Lönnberg 1899; Podgorny 1999b; Prichard 2003 [1902]; Vizcaíno 2011). Andrés Tournouër, a French explorer, even reported having seen a living sloth at a Patagonian lake (Tournouër 1901). Nevertheless, that aspect of the story was forgotten after those expeditions failed to discover any living sloths. However, the fascination with the well-preserved skin found at Cueva del Milodón persisted.

Hauthal returned to the cave for further digging in 1900 and collected materials that were studied and published by Roth (1904) and Lehmann-Nitsche (1904). Again, no stratigraphic information was presented. Hauthal's most famous proposal was that sloths were kept within a corral by humans (Figure 2.5). In other words, some kind of domestication of sloths was

Historical Background 39

considered. It was Hauthal's way of interpreting the large accumulations of sloth dung on the surface of the cave. This corral idea was never developed and without much discussion was promptly forgotten. However, the subject of the association between humans and extinct fauna was persistently debated during the twentieth century (Borrero et al. 1991; Emperaire and Laming 1954; Saxon 1976), particularly at the time of the disappearance of the sloths.

Stratigraphic work by Earl Saxon during the 1970s supported the notion of Holocene survival of sloths (Saxon 1976). Later research clarified the stratigraphy and showed the importance of the redeposition of sediments in some sectors of the cave. As a result, there was no basis for the existence of sloths during the Holocene (Borrero et al. 1991). At any rate, the idea of sloths hunted by humans in that region was prevalent at the end of the twentieth century on the basis of both presumed cut-marks and associations of bones and tools (Borrero 1986a; Nami 1994), a situation that was going to change with the incorporation of taphonomic studies (Borrero et al. 1988; Martin 2013).

Returning to the Pampas, the final research of Florentino Ameghino in the field of archaeology refers mainly to his findings at the Atlantic seashore, in which he postulates the existence of the "split stone" and the "broken stone" industries (Ameghino 1909b, 1910c, d), and attributes some burnt sediments known as *tierras cocidas* (baked earth) to hearths made by humans (Ameghino 1907, 1909c). He believed that all these materials were evidence of the human presence in the Tertiary. He defined the "split stone industry" in Punta Canteras as characterized by a manufacturing process different from direct percussion or pressure, which were the reduction techniques known at the time. This technique, which is nowadays known as "bipolar," was used for the reduction of the coastal pebbles that were found at the Pampas seashore (Figure 2.6) and was used for the manufacturing of a distinctive instrument of this industry, the *hachette-coin*, or "wedge-shaped ax" (Ameghino 1910d: 195). Ameghino claimed that the "split stone industry" was associated with the *Homo pampaeus*.

The proposal of the existence of a "split stone industry" of Tertiary age was first questioned by Outes (1909). On the basis of his fieldwork in the same area, this author stated that the bipolar products on the pebbles were synchronous with the later unifacial artifacts knapped by direct percussion on quartzite, characteristic of the Pampean inland. This interpretation is currently understood as the most likely (see Bonomo 2005).

With the name "broken stone industry," Ameghino denominated metaquartzite and subarkose pebbles from Ventania with negative scars from flaking and irregular flakes from the famous Monte Hermoso cliff, currently known as Farola Monte Hermoso (Figure 2.7a). Although during his paleontological investigations on the Monte Hermoso cliff he had found a series of flakes and broken pebbles (Ameghino 1889: 75), it was only in 1910, when he visited this locality along with Ales Hrdlička and Bailey Willis, that he paid any

Figure 2.6 Artifacts made of seashore rounded cobble attributed to the "split stone Industry" by Ameghino (1907a).

Figure 2.7 View of the Monte Hermoso cliff with the position of a metaquartzite artifact assigned by Ameghino to the "broken stone industry" in the Lower Member of the Punta Tejada Formation; (inset) detail of a "broken stone" artifact.

Historical Background

attention to these materials. Shortly after, he proposed the existence of the "broken stone industry," estimating its age in the Early Miocene, because of its stratigraphic position and the crudeness of its technology (Ameghino 1910c). Recent studies at the site point out that the pebbles used as raw material are available at some places on the coast as a product of fluvial transport of paleochannels that transported rocks from Ventania (Bayón and Zabala 1997). These lithic pieces can be found in situ in the early member of the Punta Tejada formation (Figure 2.7b), which has been estimated to have an Early and Middle Holocene antiquity (Bayón and Zavala 1997).

The third of Ameghino's archaeological pillars was the "baked earth," a material that resembled bricks, pieces found in the tertiary strata in the seashore banks (Ameghino 1907, 1909c, 1910e). For him, it was a human product made for burning grasses and maintaining the fire: this was how the human ancestor *Tetraprothomo* was able to keep hearths active in the Miocene. Currently, these geological features are interpreted as Miocene impacts by extraterrestrial materials (Schultz et al. 2006).

In short, Ameghino developed his own theory about the American origin of humanity, proposing human precursors from the Pampean region from times as old as the Early Pliocene. The interpretations of the findings attributing marks and anthropic fractures on bones of extinct fauna and his interpretations of human skeletons were the object of strong controversies throughout Ameghino's scientific life (e.g., Burmeister 1891; Lehmann-Nitsche 1907; Outes 1909; Outes et al. 1908). In no way can his ideas be considered to have been widely accepted by the country's scientific community at the time, although it must be recognized that he generated a debate that remained active for decades.

The most complete and detailed revision of the findings and Ameghino's interpretations of the human remains is Orquera's Grade Thesis (1971), which, sadly, remains unpublished. The geoarchaeological aspects have been recently discussed by Toledo (2009, 2016), while the political dimension and the historical context of production have been treated in detail by Podgorny (2009, 2021). Above all, she has revealed how the Socialist Party used Ameghino as a tool of political propaganda and how, in a way, his archaeological and paleontological enterprise was a "family business" (Podgorny 2021).

Darwin's ideas concerning the evolution of species did not play a significant role in interpreting initial archaeological observations. Darwin himself published short references to archaeological remains on the coasts of Patagonia (Darwin 1906 [1839]), but in the main, his Fuegian ethnographic descriptions – not to mention his key paleontological discoveries – were more detailed and significant. He also published pioneer taphonomic observations on guanaco remains made on the banks of the Santa Cruz River during the expedition directed by Fitz Roy in 1832 (Darwin 1906 [1839]). He observed significant accumulations of bones near the bushes and explained that, compared with other concentrations of scattered bones, they did not appear to be the result of carnivore activities. Recent taphonomic work confirmed those observations and attributed the bone accumulations to winter stress (Borrero 2009a). People such as the naturalist William Henry Hudson, a defender of Darwin's evolutionary theory, collected archaeological materials in North Patagonia without considering its implications. Their importance is mentioned in Hudson's *Idle Days in Patagonia* (1917 [1893]), but they produced no impact. These materials were analyzed in England by Augustus Lane Fox Pitt-Rivers, one of the founders of archaeological methodology (Lane Pitt-Rivers and Rudler 1875). Certainly, Pitt-Rivers used an evolutionary framework, but one more akin to Herbert Spencer's ideas than Darwin's (Franco 2019). The Ameghino brothers and many others were staunch supporters of Darwin's ideas, but they were focused on paleontology and paleoanthropology, while people like Carlos Burmeister were against those ideas. Burmeister was not a minor figure, since he was the director of what is now the Museo Argentino de Ciencias Naturales "Bernardino Rivadavia," in Buenos Aires, and the author of *Geschichte der Schöpfung* (History of Creation) (Burmeister 1843), which was a classic reference at the end of the nineteenth century in Europe. Nevertheless, his influence on Patagonian and Pampean research was not that important since people who worked with him at the museum, such as Luis Jorge Fontana (1976 [1886]), were more important as explorers, and most of his fieldwork was related to geological and naturalistic observations, rarely accompanied by information about the existence of rock paintings or stone tools (Burmeister 1891, 1892).

The turn of the twentieth century was a time when the completion of the geographical exploration of Patagonia was taking place under the impetus of people such as Francisco P. Moreno, Carlos Ameghino, Ramón Lista, Clemente Onelli, Jorge Claraz, and Carlos Moyano. These explorers described archaeological sites or collected archaeological materials, especially Moreno (1874), who promised a detailed description of sites and human remains that was never produced. Henry de la Vaulx (1901), who was influenced by Moreno's work, explored North Patagonia collecting human skeletons and archaeological artifacts today deposited at the Musée de l'Homme and Musée du Quai Branly, respectively (Vezub 2009). However, these observations were rarely followed by in-depth analysis. Paintings on rock walls were discovered and described (Bruch 1904; Burmeister 1891, 1892; Moreno 1879) and were sometimes interpreted as texts or attributed to "extinct races" (Fiore and Hernández Llosas 2008). Bruch also found human remains and pottery on the surface of one small cave with paintings (Bruch 1901). Major discoveries, like the naturally mummified human skeleton at Punta Gualicho in Lago Argentino (Echeverría Baleta 1995; Moreno 1879; Vignati 1934), acquired important museum value but were not readily incorporated into the initial archaeological discussions.

Historical Background

THE FIRST SHIFT: TOWARD A MORE SCIENTIFIC ARCHAEOLOGY

In the early twentieth century, when the main wave of European migration had already arrived, the profile of Argentinean society was changing quickly as anarchist and socialist ideas permeated the country. Hence, the ruling elites promoted criollo and Spanish Catholic values and traditions. At the same time, archaeologists started to look for the indigenous roots of Argentinean identity. The exegesis of historical documents was one of the primary sources of information. Other scholars were still discussing the origin of humankind in Argentina, which was Ameghino's legacy.

During this period, Felix Outes (1904) published the results of his research at the Hucal site, in the Transversal Valleys area, the first site discovered in the western Pampa, and recognized two "well-delimited industries" (Outes 1904). However, he only analyzed the lithics but did not collect them since they were given to him by an amateur who picked them up on the surface in the surroundings of the local train station (Berón 2013). Until the 1950s, this was the only archaeological site studied in some way in the western Pampa.

Among the first exhaustive and systematic archaeological reports produced in Patagonia were descriptions of large sets of artifacts from different areas, most of them without any context, also made by Outes (1905). Some trips with archaeological goals were also carried out (Aparicio 1937a,b). Descriptions of ethnographic objects were also published, but they produced no impact on archaeological research (Gusinde 1982 [1937], 1921; Lothrop 2002 [1928]; Outes 1906).

At this time, Torres (1911) excavated various isolated earth mounds in the Lower Delta of the Paraná River, and, just as Lista (1878) had, he considered that they had been raised by the indigenous people to avoid the recurring floods in the area and to be used as cemeteries. Torres attributed the differences observed in the pottery decoration to different ethnic groups from historical times and linked the zoomorphic appendages to the southern Arawak, known as Guanás.

In 1910 Ales Hrdlička and Bailey Willis arrived in Argentina to explore where human remains had been found and were used by Ameghino to propose his autochthonism theory. They also collected lithic material at surface level in some coastal sites, which William Holmes later studied. One by one, Hrdlička carefully analyzed the human remains studied by Ameghino and compiled the other published interpretations. Hrdlička's travel diary shows his initial skepticism despite the Ameghino brothers' enthusiastic welcome (Podgorny and Politis 2000). He strongly criticized Ameghino's ideas, with resounding success, using the same method he had used to reject the Pleistocene antiquity of humans in North America: he demanded well-documented findings, clear associations, and unquestionable stratigraphic identification (Hrdlička 1912: 19). By applying these criteria with regard to the "Early Man" in South America, Hrdlička (1912: 386) concluded that there was no evidence of geologically ancient human remains, nor of any precursor of humanity, which was concordant with his model of post-glacial peopling of America. As for the so-called split stone and broken stone industries, Hrdlička, Holmes, and Willis determined their antiquity to be very recent (a few centuries before the present time), noting that the coastal sites were in a superficial position and contained associations of artifacts of black basalt pebbles ("black stone industry") and white quartzite ("white stone industry") (Hrdlička 1912: 121). In addition, they were linked to the modern coastline, therefore corresponding to very late periods. For them, the coastal sites would have functioned as workshops and, because of that, would have been made up mainly by cores or waste produced during the knapping of the abundant pebbles available in the littoral (Holmes 1912; Hrdlička 1912). The further research of Aparicio (1932), as well as Bonomo's (2005) recent investigations in the seashore of the Interserrana area, supports this interpretation (see Chapter 6).

The causes of the quick deterioration of Ameghino's model and the acceptance of the interpretation of Hrdlička, Holmes, and Willis were multiple and complex. In the first place, success was a consequence of the dubious nature of many key findings and Ameghino's exaggerated chronological interpretations. The weaknesses of the Ameghinian model had already been pointed out, less successfully, by his local contemporaries. However, other factors played a part as well. In 1912 *Early Man in South America* (Hrdlička 1912) was published a year after the death of Ameghino; none of his followers had the energy or the capacity he had had to defend his ideas.

Nevertheless, one of the main causes was that both Hrdlička and Holmes anticipated a notable change in the interpretation standards and archaeological verification. The criteria applied to reject Ameghino's model were universally accepted in the later period: the Historical-Classificatory period, of which both authors were precursors (Willey and Sabloff 1980). The end of Ameghino's production coincided with the beginning of a period of substantial theoretic-methodological renovation. In the nascent field of professional anthropology, the crisis and eventual abandonment of the evolutionist paradigm was happening (Palerm 1977). The origins of the evolutionist crisis of the beginning of the century had multiple sources: Mendelian genetics, non-Darwinian biological evolutionism, the increaasing fieldwork by anthropologists and archaeologists, and so on (Palerm 1977). In consequence, besides the negative empirical testing of the very ancient peopling model, Ameghino's work also suffered the impact of anti-evolutionism and this paradigm's world crisis.

Hrdlička's, Holmes', and Willis' work circulated rapidly through the world, successfully bringing evidence of human modernity to the Pampean region. However, in Argentina, and especially in the Atlantic seashore, investigations

Figure 2.8 View of the Túmulo de Malacara excavated by Carlos Ameghino and Luis Maria Torres in 1913. Photo Archivo del Museo de La Plata.

continued with significant energy (Daino 1979). The topic became a domestic discussion, and many local researchers participated in it (e.g., Carlos Ameghino, Santiago Roth, Joaquin Frenguelli, Felix Outes) in favor of the high antiquity against it or adopted intermediate positions (Orquera 1971; Podgorny 2009).

During this period, the Túmulo de Malacara was discovered by Luis M. Torres and Carlos Ameghino in the course of an intensive exploration of the Pampas seashore (Torres and Ameghino 1913) (Figure 2.8). The description of the findings, which remained unpublished for almost 50 years, was made by Vignati (1960: 104–110). The site was in the seashore dunes, close to the confluence of the Nutria Mansa and Del Pescado creeks, and the excavators interpreted it as an anthropic construction. Inside, they found a minimum of 13 individuals interred in both primary and secondary burials. Based on several features, Torres and Ameghino (1913) concluded that the tumulus was relatively recent. A sample from these remains gave a date of 2710 BP, confirming the initial assumption (Politis et al. 2011a).

The discussion regarding the "split stone" and "broken stone" industries continued through the following decades. Frenguelli (1931) and Vignati (1948) questioned Ameghino's interpretations in regard to the "broken stone industry"; in their opinion, this material was much more recent. To Imbelloni

(1928), this "industry" was not as ancient as Ameghino proposed, nor as recent as Hrdlička and Holmes claimed. Fundamental was the research of Aparicio (1932) about the archaeological sites in a superficial position of the Pampean seashore. He agreed with Outes (1909) and Hrdlička (1912), claiming that the "split stone" and "broken stone" groups were recent and differentiated only by the raw material and the reduction technique used. The crude appearance of the coastal artifacts was a consequence of the low quality of the rounded cobbles available on the seashore, the low frequency of finished instruments, and the scarcity of pottery (Aparicio 1932).

In comparison, archaeological discussions in Patagonia were less vibrant at the turn of the century. The rejection of Ameghino's ideas about the origin of humans at the Pampas (Hrdlička 1912) affected the development of Patagonian archaeology, basically by negating the possibility of a great antiquity for the process of peopling. Indeed, due to the discussions about the Pampean sites, few were inclined to think about Pleistocene human occupations in Patagonia until late in the twentieth century. Influential authors such as José Imbelloni (1955) maintained a very short chronology for the peopling of the Americas. Claims of a Late Pleistocene antiquity for human remains found at Mata-Molle in North Patagonia can be counted among the few exceptions (Vignati 1957–1959). However, those remains have recently been dated to ca. 4500 BP (Fernandez 1983). The human remains recovered by Bird in association with extinct fauna at Cerro Sota Cave were for decades considered to be very old and were even described as "Paleoindians" (Turner 1992). However, they were dated to approximately 3700 BP (Hedges et al. 1992). Nevertheless, the acceptance of deep time in Patagonia occurred when evidence for human occupations associated with Late Pleistocene fauna was confirmed (Bird 1938), but it was not widely acknowledged (Figure 2.9).

John M. Cooper published a detailed compilation of Fuegian historical written sources in 1917, where he resumed, studied and commented on the results and observations made by hundreds of sailors and explorers who visited Tierra del Fuego and the adjacent territory. Regretting the paucity of archaeological information, he wrote that investigations were "urgently needed" (Cooper 1917: 218). Despite this limited panorama, he ventured some ideas concerning the order of arrival of the different ethnic groups to Tierra del Fuego. He accepted a considerable age for the creators of the shell middens and inferred that "the Magellanic archipelagos have been inhabited for a very long period" (Cooper 1917: 219). It is challenging to calibrate what was a "considerable age" at that time, but it clearly sustains the suggestion that people occupied the archipelagos well before the arrival of European sailors.

On the other hand, the results of an expedition by Charles Wellington Furlong to Tierra del Fuego in 1907–1908 included maps with the distribution of ethnographic camps. He also presented information about the distribution of shell middens – particularly at Wulaia, on the Murray Channel – as well as

Historical Background

Figure 2.9 Fell Cave. A first solid case of Late Pleistocene fauna associated with human foragers in Patagonia. Photo courtesy Fabiana Martin.

descriptions of hunting and fishing techniques used by the Yahgán and the Selk'nam (Furlong 1909, 1917a). Wulaia is a famous Yahgán camping place, well known to many travelers and famous because of the killing of members of the Missionary Society in 1859 (Chapman 2010). Furlong proposed that the Fuegian people arrived on foot by traveling down the eastern Patagonian plains, while the "fisherfolk" arrived "in their canoes down the Patagonian channel ways" (Furlong 1917b: 5), leaving little room for local adaptation. He also maintained that the canoe people "reached Tierra del Fuego before the foot peoples" (Furlong 1917b: 7), an interpretation that appears impossible to sustain today.

Work by Samuel Lothrop in Tierra del Fuego in the 1920s produced interesting descriptions of tools, estimations of refuse accumulation rates, and maps with the distribution of shell middens on the coasts of the Beagle Channel (Lothrop 2002 [1928]). He also inspected three archaeological sites in the northeast of the island and described some of the tools, emphasizing the presence of bola stones. Lothrop also accepted that people already occupied the southern archipelagos before the arrival of European sailors.

Milciades A. Vignati excavated at Río Chico in the North Tierra del Fuego in the 1920s (Vignati 1927), and also worked at Bahía Solano near Comodoro

Rivadavia, in the interior of Santa Cruz, in the coasts of Lago Buenos Aires, and in the world-famous Cueva de las Manos (Vignati 1934, 1950). Cueva de las Manos became the center of long-term research during the 1970s and 1980s, given its fantastic pictographs, particularly the hand negatives and guanaco hunting scenes. It also became one of the few archaeological sites in Argentina to be protected by UNESCO. Vignati delegated fieldwork at Cueva de las Manos to Alberto Rex González, then a young doctoral student from the University of Columbia, just returned to Argentina. The publication of the preliminary results obtained at Cueva de las Manos, including some good drawings (Vignati 1950), led to the recognition of its importance and prompted interest by other archaeologists (e.g., Gradin et al. 1976). Vignati also worked in North Patagonia, where he concentrated his efforts in the Limay basin (Vignati 1934). His Fuegian sequence at Río Chico was interpreted mainly in ethnographic terms. For example, Vignati considered the lower occupations of his sequence at Río Chico as a testimony of the presence of Haush groups, after which Selk'nam occupations followed (Vignati 1927). The unreliability of this interpretation is clear now when evidence is mounting showing the Haush as a late cultural configuration (Borrero 2011).

In the Pampas region, the period from the publication of *Early Man in South America* to the end of the 1940s was characterized by a certain empiricism, lacking a defined theoretical framework. Intense discussions on the findings on the seashore took place, and in some cases, they were plagued by ad hominem arguments and findings of dubious authenticity (see Daino 1979; Fernández 1982; Orquera 1971). Each new discovery contributed to the discussion unevenly, depending on the researcher who was interpreting it, and the methods and techniques used to produce results were, a lot of the time, mutually incompatible.

Torres' (1911) scheme of cultural development for the Paraná River Delta was later refined by Outes (1918a), who, on the basis of pottery and other elements, distinguished three successive groups from the Middle Paraná to the Martín García island in the La Plata River. The first had a "very simple" pottery, with few incised or painted samples associated with bone instruments and burials in elevated terrains, "apparently tumuli." The second group built the mounds (used for human burials) and created pottery with zoomorphic appendages, bone tools, and stone artifacts. The third group was the Guaraní, with large polychrome and corrugated funerary urns, polished stone axes, and a few bone instruments. This cultural scheme had a strong acceptance among the researchers who studied the archaeology of the Paraná River during the following decades. Around the same time, the excavation of various sites, such as the Brazo Largo II, brought new findings that showed the archaeological heterogeneity of the area (Politis et al. 2017; Figure 2.10).

The methods of stratigraphic seriation, the lithic and ceramic typology, the classification into cultural units, and the direct historical approach that prevailed in the North American archaeology of the time (Willey and Sabloff

Historical Background

Figure 2.10 Excavation of the Túmulo de Brazo Largo II in 1923 by Museo de La Plata employees Octavio Fernandez and Pablo Gaggero. Photo from the Museo de La Plata Archives.

1980) did not go through significant development when it came to the Pampas and Patagonia investigations. However, the research of Samuel Lothrop (1932) on the Lower Delta of the Paraná River and Junius Bird (1938) in South Patagonia somehow brought to the region the methodology that was being used in North America. However, it certainly was not wholly new in the area, since, in a certain way, Torres had applied it 20 years before.

Among Lothrop's contributions stand out the intention to recover the context, the exhaustive handling of the chronicles to interpret the archaeological record, and extensive excavations (by shovel and contracting local workers, as was the custom at the time) in three sites: Arroyo Malo, El Cerrillo, and Arroyo Sarandí. He basically distinguished between three cultures. The first had cemeteries with urn burials with either painted or corrugated pottery and labrets and stone celts; this culture was attributed to the Guaraní and was typified at the Arroyo Malo site. The second culture was characterized by its pottery, zoomorphic representations, and primary flexed burials placed in "artificial mounds like those of North America" (Lothrop 1932: 183). The third culture was distinguished by plain pottery with simple forms, sometimes decorated with incised patterns or painted bands. Burials were placed in naturally elevated land. This third culture is typified in the Arroyo Sarandí and was attributed by Lothrop to the Querandí people.

The impact of archaeological research by Junius Bird, representative of the American Museum of Natural History, New York, was more important. Bird was an archaeologist with extensive field experience in Arctic and subarctic lands, including the first test pit at the now-famous bison jump site Head-Smashed-In, Canada (Reeves 1978). Clark Wissler, then director of the anthropology division of the museum, was interested in constructing chronological frameworks for the different areas where archaeologists from the museum were working (Freed 2012), and accordingly, that was also one of Bird's primary goals. It was a time during which no efficient dating techniques existed, but Bird was prepared to make useful estimations calculating sediment accumulation rates, observing stratigraphic order, and using geomorphological relationships with fluctuating lakes (Bird 1938). During long field seasons, he worked at several places in the Chilean side of Patagonia and Tierra del Fuego, including an exploration of the archipelagos between Chiloé Island and Tierra del Fuego. This dangerous enterprise was accomplished in about five months in a 6-meter-long boat, "seeking and checking archaeological sites among the islands" (Bird 1988: 1). His observations were not detailed but were instrumental for the recent modeling of the use of the channels by maritime hunter-gatherers (Borrero 1982). In fact, even today very few places along Bird's route were systematically interrogated by archaeologists (see Reyes 2021). Once in Punta Arenas, Bird started a series of land explorations using a Ford Model T that included Laguna Blanca, the coasts of the Strait of Magellan, and the Pali Aike Volcanic Field. The access to most of those places, lacking roads at the time, was very difficult, a situation that was even more complicated given the harsh climatic conditions. Since the end of the 1930s, he published some of his results, which clearly suggested a Late Pleistocene age for the first inhabitants of Patagonia (Bird 1938, 1946). When the technique of radiocarbon dating was discovered at the beginning of the 1950s, Bird was among the first archaeologists to contribute samples. He sent charcoal samples from Patagonia to Willard Libby's laboratory, and the results of those analyses confirmed a Late Pleistocene age for human occupations at Fell Cave at the Pali Aike Volcanic Field, with the added significance that those humans were interacting with extinct fauna (Bird 1988). These results are basically confirmed by more recent research (Martin 2021; Waters et al. 2015). Based on his excavations in Fell and Pali Aike Caves and his tests at a number of sites along South Patagonia, Bird presented a cultural sequence organized into six periods. This sequence started with the association between humans and extinct fauna and finished with the European contact in the sixteenth century (Bird 1946, 1988). This sequence was a classic example of the cultural-historical approach that was current in the United States (Freed 2012; Harris 1983 [1968]) and provided the chronological framework for the archaeology of Patagonia for decades.

Historical Background

Unfortunately, Junius Bird never published his results in any detail, so most of his important field accomplishments remained scarcely known for decades. It was only with the editorial work of John Hyslop in the 1980s that most of Bird's results in South Patagonia began to be widely known and used (Bird 1988). Hyslop not only worked with Bird's notes and photographs from Fell Cave, Pali Aike Cave, Cerro Sota Cave, Cañadón Leona, and Cueva del Milodón, but also included information organized by Ian Tattersall about the human remains and Thomas Amorosi about the faunal remains, as well as reports about the carnivore remains and the palynologic sequence at Fell Cave (Clutton-Brock 1988; Markgraf 1988). Detailed tables compiled the basic list of tools obtained at each of the sites. Hyslop also commissioned a biography of Junius Bird by Gordon Willey (Willey 1988).

Bird also worked during the winter months in South Tierra del Fuego at the Beagle and Murray Channels and produced a basic scheme of human occupations for that area divided into two periods initially named "Shell Knife Culture" and "Pit House Culture" (Bird 1946). Later work by Menghin (1956) commented on some aspects of this scheme, but it was necessary to wait until the 1970s for intensive and significant stratigraphic work (Orquera et al. 1977). Orquera and colleagues worked in 1975 at the site Lancha Packewaia on the North Coast of the Beagle Channel, where they isolated two main archaeological components, the older reaching ca. 4000 BP. Large lithic tools, including projectile points, and bone tools, including harpoon heads, characterize these older occupations. They were associated with abundant guanaco and pinniped remains, complemented by birds, fishes, and mollusks. A different adaptation appears to be represented in the upper layers, which are dated to within the last 1,000 years. Marine mammals and bone technology dominate them. Despite these differences, later studies by the same team integrated both occupations within a single tradition. This excavation was immediately followed by research at the Túnel site, not too far from Lancha Packewaia, where they found even older occupations starting around 6,500 years ago, based on the same sets of resources, routinely accompanied by abundant bone tools (Orquera and Piana 1999).

During this period, some archaeological localities would be important in defining the first archaeological entities of the Pampas. The most important one was Goya-Malabrigo, which derives its name from the union of two of the most studied localities in the beginnings of the archaeology of the Argentine Northeast: Goya, in the Corrientes province on the left bank of the Paraná River (Ambrosetti 1894), and Malabrigo, to the southwest of the former (Frenguelli and Aparicio 1923). Early on, both type-localities were recognized as the focal points of an area with a greater abundance of zoomorphic appendages, whose distribution would reach the Paraná River's Delta, although with less density (Aparicio 1939; Serrano 1930). The Túmulo de Campana was recognized as another of the type sites of this archaeological entity as well and as its southernmost expression.

At this time, Antonio Serrano started his pioneer research in the Argentine Northeast. His early investigation was basically descriptive notes or schematic generalizations (Serrano 1930, 1934), but soon he developed integrative models (Serrano 1950, 1955) and placed his research in a cultural-history theoretical framework that he refined throughout his career (Serrano 1972). The work of Serrano was intensive and covered many areas of the Argentine Northeast. Without any doubt, he was the first to systematize the archaeological knowledge of the region, producing an impact that is still recognizable.

In 1939, long before obtaining his doctorate in archaeology at the University of Columbia, González (1947) carried out his first excavation at the archaeological site of Cerro Grande del Paraná Pavón, which differentiates itself from the aeolian elevations recognized by Frenguelli (Frenguelli and Aparicio 1923) and from the earth mounds with possible intentional addition of sediments described by Torres (1911). Like Lothrop (1932), he proposed that the site had been formed from a small natural elevation that had slowly increased its volume because of natural deposition and, in a lower proportion, because of human intervention. This site has been now attributed to the archaeological entity Goya-Malabrigo and dated to 630 BP (Bonomo et al. 2017).

In 1946, Gaspary (1950), a disciple of Serrano, started his investigations in the islands in front of the city of Rosario, where he excavated the anthropic mound Cerro Grande de la Isla Los Marinos. Interestingly, this author associated a hollow immediately adjacent to the hill with the extraction area of the sediments used for construction. The identification of the area of borrowing was something new at the time. In addition, he extracted an important quantity of human skeletons, a number of them painted with abundant red ochre. This site has been recently dated to 460, 590, and 660 BP (Kozameh et al. 2018).

THE AUSTRIAN-GERMAN CULTURAL-HISTORY SCHOOL: A NEW PARADIGM ARRIVES AT THE PAMPAS AND PATAGONIA

The arrival of foreign anthropologists such as José Imbelloni and Alfred Metraux in the first half of the twentieth century was instrumental in spreading the cultural-history approach represented in two main variants, one closer to the Anglo-Saxon cultural history (e.g., Serrano 1955), and another related more to the Austrian-German orientation (the so-called *kulturkreise* school) (Boschin and Llamazares 1984; Kohl and Perez Gollán 2002; Politis 1988). Using the framework of Anglo-Saxon cultural history, Willey (1946) and Willey and Howard (1948) synthesized what was known at the moment of the Pampean archaeology based on the published information. Their articles did not contribute significantly to the regional archaeological knowledge, and

Historical Background

their only merit was organizing and spreading published data of diverse origin and quality to the English-speaking world.

On the other hand, the Austrian-German cultural-history school represents the second period, in which a theoretical-conceptual body acquired popularity for over 30 years and marked the archaeological production in the Pampas and Patagonia from the 1950s to the 1970s. Numerous papers have been published that develop the theoretical basis of this school (Bórmida 1964; Imbelloni 1936; Menghin 1931), recognizing F. Ratzel, L. Frobenius, F. Graebner, W. Schmidt, W. Koppers, among others, as precursors at an international level. This current of thought has been the object of many critical analyses, not only from a strictly scientific point of view but also concerning its political dimension (Arnold 1990; Boschín and Llamazares 1984; Fontán 2005; Kohl and Pérez Gollán 2002; Madrazo 1985; Mederos Martin 2014; Politis 1995, 2021; Silla 2021).

In 1948, Oswald Menghin arrived in Argentina. He was a prestigious Austrian prehistorian affiliated with the Nazi regime in Austria during World War II (Fontán 2005; Kohl and Pérez Gollán 2002). Marcelo Bórmida, who had arrived from Italy a year before, became one of the most known of Menghin's disciples in Argentina. The arrival of Menghin and Bórmida at the end of the 1940s had a strong theoretical impact and opened a new field of investigation on sites related to prehistoric hunter-gatherers in the Pampas and Patagonia aimed at identifying the temporal depth of human occupation there.

Menghin was a fervent sponsor of the "theory of cultural circles" (*kulturkreise*), a diffusionist current that came to be known in South America by the name "Austrian-German cultural-history school" and was even self-described in its local version as the "Buenos Aires school" (Luco 2009). Menghin had made transcendent contributions toward the development of this school: he had written the well-known book *Weltgeschichte der Steinzeit* (*World History of the Stone Age*), and it was precisely he who proposed the existence of one of the three primal cultural cycles: the "Protolithic bone culture" (Menghin 1931). This cultural cycle provided the framework within which sites considered to represent early cultural manifestations in the Pampas and Patagonia were accepted (Menghin 1957a). Some cases led to what now may be seen as innocent interpretations of surface materials (Sanguinetti de Bórmida 1970a), while others led directly to the acceptance of bone pseudoartifacts as representatives of the cycle (Curzio 1976). Menghin's investigations in Egypt and various places in Europe had won him international prestige. His academic position, first as a professor and then as the rector of the University of Vienna, had acted as an institutional trampoline. He was, without a doubt, one of the best-known prehistorians of the time and a sizable opponent of Vere Gordon Childe. From different theoretical positions, they were discussing the world's prehistory.

In the field of Pampean archaeology, the founding research of the Austrian-German cultural-history school was carried out by Menghin and Bórmida in

Figure 2.11 View of the entrance of Gruta del Oro, excavated by Oswald Menghin and Marcelo Bórmida in 1949. Photo courtesy Agustina Massigoge.

1949, when they excavated the Oro and Margarita caves in Tandilia (Figure 2.11). The results were published the next year (Menghin and Bórmida 1950), and from that moment on, the school was the almost exclusive theoretical current until the end of the 1960s. The last archaeological synthesis framed within the cultural-history school was published in 1970 (Sanguinetti de Bórmida 1970b). However, some theoretical-methodological elements related to this school survived until the 1980s (Castro 1983; Conlazo 1983; Mesa and Conlazo 1982; Silveira and Crivelli Montero 1982).

Menghin and Bórmida (1950) excavated two trenches in the Gruta del Oro and a trench in the neighboring cave, which they named Margarita, and concluded that the scarce lithic material found in the third layer and in the roof of the fourth had been deposited around 7000 BP. Years later, Orquera and collaborators (1980) reexcavated the site and dated the organic matter of the third layer, obtaining a date of 6560 BP, considered a minimum age. Surprisingly, despite the speculative manner in which they estimated the antiquity of the archaeological level, Menghin and Bórmida had been relatively close to the probable age of the strata.

Menghin and Bórmida (1950: 34) proposed the existence in the area of "a very primitive culture of protolithic morphology" named Tandiliense Cultural Complex and carried to America by "inferior-hunters," which would have developed from around the sixth to the fifth millennium BC. This culture

Historical Background

Figure 2.12 Oswald Menghin inspecting an artifact probably recently found in the Chacra Briones site in Patagonia in 1956. His wife Margarita is standing on the left. Photo courtesy Nicolás Sanchez Albornoz.

would belong to a sui generis natural cycle named by Menghin as the "Protolithic Bone Culture." This cultural complex was considered epiprotolithic, which in Menghin's classification refers to a Late Protolithic, with the prefix "epi" added to indicate that it survived "in times much later than those of its original formation" (Menghin and Bórmida 1950: 34). The assignment to what they called "inferior-hunters" allowed them to infer a type of subsistence: generalized hunting (not centered on large prey, like "superior-hunters" were) and gathering. Last, this exiguous assembly of lithic material "seems to be an indication that most of the instruments of these cultural complexes were manufactured from other raw material, that is, wood and bone" (Menghin and Bórmida 1950: 34). And then they completed the argumentative sequence: materials from the Gruta del Oro and Eberhard Cave – which is no other than the Cueva del Milodón visited by Menghin in 1953 (Menghin 1961) – could belong to the "Protolithic Bone Culture" cycle, whose existence Menghin had been defending since 1931 with the publication of *World History of the Stone Age*. Many of the bone tools used to support this argument are now considered pseudotools (Borrero and Martin 2008).

The research of Menghin in Patagonia was also highly influential since his initial visits to the region in the 1950s, combining results from the study of surface assemblages with limited excavations (Figure 2.12). For decades, surface finds on the eastern steppes, particularly on sites along the Atlantic coast and the Río Gallegos basin, were assigned chronologies using a simplistic typological scheme mainly derived from Menghin's work (1960), in particular, his expectations concerning the crude technology that he associated with the earlier occupations. The presumed antiquity of the sediments above which the artifacts were deposited – usually fluvial or marine terraces – was taken as evidence for the age of the archaeological assemblages. In practice, those studies inevitably produced maximum dates. A number of archaeologists influenced by the Austrian-German cultural-history school organized their research along those lines, and many provided minimal variation to the original scheme at different places in Patagonia and elsewhere (Bórmida 1962, 1964; Sanguinetti and Schlegel 1972; Sanguinetti de Bórmida 1970a; Schobinger 1969). It took some time to accept that no credible chronological content existed on those surface collections (Bate 1982; Borrero 1980; Orquera 1984–1985). Menghin's research at Los Toldos cave (Menghin 1952a) was more important, followed by stratigraphic work in that and other caves that simply repeated the sequence (Cardich et al. 1973; Sanguinetti de Bórmida 1976). The scheme constructed by Bird in Chile was used, within the wider scheme of the *kulturkreise*, as a basis for Menghin's cultural sequence. As completed by his followers, this sequence was presented as a succession of industries named, from older to younger, "Level 11 Industry," Toldense, Casapedrense, and Patagoniense (Cardich et al. 1973; Gradin et al. 1979; Menghin 1952a). Generally speaking, this scheme relied more on population replacement than on innovation and changed through time, reflecting Menghin's opposition to evolutionary frameworks.

The study of human remains was one of the primary concerns of researchers working in Patagonia. These remains were basically interpreted within a diffusionist paradigm based on the shape of the skull and a typology of cranial deformation (Bórmida 1953–1954; Imbelloni 1937–1938).

At the same time, Menghin carried out several field trips in the west of La Pampa province. In 1950s he studied several sites in the localities of Carro Quemado, Estancia Chicalcó, and La Vega Lake (Berón 2013). Later on, in 1952–1953 and 1957, he excavated the Fortín Necochea site (Crivelli Montero et al. 1994) at the Interserrana area. Unfortunately, he did not publish these sites in any detail, although they were instrumental in consolidating the existence of the Tandiliense, which he later differentiated into three stages (Menghin 1963).

In later years, numerous investigations were developed that had a notable theoretical-methodological similarity. Bórmida (n.d., 1960) proposed on the basis of exhaustive typological analyses of surface findings, and the information obtained in some test pits, the existence of two "industries" derived from the Tandiliense: Bolivarense and Blancagrandense. Following the methods of this school, he interpreted ground stones, present in the Bolivarense, as "neolithizing" (*neolitizantes*) elements, an adjective used to explain certain inconsistencies in his expectations of the archaeological record of the "South American Protolithic." Obtaining relatively large lithic surface samples, particularly from the northeast coast of Patagonia, was another important line of research pursued by Marcelo Bórmida during the 1960s and early 1970s. In practice, these studies added a few new industries to the list initiated by Menghin and implanted some order into a complex archaeological whole. Those collections were systematically obtained, studied, and published (Bórmida 1964). They offered insights into the great morphological, typological, and technological variability present at the coastal sites. The most important research done in Patagonia during the last decades of the twentieth century was organized according to Menghin's scheme of successive industries (Gradin et al. 1976, 1979), which proved to be extremely resilient (i.e., Castro et al. 2016).

Amid the rise of cultural history, Bórmida (1962, 1969) and Austral (1965) applied a similar method – intensive surface collecting determining micro-areas of association and detailed typological analyses – and identified three new industries in the Pampean and North Patagonia seashore: Palomarense, Puntarrubiense, and Jabaliense. Furthermore, Sanguinetti de Bórmida (1966) proposed the existence of two "industrial contexts" called Trenque Lauquen A and B, which she interpreted as a territorial expansion of the Bolivarense. Also, Zetti and Casamiquela (1967) published the results of an archaeological survey in the Lihué Calel hills (in the Salado-Chadileuvú-Curacó area) that was influenced by the *kulturkreise* school (Berón 2013).

The popularity of this theoretical current in the archaeological investigations of the Pampas and Patagonia can be attributed to a number of causes. Initially, it effortlessly occupied the vacant place in the country left by evolutionism. Later on, long years of development in Europe and later in Argentina gave it scientific maturity and consolidated it as one of the most elaborate diffusionist currents. Third, its practitioners were prestigious and occupied important political-academic positions, which produced a quick and fluid theoretical transfer. Finally, the ascription to cultural-historical principles provided them with explicative statements that could be used even when the archaeological record was scarce. In this way, the artifactual exiguity of some of the sites could be interpreted by relying on identifying the cultural cycle to which they belong, a method derived from the theoretical framework of the school and intimately related to the diffusionist paradigm.

However, the investigations derived from the *kulturkreise* school reactivated the interest in studying the Pampas and Patagonia region beyond its maritime littoral. Furthermore, typological studies were encouraged, new sites were detected and excavated, and important efforts were carried out to systematize the surface assemblages and geologically date them. Nevertheless, extensive excavations were left aside; even when contemporaneous with other sites in Argentina, they had given very good results (i.e., Intihuasi Grotte, González

1960), and there was little interest in using the new techniques of radiocarbon dating. On the other hand, even when the findings in stratigraphy in lake banks indicated several diachronic occupations, the assemblages of artifacts found in the surface were considered synchronous (Bórmida 1960), as were the superficial associations between active dunes, without paying attention to the countless factors of disturbance and mixing (e.g., Austral 1965). Subsequent research noted anomalies in Menghin's scheme, but they were typically explained with ad hoc hypotheses, basically adding new cultural units to a more and more complex sequence (Cardich et al. 1973; Gradin et al. 1979). Using typological markers, these and other units derived from analysis of surface collections were organized in different cultural phyla remotely related to the European Palaeolithic (Menghin 1957b). It was an extremely complicated scheme that required information that was rarely available to correctly attribute any given archaeological assemblage to one of those units.

With lights and shadows, Menghin and Bórmida had a lasting influence and remained in the history of the archaeology of the Pampas and Patagonia. The epistemological principles that underpinned the cultural-historical model, as well as the empirical basis on which it was built, were criticized from the 1980s. Extreme diffusionism, together with the mechanical and arbitrary inclusion of archaeological materials in the circles and cultural cycles defined ad hoc by this theoretical perspective, did not resist the criticisms of a Pampean and Patagonian archaeology that was definitely oriented toward processualism. However, for three decades this model played a central role in the discussion of the past in both regions.

THE THEORETICAL ALTERNATIVES IN THE 1960S

While some of the investigations carried out in the La Plata River littoral and the lower course of the Uruguay River by Mario Cigliano (1963; Cigliano et al. 1971) were not framed within the *kulturkreise* school, the transition that would lead to a departure from this school's theoretical structure toward the search for alternatives to interpret the Pampean archaeological record began with Guillermo Madrazo's publications. Toward the end of the 1960s, Madrazo (1968, 1972) questioned the antiquity of the Tandiliense and its derived industries, its ascription to a category of "inferior hunters," and the underlying idea of a Pampean cultural homogeneity. He proposed a model based on the postulation of three "hunter niches" (of Pleistocene fauna, guanaco, and Pampas deer) with different temporal and spatial locations and also discussed some of the chronological problems from a stratigraphic perspective, taking a clear multidisciplinary approach. His fieldwork contributed with fresh data to the regional discussion and included the findings of blades from Quequén Chico in "Platense" sediments (Middle to Late Holocene),

Figure 2.13 Guillermo Madrazo's camp during a survey in the Ventania Hill Range in the late 1960s. Madrazo is on the right.

Fishtail projectile points from the hilltop of El Sombrero, and stratigraphic findings in the Blanca Grande lake and in several sites in Ventania and the CPD (Figure 2.13). The finding of Fishtail projectile points at El Sombrero hill marked a turn in the Pampean investigations and showed, for the first time since Ameghino, the possibility of a Pleistocene peopling in the region.

Madrazo's main contribution resided in the search for theoretical-methodological alternatives when the rest of the scientific community interested in the Pampean region was under the umbrella of diffusionism. The adaptive concepts, which produced some explicative statements, introduced by Madrazo (1973, 1979), opened up a whole new line of analysis and interpretation that flourished over the next decade (Mazzanti 2005; Politis 1988, 2005).

The contributions of Antonio Austral, framed at the beginning within the Austrian-German cultural-history school, also produced a theoretical change toward the beginning of the 1970s. In his article about the Vallejo site (Austral 1971), he proposed a new model based on the selection of "relevant taxonomic attributes of the contexts" (1971: 63): lithic projectile points, polished lithic artifacts, and pottery. Based on the presence of these elements, he identified three "industrial stages": Early Lithic, Late Lithic, and Ceramic-Lithic. In this stance of Austral's investigations, a preoccupation for incorporating novel concepts and methods is evident, but the persistence of cultural-history elements can also be detected (Austral 1971: 66).

Both Madrazo's and Austral's (after 1970) contributions are difficult to frame within a defined paradigm, perhaps because they were theoretical transition alternatives. None of these two authors carried out extensive excavations, or at the very least, they did not base their models on information obtained from them. Madrazo used test pits only at several sites and Austral published his first stratigraphic results in 1977. While Madrazo oriented his investigation toward an adaptive approach, Austral did it toward the systematization of lithic typology.

The Paraná River Delta and the northeast areas have been integrated into the cultural models and discussions of the Argentine Northeast (Lafon 1971; Serrano 1972). Under the influence of cultural-history approaches, diverse analytical–classificatory categories were built, and cultural sequences separated into two great "stages" or "periods," defined by the presence or absence of pottery, were established (Caggiano 1984; Rodríguez 2001; Serrano 1972). In the period that goes from the emergence of ceramics to the Spanish conquest, the archaeology of the alluvial plain of the Lower and Middle Paraná and the Lower Uruguay was characterized by the succession of different cultural entities; among others, "cultures" were identified such as the "Entrerriana or Basic Littoral Culture," "Ribereños Plásticos," and "Tupí-Guaraní" (Caggiano 1984; Serrano 1972), and traditions and sub-traditions such as "hunter-gatherers," "neolithic," "generalized Tupí Guaraní" (Lafon 1971), "Salto Grande," "Ibicueña," "Ribereña Paranaense," and "Tupiguaraní" (Rodríguez 1992). These archaeological units were subdivided into phases such as "Ibicuy" or "Ibicueña," and "Lechiguanas" (Caggiano 1984; Serrano 1972).

With a very different methodology from the *kulturkreise*, Omar Ortiz Troncoso studied selected surface collections from the southern plains of Patagonia, which were published with excellent drawings (Ortiz Troncoso 1972, 1973). The information offered by these and similar studies was important, but it took some time for archaeologists to recover their interest in surface samples. They were more inclined to look for sites with stratigraphy, seeking sequences of occupation. This was at least partly a reaction against some of the excesses of research made under the *kulturkreise* paradigm and constituted a clear case of throwing the baby out with the bathwater. Those studies of surface collections, together with new studies of those materials and new methodologies, constituted a solid basis on which a new understanding of the archaeology of the Patagonian lands was constructed, one in which we can take advantage of both kinds of discoveries (Alberti 2019; Borella and Cardillo 2011; Borrero et al. 1993). The archaeological exploration of the plateaus was important but limited, given the difficulties of access. Carlos Gradin, who moved around on horseback, was among the first to obtain significant information from those remote areas (Gradin 1959–1960, 1971). His discoveries included rock structures that were probably used as guanaco hunting blinds.

Historical Background 61

On the other hand, intensive explorations of large tracks of land, sometimes accompanied by testing or excavations, were made on the coasts of the Strait of Magellan and the Sea of Otway (Johnson 1976; Legoupil 1980; Massone 1979; Ortiz Troncoso 1973). The results from these explorations were fundamental in guiding fieldwork afterward. Among other issues, they contributed toward an initial understanding of the coastal distribution of green obsidian, a high-quality rock probably obtained at the Sea of Otway. Also, Massone's research confirmed the importance of coastal settings among so-called terrestrial hunter-gatherers. At the same time, intensive excavation programs were beginning at several places, including the Río Pinturas Basin (Gradin et al. 1976), the coasts of the Strait of Magellan and the Sea of Otway (Emperaire and Laming 1961; Ortiz Troncoso 1973, 1975), western Chubut (Aschero 1975), and the island of Tierra del Fuego (Chapman and Hester 1973; Laming Emperaire et al. 1972; Orquera et al. 1977). In most cases, these excavations were accompanied by archaeological surveys nearby, usually focused on the location of large concentrations of artifacts. Stratigraphic work was again taking place at Cueva del Milodón (Emperaire and Laming 1954; Saxon 1976, 1979), informing for the first time in French, Spanish, and English about the different periods of occupation of the cave by ground sloths and humans, which were not necessarily associated. As already mentioned, this information was available in Swedish since the end of the nineteenth century, as a result of the work by Erland Nordenskjöld, but was practically unknown. At any rate, since Cueva del Milodón is so big and was discontinuously used by animals and humans, new excavations always provided new information.

Beginning in the 1950s, rock art studies became systematic compared with the scattered efforts of the turn of the century (Menghin 1952b). The quest for the location of particular rock art styles and the initial discussions about their origin and significance are magnificently narrated by Carlos Gradin, undoubt-edly one of the most important Patagonian archaeologists, in his book of memories *Recuerdos del Río Pinturas* (1999). Since the 1960s, some of those studies have tried to go beyond the description of motifs and panels, establish-ing some context and initiating a serious discussion of chronology based on stratigraphic observations (Bate 1970, 1971; Gradin 1966–1968, 1978). The corpus of information recovered by these studies is nothing short of impressive (see Podestá et al. 2005).

This was also the time when Junius Bird was completing the radiocarbon dating of the whole sequence of Fell Cave (Bird 1988), thus making it stronger than Menghin's. Bird directed John Fell, the owner of the ranch where the cave was located, to recover charcoal samples from different sectors of his profiles, which he used to obtain radiocarbon dates for all his periods. He also did additional fieldwork at the cave and other sites, particularly an open-air site near Laguna Tom Gould, during the 1970s (see Massone 1989–1990). On the other hand, even when the industries defined by Menghin were recognized and dated by different research teams at different places in Patagonia, mostly caves, the initial chronological results were not consistent (Borrero 1989). Bird's scheme served well for decades, but near the end of the twentieth century, more regional approaches were preferred, and new sequences produced evidence of much more variability than that accepted by the original framework (Bate 1982; Borrero 1989; Gómez Otero 1987; Martin 2021; Massone 1981). These problems were found in both schemes and resulted from efforts made by different teams to construct a comprehensive chronology based on well-defined stratigraphic strata and organize reasonable sequences of human occupation. Then, the most important synthetic schemes were beginning to show operational difficulties. This was not unexpected since both sequences were formulated very early in the history of research. Nevertheless, in the 1980s, it was becoming clear that fidelity to those schemes was an invitation to stagnation. Given that Bird's scheme was published in English in the highly visible *Handbook of South American Indians* (Bird 1946), it was more widely cited outside Chile and Argentina (i.e., Willey 1971). In contrast, Menghin's papers written in Spanish and German were rarely mentioned outside the Southern Cone. With few exceptions, these systems have been no longer in use since the end of the twentieth century, given their logical, chronological, and field inconsistencies (Borrero 1980; Boschin and Llamazares 1984; Orquera 1980, 1984–1985). In retrospect, it can be said that they were important schemes to organize the archaeology of a poorly known region.

Archaeologists from the French Patagonian Mission working in south Chile during the 1960s and 1970s (Laming-Emperaire 1968, 1972) produced important stratigraphic and chronological results at crucial localities like Marazzi in Tierra del Fuego (Laming-Emperaire et al. 1972) (Figure 2.14) and Englefield in the Sea of Otway (Emperaire and Laming 1961). Both indicated important Middle Holocene occupations based on hunting guanacos at Marazzi and the exploitation of marine resources at Englefield. The results of these excavations clearly showed that human occupation of the Patagonian coasts was much older than expected and constituted the basis on which the excavation programs led by Ortiz Troncoso in Chile and Luis A. Orquera and Ernesto L. Piana in Argentina began. The French Mission also made complementary studies at Fell Cave, which helped in the understanding of the history of occupation of that site, which at the time was only sketchily known (Emperaire et al. 1963). Notably, these studies also included a relatively detailed presentation of the fauna (Poulain-Jossien 1963). The sustained efforts by members of the Mission were concentrated on the archaeology of maritime hunter-gatherers but also contributed useful studies that helped clarify the interaction between terrestrial and maritime hunter-gatherers at places like Ponsonby or Marazzi (Laming-Emperaire 1968; Laming-Emperaire et al. 1972). One important result was an understanding of the geographical variation existent within maritime adaptations, which was accompanied by

Historical Background 63

Figure 2.14 Marazzi, Tierra del Fuego, Chile. Photo courtesy Flavia Morello.

differences in adaptation, which were later detected by different research teams (Orquera et al. 1977; Ortiz Troncoso 1975).

THE DECADE OF THE 1980S: NEW DIRECTIONS

Toward the beginning of the 1980s, a significant theoretical change came about in Pampean and Patagonian archaeological investigations. This change is based fundamentally on adopting methods, concepts, and interpretative tools coming from the so-called ecological-systemic paradigm or processual archaeology (Binford and Binford 1968). These new ideas gave a new impetus to archaeological research in both regions. Archaeologists started to look more carefully at the environmental distinctions in the Pampas and Patagonia and began to discuss these differences in terms of adaptive strategies. Moreover, there has been a marked increase in researchers who systematically investigate both regions. New generations have increasingly become interested in these regions, and new methods and theoretical perspectives emerged. During the late 1970s and throughout the 1980s, the intensity of Patagonian archaeological research under the processual paradigm increased substantially, and beyond producing a multitude of cultural-historical sequences, it clearly showed that there was much more variation than that encapsulated in Bird's or Menghin's sequences (Borrero 1989).

In his synthesis of the archaeology of the Pampas and Patagonia, Orquera (1987: 346) agreed with this view, recognizing that since 1980 the archaeology of both regions has "achieved a solid scientific foundation." In this article, devoted mainly to Patagonia, one can notice a shift, since there is no mention of the *kulturkreise* units whatsoever. In the same vein, most of the regional syntheses written since the 1980s recognized this paradigmatic change (Berón and Politis 1997; Borrero 1989; Crivelli 1999; Politis 1988; Politis and Madrid 2001; Salemme 1994).

Toward the beginning of the 1980s, most of the new researchers interested in Pampean archaeology avowed that there is a great ecological and cultural diversity, and therefore it cannot be assumed to be a homogenous development as was stated before. Also, different areas can be recognized in the region from an environmental point of view, and each of these presents certain differences in the archaeological record. However, this mosaic was not considered a priori as representing ethnic frontiers. Finally, and probably due to the ecological perspective, research projects posed a multidisciplinary approach with geologists and paleontologists' active participation. At the same time, archaeologists specialized in analytical procedures, and therefore lithic analysts, zooarchaeologists, taphonomists, and others proliferate. Site formation processes, detailed rock art studies, and site functionality were new approaches emerging in the 1980s.

As mentioned, most of the initial efforts made by archaeologists in Patagonia focused on obtaining sequences. Those from the Pinturas River Basin (Gradin et al. 1979) and the Beagle Channel in Tierra del Fuego (Orquera et al. 1977) were among the most important, because they helped to organize the long history of human occupation. This was true despite the initial use of Menghin's scheme to describe the key sequence of the Cueva de las Manos (Gradin et al. 1976). With the passage of time, the use of those cultural labels – the industries – in both the Pampas and Patagonia was more of a burden than a help.

All the research done during the 1960s and 1970s in Patagonia was useful and produced a necessary basis on which new goals began to be selected. The slow incorporation of new questions, like those related to the extinction of the megafauna, the adaptations to the southwestern channels, or the divergent cultural trajectories on both sides of the Strait of Magellan, prompted a number of changes in methodology, particularly in research designs. As mentioned, mostly regional approaches began to be selected since the 1970s, which inevitably began to change the previous focus on large archaeological sites into a search for the different classes of sites (Figure 2.15). One important result was the incorporation of evidence of functional variation. Most of these studies concentrated on the search for variability, which opened the field beyond the analysis of lithics and the counting of bones. A new emphasis on

Historical Background

Figure 2.15 View of San Martín Lake Basin, with Cach Aike Hill in the background. Photo courtesy Juan Bautista Belardi.

archaeozoological studies and a replacement of typological concerns with technological questions was spreading fast (Mansur-Franchomme 1983; Mengoni Goñalons and Silveira 1976; Nami 1986; Silveira 1979). The importance of these studies was demonstrated by the discussion concerning the presence of dogs during the Late Pleistocene or Early Holocene of Patagonia, one of many debated issues at the time. According to Juliet Clutton-Brock's analysis, the canid remains found by Bird at Fell Cave were interpreted as dogs (Clutton-Brock 1977, 1988), and canid remains recovered at Los Toldos were also interpreted as dogs (Cardich et al. 1977). Later work determined those remains as pertaining to the extinct *Dusicyon avus* (Caviglia 1976–1980; Prevosti et al. 2011).

The important work from foreign researchers in Patagonia, like the French and the Spanish Missions, collaborative work with Norwegian archaeologists, or the relatively isolated works of Samuel Lothrop or David Yesner in the southern archipelagos, do not have a massive impact on regional archaeology. As noted, the input of the cultural-historical approach had a longer effect in both the Pampas and Patagonia, but as a result of the theoretical turn at the end of the twentieth century, it was clear that processual archaeology predominated in both regions. Many of these regional projects that regularly included archaeozoological, and sometimes botanical, components were increasingly combined with multidisciplinary studies. This trend shaped the interpretation of the past in both regions, and what is called "archaeological sciences" and archaeometric analysis increasingly had a more prominent role. However, other theoretical currents had their influx: Felipe Bate, Assumpció Vilá, and Jordi Estevez used Marxist categories to interpret the archaeology of Patagonia, while some issues from the post-processual agenda, such as agency, symbolism, and political dimensions, were present in Pampean archaeology. These influences can also be seen in Patagonian rock-art studies, which are reformulating previous discussions focused on the definition and distribution of styles. Also, processual-plus/neo-processualism approaches were slowly being incorporated within the research programs of several teams. In both regions, landscape-oriented studies have increasing importance. Evolutionary and neo-Darwinian approaches were also developed in the 1990s, especially from the Universidad de Buenos Aires. Many of these discussions incorporated phylogenetic studies, particularly since the beginning of the twenty-first century.

Finally, the impulse for archaeology and other sciences, which occurred due to the return to democracy in Argentina at the end of 1983, also benefited Pampean and Patagonian archaeology. New degree programs in archaeology were opened in universities in different provinces, and the Consejo Nacional de Investigaciones Científicas y Técnicas (CONICET) incorporated many archaeologists in permanent positions. New professionals started research in both regions, resulting in an exponential increase in archaeological fieldwork, material analysis, and overall generation of fresh and abundant data and models. The outcome of these growing research activities in the last 40 years, which are the core of modern Pampean and Patagonian archaeology, is summarized and discussed in the following chapters.

CHAPTER 3

RESOURCES: PREY, PLANTS, AND STONES

Since cultivation was late and marginal and there were no domestic animals (except the dog) in the Pampas and Patagonia, indigenous people in both regions depended almost exclusively on wild animals, both terrestrial and aquatic, and undomesticated plants. At the same time, stones were also crucial for making the tools to kill and butcher the prey and to process the plant products. As we will show, bone technology was secondary in most of the Pampas and significant only among coastal, both maritime and riverine, and Paraná Delta people. Therefore, wild natural resources were the key elements for human subsistence in the Pampas and Patagonian and, in some way, shaped their adaptive patterns.

In this chapter, we summarize the characteristics and availability of faunal and floral resources. We also pay special attention to the lithic raw material since rock acquisition, management, and transport provide valuable information to understand many dimensions of Pampean and Patagonian hunter-gatherer behavior. In the archaeological study of hunter-gatherers, lithic raw material has been crucial to addressing the central topics of these societies, such as lithic technology, mobility and territory, symbolic and ideational aspects, and identity and social boundaries. This chapter addresses the study of lithic raw material, its localization, and its spatial distribution. We summarize the quarry/workshop sites that have been detected in both regions. We start from the premise that most of the current lithic resources have been available since the late Pleistocene, although there may have been some variation in the accessibility of Atlantic littoral coastal pebbles (Zárate 1999) and some secondary fluvial deposits. That said, with some exceptions, the toolstone used by indigenous societies of the Pampas and Patagonia was located in the same places as they are today, and most likely with the same abundance and accessibility. Quarries are sites with a very low resolution, and their exploitation most likely involved recurring events of extraction through millennia.

Pampean and Patagonian quarries were exploited trans-generationally from the Late Pleistocene to the Late Holocene. Despite this, some quarries have been dated to at least allow us to determine a *terminus post quem* for their exploitation. In others, artifacts made out of raw materials foreign to the quarry have been found with some techno-typological clues to track the groups that were exploiting them.

FAUNAL AND FLORAL RESOURCES

The Pampas

In terms of phytogeography, the Pampas region belongs to the Chaco Domain of the Neotropical region, where four districts have been distinguished: Uruguayense, Eastern Pampean, Western Pampean, and Southern Pampean (Cabrera 1980). On the other hand, Soriano et al. (1992), following Burkart (1975), divided the grasslands region into two subregions: the first under the name of Pampa, which extends through the province of Buenos Aires and in parts of the Entre Ríos, Santa Fe, Córdoba, La Pampa, and San Luis Provinces (Soriano et al. 1992), and the second they refer to as Campos and it is found in Uruguay and the southern part of the Rio Grande do Sul state (Brazil).

The geographical limits of the grasslands are determined where contact with the xerophytic forest of the Spinal Province occurs (Figure 3.1). These forests form an arch that surrounds the Pampas grasslands (except to the east) and are characterized by the dominance of tree species such as *Prosopis*: *P. affinis* (*ñandubay*), *P. caldenia* (*caldén*), *P. nigra* (*algarrobo negro*), and *Geoffroea decortiocans* (*chañar*). These trees have been very important food resources, especially in the western Pampa. Seeds were the primary product, while the fruits were fermented to produce a low alcoholic beverage. The most important gallery forests are found at the Paraná and Uruguay Rivers and on the western margin of the La Plata River. These forests include trees with edible products such as *algarrobo* (*Prosopis* sp.) and *tala* (*Celtis tala*). In association with the Lower Paraná and Uruguay Rivers, there are also *pindó* (*Syagrus romanzoffiana), yatay* (*Butia yatay*), and *caranday* (*Trithrinax campestris*) palm groves, which are generally scattered. Palm fruits from *pindó* and *yatay* were also complementary food resources during the Late Holocene in Paraná Delta (Acosta and Ríos Roman 2013; Torres 1911). Nowadays, palm groves are heavily depleted and have a very restricted distribution. In the Campos of Uruguay and southern Brazil, these palms are also present and were frequently consumed.

There is also shrub vegetation in the rocky areas of Ventania and Tandilia hills and in the dorsal stripe of the Las Encadenadas lakes (Soriano et al. 1992). In the west, in the provinces of San Luis and La Pampa, the grassland limit is hard to define as a precise border because it is a zone where agricultural activities have completely altered the natural vegetation. The change in the border is

Resources: Prey, Plants, and Stones

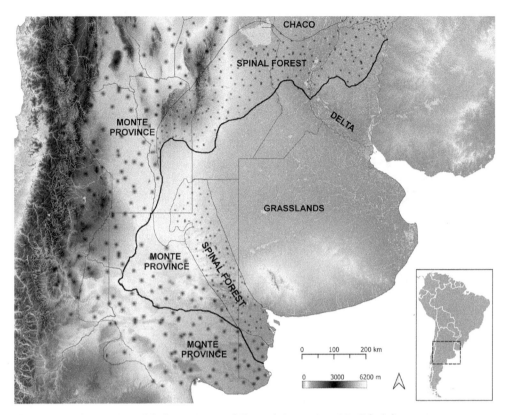

Figure 3.1 Phytogeographical provinces of Central Argentina. Modified from Burkart (1975), Cabrera (1980), and Soriano et al. (1992).

distinguishable in the province of Entre Ríos, in which the flat grasslands to the south of the 32° parallel contrast with the forests that extend to the north over the gentle undulations, locally known as *cuchillas* (Soriano et al. 1992).

On the coast of the estuary and the La Plata River, up to 5 masl, a marine plain extends, in which there are parallel seashell ranges, a remnant from the Middle Holocene Marine Ingression. On these ranges, there are *tala*, *molle*, and *coronillo* dense forests. These trees have been exploited during the Late Holocene, especially the *tala*, which has edible small fruits (Paleo and Perez Meroni 2004).

The zoogeographical territories are usually associated with phytogeographical ones. Ringuelet (1955) and Ringuelet and Aramburu (1957) proposed that, zoogeographically, the Pampas region is a transitional zone between the Guyanese-Brazilian subregion of the Subtropical Domain and the Austral subregion. Ringuelet (1955) considered the fauna of the Lower Paraná and Uruguay-La Plata Rivers as a subtropical intrusion from the north. Regarding the rest of the biogeographical province, fauna elements are mainly Brazilian, although a strong Patagonian influence can be observed in the southern sector (Cabrera 1980).

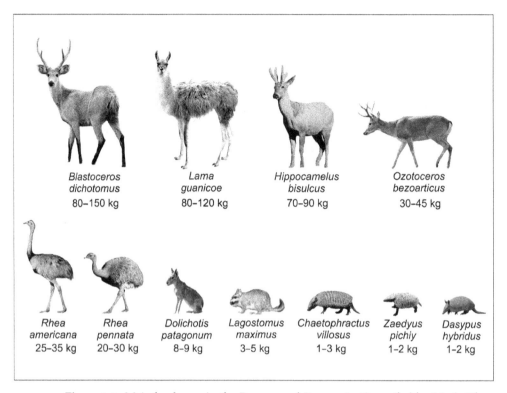

Figure 3.2 Main land prey in the Pampas and Patagonia. Compiled by María Clara Álvarez.

In the Pampas, the more conspicuous mammals are the plains viscacha (*Lagostomus maximus*, Figure 3.2) and some marsupials, like the opossum (*Didelphys azarae*), the lesser grison (*Galictis cuja*), and the neotropical river otter (*Lontra longicaudis*). There are numerous rodents, like the mara or Patagonian hare (*Dolichotis australis*), the tuco-tuco (*Ctenomys*), the wild cavy (*Cavia, Microcavia*), and the coypu (*Myocastor coypus*). Among these, the coypu stands out because it was a key resource in the aquatic environments in the Northeast Area and in the lower sector of the Salado River Depression. The biggest rodent, the capybara (*Hydrochoerus hydrochoerus*), is abundant in the Northeast area (Cabrera 1980) although despite its high meat yield it was only occasionally exploited. Armadillos from different genera (*Dasypus, Chaetophractus, Zaedyus*, etc.) were abundant in almost all areas. Most of these medium and small-sized mammals have been consumed by Pampean indigenous people. Although they do not provide abundant meat, their high density in many places and ubiquity make them reliable secondary resources. Ethnohistorical accounts are very informative about the importance of the armadillos in the diet of Pampean hunter-gatherers.

There were three species of cervids (Figure 3.2): Pampas deer (*Ozotoceros bezoraticus*), marsh deer (*Blastoceros dichotomus*), and brocket deer (*Mazama gouazoubira*). The former two were abundant in the past in some areas but

Resources: Prey, Plants, and Stones

Figure 3.3 Pampas deer in a typical grassland in the Northwest area.

currently live only in relictual zones (Merino 2003; Politis et al. 2011). The Pampas deer is a typical cervid of the open areas south of the Amazon River Basin. It is a gregarious mammal weighing between 30 and 45 kg, and it occupies places where green grass is available (Figure 3.3). The distribution area up until the mid-nineteenth century covered central and southeastern Brazil, southeastern Bolivia, Paraguay, Uruguay, and central and Northeast Argentina. It was abundant in the Pampas region, but vigorous hunting introduced diseases, and the alteration of the habitats due to agro-pastoralism resulted in a sharp reduction of its population. It was a significant resource, although not the main one, in the whole Pampas region throughout the Holocene. As we will show, the Pampas deer became more important in the human diet toward the Late Holocene in almost all areas.

The marsh deer is a large cervid, between 80 and 150 kg, which lives in floodplains (with a water depth no greater than 60 cm) with low vegetation (estuaries, reservoirs, and marshes) in the south-central region of South America, where the average rainfall exceeds 1,000 mm per year (Pinder and Grosse 1991; Piovezan et al. 2010). In Argentina, this species was distributed along the Paraná, Paraguay, and lower Uruguay basins, including the Iberá marshes and the delta of the Paraná River. Due to hunting and habitat modification, the marsh deer is currently limited to a few localities (Piovezan et al. 2010; Politis et al. 2011). This cervid was an important resource during the Late Holocene only in the Lower Paraná and Uruguay Rivers since their habitat was restricted to aquatic environments. The brocket deer was always confined to a few sectors in the northeastern area, although it was more abundant in the Campos of Uruguay and Southern Brazil. Its record in the archaeological sites in the northeastern area is very low.

There are a few carnivores: skunks (*Conepatus*), foxes (*Dusicyon*), Geoffrey's cats (*Felis geoffroyi*), and the Pampas cat (*Lynchailurus pajeros*). The Northeast of the region is also inhabited by the yaguarundí (*Herpailurus yagouarundi*) and two fox species: crab-eating fox (*Cerdocyon thous*) and *aguará guazú* or maned wolf (*Chrysocyon brachyurus*). Until the nineteenth century, two of the biggest felines of South America lived in the Pampean region: the cougar (*Felis concolor*) and the jaguar or *yaguareté* (*Pantera onca*). The first was very abundant and still inhabits various areas, while the second, much less frequent, is nowadays virtually extinguished from the region. Carnivore bones are regularly recorded in very low quantities in the archaeological record in the Pampean sites, but evidence of human consumption is exceptional. Their presence has been interpreted as the result of uses other than food (e.g., fur, teeth, bones for tools, etc.)

There is a large number of arboreal and aquatic birds (*Phalacrocoracidae, Ardeidae, Podicipedidae, Rallidae, Psittacidae*), like partridges of the genera *Rynchotus* and *Nothura*, martinetas (*Eudromia* sp.), and ducks (*Anas* and *Netta*), among others (Cabrera and Willink 1980). The greater rhea (*Rhea americana*) is the largest bird in the region and was certainly a resource for the Pampean hunter-gatherers. Although its presence in the archaeological bone assemblages is low, probably due to taphonomic factors, ethnohistorical accounts frequently mention greater rhea hunting. Shell eggs from this bird are present in archaeological record since the Middle Holocene (Chapter 5), suggesting consumption. Complete greater rhea eggs with a hole in one pole have been found in the Central Pampas Dunefield, indicating their use as liquid containers (see Chapter 5). The ethnohistorical record also shows intense use of greater rhea eggs for food.

Other fauna includes reptiles (*Tupinambis merinae* and *Caiman latirostris*) and mollusks (*Diplodon* sp., *Ampularidae*). In the Paraná and Uruguay Rivers, there is a great abundance and variety of fish, with around 300 species of the *Characiformes* and *Siluriformes* orders (López 2001). Most of the pisciform vertebrates are subtropicals that arrive at the region through the Paraná and Plata basins. The lamprey (*Geotria australis*), the swamp eel (*Synbranchus marmoratus*), and the pejerrey (*Basylichtys*) are the species that stand out the most (Cabrera 1980). During the second half of the Late Holocene freshwater fish from the Lower Paraná and Uruguay rivers were the base for the subsistence of the riverine indigenous people in the northeastern area (Acosta 2005; Bastourre and Azpelicueta 2020; Caggiano 1977).

Resources: Prey, Plants, and Stones   73

Until the nineteenth century, there were several rookeries at the coast of the Pampas region, to the west of the Cabo Corrientes. They were formed by the southern fur seal (*Arctocephalus australis*) and the southern sea lion (*Otaria flavescens*) since the ranges of these two otariids are sympatric (Redford and Eisenberg 1992). While fur seals prefer rocky areas and sea lions sandy beaches, they often haul out together (King 1983). Sea lions are the larger of the two species, with some overlap in weight and length between female sea lions and male fur seals. Both species have been exploited since the Middle Holocene on the southwestern coast of the Pampas, although few sites testified to this exploitation (Bayón and Politis 2014; Bonomo and León 2010; see Chapter 5). Additionally, there are important rookeries in the Isla de Los Lobos at the entrance of the La Plata River estuary, where both species cohabit. On the Pampean coast, there occasionally is cetacean stranding of different species: southern right whale (*Eubalaena australis*), humpback whale (*Megaptera novaeangliae*), and a few others, which can also occasionally penetrate the La Plata River.

Without a doubt, the most important species for the subsistence of the indigenous populations of the Pampas and Patagonia was the guanaco (Figure 3.2). This camelid weighs between 80 and 120 kg, depending on the region (Barberena et al. 2009). It was the most widely distributed ungulate in the south of the continent from the Pleistocene until the introduction of cattle. The guanaco covers all spectrums of aridity, reaching humid areas of over 750 mm of annual rainfall in Tierra del Fuego, at altitudes from 0 to 800 masl in the south and from 150 to 4,500 masl in the north. They strongly prefer open spaces (grasslands and low and middle shrublands) and only exceptionally occupy forests, for example, the *caldenar* in the Pampas and the cold forests in Tierra del Fuego. The highest abundance of guanacos in Argentina is in Patagonia, while in the Pampas, there are confined populations in the Ventania hills (Figure 1.8) and more established herds in the southern area.

The pre-Hispanic and historical distribution of the guanaco in the Pampas has been subject to a vivid discussion since Madrazo (1973) proposed that this ungulate would not have inhabited the Salado Depression and the Rolling Pampa due to ecological constraints. This hypothesis was resumed by Tonni and Politis (1980), who concluded that the guanaco inhabited the eastern Pampa during the Late Pleistocene and most of the Holocene, but that when the Spaniards arrived in the sixteenth century, this camelid no longer occupied this subregion (except for the Ventania hills). They proposed that the guanaco retraction during the Late Holocene was a consequence of ecological causes related to climatic changes. Later research by Politis and Pedrotta (2006) supported this hypothesis and suggested that guanaco retraction to the west and the south might be related to the environmental conditions between the eighth and twelfth centuries known as the Thermal Medieval Maximum. Politis et al. (2011) used the Maxent program and compared the ecological conditions of the guanaco with those of Pampas deer and marsh deer. This study showed that guanacos and marsh deer have no area of overlap but are clearly separated by a strip of land of variable width, always greater than 100 km, which indicates that the species are most likely allopatric. Therefore, the presence of bones from both species in the same context in the archaeological record would indicate long-distance human transport.

Based mainly on historical accounts, Loponte (1996–1998; Loponte et al. 2004) proposed that guanacos did inhabit the eastern Pampa in historical times and that this species was the main hunting prey of the Querandí Indians who forayed in this subregion (Loponte et al. 2004). However, no historical mentions refer to the hunting of guanacos by the Querandí Indians in the eastern Pampa. The historical accounts summarized by Loponte cannot be placed in the east of the Pampas region since the locations mentioned in these quotes are vague or even belong to regions other than the Pampas. Furthermore, some of the historical quotes mentioned by Loponte refer not to the guanaco but rather to domesticated camelids (Cornero 2021; Politis and Pedrotta 2006).

During the Late Pleistocene, a rich fauna inhabited the Pampas with a high percentage of megamammals. Analysis of mammal diversity in the region shows a maximum peak of around 14,000 BP, after which it declines (Prado et al. 2015). Megamammals include proboscideans, giant ground sloths, glyptodonts, toxodonts, equids, and paleo-camelids (Barnosky and Lindsey 2010; Cione et al. 2009; Prado et al. 2021). The archaeological record shows the association with *Megatherium americanum*, *Hippidion principale*, *Equus (A.) neogeus*, *Paleolama* sp., *Macrauchenia patachonica*, *Toxodon platensis*, *Doedicurus clavicaudatus*, *Glossotherium robustum*, *Neosclerocalypus* sp., *Glyptodon* sp., and *Eutatus seguini*. However, only *Megatherium*, *Doedicurus*, *Equus*, *Hippidion*, *Macrauchenia*, and *Eutatus* have evidence of human exploitation. Almost all these mammals became extinct during the Late Pleistocene to Holocene transition for causes that are still under debate (among many others, Barnosky and Lindsey 2010; Barnosky et al. 2016; Cione et al. 2009; Prado et al. 2021; Prates and Perez 2021). Only the giant armadillo, *Eutatus seguini*, and the extinct canid *Dusicyon avus* survived until the Holocene.

Patagonia

The phytogeographic diversity observed along the 1,600 km of the western archipelagos clearly indicates that they offer a variety of heterogeneous habitats. Important water barriers separate some of the archipelagos, principally the Gulf of Corcovado. Accordingly, the Chonos Archipelago, south of Chiloé, is relatively isolated. It forms a net of channels and fjords with narrow and abrupt coastlines, whose exploitation necessarily requires particular effort (Reyes et al. 2016). All

Resources: Prey, Plants, and Stones 75

these lands have in common the harsh climate and their vulnerability to earth-quakes and tsunamis (Reyes et al. 2018). For those reasons, plus the presence of extensive peatlands, the archipelagic islands are places in which it is extremely difficult to work. Finding archaeological sites requires intense sampling by coring and test pits because visibility is very low. Information concerning the important changes in the Holocene coastlines is also crucial in this quest.

The Northern Andes present two very different forests. In the northern limit with Cuyo, the Araucarian forest offers a high productivity environment, with pines providing a seasonal harvest of nuts that humans exploited. South of these pine stands, the Valdivian evergreen forest is less attractive. It is particu-larly developed on the west side of the Andes but is also present at high precipitation patches on the east side (Cabrera and Willink 1980). The Valdivian forests constitute green barriers, where the dense understory of bamboo makes human navigation very difficult.

In the south, deciduous forests of *Nothofagus pumilio* and *N. antarctica* dominate the Andean slopes up to 600 masl, while more closed forests of evergreen *N. betuloides* characterize the humid valleys in the west (Dollenz Alvarez 1995; Heusser 2003). These forests are also present in the center of Tierra del Fuego, following the west-east axis of the Fuegian Andes (Pisano 1977). In the northwest of the Isla Grande de Tierra del Fuego, north of Bahía Inútil, there is an isolated forest of *Drimys winteri* and *Maytenus magellanica*, notable for the absence of Fagaceae (Dollenz Álvarez 1995: 23). These forests support high precipitation, in stark contrast with the Patagonian or Fuegian steppes, where precipitation is less important. Hunter-gatherers from Tierra del Fuego make use of all these environments.

Most of Patagonia is characterized by vast steppes of alternating xeric grasslands of *coirón* (*Festuca gracillima*), *Stipa* sp., and *calafate* (*Berberis buxifolia*) in the east and humid or mesic grasslands characterized by *Festuca* sp. and *Lepidophyllum cupressiforme* in the west (Figure 3.4). These steppes show changing proportions of shrubs, particularly *mata negra* (*Chiliotrichum diffusum*, *Verbena tridens*), reaching up to 1.5 m in the extensive plateaus between river basins. All these environments were exploited by guanacos, the mainstay of local hunter-gatherer populations. High-elevation wetlands and tundra vege-tation exist at some of the more western plateaus, such as the Meseta Latorre (Ercolano et al. 2020).

The modern biomass of the Patagonian steppes is relatively homogeneously distributed, with few exceptions. The summer occupation of the plateaus by guanacos is one of Patagonia's most significant ecological rhythms since it determined human displacements following the herds. The plateaus consti-tuted recurrently used places to hunt guanacos, to the point that during the Late Holocene, they were equipped with hunting blinds.

The most important faunal contrast is between those from the steppes and the humid western forests and the coastal environments. The diversity of large

Figure 3.4 View of Potrok Aike Lake, Pali Aike Lava Field, Argentina.

Patagonian vertebrates is extremely limited in comparison with northern regions in South America. The largest and more abundant terrestrial vertebrates are guanacos and both greater and lesser rhea *(Rhea americana, R. pennata)*. Huemul *(Hippocamelus bisulcus*, Figure 3.2) and pudu *(Pudu puda)* can be found in some Andean forests in very low densities. The former has a relatively extensive latitudinal distribution, while the latter is only present in the North Patagonian forests. There are few carnivores, of which the largest is the puma *(Felis concolor)*, which hunts guanaco, huemul, and smaller prey. Also, small wild cats *(Felis geoffroyi, F. colocolo)*, foxes *(Lycalopex culpaeus, Lycalopes griseus)* and Mustelidae are present. Rodents are abundant and diverse, some of them with very strict ecological requirements, making them good markers for past conditions. *Ctenomys* sp. was abundant and consumed by humans in several Patagonian regions. Bats complete the basic list. The most widely distributed reptile is *Liolaemus* sp., whose remains are sometimes recovered within archaeofaunas, but are not necessarily the result of human activities (Albino 2016).

The coasts of the Atlantic and Pacific Oceans are characterized by rookeries of two pinnipeds, where the large *Otaria flavescens* is predominant today. Given the massive exploitation of the smaller *Arctocephalus australis*, this species presents today a highly restricted distribution. The largest concentration of

Resources: Prey, Plants, and Stones

rookeries exists at the Peninsula Mitre, in the southeastern extreme of Tierra del Fuego. A few rookeries of the largest phocid in the world (*Mirounga leonina*) exist. These animals weigh up to 3 tons, thus offering substantial quantities of meat and fat, but they were rarely exploited in the past. It is today relatively abundant in Peninsula Valdés, Argentina, and Seno del Almirantazgo, Chile. Marine mammals from Antarctica such as *Hydrurga leptonix* (Markham 1971) or *Arctocephalus gazella* are occasional visitors to the coasts of Tierra del Fuego. The Patagonian coasts are also seasonally visited by large whales, some of which reproduce on the coasts of Chubut, such as *Eubalaena australis*. Concentrations of *Physeter catodon* and smaller cetaceans are also observed. Sometimes these different whales have massive strandings in areas with flat intertidal substrates such as Bahía San Sebastián or Bahía Lomas (Borella 2004). Dolphins are regularly seen on the coasts, particularly *Cephalorynchus commersonii*, *Lagenorhyncus australis*, and *Orcinus orca*. The Strait of Magellan is an important microregion in itself because some sectors – particularly near San Gregorio and the mouth of the Jerónimo channel – are characterized by very high productivity, and seasonal concentrations of whales occur (Gibbons et al. 2000).

Sea mammals constitute the primary prey for humans in the channels, but they can be found in high numbers only at selected locations. On the Pacific front, those locations are on the more western islands, which are also characterized by high numbers of resident birds. The combination of places where eggs can be gathered in numbers and marine mammals can easily be hunted or scavenged makes these outer islands a crucial seasonally occupied habitat for maritime hunter-gatherers. Excepting occasional visitors, the fauna from the western channels include very few vertebrates (Markham 1971). Small carnivores with restricted distribution, such as *Lutra* sp., are present at very exposed coasts.

A diversity of mollusks can be found in the different coastal habitats of the Atlantic and Pacific Oceans (Forcelli 2000). Birds are quite abundant in all the main habitats, including dozens of migratory species (Tivoli 2010; Vuilleumier 1993). In terms of human subsistence, *cauquenes* (*Chloephaga picta*), shags (*Phalacrocorax* sp.), and the mentioned flightless species were the most important birds. Penguins (*Aptenodytes patagonico*, *Spheniscus magellanicus*) played a minor role in subsistence on the coasts.

As already mentioned, for the Pampas, guanacos are the most important vertebrates for human subsistence. Without any discussion, guanacos were available practically everywhere in Patagonia. Despite its importance, there are a few regions in arid Patagonia where the archaeological record is not focused on their exploitation, like the Middle Limay and Negro basins. This ungulate forms familiar groups, male groups, and in some places, female groups. Even when guanacos are not characteristic of the forests, they can make a living there, as exemplified by the case of Tierra del Fuego, where guanaco populations are abundant in several forest habitats (Raedeke 1978).

As mentioned, in terms of human subsistence, the presence of huemul (Figure 3.2) and pudu is the main characteristic of the forest. Several potentially attractive plants and mushrooms must also be added, but with few exceptions, their importance in the past is not well known (Belmar 2019). The distribution of the huemul is basically confined to the western forests, even when some authors suggest its presence in the eastern steppes in the past (Diaz 1993). The distribution of skeletal remains, particularly horns, indeed indicates their fossil presence at places far away from the forests, such as the middle course of the Gallegos River or the mouth of the Santa Cruz River (Carballo Marina et al. 2008; Cruz et al. 2010; L'Heureux and Borrero 2016). To explain these findings, the existence of hunting expeditions from the steppe was considered (Díaz et al. 2007), although they are better explained as the result of the transport of horns. The use of huemul skins for armatures and other objects, and horns for tools, was recognized in the ethnographic and archaeological records (Díaz and Smith-Flueck 2000), and this probably was one of the reasons for huemuls' attraction. Significantly, huemuls differ substantially from the guanacos in both behavior and abundance. They are solitary animals or move around in small groups of five to eight individuals (Diaz and Smith-Flueck 2000; Guineo et al. 2008). A few historical references suggested that larger groups may have existed in the past (Prichard 2003 [1902]). Attractive as they were when available within normal hunting ranges, huemuls' social organization, demography, and size make them a less preferred target than the guanaco (Fernández et al. 2016). Also, their meat is considered meager, but this is also the case for guanacos.

Pudus are less abundant and very small in size, about 0.4 m high and with a mass of about 10 kg. This small cervid lives in small family groups and selects little disturbed habitats, sometimes preferring *Nothofagus pumilio* forests in sloping humid terrain. They can be sympatric with huemul in the same places and were rarely exploited by humans.

During the Pleistocene, the list of animals was longer since a number of extinct species were still available. Among the herbivores, we must mention the American horse (*Hippidion saldiasi*), a substantial subsistence resource for the first hunter-gatherers; ground sloths (*Mylodon darwini*); camelids (*Lama gracilis*); and one Notoungulate, *Macrauchenia* sp. The list of extinct carnivores includes short-faced bears (*Arctotherium* sp.), two extinct felines, the saber-tooth cat (*Smilodon*), the Patagonian panther (*Panthera onca mesembrina*), and an extinct canid (*Dusicyon avus*). The latter is the only extinct mammal for which there is good evidence of Holocene survival in Patagonia (Prevosti et al. 2011).

LITHIC RAW MATERIALS

A diversity of rocks available in primary and secondary sources characterized the Pampean and Patagonian landscapes, many of them routinely selected for

Resources: Prey, Plants, and Stones

tools in the past. The provenance of those stones interested archaeologists of both regions. However, it was only after Hugo Nami's and Nora Flegenheimer's pioneer work on sources and quarries that a systematic approach to discussing raw materials' provenance began to be used (Flegenheimer 1991; Nami 1986, 1992). Together with other regional approaches (Ericson 1984), they were intensively used in the Pampas and Patagonia. Research on the transport of different raw materials with known provenance provided major vectors for mobility and interaction at different temporal and spatial scales. Secondary sources, in which only rarely is origin discussed in any detail, were not ignored and significantly added to the discussion (Bayón and Zavala 1997; Bonomo 2005; Catella 2014; Franco 2002a, 2004).

Beyond the distinction between primary and secondary sources, focal distributions of rocks occur when they are spatially restricted. Focal sources are particularly important: (1) Since spatially restricted sources are more difficult to discover, the earliest appearance of a particular rock in the archaeological record informs the degree of knowledge of the environment; (2) they are useful to assess possible networks of connection between places; and (3) some raw materials from focal sources are of high quality, which not only helps to explain their wide distribution but transforms them to magnets attracting people through time. While most raw materials used in Patagonia were obtained from secondary sources and are more abundant, in the Pampas, primary sources seem to be more exploited. Together, both classes of sources contribute to our assessment of human adaptations. Anthropologically oriented questions, provided that they are phrased in archaeological terms, offer different models to explain the observed distributional patterns. Accordingly, models of exchange, visits, and other interaction mechanisms used to explain them are regularly invoked. In the Patagonian literature, it is usual to take the abundance of nonlocal raw materials to measure the importance of exchange, which is not an inference to be made lightly. In the Pampas, the focus was on the distance to the known quarries since extra-regional toolstones are rare. The notion of exchange as a means of obtaining exotic goods in Patagonia was recently discussed by analyzing distance-decay patterns in the frequencies of black obsidian and marine materials, and it was found that there is much intermediate variation that is not explained by the ideal extremes of exchange or direct acquisition via mobility models (Pallo and Borrero 2015a). Accordingly, it was suggested that there are a number of conditions under which the distribution of raw materials over large distances relates to other processes that need to be explored. The critical information is not the fall-off itself but the spatial scale of this pattern. This is why analysis of large spaces is preferable, perhaps including areas where no known manifestations of the item under research are present (e.g., Molinari and Espinosa 1999). This is a consideration that was not always easy to follow (Cassiodoro et al. 2020;

Guraieb et al. 2006), limiting the significance of the analysis. A more secure inference is that the spatial scale of those distributions is a measure of social communication or interaction in which more than one acquisition mode was operating (Borrero 2012; Santos Valero and Martínez 2019). This broader concept admits variants, such as visiting or other types of social interaction associated with open social formations. It can be maintained that these mechanisms can be more clearly discussed using raw materials with known sources of provenance (Barros et al. 2015; Borrazzo et al. 2018; Borrero et al. 2009; Méndez et al. 2018; Nami 2017; Pallo and Borrero 2015a). We return to this subject in Chapter 7.

There are important technical considerations for analyzing lithic sources, beginning with the identification of the rocks. This is sometimes conducted visually based on macroscopic properties such as color or texture, among many other observational variables, but usually requires a more technical approach. Among the techniques used are petrographic descriptions of thin sections, trace elements, X-ray fluorescence analysis, or geochemical analyses. As a result of using these techniques, most long-term projects constructed reference lithotheques that cover the most important lithic sources for the Pampas and Patagonia. But there are always difficulties stemming from the use of different classificatory systems (Barros et al. in press; Berón 2006; Cattáneo and Dilello 2000; Ratto and Belardi 1996) to the point that even a gazetteer of lithic raw materials was published to facilitate communication (Alberti and Fernández 2015).

Flaking properties are a logical consideration when discussing the selection of raw materials (Aragón and Franco 1997; Bayón et al. 2006), even when recent studies suggest that this variable is not definitive (Eren et al. 2011). Many other factors condition the selection and use of lithic sources, especially the availability of local stones or access routes (Belardi et al. 2006; Colombo 2013; Méndez Melgar 2004; Pallo and Borrazzo 2016). The Pampas showed that color could be a selecting variable (Flegenheimer and Bayón 1999), and similar considerations were made for Patagonia (Hermo and Miotti 2010). Most sources were likely more accessible when there was no snow or ice cover, as happens during the long winter months in or near the Andes, sometimes located at more than 3000 masl (Belardi et al. 2006; Durán et al. 2004). This problem also exists for locations on the eastern Patagonian steppes, where for a couple of months, most secondary sources are covered by snow and ice, and only some outcrops remained available (Cattáneo 2004), or the southwestern channels where green obsidian probably was collected during the warmer months (Morello et al. 2001). Of course, research can change some of these perceptions. For example, the discovery of obsidian nodules away from their sources completely changed previous interpretations of exclusive access to rocks during certain months (Belardi et al. 2006; Fernández et al. 2017; Franco et al. 2017a). Also, the recent discovery of a quarry site of high-quality orthoquartzite in the northwestern extreme of Tandilia substantially

Resources: Prey, Plants, and Stones

modified the minimum distance to the source from the western Pampean sites (Barros et al. 2021). Other seasonal limits are established by intense precipitation that covers sources with mud at gullies and canyons (Cattáneo 2004). Then, in many cases, there were short windows of utilization for those sources, a condition that requires long-term planning by people using them.

On the other hand, there are cases responding to other rhythms, like Punta Pórfido on the coast, accessible only at low tide (Alberti et al. 2015), a situation shared by many sources along the Atlantic coast (Bonomo and Prates 2014). Long-term changes are also important, for example, the patterns of disappearance and redistribution of lithic sources in coastal locations (Borrazzo 2009, 2010, 2012). The contrast of all these cases with sources available year-long is basic for the interpretation of regional patterns of human mobility and settlement.

One problem in the identification of the raw materials is the different names given in the literature to the silicious rocks. There is a microcrystalline silica, fine-grained radiolarian chert that is whitish, gray, or smoky, which outcrops in several places in Tandilia. This has been called chalcedony, but based on the mineralogical analysis, it is currently named phtanite (the name we will maintain) and sometimes chert. In other cases, some cherts with specific characteristics made them recognizable, such as the "silicious chert" of the El Fresco Plateau. Finally, other cherts cannot be referred to more specifically, and therefore, we simply maintain the generic denomination of chert as the original authors mentioned it.

A very significant feature in the Pampas is that most outcrops of knappable stones are in the southern and western portion of the region, while in the rest of the region there exist tens of thousands of square kilometers of loess and sand with no available toolstones (Figure 3.5). In this immense land, the harder rock is the calcrete, the white calcium carbonate occurring in loess, which was only exceptionally used for low-quality bola stones (Massigoge et al. 2021; Vecchi 2016) and to signalize human burials (Politis et al. 2014). This means that approximately two-thirds of the region is a stoneless grassland. This, without any doubt, affected lithic strategies and mobility patterns.

LITHIC RAW MATERIALS IN THE PAMPAS

Until the 1980s, knowledge about the sources of raw material was very general, and essentially only the fine-grained quartzite from Tandilia, the coarse-grained from Ventania, the phtanite from Tandilia, and the coastal pebbles of the Atlantic coast were identified (e.g., Bórmida 1962; Madrazo 1979; Politis 1984). Quarries and workshops were not detected, and direct access to the raw materials within an embedded strategy was assumed (Politis 1984). With few exceptions, there was no precision on the source of each rock. In the early 1990s, there was a substantial change since a regional lithic resources base started to be developed, and quarries of different raw materials

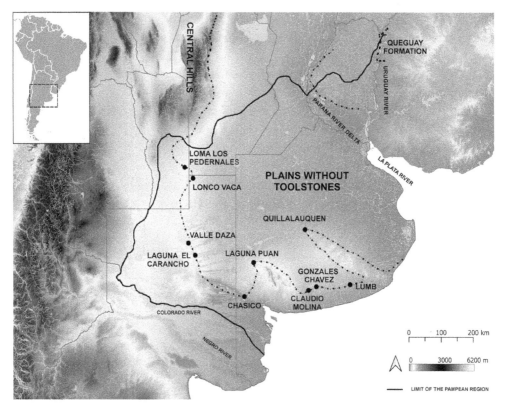

Figure 3.5 Map of the Pampas showing the plains without any toolstone.

were identified in Tandilia (Barna and Kain 1994; Flegenheimer 1991; Flegenheimer et al. 1996, 1999; Flegenheimer and Bayón 1999; Lozano 1991; Pupio 1996), Ventania (Oliva and Moirano 1997; Oliva et al. 1991), and in the western Pampa (Berón 1999; Curtoni 1999). Quarries and specific outcrops also start to be correlated with the sites' lithic tools (Bayón and Zabala 1997; Franco 1994; Madrid and Salemme 1991; Ormazabal 1999). In this period, Flegenheimer and Bayón (1999, see also Bayón and Flegenheimer 2004) developed the foundations for building a lithic resources base in the Pampas region and published a guide for identifying quartzite. From the 2000s onward, researchers on the subject notably increased, and new quarry and workshop sites were recorded in both hill systems (Barros and Messineo 2006; Catella et al. 2010; Messineo et al. 2004; Paulides 2005) and El Fresco Plateau (Berón 2004, 2006; Berón and Curtoni 2002; Curtoni et al. 2004). The secondary deposits of the Atlantic coast (Bonomo 2005), the courses of the Ventania rivers and creeks (Catella 2014; Catella et al. 2010), and the Colorado River (Armentano 2012) were studied in more depth. During this period, a base of lithic resources for western Pampa (Berón 2006) and the northeastern area (Bonomo and Blasi 2010) was built. Finally, several doctoral theses were completed in the last decade, which contribute to the base of Pampas lithic resources. Mariano Colombo's (2013) study was dedicated to the quarries of orthoquartzite in Barker-La Numancia zone in Tandilia; Luciana Catella's (2014) to the deposits of the western slope of Ventania; and Rodrigo Vecchi (2011a) and Alejandra Matarrese (2015) studied the rocks used for the instruments modified by abrasion and polishing such as ground stones, pestles, and bola stones. The chapters on lithic resources and the petrological analyses of Carrera Aizpitarte's thesis (2014) on the exploitation of lithic resources from the western Pampa and the ones from Armentano (2012) and Santos Valero (2017) about the use of raw material in the lower valley of the Colorado River are also relevant. Finally, the contribution of the toolstones in the northwestern area as described in the doctoral thesis of Heider (2015) provided abundant systematic information. Building upon these many studies that significantly increased the quality of the archaeology of the Pampas, a complete panorama of the lithic resources available in the region has been built.

The Raw Materials in the Eastern Hill Systems

There are two hill systems in the Pampas region: Tandilia, Ventania, and several minor isolated hills in the south, such as Lihué Calel and Choique Mahuida. Tandilia seems the most important one because rocks from this hill system are of high quality and are widely distributed throughout the Pampas; it is also where most of the research has concentrated. The second one is Ventania, where an important variety of rocks can be found, some of which have been transported great distances.

Tandilia. This hill system is an elongated range of 340 km in length by a maximum width of 60 km, which runs southeast-northwest (Figure 3.6). Three main units have been determined: the Proterozoic crystalline basement (Buenos Aires Complex), the Precambrian and Paleozoic sedimentary stones (Sierras Bayas Group and Balcarce Formation, respectively), and the Cenozoic sedimentary complex (Dalla Salda et al. 2006; Iñiguez et al. 1989). The hill relief presents two different morphologies: the crystalline basement's hills, shaped like domes with an irregular curvilinear silhouette, and the Precambrian sedimentary rock's plateau-shaped hills, elongated and flat. The entire relief is low, the highest point being La Juanita hill (525 masl).

The crystalline basement is formed by igneous (granites) and high-grade metamorphic rocks (migmatites, gneisses, and amphibolites). From the basement come most of the rocks that have been used as raw material for the making of bola stones, mortars, and pestles (Matarrese 2015; Vecchi 2016). The Sierras Bayas Group (SBG) is formed by siliciclastic sedimentary rocks, among which layers of carbonate rocks (dolomites and limestones) are interspersed. From this group come some of the best and most popular toolstone of the Pampas region:

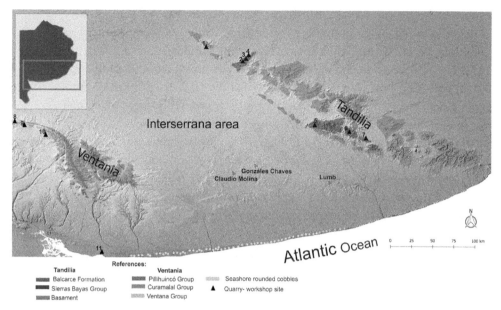

Figure 3.6 Geological map of Tandilia and Ventania Hill Ranges. (1) Don Guillermo; (2) Tres Lomas; (3) Núcleo central; (4) Cerro Aguirre; (5) Barker; (6) La Numancia and Arroyo Diamante; (7) San Manuel (La Liebre); (8) Laguna de Puán; (9) Abra de Saavedra- La Ermita; (10) Arroyo Saudade; (11) Farola Monte Hermoso. Drawn by Rocío Torino.

orthoquartzite, phtanite, and silicified dolomite (Barros and Messineo 2006; Bayón et al. 1999; Colombo 2013). The Balcarce Formation is integrated too by siliciclastic sedimentary rocks, but of lower quality for flaking, that outcrop in the western ridge along Tandilia. However, as discussed below, the recent discovery of the Don Guillermo quarry in the Curicó hills, in the northwestern sector, in supposedly Balcarce Formation outcrops (this has to be confirmed) shows that it would have high-quality quartzite (Barros et al. 2021, Figure 3.7).

The main quarries of the Pampas have been found in the orthoquartzites of the SBG. It is a series of quarries and workshops that encompass an area of a couple of tens of square kilometers and concentrate between the localities of Barker and La Numancia (Colombo 2011; Flegeheimer et al. 1996) (Figure 3.8). In the last decade, Colombo (2011, 2013) identified two dense centers of availability and exploitation of orthoquartzites around these localities and isolated findings of lower-quality rocks in the region of San Manuel. Fifty-six sites located in a broad sector of outcrops with evidence of extraction (quarries) and later processing (workshops) are interconnected along ca. 35 linear km. The size of the extraction and knapping locus is variable: there are areas of 10 m^2 with fractured nodules and others of up to 7,000 m^2 with a continuous accumulation of knapped waste. The presence of a Fishtail point at a quarry suggests exploitation of these outcrops since the Late Pleistocene (Colombo and Flegenheimer 2013; Flegenheimer et al. 1999).

Resources: Prey, Plants, and Stones

Figure 3.7 View of the orthoquartzite quarry Don Guillermo. Photo courtesy Cristian Kaufmann.

Three types of procurement were detected: exploitation of loose clasts in primary position, exploitation of veins and great rock masses, and places where holes implied the excavation of semi-buried raw material of special characteristics (quality or color) (Colombo 2011). These holes can be up to 70 cm deep, and they are of variable shape and diameter, although there is a predominance of subcircular ones around the mass of rock used. There are others shaped like a foxhole, following the natural veins. High proportions of tested nodules can be found in all these quarries, as well as undifferentiated waste, fractured flakes, and dehusking flakes, which suggest tasks oriented toward the first stages of lithic reduction. Although in these kinds of deposits the instruments are few, here they appear with relative frequency. On the other hand, very few hammerstones were found (Colombo 2011, 2013).

In this quarry and workshop zone, other toolstones were also found: chert, silicified dolomites, and quartz. The first ones are in all locations, both in the shape of small pebbles (>5 cm) and in great blocks and veins. The dolomites

Figure 3.8 Quarries of La Numancia in the Tandilia Hill Range. Photo courtesy of Pablo Messineo.

are less frequent. These two raw materials are found in low proportion, not in specific quarries/workshops, like those in Sierras Bayas, but rather inside the orthoquartzite exploitation loci (Colombo 2011). Only in the southeastern region of Tandilia has a quarry workshop of silicified dolomite and pigments been identified, at the site of La Liebre (Flegenheimer 1991), which dates back to 1630 BP. Last, quartz, located in the northern region of Barker, has also been exploited.

The Balcarce Formation orthoquartzite has also been exploited, but its use has been mostly local (Bayón et al. 1999; Bonnat 2016; Donadei 2020; Mazzanti 1997; Valverde 2002). In some exceptional cases, it has traveled great distances (up to ~ 500 km) since a recovered flake in the Campo Monaldi site in the Colorado River was identified as an orthoquartzite from this formation (Santos Valero 2017: 120).

In the Sierras Bayas, in the northwestern sector of Tandilia, the complete Precambrian stratigraphic column is formed by the crystalline basement (Buenos Aires Complex), the sedimentary sequence of the Sierras Bayas group, and the clays of the Cerro Negro Formation. These hills are composed of sedimentary rocks were phtanite is present as a breccia that protrudes over the slopes and outcrops in three levels. The first level is in the lower sedimentary

Figure 3.9 Phtanite quarry of Cerro Aguirre. Photo courtesy of Pablo Messineo.

sequence, or Villa Mónica Formation (Poiré 1993; Poiré et al. 2001); the second level is found at the base of the second deposit sequence, or Cerro Largo Formation. This level is the one that outcrops in all the prospected hills and in which archaeological quarries and workshops have been detected (Barros and Messineo 2004; Lozano 1991; Messineo et al. 2004). In the Sierras Bayas hill, silicified dolomites were also recorded in the Villa Mónica Formation, in primary outcrops of breccias (Barros and Messineo 2006).

Three quarry localities have been found in the Sierras Bayas hills: quarry/ workshop of silicified dolomite of the Cerro Tres Lomas 1 site; the phtanite workshops of the Cerro Núcleo Central 1 (Messineo and Barros 2015), El Mirador, Boca de la Sierra, and Malegni (Barros 2009; Barros et al. 2015; Messineo 2008: Messineo et al. 2004); and a phtanite quarry in Cerro Aguirre (Lozano 1991) (Figure 3.9).

There are outcrops of phtanite and silicified dolomite also in the eastern range of Tandilia, in the Sierras Bayas Group, in the Barker-San Manuel sector

(Colombo 2011; Flegenheimer 1991; Paulides 2005). Besides the Barker–La Numancia zone, the cherts are present in primary outcrops in isolated rock breccias but with relative abundance, and phtanite pebbles have been recorded in secondary deposits, carried forward by the riverbeds, although only in the heads of the valleys (Flegenheimer et al. 1996; Paulides 2005). This rock – called microcrystalline silica by Barna and Kain (1994) – outcrops in a primary conglomerate at the base of the sedimentary sequence of the Balcarce Formation.

Quartz has also been recorded with some frequency in pebbles in breccias from the Balcarce Formation (Donadei 2020) and in slender veins inside the granites of the Buenos Aires Complex (Politis and Gutiérrez 1998). In the outskirts of the La Moderna site, some quartz veins have been found with points of impact and stepped fractures, which suggest extraction activities (Politis and Gutiérrez 1998).

In the central sector of Tandilia, in the Buenos Aires Group, outcrops of andesite, diabase, granite, granodiorite, and tonalite have been recorded, but no quarries/workshops have been identified (Arislur et al. 2020). All these rocks have been used to make bola stones and grinding stones (Matarrese 2015; Matarrese and Poiré 2009; Vecchi 2011).

Other toolstone outcrops in Tandilia are (1) silicified pelites, (2) dacite (Donadei 2020), (3) amphibolites (Dalla Salda et al. 2005), and (4) ferrilita (Matarrese 2015). There are also iron oxides and hydroxides in various geological units of Tandilia (hematite and goethite, respectively) (Di Prado et al. 2007; Flegenheimer 1991; Messineo 2008). In the Pampas region, there are various mentions of the use of ochres in early periods (Mansur et al. 2007; Mazzia et al. 2005; Scalise and Di Prado 2006) and then already throughout the Holocene in all areas of the region, particularly – although not exclusively – in mortuary contexts (Kozameh et al. 2018; Politis et al. 2014; Scabuzzo et al. 2015), rock art (Madrid and Oliva 1994; Oliva et al. 2010a; Porto Lopez and Mazzanti 2010), ceremonial sites, like Calera (Politis et al. 2007), and as paint or pottery engobe (González 2005; Matarrese et al. 2011; Politis et al. 2001).

Ventania. The other important source of lithic resources in the Pampas region is in the hill system of Ventania (Figures 1.8 and 3.6). This system is formed by a continuous hill range of ca. 180 km of length southeast-northwest, and 60 km of width in the central part, with heights of over 1,000 m (maximum altitude being the Tres Picos hill at 1,239 masl). This hill system is composed of Paleozoic sedimentary rocks, predominantly quartzites, and to lesser degree granites, and Precambrian rhyolites (Harrington 1970; Sellés Martínez 2001).

The Ventania system is formed by three geologic groups, each of them with four formations: the Curarmalal Group with the La Lola, Mascota, Trocadero, and Hinojo Formations; the Ventana Group with the Bravard, Napostá, Providencia, and Lolén Formations; and the Pillahuincó Group with the

Resources: Prey, Plants, and Stones 89

Sauce Grande, Piedra Azul, Bonete, and Las Tunas Formations. In these geological units, the most abundant rocks are the metaquartzites and ortho-quartzites; the formations with rocks most fit for knapping are the Mascota, Napostá, Providencia, Trocadero, and Bravard Formations (Catella et al. 2010). It has been assumed that metaquartzite's quality for knapping is less than the orthoquartzite's, but it can still be considered high (Bayón et al. 1999). However, Catella (2014: 315) stated that the quality of some Ventania orthoquartzite is as good as the SBG orthoquartize and cautions about the danger of determining the source of the quartzite based only on macroscopic observation or in the presence/absence of metamorphism.

In contrast to Tandilia, the primary sources of these quartzites have been difficult to identify. On the one hand, they could be less accessible and have therefore not been recorded yet. On the other hand, there had likely been procurement of raw material from secondary deposits of the rivers and streams that come down from the hills (Catella 2014). Until now, only two primary procurements of quartzites have been recorded: the Puán island (Oliva and Barrientos 1988) and the headwaters of the Naposta stream (Oliva 2000) (Figure 3.6). Also, a procurement site of high-quality quartzite rocks has been detected in the Arroyo Saudade site 2 (Catella et al. 2013).

Another toolstone in Ventania is the rhyolite that outcrops in La Mascota (outskirts of the Abra de Saavedra) and La Ermita, in the form of small hills that, in some cases, were interpreted as quarry/workshop sites (Oliva and Moirano 1997). Secondary deposits with very little spatial dispersion have been found around these primary outcrops (Oliva 1991; Oliva and Moirano 1997, 2001). Rhyolite is also found in pebbles, which make up a minority of the La Lola Formation conglomerate (Catella et al. 2017).

Besides the primary sources of these raw materials in the hills, rounded cobbles are transported through the streams from the slopes and carry a great number of rocks (metaquartzites, orthoquartzites, rhyolites, etc.) through tens of kilometers (Catella 2014). There are some courses, like the Chasicó basin, in which secondary deposits are composed almost exclusively of quartzites (Catella et al. 2017; Oliva 1991). Another important secondary source of metaquartzites and subarkoses is the current channel and the paleochannels of the Sauce Grande River, which have been exploited at least since the Middle Holocene (Bayón and Zavala 1997) (Figure 3.6).

Coastal Deposits and Primary Outcrops of the Interserrana Area

A locally important source of raw materials in the southeastern Pampa is made up of the secondary deposits of pebbles located in the coastal beaches. These pebbles have an extra-regional origin from three different sources: the Patagonian Shingle Formation, the fluvial clasts transported to the Atlantic coast by the Patagonian rivers, and the accumulations of clasts formed on the continental shelf during the marine regressions of the Quaternary (Bonomo and Prates 2014). The three have similar lithologies but with different processes of transportation and rework, and they have been redeposited in a west-east direction in the Pampas seashore by longshore drift (Bonomo and Prates 2014; Parker et al. 1997: 85). Sea transportation generates elliptical and flat shapes in the pebbles (Isla 1984; Spalletti 1980), which determined the technique of core reduction. In this way, they became a lower-quality resource but locally abundant, particularly in the south and southeast of the Pampas (Aparicio 1932; Bonomo 2005; Hrdlička1912; Politis et al. 2003b).

By "coastal pebbles" we mean the banks and isolated deposits found in the beaches (particularly in the intertidal zone) on the coasts of the Interserrana and southern areas of the Pampas (Bonomo 2005). North of Cabo Corrientes they are smaller and scarce, and only one volcanic gravel deposit has been detected in the area surrounding Villa Gesell (Isla et al. 1998). To the south, there are abundant deposits in the mouth and paleodelta of the Colorado River and the San Blas peninsula (Armentano 2012; Bórmida 1969; Santos Valero 2017).

Bonomo (2005) determined that the most abundant raw material forming the coastal pebbles is andesite, followed by rhyolite and basalt. Other raw materials are also present in low percentages: tuff, dacite, silica, and quartz. Also, there is a sector between Farola Monte Hermoso and Pehuen Co where a different composition was recorded: fluvial metaquartzite and subarkose pebbles from the Ventania transported by the ancient channels of the Sauce Grande River (Bayón and Zavala 1997). There is a great frequency of pebble workshops recorded in the dunes close to the beach, where the first stage of reduction and the recurring presence of artifacts and bipolar nodules was detected (Aparicio 1932; Bonomo 2005; Politis et al. 2003b, see Chapter 6).

In the Interserrana area, some outcrops have been linked to the Las Tunas Formation from the Pillahuincó Group of Ventania (Roselló 2016). Silicified tuffs (limolites) have been identified in the outskirts of Gonzales Chaves and Mariano Roldán (Barros et al. 2021; Madrid and Salemme 1991). Quartzite sandstones (Furque 1965) and coarse grain quartzites (also from Las Tunas Formation) outcrop in Lumb and have been used for the manufacturing of bola stone and ground stones (Matarrese and Poiré 2009; Ormazabal 1999; Politis 1984).

The Northeast Area or Mesopotamic Pampa

This is an area with a low-intensity use of lithic material. The procurement of most toolstones was likely made by collecting loose blocks or fluvial pebbles, which is the case for the Ituzaingó and Paraná Formations. There are also superficial pebble accumulations in some watercourses that go across the layers of these formations (Apolinaire et al. 2019; Bonomo and Blasi 2010). However, no quarries or workshops have been identified in any of these outcrops.

There are six defined formations that contain toolstones: Ituzaingó, Paraná, Queguay, Serra Geral, Boticatú, and Salto Chico. The biggest presence in the region is the Ituzaingó Formation, which can be found in the ravines or the subsoils of the Uruguay, Gualeguay, and Gualeguaychú Rivers (Torra 1999). Although the Ituzaingó Formation has extensive exposure areas, hundreds of square kilometers, it presents outcrops with materials fit for flaking artifacts only when the sandstones have been cemented by opal (Bonomo and Blasi 2010). Artifacts knapped from this raw material have been detected on various sites of the Upper Delta Superior of the Paraná River. The Paraná Formation has a more restricted distribution and outcrops in the ravines of the Paraná River between the Feliciano creek and the Nogoyá River (Aceñolaza 2000).

The Serra Geral Formation (White 1908), or Arapey Formation, in Uruguay (Bossi 1966) outcrops in the area only at some points of the middle course of the Uruguay River (SGEMAR 1995). This formation is composed of the lava flow of tholeiitic basalt and their geodes with chalcedony (Gentili and Rimoldi 1979). The weatherization and erosion of the basalts generated large pebble deposits transported by the Uruguay River (Iriondo and Kröhling 2009).

The Puerto Yeruá Formation, also named Queguay limestones (known as Mercedes Formation in Uruguay; Martínez et al. 1997), lays on erosion unconformity on the Serra Geral Formation, and is made up of clastic and carbonate deposits (Tófalo and Pazos 2002). It contains limestones that present characteristic microfossils – the oogonia of Characeas (Bonomo and Blasi 2010; Nami 2017). They have been recorded in the El Palmar National Park and in other sectors of the northeastern border of the Pampas (Aceñolaza 2007; Apolinaire et al. 2019; Loponte et al. 2011), as well as several outcrops in the Campos of Uruguay (Nami 2017). This is one of the best-quality materials in the region, and it was used from the Late Pleistocene to the Late Holocene (Castiñeira 2008; Flegenheimer et al. 2003; Nami 2017).

Outcrops and Fluvial Deposits in the South and West of the Pampas Region

In this sector, various outcrops of abundant quality toolstones have been detected (Figure 3.10). There are two main sources of raw material: El Fresco Plateau (Meseta del Fresco) and the Patagonian Shingle Mantle (Manto Tehuelche). There are also abundant secondary deposits of pebbles, mostly on the channels and paleochannels of the Colorado, Negro, and Salado-Chadileuvú-Curacó Rivers.

El Fresco Plateau. It is a low plateau ~ 42 km long and ~ 13 km wide, 60 m above the surrounding plains (Figure 3.11). A characteristic silicified limestone (chert) is recurrently found in the sites of the western Pampean outcrops here

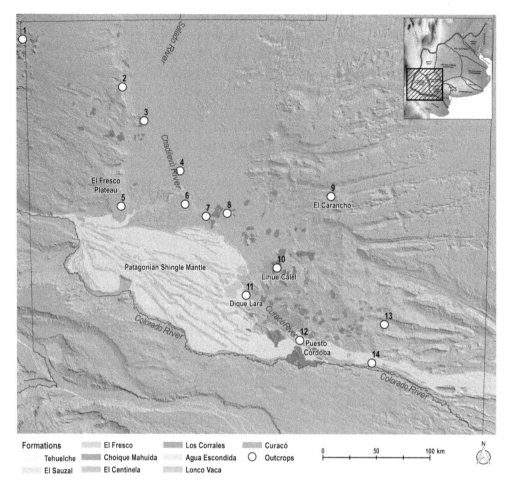

Figure 3.10 Geological map of the western Pampas with main outcrops and quarries. (1) La Escondida-Piedras de Afilar; (2) Cerro Guanaco; (3) Cerro La Ramada-Cerro Las Matras; (4) Limay Mahuida; (5) Meseta del Fresco; (6) Cerro Pichi Mahuida; (7) Cerro Carpacha Grande; (8) Cerro Carpacha Chico; (9) El Carancho; (10) Lihué Calel; (11) Dique Lara; (12) Puesto Córdoba; (13) Cerro de Los Viejos; (14) Sierra Pichi Mahuida. Based on *Mapa Geológico de la Provincia de La Pampa, Secretaria de Industria, Comercio y Minería* (1999) and Carrera Aizpitarte (2014).

(Carrera Aizpitarte et al. 2015). In this plateau, the exposed silicified limestone shows variability in color and in the degree of silicification (Berón 2006; Berón and Curtoni 2002; Curtoni et al. 2004). Quarries have been identified in the plateau in the southern end foothill (top of Estribación Sur) and western slope in the sites Memoria del Fresco WP 75 and WP 76 and Cima del Cerro WP 81 (Carrera Aizpitarte and Berón 2021; Carrera Aizpitarte et al. 2015). These rocks are of high quality for flaking artifacts.

Another source of silicified limestone has been found in the Valle Daza (department of Utracán) in the calcrete ridge of the Estancia La Gama (Charlín

Figure 3.11 View of El Fresco Plateau in the Salado-Chadileuvú-Curacó area. Photo courtesy Manuel Carrera Aizpitarte.

2002). However, this resource is very scarce and has little visibility (Carrera Aipitarte 2014).

The Patagonian Shingle Mantle. One relevant geological feature in the southern Pampa and Patagonia is the Patagonian Shingle Mantel, which is an accumulation of gravelly clasts, sometimes cemented, with a dominant size fraction of pebbles and cobbles (Martínez et al. 2009) (Figure 3.12). These gravel deposits of Andean origin extend discontinuously throughout most of Patagonia, from the mountain range to the Atlantic coast and from the Colorado River to Tierra del Fuego (Fidalgo and Riggi 1965, 1970). Ever since Darwin discovered them on his trip to Patagonia, multiple hypotheses have been proposed for the origins of these shingles (see summary in Martínez et al. 2009). The lithology of the Patagonian pebbles is quite varied due to the different sources of origin, including a variety of basalts, andesites, rhyolites, riodacites, dacites, granites, granodiorites, tonalites, garbos, aplites, pegmatites, phyllites, quartzites, amphibolites, limestones, sandstones, tuffs, and quartz. While the sediments deposited at the bottom of the Colorado and Negro Rivers cannot be equated to the ancient levels of Patagonian Shingle Mantle, this does not exclude the fact that a lot of them could come from original clasts from that formation redeposited by fluvial action (Bonomo and Prates 2014). Despite the lithological similarity, some differences can be observed between these groups of pebbles, among which size is the most notable one. During the

Figure 3.12 Different views of the outcrops of the Patagonian the Shingle Mantle. Photo courtesy Luciano Prates.

Middle Holocene, pebbles from the coast were preferred but were replaced during the Late Holocene by the Patagonian Shingle Formation (Martínez and Santos Valero 2020; Santos Valero 2020; Santos Valero and Armentano 2017).

In southwestern Pampa, the Patagonian Shingle Mantle, locally named El Sauzal and Tehuelche Formations, is one of the most important raw material sources. It is formed by a ~ 6-m-thick conglomerate of rocks, mostly volcanic, but also contains quartz, quartzites, and silicas. In the low erosive areas, there are "fields of pebbles," smaller in size (~ 5 cm), the result of the alluvial drag (Berón 2006). In the Patagonian Shingle Mantle, many sectors have been detected that present evidence of exploitation. One of the most important is the quarry/workshop Puesto Córdoba, on the right margin of the Curacó River (Figure 3.10). It is a source of high-quality rocks, many of which have been recorded in nearby sites (Berón et al. 1995; Carrera Aizpitarte and Berón 2021).

Abundant clasts of basalt have also been found in the Santa Isabel Formation, on which the Salado-Atuel-Chadileuvú Rivers flow (Carrera Aizpitarte 2014). Basalt was used basically at the end of the Middle Holocene, and its frequency lowers while the use of silica rises, which is evident in the Tapera Moreira site. The exploitation of chert does not seem to suffer from any drastic differences through time, except in the early exploratory period when it is absent (Carrera Aizpitarte and Berón 2021).

Orthoquartzites. Orthoquartzite outcrops have been found in the west, in the Agua Escondida Formation. Charlin (2002) surveyed Cerro Guanaco and found that the best conditions for the provision of quartzites are at its base. However, she concluded that because of its hardness and form of presentation, it would not be fit for flaking, although it would be for manufacturing polished and abraded artifacts. Although it would seem that this quartzite was not used in the region (Berón 2006), a large core of this rock has been found in the Laguna Santa, some 320 km east from the outcrop (Tapia et al. 2020).

Opalized Clay (Traru Lauquen Lake). This is a high-quality raw material source, in the Close Basins area, very specific, and with precise localization. It is a partially opalized clay that constitutes almost 100% of the raw material used in the El Carancho workshop site (Berón and Curtoni 2002).

Chert. There are very few sources of this raw material in the western Pampa. A small outcrop has been recorded on a hillock close to Dique Lara in the Salado-Chadileuvú-Curacó area, where numerous cores that would indicate its exploitation have been recovered (Berón 2006). Also the geological literature mentions banks in the San Jorge hill, where small (<5 cm) chert nodules can be found, but this outcrop could not be localized (Carrera Aizpitarte 2014).

Quartz. Quartz is recorded in various formations in the Curacó area, in the pebbles of the Patagonian Shingle Mantle, in Dique Lara, and in veins inside the granite outcrops close to the Lihué Calel Hills (Carrera Aizpitarte 2014). Also, in the northwestern area, quartz has been recorded in the Loma de Los Pedernales site (Heider and Demichelis 2015).

Granite. Numerous granite outcrops with various characteristics have been detected, and they were assigned to four formations: Curacó, Lonco Vaca, Zúñiga, and Piedras de Afilar (Berón 2004a, 2006). These outcrops follow a north-south vector, from Cerro Varela, Cerillo de Las Salinas (Guillermo Heider, pers. comm.), and the Lonco Vaca hills to the Pichi Mahuida hills. These outcrops were also detected on the Colorado and Curacó Rivers, in Valle Daza and in Cerro Las Matras (Berón 2006; Carrera Aizpitarte 2014; Tapia et al. 2020).

Silicified Wood. There are only three places in the western Pampa where this raw material has been identified: the Patagonian Shingle Mantle, the Calencó Hills, and the Carapacha Chica hills. None of the three locations has evidence of raw material exploitation (Carrera Aizpitarte 2014).

Rhyolite. Rhyolite is relatively abundant, especially in the south since it is present in the Choique Mahuida Formation, which outcrops in various places, and presents a certain variability (Linares et al. 1980; Llambías 1975). It has also been detected among the pebbles of the Patagonian Shingle Mantle and in the Cortado hill (in the Lihué Calel hills, Berón 2006). There is also brown rhyolite in three isolated hills in the northwestern area: Lonco Vaca, Cerro Varela, and Cerrillo de Las Salinas, on the border of the Pampas (Guillermo Heider, pers. comm.).

Andesites. In the southwestern sector of the Pampas, 21 outcrops of andesite have been identified. Among these the ones that stand out the most are from El Centinela and Choiqué Mahuida Formations, Lomas de Olguín, and to the south of the Carapacha Grande hill (Berón 2006; Charlin 2002; Vecchi 2016).

Chalcedony. Microcrystalline silica characterized as "long-slow chalcedony" has been detected in the Loma de Los Pedernales (Heider and Demichelis 2015). Clasts of nodules of this rock are available at low frequencies and with different proportions on the slope of the knoll. The predominant color is a gray cloud with milky white tones and characteristics of empty holes (microgeodes) (Heider and Demichelis 2015).

Río Negro Sandstones. These are found in the ecotonal area between the southern Pampa and North Patagonia (Cappannini and Lores 1966). This formation does not have good quality rocks for flaking, but its rocks have been used for the manufacturing of grinding stones and bola stones. Outcrops of these sandstones have been detected in the southeast of the Pampas (Martínez 2004).

LITHIC PROCUREMENT IN PATAGONIA

Obsidian

Obsidians are usually considered attractive for a variety of reasons, among them their usual high flaking quality (Cortegoso et al. 2012; Hermo and Miotti 2010). But obsidians do not offer universal solution, and sometimes they are even too brittle for flaking, as with the obsidians from Río Cisnes (Méndez et al. 2008–2009, 2012) or Volcán Payún Matrú (Durán et al. 2004).

Obsidian from North Patagonia

Several studies demonstrated the tremendous variety of obsidians used in south Cuyo and Neuquén, including across the Andes. Potential sources of obsidian in south Mendoza and Central Chile were recorded (Barberena et al. 2011, 2019; Cortegoso et al. 2012; Durán et al. 2004, 2012; Fernández et al. 2017, 2019; Giesso et al. 2011; Neme et al. 2011; Salgán et al. 2012, 2014, 2015; Seelenfreund et al. 1996). Volcán Payún Matrú, at 3,600 masl, offers low-quality obsidians that occasionally include good nodules. Its limited use is particularly interesting given the level of selectivity required to obtain them. Laguna del Maule, at 2,500 masl, is a source of relatively small pebbles used since the arrival of people to the area. These obsidians were widely distributed along the Andes, with distances up to 230 km to Cajón del Maipo, Chile

(Cornejo and Sanhueza 2003). Obsidians have been located at several Early Holocene sites, and one sample from the earliest levels at Cueva Huenul is from Laguna del Maule (Cortegoso et al. 2012; Giesso et al. 2011; Neme et al. 2011).

Although there are no primary resources of obsidian in the Pampas region, some secondary deposits in the southern border have small, rounded cobbles of this raw material. Barberena and collaborators (2019) indicate the presence of nodules from Cerro Huenul and Laguna Maule 2-Barrancas sources in the upper Colorado River basin. The record of small-sized pebbles close to the Tapera Moreira archaeological locality could extend the availability of these obsidians to the middle Colorado River and would imply a closer and, therefore, less expensive access (Berón et al. 2018). One obsidian tool from the Huenul source was even recorded at the lower Colorado River, around 700 km east of the sources. Prates (2008) found only one obsidian artifact along some 150 km of the río Negro basin.

The obsidian sources Laguna del Maule and Las Cargas, located in the highlands and usually interpreted as only accessible during summer, are contrasted with sources like Cerro Huenul and El Peceño, which were accessible year-long (but see Fernández et al. 2017). Several sources were identified in Neuquén (Pérez and López 2007; Pérez et al. 2015; Silveira et al. 2010).

Porphyritic gray obsidian from the Chaitén volcano was widely distributed in western Patagonia along maritime hunter-gatherer circuits (Méndez Melgar et al. 2010; Reyes et al. 2007a, 2016, 2019; Stern 2018; Stern et al. 2002). A few small fragments were found as far away as Monte León and Pali Aike (Caracotche et al. 2005; Charlin 2009a) about 1,100 km southeast, testifying to the asymmetrical patterns of circulation of raw materials in maritime versus terrestrial environments (Stern et al. 2012).

At least six types of obsidian were recognized on the NE Atlantic coastal sites, some obtained nearby (<100–250 km), and some as far as 300–400 km away at Sacanana, or 500 km away at Lago Lolog. Obsidian was found only at sites on the west coast of Gulf San Matías, albeit in very low frequencies (Favier Dubois et al. 2009a; Gómez Otero and Stern 2005; Stern et al. 2000, 2007, 2013).

Work in northwest Chubut recorded transport of obsidian from sources between 300 and 800 km away (Banegas et al. 2015; Bellelli and Pereyra 2002; Boschin and Massaferro 2014; Gómez Otero and Stern 2005; Stern et al. 2007), plus obsidians from unknown sources (Bellelli and Pereyra 2002; Bellelli et al. 2006; Cortegoso et al. 2012; Favier Dubois et al. 2009a; Stern et al. 2000, 2007).

Exotic obsidians from the eastern steppes arrived at Aisén in very low frequencies. Pampa del Asador (PDA) obsidian appears only in Early Holocene levels at Baño Nuevo 1 and El Chueco 1, about two millennia after the first human presence (Méndez et al. 2018). At El Chueco 1 PDA obsidian (ca. 370 linear km from the source) appears together with obsidian from Somuncura ca. 445 linear km northeast (Méndez et al. 2012, 2018). At Casa de Piedra Rosello, in West Chubut, obsidian artifacts were found in all layers (Castro Esnal et al. 2012, 2017). These exotic obsidians were of higher quality than the local obsidians from the headwaters of the Cisnes Basin (Méndez et al. 2012). Obsidian from PDA is the more important type at sites relatively close to the sources, like some of the major Aisén hydrographic basins (Méndez et al. 2008–2009) and the Chalía basin.

Obsidians from South Patagonia

PDA is a secondary source of large black rhyolitic obsidian and a brown-banded variety available near the Andes (Espinosa and Goñi 1999; Stern 1999, 2000, 2004, 2018). It covers >1,200 km², at 1,100–600 masl. Charles Stern determined several different types of chemically distinctive obsidians, whose distribution as tools covers a large part of Patagonia. Although Pampa del Asador is technically a secondary source, it was often treated as a focal source because of its relatively restricted spatial expression. Recent work expanded the availability of obsidian some 65 km east and 75 km northeast, completely changing the analysis of provenance distances for PDA obsidian. For example, Cueva de las Manos, with a relatively high frequency of obsidian, was located 47 km from the PDA source instead of the 98 km previously computed (Belardi et al. 2006; Civalero 1999).

Another secondary source of geochemically similar obsidian pebbles – the 17 de Marzo locality – was found about 170 km southeast from PDA as part of the Patagonian Shingle Formation (Figure 3.13). These obsidian pebbles were transported along the ancient Chico River valley. This discovery has interesting implications for the study of the eastern distribution of obsidian tools. Moreover, it is possible that other distal PDA obsidian sources just await discovery (Franco et al. 2017a).

Cerro Tres Tetas (Cueto et al. 2016; Paunero 2003a) and La Gruta 1 (Brook et al. 2015; Franco et al. 2010a) are sites with the earliest evidence of PDA obsidian utilization, located ca. 97 km and 114 km, respectively, from the eastern margin of PDA. Very small obsidian tools represent only about 1% of the total sample (Cueto et al. 2016, 2018; Franco et al. 2017a). The only obsidian flake recovered at La Gruta 1 is smaller than many of the pebbles found at the 17 de Marzo source located only 18 km away (Brook et al. 2015; Franco et al. 2015, 2017a). Then, at least one of the early sites can be easily related to that source. Recent references to small amounts of obsidian present at sites at La María locality maintain that it was obtained at the main source more than 100 km west, ignoring the presence of nearby sources (Frank et al. 2020).

Figure 3.13 View of 17 de Marzo source of black obsidian, Deseado Massif, Argentina. Photo courtesy Nora V. Franco.

It is only during the Early Holocene that large obsidian artifacts are found in the southern Deseado Massif. Effectively, evidence from La Martita 4 (Aguerre 2003) suggests knowledge of the main PDA obsidian source, ca. 9000–7000 BP. This was probably when this source was widely known at the Deseado Massif and when human occupation near Western Patagonia began (Franco et al. 2017a: 240; Goñi et al. 2011).

Claims for the early use of this obsidian south of PDA and the Deseado Massif near the Andes corresponds to the Early Holocene (Borrero et al. 2019a; Civalero and Franco 2003; Franco and Borrero 2003; Méndez et al. 2018). No obsidian was found at the earlier layers of Fell Cave. Only during Bird's Period III is PDA minimally present (Bird 1988; Stern 2000). Obsidian found at Pali Aike Cave is probably of Early Holocene age. PDA continues to be present in low frequencies during the Holocene and is even found as far south as the Strait of Magellan and Tierra del Fuego (Morello et al. 2012), and as far north as Peninsula Valdés and Puerto Madryn (Gómez Otero and Stern 2005; Molinari and Espinosa 1999), always in very low frequencies.

It was recently claimed that since obsidian from PDA was known during the earlier occupations of the Deseado Massif, it is significant that there are no Fishtail projectile points made of that raw material (Flores Coni et al. 2020).

However, this is not totally unexpected given that the minimal presence of PDA at the Deseado Massif could be easily related to the use of local sources like 17 de Marzo. Flores Coni and collaborators dismiss the importance of this source, explaining that it "does not present the characteristics of a quarry ... there are no flakes and no cores ... pebbles are very small, no bigger than 48 mm" (Flores Coni et al. 2020: 9). However, Franco and collaborators (2017a) found that the dimensions of the pebbles are adequate to explain the size of the PDA obsidian tools found in the Massif during the late Pleistocene. This size concordance is a strong reason to claim that this or similar sources explain the findings at the Massif more economically than access to the main source. There is no support for the claim that the primary PDA source was known to the first human explorers of Patagonia, as suggested by Flores Coni and collaborators (2020). Knowledge of the main source by hunter-gatherers is manifested during the Early Holocene (Méndez et al. 2012; Stern 1999, 2004; Stern et al. 2013).

The Late Holocene distribution of obsidian from Pampa del Asador presents a general fall-off from the source. It constitutes >60% of lithic assemblages at nearby sites up to 50 km from PDA, and then varies between 60 and 10% for sites up to 125 km from the source. Sites in Aisén, the Deseado Massif, and north of the Santa Cruz River present black obsidian between 1 and 13%, while on the South Atlantic coast it is limited to 1–5% of lithic assemblages (Ambrústolo et al. 2015; Méndez et al. 2018; Pallo and Borrero 2015a).

In summary, the earlier uses of PDA obsidians in Patagonia can be explained by the use of the 17 de Marzo or similar sources. The main source appears to have been discovered during the Early Holocene. During the Late Holocene, regular use of this obsidian is recorded at the Deseado Massif, with a highly discontinuous distribution marked by fall-off curves (Cueto et al. 2018).

Green Obsidian. The precise location of the source of green obsidian is still unknown, but several indicators confine it to primary and secondary sources in the Otway Sea and Riesco Island, Chile (Morello et al. 2001, 2004). The contrast between the proportion of obsidian at sites in the Otway Sea and the eastern steppes is drastic and goes from 96–88% to 0.02–1.2% (Morello et al. 2001; Stern 2000). This distribution clearly points to a source located within the range of maritime hunter-gatherers, who probably were the initial pushers of their dispersal. Green obsidian is particularly useful to measure the interactions between people from the channels and the eastern steppes (Morello et al. 2015). The Ponsonby site, near the Fitz Roy Channel at the edge of the steppes, is crucial because, despite being located near the source, it presents very low percentages of green obsidian (Legoupil 2003). This is in agreement with the general observation that the frequency and size of green obsidian reaching the eastern steppes was small (Charlin et al. 2018). Notable are findings at Morro Chico (Stern and Prieto 1991) and relatively large nodules at Mala Cueva, PALF (Martin and San Román 2010) in contexts

Resources: Prey, Plants, and Stones

suggesting a significance beyond subsistence. In the East it is always present in low numbers, basically as the remains of late-stage reduction techniques. Small projectile points made of green obsidian were also found in an arc from the piedmont of Cancha Carrera and Lago Argentino to Pali Aike, including one projectile point found at Amalia 4 in the steppes of eastern Tierra del Fuego (Oría et al. 2010).

The main concentration of green obsidian is along the Strait of Magellan and the Otway and Skyring Sounds (Legoupil 1989; San Román 2013), confirming that green obsidian probably was exploited and distributed by maritime peoples (Borrero et al. 2008a, 2019b; Morello et al. 2012, 2015; Orquera and Piana 1999). Use of this obsidian is dominant during the early occupations of the channels, after which it stopped being used for more than 2,000 years, returning during the last 2,000 years up to historical times (Legoupil 2003; Morello et al. 2012, 2015; San Román and Prieto 2004; San Román et al. 2016), a remarkable fact that invites consideration of cultural or populational discontinuity.

Banded Gray-Green Obsidian. The provenance of banded gray-green obsidian is not known with precision, but it is located at the Baguales Range (Stern and Franco 2000). Compared with other obsidians, it is a little-used rock, but it was found as far east as the mouth of the Santa Cruz River and Cabo Vírgenes (Borrero et al. 2008a; Caracotche et al. 2005) and, surprisingly, is the most abundant obsidian found at Pali Aike Volcanic Field (PAVF). This situation requires an understanding of the links between PAVF and the Baguales Range and led researchers to consider that other circulation mechanisms beyond exchange were probably in place, perhaps including direct acquisition (Charlin 2009b; Franco 2002a). Pallo (2016) analyzed potential routes for direct acquisition and found that there are several whose optimality was dependent on changing palaeoenvironmental conditions through the Holocene. This makes sense in terms of the distances involved, but direct acquisition does not fare well with our knowledge of existing networks of people moving around derived from the study of lithics, maritime items, stable isotopes on human bones, and provenance of a variety of rocks (Borrero et al. 2009). At any rate, the older record for this obsidian is from the lower layers of Punta Santa Ana 1, ca. 6500 BP, on the Strait of Magellan (Morello 2016), indeed a time at which conditions for human circulation probably were relatively relaxed. Pallo (2016) evaluated the possibility of the original access to that obsidian as an unplanned result from other activities, with later special or embedded access.

OTHER STONES IN PATAGONIA

North Patagonia

A variety of stones can be mined at plateaus or collected as pebbles in rivers and were used (Barberena et al. 2015; Crivelli et al. 1993), but preferences are not always clear. The minimal use of excellent but scarce local siliceous stones during the early occupations at Huenul Cave is significant. Basalt and chalcedony were the most frequently used rocks during the Holocene, with the latter increasing through time.

As already mentioned, a huge part of eastern Patagonia is covered by the Patagonian Shingles. These pebbles can be found over broad areas of the steppes, forming extensive gravel tablelands between the Andes and the Atlantic (Clapperton 1993; Feruglio 1950; Martínez et al. 2009). In the middle Negro River basin, fluvial pebbles were preferred, and stones from the Shingle Formation were selected only exceptionally (Prates 2008).

Four primary rock sources were identified on the west coast of the Gulf of San Matías, two of which show evidence of human use (Alberti et al. 2015). They differ in their flaking properties, and one of them was only available with low tide. Coastal landforms like littoral cordons are rich in rocks, providing alternative lithologies and qualities that can be found within 5–10 km of the known sites (Alberti and Cardillo 2015). Those conditions invite us to consider that the few exotic rocks are not necessarily the result of systematic social interactions. Indeed the evidence emphasizes the use of local rocks (Alberti 2019; Favier Dubois et al. 2009b). In both the north and west coasts of the Gulf of San Matías, intensively used secondary deposits of gravels located above the cliffs and at the littoral cordons are mainly implicated (Cardillo 2009; Cardillo and Scartascini 2007; Cardillo et al. 2007; Favier Dubois et al. 2009a). The best examples are rhyolites and dacites, as well as the abundant tabular nodules of chalcedony (Cardillo and Scartascini 2007). However, a group of rocks of diverse origin characterized by their dark color and fine grain, regionally known as RGFO (Charlin 2009b), are more abundant as secondary deposits in the north coast.

The lower valley and mouth of the Chubut River and Atlantic coast provide secondary deposits of pebbles of diverse quality (Banegas et al. 2015). Nodules of varied size, shape, and quality characterized the different landforms and were intensively used. A reduced variety of nonlocal raw materials, such as obsidian, slate, hematite, and petrified wood, is also present at the sites, while basalts from Somuncurá Formation were used for hammerstones, spheroids, and millstones (Banegas and Gómez Otero 2020; Banegas et al. 2015; Favier Dubois et al. 2008; Gómez Otero et al. 1999).

Central Patagonia

South of the Deseado River coastal primary sources predominate, with intensively exploited veins, outcrops, and vesicles of high-quality red chalcedony (Ambrústolo et al. 2009, 2015). Negatives on the outcrops of some of these sources testify to extractive activities. The exploitation of a primary source of

Figure 3.14 Primary source of red silex, Oso Marino Bay, Argentina. Photo courtesy Pablo Ambrústolo and Mikel Zubimendi.

red chert is well represented at the Bahía del Oso Marino (Ambrústolo and Zubimendi 2019) (Figures 3.14 and 3.15). At any rate, as usual in Patagonia secondary sources at marine and fluvial terraces as well as colluvial and alluvial sandy gravels are dominant.

In central-western Patagonia, the regional lithic resources base presents a high frequency and variety of widely available excellent raw materials (Cassiodoro et al. 2015; Espinosa et al. 2015). Siltstone is a local, high-quality raw material, abundant on the northwestern coast of the Cardiel Lake, which can be found at both primary outcrops and secondary deposits (Belardi et al. 2015). Other local, albeit less used, rocks in the hinterland are basalts and silicified tuff.

There are anomalous high percentages of PDA obsidian in sites at the Tar and San Martín lake basins, but many other rocks from different sources were also used, such as local green silicified tuff and basalt (Espinosa et al. 2019). These local raw materials were used widely, but their circulation was apparently rather restricted (Espinosa et al. 2015).

Barrientos and colleagues observed that the distribution of tools made of siltstones indicates "the presence of a single, already known source area located

Figure 3.15 Detail of red silex source, Oso Marino Bay. Photo courtesy Pablo Ambrústolo and Mikel Zubimendi.

at the northwestern margin of the Cardiel Lake" (Barrientos et al. 2018). Interestingly, given its high-quality knapping, the rocks show a restricted area of use, probably the result of competition with other high-quality rocks, principally obsidians and "opaque siliceous rocks" (Barrientos et al. 2018).

In general, arcs of moraines located east of the Andes are important sources of rocks, sometimes surrounding the distal limits of peri-cordilleran lakes. For example, the moraines near Bajo Caracoles and old hydrological systems (Belardi and Carballo 2005) provided a rock known as "Basalto Posadas," which geochemically corresponds to andesite recognized at the Salitroso and Posadas lakes (Cassiodoro et al. 2004).

Victoria Fernández (2015; Fernández and Leal 2014) shows the variability of raw materials in the valleys south of Buenos Aires lake, with incidental exploitation of local resources and more frequent use of nonlocal rocks.

The Deseado Massif is a vast area where several sites spanning the Late Pleistocene to Early Holocene transition were excavated. Volcanic rocks of high siliceous content, fossil woods, and a large variety of good-quality rocks can be found at most localities (Franco et al. 2011a; Hermo 2008, 2009; Hermo et al. 2015; Skarbun 2011; Skarbun and Páez 2012; Skarbun et al. 2019; Vetrisano et al. 2020). Important work near Piedra Museo, a site occupied since ca. 11,000 BP, and at Maripé, Cerro Tres Tetas, and La Gruta (Cattáneo 2002, 2004; Cueto et al. 2016, 2018; Franco et al. 2012a, 2015; Hermo 2008; Magnin 2010), found the predominance of volcanic geologic formations rich in siliceous rocks. Cattáneo's (2002, 2004) work near Piedra Museo found rock outcrops presenting high silicification and vitrification, as well as sedimentary formations with siliceous clasts and fossilized woods and basalts.

All the rock sources analyzed by Hermo between 200 m and 11.6 km from the Maripé site (Hermo 2008, 2009; Hermo and Lynch 2015) were probably used and represented by artifacts. Magnin also studied the distribution of rocks and isolated tools near Maripe and found that secondary deposits were continuously used (Hermo et al. 2015; Magnin 2010, 2015). Four artifacts from the Maripé site were analyzed by neutronic activation and compared with known sources, three of which were manufactured on raw materials from the D9 quarry, located 5.7 km away. The fourth artifact was made of an unknown source (Hermo et al. 2020). Small amounts of PDA obsidian were found at Maripé, leading to speculation about their relatively high value (Hermo 2008; Hermo and Miotti 2010), an interpretation that was not widely shared by others dealing with similar records (Cueto et al. 2018; Favier Dubois et al. 2009a).

At the southern end of the Massif, the Baqueró and Bajo Grande Formations are characterized by limited and minimally visible primary and secondary sources of silicified wood. The use of fossilized wood is higher in the north of the Deseado Massif and is present in low frequencies at several sites (Cattáneo 2005; Durán et al. 2003; Franco et al. 2010a; Frank et al. 2013; Paunero 2003b; Skarbun and Páez 2012; Vetrisano et al. 2020).

The La Gruta area is rich in primary and secondary potential sources of siliceous rocks (Franco and Vetrisano 2019: 15–16). West of La Gruta, the presence of veins with siliceous infills, including quartz, chalcedony, and opal, was identified. Occasional and seasonal flooding of lagoons could also expose secondary sources of raw materials (Franco and Vetrisano 2019: 17). In the case of La Gruta, sinters – stone outcrops originating from the deposition of siliceous materials in a hydrothermal environment – of chalcedony of good to very good quality were identified (Franco et al. 2020).

The Viuda Quenzana locality yielded a highly localized hot spring with a low-visibility dispersion of high-quality chalcedony and siliceous rocks extending over a surface of about 100 m^2 (Franco et al. 2011a, 2012a). Then, the environment is highly heterogeneous in terms of the quantity, size, quality, and visibility of available rocks. Heterogeneity is even more marked if we also consider the mouth of the Santa Cruz River with an almost absolute dominion of good-quality dacites and the presence of RGFO and fossilized wood (Vetrisano et al. 2020).

South Patagonia

Nora Franco developed an intense sourcing program south of Lago Argentino. The most frequent rock used in the East is the gray dacite, while green dacites are dominant in the west. Since gray dacites are less abundant in the area, their selection in Lago Argentino and passes through the Baguales range indicates a clear preference. Indeed, Franco found that while green dacites were basically used expediently, tools in gray dacite were mostly curated. Most of the basalt artifacts – probably mined at the Baguales Range and Las Vizcachas plateau (Franco and Aragón 2004) – were probably introduced as finished tools. Franco detected a pattern of variation in the availability of rocks from the distal end of the lake toward the west, at the foot of the Southern Ice Cap. The most frequent good flaking quality rock is green dacite, abundant near the location of the primary source west of Brazo Sur. It was extensively used locally and was transported as nodules or finished tools. The Ice Caps and seasonality constrained its access. The best gray dacites are found west of Brazo Sur and at La Angostura, in Lago Roca, but their flaking quality is inferior compared with the archaeological tools, suggesting a process of selection of nodules and blocks. All this evidence suggests a good knowledge of the structure of the local lithic resources (Franco and Aragón 2004). Other rocks, like basalts and chalcedony of unknown origin, were also important.

The pattern of dominant use of local rocks complemented with allochthonous rocks characterizes the Baguales Range (Figure 3.16). During late times RGFO rocks were dominant, particularly sedimentary and volcanic rocks that were microscopically identified as lutites and fangolites (Borrazzo 2006; Borrero et al. 2006; Charlin 2005). They are of good quality, and their large size makes them attractive for flaking. Abundant evidence of their use was recorded even away from Baguales (Balirán 2020; Borrazzo 2006, 2008).

Different sources of raw materials were identified at the eastern end of the Baguales Range in the south slopes of Tridente Hill. These include a primary source of a colorless volcanic chalcedony for which no evidence of use was found. A second class of colorless chalcedony exists as a secondary source (Franco and Aragón 2004). It is macroscopically undistinguishable, but its origin is sedimentary. They have very good to excellent flaking qualities, and cores were locally recorded.

The Pali Aike Volcanic Field (PAVF) is a topographically varied area with caves and rock shelters, seasonal lagoons, and some year-long freshwater sources. Varied lithic raw materials can also be found, making the area highly attractive for human inhabitation since the Late Pleistocene. Judith Charlin

Resources: Prey, Plants, and Stones 107

Figure 3.16 Lithic sources in moraines at Estancia La Verdadera Argentina, Baguales Range, Argentina. Photo courtesy Karen Borrazzo.

(2009b) developed an intensive analysis of lithic sources. After observing the available variation, she defined the already mentioned RGFO (fine-grained dark rocks) category describing rocks that can be volcanic, sedimentary, or metamorphic and can be found at the PAVF and most of South Patagonia (Balirán 2020; Charlin 2005, 2009b, 2012; Cirigliano et al. 2020).

Provisioning distances were assessed using different archaeological sequences of the region, and spatial models were discussed and tested on that basis. Charlin and Pallo (2015) also worked at the north coast of the Strait of Magellan and the Zone of Morros, west of PAVF, allowing a wider supra-regional scale to discuss hunter-gatherers' mobility, provisioning costs, and landscape use in southernmost Patagonia (Balirán 2020; Borrero et al. 2009; Charlin and Pallo 2015).

A particular class of volcanic RGFO, the "Potrok Aike type" (PKA), was identified. It is a black, shiny vitreous dacite of very good flaking quality, particularly abundant at lagoons between the Gallegos and Chico Rivers (Figure 3.17), at the core of the PAVF (Borrazzo et al. 2019; Borrazzo and Cirigliano 2020; Charlin and D'Orazio 2015; Charlin and Pallo 2013, 2015). It was probably systematically acquired by direct access at the numerous secondary sources. The available rocks at the zone of the Morros are basically

Figure 3.17 Potrok Aike Lake, Pali Aike Volcanic Field. The main source of the "Potrok Aike type" (PKA) of RGFO.

dacites of different colors and sedimentary RGFO – lutites and fangolites, and also andesites, basalts, and rhyolites (Charlin 2012; Charlin et al. 2011; Cirigliano et al. 2020). The area between Laguna Cóndor, the PAVF, and the nearby oceanic coasts is seen as a population circulation area characterized by the use of RGFO-PKA (Cirigliano et al. 2020). In contrast, the area northwest of Laguna Cóndor, with evidence of use of sedimentary RGFO and laminar technology, belongs to a different human hinterland circulation sphere (Borrero and Charlin 2010; Charlin et al. 2011).

Tierra del Fuego

Systematic work on potential raw material sources was initially focused in the area between San Sebastian Bay and Espíritu Santo Cape (Borrazzo 2012; Borrazzo et al. 2010, 2015, 2018; Franco 1998; Franco and Borrero 1999; Ratto and García 1996). Other projects explored the hinterland at the Grande and Chico Basins (Oría 2019, 2012; Turnes et al. 2016). There were changes in the availability of sources through time, related to eroding cliffs and prograding coasts (Borrazzo 2009; Favier Dubois and Borrero 2005; Ferrero

Figure 3.18 Lithic workshop at Playa Donata, Atlantic coast of Tierra del Fuego. Photo courtesy Martín Vázquez.

1996). These processes created new lithic sources such as the Paramo spit (Borrazzo 2011, 2016; Bujalesky 2007; Vilas et al. 1999) and buried old quarries (Franco 1998). Secondary deposits of good-quality rocks of glacial, fluvial, or marine origin are abundant and were predominantly used, particularly rhyolitic and silicified rocks (Borrazzo 2010, 2013; Franco 1998; Oría 2012; Oría and Salemme 2016; Santiago et al. 2007; Turnes et al. 2016) (Figures 3.18 and 3.19). Siliceous rocks such as chalcedony, opal, and silicified wood were also used in different parts of the island (Borrazzo 2010, 2013; Borrazzo and Etchichury 2013; De Ángelis 2015; Oría 2012). All these studies confirm that the selection of rocks was not primarily influenced by availability but often is directed by special requirements, such as manufacturing bola stones, polishers, or projectile points. The existence of relatively large areas naturally devoid of rocks, like the intertidal flats and clay dunes of northern San Sebastian Bay, must be noted (Borrazzo 2013).

Toolstones were routinely mined at several secondary sources at glacial landforms, the foot of the Andes, and the oceanic coasts (Álvarez et al. 2010; Borrazzo 2012; Orquera and Piana 1999; Turnes et al. 2016). The principal lithic sources in the island's center are fluvioglacial quaternary deposits, conformed with rocks from the Lemaire and Yaghan Formations of varied size and

Figure 3.19 Gallegos hydrographic basin. Fluvial source of toolstones, Argentina.

quality (De Angelis 2015; Mansur et al. 2020). The most abundant raw material is rhyolite, followed by cinerite and slate. Quartz is found as veins or as small round pebbles in the interior forests and the Beagle Channel (Álvarez et al. 2010). Raw materials are heterogeneously distributed in this area, being more visible at lakes or river banks (De Angelis and Mansur 2015; Mansur and De Angelis 2016). The coasts of Fagnano Lake present particularly attractive large pebbles predominantly of good flaking quality.

Most of the raw materials used at the Beagle Channel are found at the Lemaire and Yahgán Formations (Álvarez 2004; Salvatelli 2012; Terradas 1996). The former offers a variety of volcanic and sedimentary rocks such as cinerite, rhyolite, and lutite, whereas the latter includes slates, lutites, and other vulcanites, which were occasionally used. These materials can also be found at fluvioglacial secondary deposits, a reason Salvatelli (2012: 228) used to suggest that the costs of its exploitation were not high. She mentions selective provisioning of rhyolites and cinerites and fine-grained tuffs from the Lemaire Formation. These rocks can be found at secondary deposits on the coast of the Beagle and are not abundant.

Altos del Varela I is one of the few sites associated with the exploitation of rocks, in this case, rhyolites, over a hill of the Lemaire Formation (Álvarez et al. 2010). Two workshops were located on Navarino Island, Cerro Bandera 1 and Paso Laguna del Salto 2, both associated with the Yaghan Formation (Morello 2018).

Miraflores

Chorrillo Miraflores is the source of two classes of rocks with a common geologic origin – rhyolitic tuff and silicified tuff – used in Tierra del Fuego (Prieto et al. 2004). The source comprises some 12 different outcrops, mostly clustered in a radius of 3 km from the Miraflores Spring, covering from 5,000 to 60,000 m² (Borrazzo 2012; Borrazzo et al. 2010, 2015, 2018; Borrazzo and Pallo 2015; Pallo and Borrazzo 2016).

Karen Borrazzo undertook an extensive sampling of Fuegian artifact collections and found that Miraflores was recorded at different locations in the island during the last 4,000 years. She found that the numbers are low, with only one case of a high frequency of Miraflores rocks away from the source (De Angelis 2012) and a few locations outside the Isla Grande (Borrazzo et al. 2015). The archaeological study of the Miraflores rocks also served to explore models of lithic transport in Fuego-Patagonia during the Late Holocene. Both rocks were transported up to 320 km away from their source. One important observation was that their distribution is discontinuous.

Tuff was exclusively used for the manufacture of polishers, probably "deposited as site furniture in settlement nodes, which are primarily located on the coast," while silicified tuff was mostly used for endscrapers that were carried as personal gear (Borrazzo et al. 2015). Use as polishers was the probable reason behind the exploitation of the Miraflores source, an alternative supported not only by its archaeological distribution and use but also by ethnographic sources (Chapman 1986: 64). Accordingly, it was concluded that most of the silicified tuff only represent incidental by-products of mobility. The earliest archaeological occurrence of tuff, even when it is an inland resource, was recorded in small islands of the Strait of Magellan, which suggest that the canoe people had a central role in its spread, and it is tempting to consider that it can be associated with cultural configurations whose lifestyles were not strictly terrestrial nor maritime, but mixed. In addition, the primary coastal distribution of Miraflores polishers suggests that its use was related to the exploitation of sea resources, probably sea mammal bones for tools and maintenance (Gusinde [1937] 1982: 455–456; Lothrop [1928] 2002: 76). The fact that the larger sites are located on the coast should not be dismissed, not only in terms of sampling effects but also because most of these sites appear to be important habitational hubs. However, Least Cost Paths modeling suggested that the provisioning of Miraflores rocks within the island probably operated without recourse to maritime mobility (Pallo and Borrazzo 2016): for only a few cases of findings on the islands of the Strait of Magellan or the mainland was navigational technology implicated. In conclusion, both Miraflores rocks were never really abundant but widely used. They minimally cover an area of some 28,000 km² of the Isla Grande of Tierra del Fuego, an area that can be plausibly treated as a significant part of the annual range of individuals (Borrazzo et al. 2018).

FINAL REMARKS

In this chapter we describe the main prey for the Pampas and Patagonia hunter-gatherers, among which the guanaco stands out. Without any doubt this camelid was a key resource along the Holocene in both regions. Its importance during the early periods at the end of the Pleistocene is still under debate. Guanaco provides not only meat but also leather for the *toldos* (typical Pampean and Patagonian tents) and *quillangos* (blankets made with the leather of the newborn guanaco), fat, tendons for cords, and bones for tools. This camelid has a centrality in the life of the indigenous people of the Pampas and Patagonia, which was hard to replace. Pampas deer, huemul, armadillos, and greater and lesser rhea were also important resources, but never as important as guanaco. Only in the Southern Channels, including the Beagle Channel, did marine resources (seals and sea lions, fish, mollusks) predominate and define an adaptive pattern. In the Pampas, sea mammals and fish were not so prominent and were exploited only in combination with the land mammals in mixed diets (see Chapter 5). Freshwater fish were abundant in the lower Paraná and Uruguay Rivers during the Late Holocene and were fully consumed. They were also captured in the littoral of the La Plata River, in the lower sector of the Salado Depression, and in the lower Colorado River. In the inland Pampean lakes, fish were scarce, less diverse, and consumed in very low quantities.

Except for the guanaco, most of the other small and medium-size mammals, *Rhea*, and fish were also exploited in the Campos of Uruguay (Moreno 2016). In general terms, the consumed resources in this region were similar to the northeast, Rolling Pampa, and Salado River Depression areas. In regard to faunal exploitation, there is not a sharp difference between the Campos and these Pampean areas.

Seeds, fruits, and tubers were gathered by Pampean and Patagonian indigenous people, although their presence in the archaeological record is still elusive due to poor preservation and the limited use of flotation techniques. Difficulties for the quantification of plant resources make it complicated to compare their importance with that of animals, but it can be defended that special knowledge was required for its exploitation, which needs to be included when the cultural geography of hunter-gatherers is studied (Belmar 2019). The importance of roots and tubercles for food is well demonstrated, and the presence of plant residues on lithic tools or human teeth is among the best evidence of culinary importance. Plants were not only used for food, being particularly important in constructing so-called floors or sleeping places. The limited available studies basically indicate the consumption of local plants, but taxonomic studies help to recognize human visits to particular zones or eventual cases of exchange. In Patagonia, the fruits of the Pehuén forest in the northwest are among the most important resources, while varied plants were exploited in the steppes and the plains of Tierra del Fuego (Ancibor and Pérez

Resources: Prey, Plants, and Stones 113

de Micou 1995; Belmar et al. 2017; López et al. 2020). In the Pampas there are three areas with abundant edible plant resources: the Spinal in the southwestern Pampa (the *caldenar*), the Paraná and Uruguay subtropical gallery forest, and the *tala* woods in the littoral of the La Plata River and its estuary. These plant resources provided abundant, seasonal food, although in none of the Pampean and Patagonian societies did wild vegetal products constituted the predominant component of the diet year-round.

This chapter also summarized the sources and the exploitation of the lithic raw material in the Pampas and Patagonia. There are some differences and similarities between these two regions. In the Pampas, there are two hill range systems, Tandilia and Ventania, where abundant primary sources can be found. From there come most of the raw material with which the eastern Pampean hunter-gatherers made their lithic artifacts, both by flaking (projectile points, scrapers, knives, etc.) and by abrasion and eventually polishing (bola stones, mortars, pestles, etc.). The most intensively exploited quarry sites in the region are from SBG orthoquartize and phtanite. The rhyolite form Ventania also seems to be a valuable toolstone that was transported toward different areas. However, quarries in Ventania are very scarce, suggesting provisioning – at least in part – from secondary deposits. Two other important sources are in the southwest: the silicified chert of the El Fresco Plateau and the secondary deposits of the Patagonian Shingle Formation. There are also some other specific outcrops, which have had a more restricted use (Valles Daza, Laguna del Carancho, Loma de Los Pedernales, etc.), although they were highly ranked on an areal scale. In other cases (like the Interserrana outcrops, the secondary deposits of the Monte Hermoso cliff, or Lihué Calel), their use was almost exclusively local. On the contrary, the Queguay silicified limestones, which had been used during the Late Pleistocene in the Tandilia and Interserrana areas, traveled longer distances (>400 km). Last, there were many secondary sources like the rounded cobbles found in the Atlantic coast of the Interserrana area, in the channels and paleochannels of the rivers that come down from the Ventania System, and in the valley of the Colorado River.

There are very few extra-regional toolstones. Except for the obsidian pebbles from the Colorado River, all other – exceptional – obsidian findings in the Pampas have been considered of extra-regional origin coming from the Andes (Berón et al. 2018; Stern and Aguerre 2013). Also, some quartz and granitoids recovered in the northwestern area have an extra-regional origin (Central Hill).

The first important contrast between the availability of stone tools in the Pampas and Patagonia is that there are relatively few areas devoid of potential sources in the latter. These areas are not very large and rarely extend beyond a few kilometers. In fact, the panorama at most places is so diverse that different combinations of sources are usually possible. The Patagonian case also differs in that secondary sources – most of them of high-quality – supply most of the selected raw materials.

As discussed in detail in this chapter, different kinds of obsidian from both primary and secondary sources were instrumental in analyzing human mobility. Both varieties of the Miraflores rocks accomplished the same role in North Tierra del Fuego. All these rocks with focal provenance constituted the best entry for constructing models of the use of space, sometimes complemented with other items of known provenance like marine mollusks or mammal bones. As we saw, conclusions derived from these models sometimes include important clues concerning the initial exploration of large portions of land. Indeed, they constitute some of the best arguments supporting the notion that Patagonia's early human exploration and colonization began away from the Andes in the eastern steppes. This is derived from the late use of the Pampa del Asador black obsidian and the even later use of the Otway Sound green obsidian.

The best toolstones, like obsidians and a variety of siliceous rocks, were heavily exploited at the regional scale but are rarely important at distances over 100 km. This is true even for rocks used by maritime foragers, people who probably circulated in canoes. This information is important to substantiate the notion that direct acquisition probably was the preferred method of accessing sources in most Patagonian areas.

CHAPTER 4

THE EARLY PEOPLING: THE LATE PLEISTOCENE TO EARLY HOLOCENE

As we show in Chapter 2, there has been a long tradition of the archaeological research in both the Pampas and Patagonia since the end of the nineteenth century. From the very beginning of the investigations, the Late Pleistocene human occupation was at the top of the research agenda in both regions. Giant ground sloth skins from Cueva del Milodón and human skulls supposedly found in very ancient (Tertiary) layers in the Pampas seashore ignited the imagination of scientists of those times, and fieldwork looking for spectacular findings as well as reckless interpretations abounded. Since then, the first human occupation has been the main focus of the archaeological investigation in both regions. This chapter summarizes and discusses the results of this almost continuous, intense, and fertile archaeological research.

It can be maintained that the dispersal of small foraging bands into the Pampas and Patagonia occurred at the end of the Pleistocene. Their specific origin is unknown and is not necessarily restricted to one entry. Independently of how fast the process of human peopling was, probably several generations of people interacting with the environments and the local climates were necessary to succeed. The earliest known occupations in both regions consist almost exclusively of lithics, animal bones, and, more rarely, bone tools. The tool kits and the prey list of these pioneers were relatively homogeneous, but the distribution and placement of sites are informative.

THE PAMPAS

The early traces of humans in the Pampas are dated back to ~ 12,170 BP (~ 14,000 cal BP), indicating that at the end of the Pleistocene, foragers were living at least in the eastern Pampa (see Supplementary Table 1, Figure 4.1).

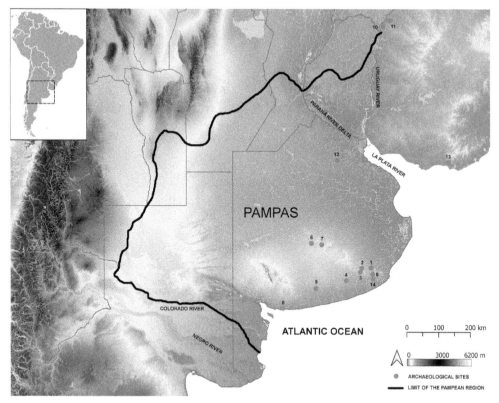

Figure 4.1 Map showing the Late Pleistocene sites in the eastern Pampas mentioned in the text. (1) Los Pinos and El Mirador; (2) Cerro El Sombrero and Cueva Zoro; (3) Cerro La China 1–3; (4) Paso Otero 5; (5) Cueva Tixi; (6) Campo Laborde; (7) La Moderna; (8) Pehuen Co; (9) Arroyo Seco 2; (10) Tigre (K87); (11) Pay Paso; (12) Arroyo de Frías; (13) Cerro de Los Burros; (14) La Amalia 2.

Between 10,800 to 10,000 BP archaeological evidence multiplies in some areas, which, as we will see below, is associated with the spread of a particular type of projectile point, named after Bird (1938), as the Fishtail projectile point. Since Bird excavated the Fell's cave in South Patagonia, this type of point, also called Fell 1, has been a chronological marker for Late Pleistocene sites in South America. Although the type includes significant morphological and technological variability (Castiñeira et al. 2011; Hermo and Terranova 2012; Nami 2013; Politis 1991), we will follow the classic definition of Bird for characterization of this iconic artifact: "a barbless, stemmed form with and without fluting, with rounded shoulders, the stem tapering towards a concave base, the stem sides generally but not always terminating in slightly expanded, rather sharp prongs or corners" (Bird 1969: 56–57).

Sites both with and without Fishtail points have been documented in some areas of the Pampa, providing critical information to understand the early settlers in the region, as we summarize in the following sections. The first scenario that the evidence shows is that not all areas were occupied during the

The Early Peopling

Figure 4.2 (a) Aerial view of the excavation in Arroyo Seco 2; (b) lithic artifacts from the older component.

initial demic pulse, but once people arrived in the region the process was fast and relatively homogenous in the western areas.

The Interserrana Area

The earliest dated site in the region is Arroyo Seco 2 (AS2) (Politis et al. 2014, 2016), located in the Interserrana area (Figure 4.2). It is a large, geologically stratified, multicomponent, Late Pleistocene through Late Holocene site. Numerous occupation events have been uncovered, although identifying discrete occupation layers (or "living floors") has been virtually impossible.

There are currently 55 radiocarbon dates for the site (see Supplementary Table 1). Twenty-five dates correspond to Early to Middle Holocene human skeletons (~ 7819 to 4487 BP; see Chapter 5), and 21 from extinct Pleistocene mammals (~ 12,240 to 7900 BP) that include two genera of ground sloth (*Megatherium* and *Glossotherium*); *Toxodon*, *Hippidion*, *Equus*, and *Eutatus*; and one family (Camelidae cf. *Hemiauchenia*) (Rafuse 2017; Salemme 2014).

The earliest human evidence is placed in ~ 12,170 BP. At this time, Pampean hunter-gatherers hunted/scavenged an extinct horse (*Equus neogeus*) and a giant ground sloth (*Megatherium americanum*) along the border of the small lake located nearby. Field-butchered units were probably transported from the kill site nearby to the upper part of the knoll, where the processing was finished later. This area would have functioned as a short-term/carcass-processing camp (sensu Fisher Jr. 1993). Over 100 formal artifacts and thousands of small debitage were recovered in these lower levels; the majority were from the SBG orthoquartzite (Leipus 2006; Leipus and Landini 2014). Phtanite and seashore cobbles were also used. No projectile points were recovered at these levels, and considering the large surface excavated (ca. 300 m²), this absence does not seem like a sampling bias.

The hunting/scavenging events of the early hunter-gatherers at the site were repeated at least once. Two Americas horse species (*Equus* and *Hippidon*) were butchered at ~ 11,180 BP. Remains of other megamammals (*Toxodon*, *Hemiauchenia*, and *Glossotherium*) were recovered at the site, although there is no evidence of human modification to the bones.

After the occupation of AS2, there is a solid human signal in both the Interserrana and Tandilia areas. In the former, two sites, Paso Otero 5 (PO5) and Campo Laborde (CL), also show the exploitation of megafauna, but in both cases, using lithic projectile points. A third site, La Moderna, located in a broad valley in the Tandilia hills, would be included in this group, although its chronology is still under discussion (Politis et at. 2019).

PO5 is located on the banks of the Quequén Grande River (Martínez and Gutiérrez 2011). The site might represent a secondary processing locus and consumption of hunted/scavenged extinct megamammals where two fragments of Fishtail projectile points, a few instruments, and several flakes were found. These artifacts were associated with various burnt bones from at least 10 extinct species, including a giant ground sloth (*Megatherium americanum*), other ground sloths, *Equus* sp., *Macrauchenia patachonica*, and *Hemiauchenia* sp. (the only species with a possible human fracture). A large amount of burnt/calcinated and mixed thermal alteration stage of bones seems to result from using megamammals as a food resource and their bones as fuel in greater amounts. Currently, the accepted dates for the site are 10,440, 10,190, and 9560 BP. A wide variety of raw materials were used, including some artifacts made of the Queguay silicified limestone (see Chapter 3, Figure 4.3).

Campo Laborde is located on a small tributary in the upper basin of Tapalqué Creek (Politis and Messineo 2008; Politis et al. 2019; Figure 4.4). The site is interpreted as a giant ground sloth kill and butchering site on the border of a Late Pleistocene swamp. The lithic artifacts recovered suggest that hunters knapped (resharpened tools) directly around the carcass (Politis et al. 2019). Beyond the giant ground sloth, bones from other species were found (*Neosclerocalyptus* sp., *Doedicurus* sp., Patagonian hare, Plains viscacha, etc.), but butchering and processing evidence was found only on the giant ground sloth and the Patagonian hare bones. Lithic material included a lanceolate bifacial projectile point stem, a side scraper, and a knife manufactured on a biface (Politis et al. 2019) (Figure 4.5).

Initially, the authors proposed that the site supported the Holocene survivals of megafauna since seven (out of 12) megamammal bones had detectable collagen, and yielded ages ranging from ~ 9700 to 6740 years BP. However,

The Early Peopling

Figure 4.3 (a) View of the excavation of Paso Otero 5; (b and c) broken Fishtail projectiles points. Photo courtesy Gustavo Martínez and María Gutiérrez.

Figure 4.4 Campo Laborde. View of the archaeological level showing the *Megatherium americanum* bones.

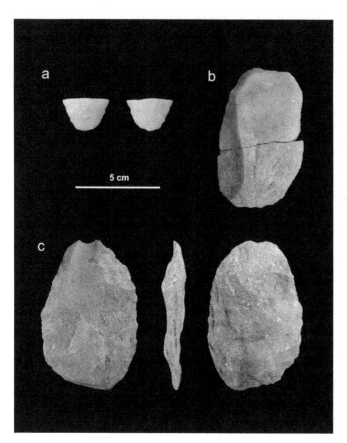

Figure 4.5 Artifacts from Campo Laborde. (a) Lanceolate bifacial projectile point stem; (b) side scraper (found in two pieces 3.2 m apart); (c) knife manufactured on a biface. Photo courtesy Pablo Messineo.

a new AMS radiocarbon dating program (with the application of XAD-2 resin purification) on *Megatherium americanum* bones generated ages of ~ 10,650 BP (Supplementary Table 1), challenging the idea of the Holocene survival of Pleistocene megamammals and providing original and high-quality chronological information (Messineo et al. 2021a; Politis et al. 2019).

La Moderna is an open-air site located on the banks of the Azul creek, where a close stratigraphic association between lithic artifacts (expedient tools of crystalline quartz and some curated tools of orthoquartzite and chert) and bones of a glyptodont, *Doedicurus clavicaudatus*, was recorded (Palanca and Politis 1979). La Moderna is interpreted as a hunting/scavenging site where, during a single event, a *Doedicurus clavicaudatus* was butchered at the edge of an ancient swamp (Politis and Gutierrez 1998). The chronology of this event has always been problematic and controversial, providing ages between 12,350 and 6550 BP. Most samples of *Doedicurus* bone collagen and organic sediments gave ages between ~ 7000 and ~ 7500 BP, considered the more reliable time span. The 6550 BP date was considered too young, while the 12,350 BP age was

The Early Peopling

rejected as too old; both dates were interpreted as outliers (Politis and Gutiérrez 1998). However, given the result from the new analysis in Campo Laborde, none of these ages could be rejected or accepted since none of them used amino acid-based methods and, therefore, may also be contaminated. Until new radiocarbon analyses are performed, the age of this site remains uncertain.

Late Pleistocene sites in the Interserrana area might result from hunting strategies or hunting events in conjunction with band mobility and raw material acquisition. It is probably that the combination of these factors determined the location of AS2, which was occupied at least twice during this period (Politis et al. 2016). The site's strategic location, roughly equidistant to the primary toolstone resources in the eastern Pampa (Tandilia and Ventania) and the Atlantic seashore, certainly would be an advantage for accessing the high-quality raw material. The few close outcrops in the Claromecó basin (Gonzales Chaves, Claudio Molina) would also provide good-quality rocks such as tuff or silicified sandstones (see Chapter 3). The setting on the border of a shallow lake would also be functional for a prey attractor, and swamp borders would help for hunting heavy and slow mammals such as the Xenarthra.

Paso Otero 5, Campo Laborde, and La Moderna shared some environmental and topographic traits. They are on the border of an ancient swamp, in the plains where megamammals were relatively abundant and are not far (<100 km) from high-quality rocks from Tandilia. They functioned as kill/procurement sites or field processing stations. The swamp substratum could be used as an advantage for hunting the megamammals, at least in Campo Laborde and La Moderna. No deposit representing massive hunting events has been identified.

Tandilia

In the southeastern half of the Tandilia hills, a cluster of sites has been systematically excavated and consistently dated between ~ 10,800 and 9500 BP (Flegenheimer and Mazzia 2013; Flegenheimer et al. 2003; Mazzanti 1999, 2003). They are mostly rock shelters occupied at the end of the Pleistocene, probably by small foraging bands with a well-developed bifacial technology, and using Fishtail projectile points. They can be grouped into two clusters. One in the central-eastern sector (the Sierras de Lobería) was excavated by Nora Flegenheimer and her team (among many others, Flegenheimer 2003, 2004; Mazzia 2013; Mazzia and Flegenheimer 2013; Weitzel et al. 2014) and includes Cerro La China (LCH) S1, S2, and S3; Cerro El Sombrero Cima (CoSC) and the rockshelter (A1); and Cueva Zoro. The other sector, toward the south (Sierras del Balcarce and Sierras de Mar del Plata), encompasses several rock shelters excavated by Diana Mazzanti and collaborators: Cueva Tixi, La Amalia

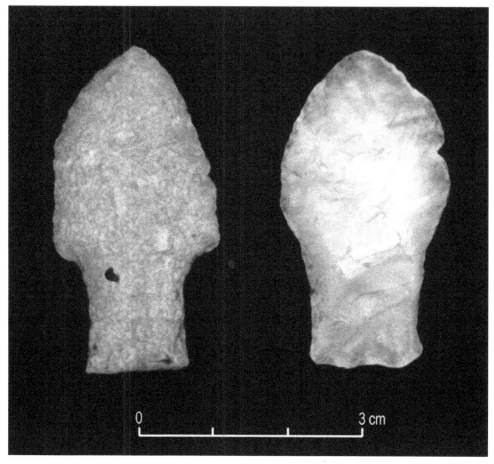

Figure 4.6 Fishtail projectile points from Cerro La China 2. Photo courtesy Nora Flegenheimer.

site 2, Cueva Burucuyá, Cueva El Abra, and Cueva La Brava (Mazzanti 2003; Mazzanti et al. 2010, 2012, 2013). Except for the date of 11,150 BP from Cerro La China 2, which can be considered an outlier, all the other dates in Tandilia are younger than 10,804 BP (see Supplementary Table 1).

The Cerro La China locality is composed of three sites, LCH1, LCH2, and LCH3. LCH1 is a medium-sized rock shelter, where systematic excavations have uncovered two stratigraphic units bearing archaeological remains. Unit 3, dated between 10,804 and 10,525 BP, contained a Fishtail preform, flakes, cores, red ochre, and white clay, as well as bones of extinct armadillo *Eutatus seguini* and plains viscacha (*Lasgostomus maximus*). LCH2 is an open-air site related to hunting activities, where two Fishtail projectile points (Figure 4.6), a core, and some flakes were recovered. Two radiocarbon dates from this level produced ages of 11,150 and 10,560 BP (Flegenheimer 2004; Flegenheimer et al. 2015a), although the former one, as we said, can be an outlier. LCH3 is also an open-air site, dated to 10,610 BP, where a variety of tool types (but not Fishtail projectile points), flakes, cores, and red ochre were recovered. It has been interpreted as a multipurpose site where domestic activities were performed (Flegenheimer et al. 2015a).

The other important locality in central-eastern Tandilia is Cerro El Sombrero, formed by two sites (Figure 4.7). The one on the hilltop (429 asl), named CoSC, comprises a great amount of lithic material lying on the flat surface (Flegenheimer et al. 2015a). In this location, 37 m^2 were excavated, uncovering the same type of artifacts as on the surface. Both assemblages represent the biggest Fishtail projectile point collection ($n = 138$) in the region, as well as ~ 1,300 tools, more than 9,000 flakes, and 11 ground artifacts, including one engraved discoidal stone. Most of the tools (90%), including the Fishtail points, are broken (Weitzel et al. 2014). The high percentage of point stems recovered has been interpreted as the result of tool kit repairing and replacement (Flegenheimer and Cattáneo 2013). Also, the presence of small, poorly manufactured complete Fishtail points found at the site (Flegenheimer and Mazzia 2013) was interpreted by Politis (1998, 1999), based on archaeological expectations derived from his ethnoarchaeological research among the Nukak, as children's artifacts (toys) produced during the learning process while their parents were knapping Fishtail points to replace the broken

Figure 4.7 View of the Cerro El Sombrero. Photo courtesy Pablo Messineo.

ones. These mini-Fishtail points were also recovered in Cerro Amigo Oeste (Miotti and Terranova 2015, see below) and in the Middle Negro River basin in the Uruguay Campos (Nami 2013, 2014). The small size, poor technology, low labor investment, and asymmetry made them a low-quality product that was not functional for hunting or any other utilitarian task. Nami (2014) arrived at the same interpretation for the three mini-Fishtail points from the Rio Negro Basin in Uruguay and also recognized that they show abrasion around their perimeter, a trait made to avoid injuries in the children (Nami 2007).

More recently, Flegenheimer et al. (2015b) proposed a different interpretation for CoSC mini-Fishtail points and characterized them as miniatures (sensu Mills 2010). All mini-Fishtail points analyzed by Flegenheimer and collaborators (2015b) are complete, contrasting with the 86.5 breakage ratio for full-size Fishtail points. In the detailed description of the tiny points, they confirmed that they are asymmetrical and poorly made. All of these characteristics are compatible with objects made by unskilled people, or apprentices, who in hunter-gatherer societies are the children. On the contrary, Flegenheimer and collaborators (2015b) do not favor the toy/children-made interpretation based on two arguments. First, the fact that the small points were complete, with no impact damage and no traces of use would indicate that they might not be toys because toys are used to play. This is not a strong argument since expedient children's artifacts can be used for a short period and then discarded without visible damage (Langdon 2013; Politis 1999). The lack of damage or use wear does not invalidate their function as toys. The second argument refers to the fact that the tiny points were recovered at the top of the hill in a weapon-refurbishing place, not on a campsite, where children spend most of their time. For Flegenheimer and collaborators (2015b), although it is an easy walk, access to the site might be restricted to some band members, and, therefore, children might be excluded. This argument is weak. While it is true that hunter-gatherer children spend a long time at the campsite, they also travel with their parents on daily foraging trips (Politis 2007; Politis et al. 2013) and can inhabit logistical camps or visit special-purpose sites (such as quarries; Hampton 1999). As many ethnographic examples show, even when men perform gender-specific tasks such as hunting, women and children are integrated with the party (Politis et al. 2013). So, the presence of children at the top of the hill cannot be ruled out.

Flegehnheimer et al. (2015) explored alternative phenomenological interpretations about the tiny Fishtail of the CoSC, proposing that "One of their meanings could include the protection of full-sized point. In this case, they strongly link meanings with a special place." It is not clear why they favor this somewhat vague interpretation over the children-made alternative. Fishtail points could be individually symbolic in themselves (as any artifact), but why only the projectile point and not all the hundreds of other artifacts found at the

The Early Peopling 125

top of the hill? Why were the Fishtails primarily functioning in an ideational or social dimension and not in a techno-utilitarian one?

Flegenheimer and collaborators' (2015) analysis fails because they do not make a crucial distinction in the miniatures between refined and poorly manufactured miniatures. Well-made miniatures, those that would usually have deep meaning and operate in the social or ideational dimension, usually require elaborate technical skills, even higher than the ones needed to make the full-size object (e.g., Hampton 1999; Sillar 2016). Both the well and the poorly made artifacts are generally the reduction of full-size objects, but the technical skill required to manufacture each one is a key element to define function and condition. The mini-Fishtail points from CoSC indicate certain incompetency resulting from the underdeveloped motor and cognitive skills usually associated with children's hands.

The other site in the Cerro El Sombrero locality is a small rock shelter (A1) on the hill slope dated between 10,725 and 10,270 BP (Flegenheimer et al. 2015a). A variety of artifacts were recovered at the site, including two Fishtail points, cores, flakes, and a possible cache of red ochre. Both sites A1 and CoSC were probably occupied simultaneously and are considered to be related. However, an obvious difference in the spatial scale should be noted. While the hilltop can be simultaneously occupied by a large number of people (many bands) and the density of debris suggests an intense occupation, the shelter might harbor a family or little more.

The other set of sites, located in the southeastern sector of Tandilia, are comparable with the ones summarized above and are probably linked. These sites included a variety of caves and rock shelters: Cueva Tixi (Figure 4.8), Abrigo Los Pinos, Amalia S2, Cueva Burucuyá, Abrigo La Grieta, Cueva El Abra, Laguna La Brava, and Lobería 1 (Mazzanti 1999, 2003; Mazzanti and Bonnat 2013; Mazzanti et al. 2010, 2013). The earliest levels of these sites have dates between ~ 10,700 and ~ 9500 BP (see Supplementary Table 1). On the one hand, the lower levels of Cueva Tixi, Abrigo Los Pinos, and Cueva El Abra are interpreted as the result of multiple long-term occupations. On the other hand, Cueva Burucuyá, Cueva La Brava, Amalia S2, Alero El Mirador, and Abrigo la Grieta suggest ephemeral occupations (Bonnat and Mazzanti 2015; Bonnat et al. 2015; Mazzanti et al. 2012). Bifacial technology was present in these sites, but only one complete Fishtail and a Fishtail stem were recovered in Los Pinos and La Amalia S2 sites, respectively (Mazzanti and Bonnat 2013). In these sites, a variety of faunal remains indicates a generalized economy. The prey included guanaco, Pampas deer, plains viscacha, coypu, several species of armadillos, and greater rhea (Mazzanti et al. 2012). A few extinct mammals were also found: *Eutatus seguini* and *Canis avus* and a small local rodent first identified at Cueva Tixi site: *Galea tixiensis* (Mazzanti 1997; Mazzanti and Quintana 2001). *Eutatus* bones are burned, which would indicate consumption

Figure 4.8 (a) View of the entrance of Cueva Tixi; (b) artifacts from the Pleistocene levels of Cueva Tixi. Photo courtesy Diana Mazzanti.

Although the same cultural group might generate all these sites, there are several similar traits and some differences between the two sectors of Tandilia despite being very close. Extra-regional lithic resources, basically the Queguay silicified limestone (see Chapter 3), are found at very low frequencies (less than 5%) and in artifacts that indicate the final stage of the operational chain (Nami 2017). This raw material is identified in most early sites of Tandilia (Bonnat et al. 2015; Flegenheimer and Mazzia 2013; Flegenheimer et al. 2003; Mazzanti 2003; Mazzanti et al. 2012; Valverde 2002, 2003). SBG orthoquartzite was used in greater proportions to manufacture various instruments, among which double and simple edges on medium to small flakes stand out (Bonnat et al. 2015). There is evidence for mobility or interactions of groups that transferred cobbles from the Atlantic seashore in both micro-regions. Another similar trait is that the rock shelters have functioned as small short-term residential camps or places for ephemeral occupations (brief stops for specific purposes or overnight camps).

A very striking difference is the faunal record. While in the central-eastern sector of Tandilia, almost no bone has been recovered (the exceptions are the few *Eutatus* and plains viscacha bones found in LCH1) in the southeastern sector, faunal remains are abundant in some sites and in great variation, but with the absence of Pleistocene megamammals. The lack of this fauna does not seem to be related to taphonomic processes (other faunal remains are present,

The Early Peopling

see, e.g., Cueva Tixi, Mazzanti and Quintana 2001), and, therefore, it seems that megamammals were not present or were not hunted during the occupation of the hills' sites.

Spatial patterns point to the preference for occupying the hill valleys, probably due to their resources: access to the lithic raw material and permanent streams and springs. Topographic facilities for hunting tactics would be another advantage of these geographical traits. Diverse vegetation (grasses, shrubs, some trees, etc.) would also be attractive (Brea et al. 2014; Mazzanti and Bonnat 2013). Among them, the forest of *currumamuel* (*Colletia paradoxa*) could be of great value since this shrub formed extended and dense forests in the hill range. Due to its abundant resin, it burns quickly and produces large flames, although it does not last long. Given the scarcity of wood for fuel, *currumamuel* was probably one of the best alternatives. However, knowledge about the use of wood and vegetal resources is still incipient in the Pampas, and a bias in favor of faunal exploitation is probably tainting the reconstruction of the SUBSISTENCE of the early hunter-gatherers.

What seems clear is that Tandilia was part of a circuit that included the neighboring Interserrana area as well as the Atlantic seashore (Mazzanti and Bonnat 2013; Politis 1984). Hunting-gathering bands probably had a flexible territorial behavior, which allowed people to freely move around during the annual range and exploit the different resources from each area under low human density. Regarding the seashore, the most frequent resource exploited was the rounded beach cobbles since they were registered in almost all the early sites. Shells were gathered and circulated inland (Politis et al. 2003b), while marine mammals and fish were exploited only on the coast since the Middle Holocene (Bayón and Politis 2014; Bonomo and Leon 2010). However, we should consider that the Pampas seashore during the Late Pleistocene was more than 100 m below the current sea level. Therefore, it remains inaccessible for archaeological investigation, or it was destroyed by the rise of the sea. This situation prevents a well-funded discussion about the use of marine resources and the occupation of the coast during the Late Pleistocene.

Other Areas

In the Atlantic seashore of the Interserrana area, some striking traits are found in the clay levels in the paleoichnological site of Pehuen Co, which suggest a human presence in the Late Pleistocene. The site, nowadays in the sea beach, was a Late Pleistocene continental shallow freshwater lake. It is world-famous for its palaeoichnological record, which shows more than 100 trackways and hundreds of isolated footprints of various extinct animals (Manera de Bianco et al. 2008). Dating of organic matter from the intermediate levels produced an age of 12,000 BP (Aramayo and Manera Bianco 1996). However, this age is still tentative due to the nature and uniqueness of the sample and the lack of information about the obtained radiocarbon date,

There are three human traits among the animal footprints: two isolated footprints and a trackway. The two isolated footprints (both a left foot) were found on large pieces of clayey sediment separated from the layer by the tide. The third is a track of 13 consecutive footprints, with alternated traces of the right and left foot, as if an individual was walking. In the same layer of this trace, there is *Megatherium* trackway and *Macrauchenia*, Artiodactyla, and flamingo trackways that cross the human one in different directions. The trackway could not be reanalyzed because the sand beach covered it almost immediately after discovery, and it is usually below sea level even at normal low tide. Although still weak, this evidence indicates that most of the large- and medium-sized Pleistocene mammals were still living in the Pampas when the first human beings arrived in the region.

One isolated finding in the Rolling Pampa assigned to this period is the Arroyo de Frías human skeletons dated to 10,300 and 9520 BP (see Chapter 2). The oldest date seems to be more reliable since the collagen was purified by XAD2 resin (Politis et al. 2011a). Despite the difference between both dates (~ 780 ^{14}C years), the skeleton is placed in the Pleistocene to Holocene transition and is one of the earliest human skeletons in South America.

To conclude with the Late Pleistocene human occupation of the region, we have to mention the finding of isolated Fishtail points in surface assemblages in the eastern Pampa (Messineo et al. 2019; Weitzel et al. 2018). They have a discontinuous distribution, which has been interpreted as the result of items discarded in paths or communication routes between more populated areas such as Tandilia and the Uruguay Campos (Weitzel et al. 2018). In western Pampa, only two Fishtail points were recorded, at Tapera Moreira 1 and El Carmel. They might represent an ephemeral exploratory phase that did not turn into a more effective occupation (Berón et al. 2015). No other early archaeological remains have been recorded in these areas. Very dry conditions and concomitant low biomass were probably limiting factors for permanent human occupation in the western sector of the Pampas during the Late Pleistocene.

In the Uruguay River, in the boundary between the Pampas and the Campos, the reexcavation of two early localities, Pay Paso and Tigre/K-87, has provided relevant data for the Late Pleistocene peopling of the region (Suárez 2014, 2017; Suárez et al. 2018). At the Tigre/K-87 site, three earliest dates between 11,355 and 11,315 BP in association with a biface fragment were recorded. A second group of ages is placed between 10,955 and 10,410 BP and dates a level containing fractured preforms and a fractured point resembling Fishtail morphology (Suárez et al. 2018). The third set produced ages between 10,075 and 9615 BP in association with Tigre projectile points. The latter type is the more frequent in the area and has been defined by Suárez and

The Early Peopling

collaborators (2018: 253) based on the following traits: "a wide stem with a convex base or slightly convex stem sides, with expanded notches with angles between 45° and 60°, with prominent barbs at the beginning of use-life."

The other site, Pay Paso 1, is located on the left margin of the Cuareim River, close to the Uruguay River (Austral 1995). Recent research led to the recovery of an early archaeological sequence dated between ~ 11,000 and 8500 BP (see Supplementary Table 1). Faunal remains include extinct horses (*Equus* sp.) and extant species. No projectile points were recovered, but ~ 10 m away from the excavation, a Fishtail point made of fine-grained silicified sandstone was found. Suárez (2015) proposes that it might be associated with this context. Two Tigre-type projectile points were recovered in the second component, while in the third component, a new type of projectile point named Pay Paso was found. This type is relatively frequent along the middle Uruguay and Cuareim Rivers (Suárez 2015) and is defined by the following characteristics: "short stem, profoundly concave stem base, divergent concave stem edges expanding toward the base, stem edges with abrasion, convex or straight blade edges, regular laminar retouch of the blade, and very careful basal thinning of the stem done by triangular and short flake scars" (Suárez 2015: 98).

A variety of Fishtail projectile points has also been found on the surface in the Campos of Uruguay (López Mazz 2013; Nami 2017, 2020; Suárez 2015). It is not clear if this abundance reflects demographic density coupled with stylistic and technological preferences or, on the other hand, is the result of high archaeological visibility in certain areas associated with an intense survey by amateurs and archaeologists. However, despite this relatively high density, only two Fishtail points come from a dated stratigraphic context (Cerro de Los Burros site, Meneghin 2004, and Tigre site, Suárez et al. 2018). In the northeastern area of the Pampas, a few Fishtail points have been found on the surface in the neighborhood of the Uruguay and Gualeguay Rivers (Capeletti 2011; Castro 2017; Castro and Terranova 2015; Mujica 1995).

Although the distribution is more restricted when compared with the Fishtail points, the Tigre points are well distributed in the Campos of Uruguay and southern Brazil (Suárez 2015; Suárez et al. 2018), and a few were recorded in northeastern Pampa in the Gualeguay River (Castro 2017). It is not clear yet what the relation is between the groups who used these two types of projectile points. Since the Tigre points are slightly younger than the Fishtail and shared "some social, technological and behavioral characteristics" with them, it has been suggested that they are the result of an early regionalization of the Fishtail in the Uruguay River basin (Suárez et al. 2018: 258).

Finally, in regard to faunal exploitation, Martínez and Gutiérrez (2004) proposed a generalized regional economy for the Late Pleistocene to Early Holocene period in the Pampas. A broad spectrum of resources (including extinct megamammals) would have been exploited by hunter-gatherers as suggested by the presence and diversity of faunal species consumed during this period: among 38 species found in the archaeological record, at least 16 were consumed. Both taxonomic diversity and richness are greater when compared with the following period (Middle Holocene). The real significance of guanaco in the Late Pleistocene hunter-gatherers' diet is not clear and needs careful examination.

The Early Holocene

During the Early Holocene, traces of human occupation can be detected in most areas of the Pampas, suggesting more flexible and successful adaptive strategies. In the Interserrana area, the El Guanaco locality presents a good record of Early Holocene occupation in the Pampas (Flegenheimer et al. 2010). Two sites, 1 and 2, containing bones of megafauna and humans, have been recovered. The lowest levels of site 1 (dated to 9250 BP) include faunal remains of guanaco, plains viscacha, fox, other extant species, and two Pleistocene fauna – *Equus* sp. and *Macrauchenia patachonica* – but they do not show evidence of human action. These remains are associated with quartzite artifacts. The lower levels of Site 2 include scarce flaked lithic artifacts and a grinding stone used for processing seeds. Four dates yielded Early Holocene ages between 9140 BP and 8411 BP (see Supplementary Table 1). These early levels have been interpreted as a residential camp where greater rhea, guanaco, and Pampas deer were processed and consumed (Frontini 2008). No extinct fauna and no projectile points were found. In the lowermost levels, two human individuals, dating to 8123 and 8433 BP, were recovered (Flegenheimer et al. 2010).

The Paso Otero 4 (PO4) site, also in the Interserrana area, on the banks of the Quequén Grande River, shows an Early Holocene occupation with some distinctive traits (Martínez and Gutiérrez 2018). The faunal assemblage includes the typical Pampean prey (guanaco, Pampas deer, plains viscacha, armadillos, greater rhea, etc.) as well as *Eutatus seguini*, all with traces of human action (Álvarez et al. 2013). The potential survival of *Eutatus seguini* is sustained by associated dates on soil organic matter residues, which provided ages between 8913 and 7729 BP. This is the only Pampean assemblage where the number of identified specimens (NISP) of plains viscacha is bigger than that of guanaco (Álvarez 2014) and has been interpreted as a succession of short-term residential and multipurpose activity camps (Barros et al. 2014).

There is also a remarkable feature at the site: a water well was dug at ~ 8700 to 8000 BP during dry pulse events along the Early Holocene (Figure 4.9). The hole was dug into the sediments of the Río Salado member's lower section and the Guerrero member's upper section (both belong to the Lujan Formation). This unique finding for the Pampas shows that humans had a strategy to cope with droughts during the Early Holocene (Martínez et al. 2015).

The Early Peopling

Figure 4.9 Paso Otero 4 site. The filled hole (dark area) is interpreted as a water well. Photo courtesy María Gutiérrez and Gustavo Martínez.

The Central Pampean Dunefield (CPD) was occupied for the first time in this period. The oldest human evidence is dated between 8971 and 7746 BP (see Supplementary Table 1) in Laguna de Los Pampas (Messineo et al. 2018; Politis et al. 2012), Laguna El Doce (Ávila 2011), and La Susana 1 (Scheifler et al. 2017). The sites are located on the margins of shallow lakes (which would be seasonally salty), and most of them are multicomponent sites with recurrent hunter-gatherer occupations through the Holocene. This evidence represents the first stage of human presence in an area that was probably an unoccupied space during the late Pleistocene (Messineo et al. 2019). The toolstones in the CPD are characterized by a predominance of SBG orthoquartzite, phtanite, and silicide dolomite from Tandilia (see Chapter 3), while other low-frequency raw materials come from Ventania, the Patagonian Shingle Mantle, and western Pampas. The presence of exhausted orthoquartzite and chert cores suggests maximizing these high-quality distant rocks (Messineo et al. 2019). Primary human burials were recovered at Laguna de Los Pampas and Laguna del Doce.

In central-eastern Tandilia, a few other sites, such as Cueva Zoro, Los Helechos, and El Ajarafe, have been dated to the Early Holocene (10,253 to 8574 BP). No diagnostic artifacts have been found, and they have been interpreted as the result of ephemeral occupations (Flegenheimer et al. 2015a; Mazzia 2011, 2013). In the eastern sector, there are also several occupations for this period in rock shelters dated between 9834 and 7670 BP: Abrigo Los Pinos, Cueva El Abra, Cueva La Brava, Lobería S.1, Cueva Alí Mustafá, and Amalia S.2 (Mazzanti et al. 2012, 2015). Abrigo Los Pinos and Cueva El Abra show evidence of multiple long-term activities. Faunal association includes only extant fauna: guanaco, Pampas deer, plains viscacha, coypu, and others.

Finally, in the southwestern Pampa, on the border with Patagonia, hunter-gatherers, using end scrapers, some "core-choppers," and abundant crude basalt and chert flakes, occupied the terraces of the Colorado River at ~ 8600 BP in the Casa de Piedra site (Gradin 1984). Other areas of the western Pampa had a very low-density human occupation, suggesting that the scarcity of freshwater during the Early Holocene was a critical factor that prevented a continuous settlement.

PATAGONIA

The confirmed Late Pleistocene and Early Holocene sites are concentrated in a few regions. Clusters of sites are known in Northwest Patagonia, in central-western Patagonia, the Deseado Massif, the Pali Aike Volcanic Field, Última Esperanza Sound, and North Tierra del Fuego (Figure 1.14). At each of these regions, there is important Late Pleistocene and Early Holocene evidence

The Early Peopling

relevant to discuss the settlement of Patagonia. The chronological information shows that the older occupations are concentrated on the steppes of extra-Andean Patagonia, particularly at the Deseado Massif, and that the later expansion toward the Andes was a discontinuous process in both time and space (Borrero 2004). The potential importance of lands now drowned under the sea was often considered (Miotti 2003), but to this day, the area has not been researched, and there is no supporting evidence.

Northwest Patagonia

The evidence from Northwest Patagonia is restricted to the Early Holocene, a fact that does not support the model of initial dispersal from the Pacific coast. This is particularly important since Monte Verde II, west of this region, is widely accepted among the earliest sites in South America, usually associated with the idea of colonization along the Pacific coast (Braje et al. 2020, but see Prates et al. 2020). Work at a number of sites in South Cuyo and Neuquén indicates low-intensity human occupations during the Early Holocene (Barberena et al. 2015; Diéguez and Neme 2003; Garvey 2021; Neme et al. 2011) (Figure 4.10). No evidence of association with megafauna was found despite the existence of a few Late Pleistocene bone assemblages (Neme and Gil 2008; Praderio et al. 2012). An extremely disturbed stratigraphy at Gruta del Indio inhibits discussion of a potential association between Late Pleistocene megafauna and humans (García 2003; Lagiglia 2001). Early short and low-intensity occupations were identified at Cueva Huenul at 1,000 masl, where lithics, one hearth, guanaco bones with cut-marks, and evidence of processing plants like *Prosopis* sp. are dated ca. 10,155–9200 BP (Figure 4.11). Lithic artifacts are represented mainly by final reduction stages and were basically made of the local Huenul obsidian (Barberena et al. 2011, 2015). A common pattern of finding the earlier human occupations resting above paleontological Late Pleistocene layers is manifested here (Barberena 2014).

A cluster of Early Holocene sites in South Neuquén, with dates around 9000 BP, testify to the human settlement near the Andes. Traful, Cuyín Manzano, Valle Encantado I, and Arroyo del Corral I and II caves are located in the forest or forest-steppe ecotone near the headwaters of the Limay River basin. El Trébol rock shelter, also in the forest, south of Lago Nahuel Huapi, is potentially older. Some 100 km east of the ecotone – in the steppe – is Cueva Epullán Grande, another important site with quite different Early Holocene occupations.

Traful Cave is at the foot of a cliff near the Traful River, at ca. 760 masl. The initial and ephemeral occupations are dated 9400–9300 BP (Crivelli Montero et al. 1993: 33). A lithic assemblage consisting mainly of unretouched flakes was found. Even though no bifacial tools were recovered, some bifacial-reduction flakes attest to their existence (Cuneo 1993: 165). The faunal

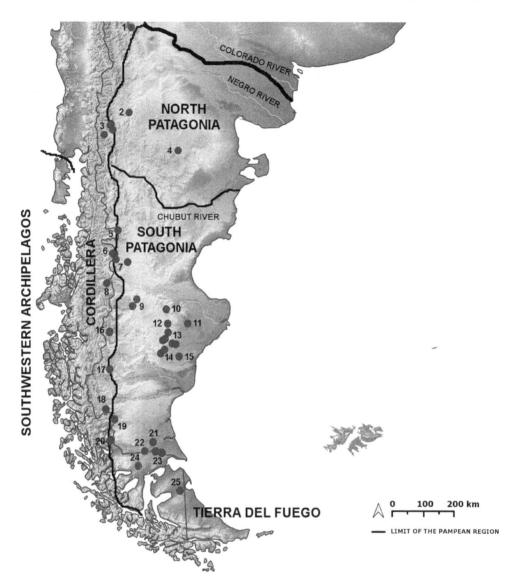

Figure 4.10 Map showing the Late Pleistocene and Early Holocene sites in Patagonia mentioned in the text. References: (1) Cueva Huenul; (2) Cueva Epullán Grande; (3) Cueva Traful, Cuyín Manzano, Valle Encantado I, Arroyo del Corral I and II, El Trébol; (4) Cerro Amigo Oeste; (5) El Chueco 1; (6) Cueva de la Vieja, Baño Nuevo; (7) Casa de Piedra de Roselló, Alero Dásovich; (8) Las Guanacas; (9) Cueva de las Manos, Arroyo Feo; (10) Los Toldos 3; (11) Piedra Museo; (12) Cueva Maripé; (13) El Ceibo 7, Cerro Tres Tetas, Casa del Minero 1, La Martita, Cueva Túnel; (14) La Gruta, El Verano; (15) Cerro Bombero; (16) Cerro Casa de Piedra 5 and 7; (17) Bloque 1-Oquedad; (18) Chorrillo Malo 2; (19) Cerro León 3; (20) Milodón Cave, Cueva del Medio, Cueva Lago Sofía 1; (21) Las Buitreras; (22) Juni Aike; (23) Fell Cave, Cerro Sota, Cueva de los Chingues, Pali Aike; (24) Cañadón Leona; (25) Tres Arroyos 1.

The Early Peopling

Figure 4.11 Cueva Huenul 1, Argentina. Photo courtesy Guadalupe Romero Villanueva.

assemblage is dominated by small mammal bones, with a few splinters of guanaco. Bones of gray and red foxes (*Lycalopex griseus* and *L. culpaeus*), both with cut-marks, are frequent, and there are also bones of other small mammals, birds, and fishes (Cordero 2011). Immediately after the initial occupation, relatively more intense occupations occur ca. 7850–7300 BP, with well-defined hearths and lithic artifacts, including triangular projectile points (Crivelli et al. 1993). Guanaco remains more important at this time, complemented by *Lagidium* sp., fox, and small rodents, the latter primarily natural contributions resulting from the activities of birds (Cordero 2011).

Cueva Cuyin Manzano is located near a small tributary of the Traful River. The lower occupations were relatively more intense than those of Traful (Crivelli et al. 1993: 39) and were tentatively related to the region's exploration by Boschín (2009: 67). They are dated by a single standard radiocarbon analysis to 9920 BP, and constitute another sad case of an intensively excavated site whose materials were never fully published. The faunal remains include guanaco, which is not abundant. Bifacial artifacts are absent, but the frequency of end scrapers is relatively high (Ceballos 1982).

Cueva Epullán Grande in the eastern steppe was intermittently occupied between 9970 and 7550 BP, probably from a distant base (Crivelli et al. 1996). The availability of water near the cave was probably scarce, which surely was an important constraint for its use. Bones of guanaco, skunk, red and gray fox,

Felidae, and Rheidae were recovered (Cordero 2009). In contrast with sites in the forest, bifacial work was important at this site. Several human burials were recovered (Crivelli et al. 1996). Their chronology is based on charcoal found near the burials, which suggested dates around 8000 BP. Of course, dates on the bones are needed. With one exception, the skeletons were placed on beds of rocks or grass, and ochre was extensively used. Engravings on the basal rock – although some expressed some doubts about their interpretation (Boschín 2009) – can be associated with the initial occupation of the site.

A Spanish-Argentine team worked at the Arroyo Corral II site for several seasons, but there are no detailed publications to assess the claims for association with megafauna or the early presence of hearths and a dwelling structure over the original floor of the shelter (Arias Cabal et al. 2012). Some evidence of burning was uncovered at the base of the sequence and interpreted by the excavators as the result of vegetation burning, an explanation that certainly requires more discussion. The archaeological status of the site is clear since bifacial tools were recovered, but the contexts remain poorly described. Arroyo Corral I nearby presents *Mylodon* remains during the Last Glacial Maximum and scarce archaeological shreds of evidence (Arias Cabal et al. 2012: 31). At Valle Encantado, evidence of ephemeral occupations attributed to the Early Holocene was recovered (Hajduk and Albornoz 1999).

The evidence from El Trébol informs about the potential association between humans and extinct mammals in a forest environment, on the basis of ca. 10,000 BP radiocarbon dates (Hajduk et al. 2004, 2006, 2012; Lezcano et al. 2010). The human presence is ephemeral at this rock shelter, located at the base of a volcanic rock outcrop. Cut-marks were observed on Mylodontidae osteoderms, which still require contextual discussion. The significance of the association – based on the cut-marks – was never fully discussed. This attractive accumulation of bones and tools occurs at a lower layer of the rock shelter, where evidence of rockfalls probably associated with an earthquake accompanied by volcanic activity was found. The lower anthropic evidence physically associated with extinct fauna was recorded among the interstices between rocks contained within the volcanic sand matrix (Hajduk et al. 2004, 2010). Only teeth fragments and 137 Mylodontinae osteoderms were recovered, 40 of which are affected by fire, and nine have cut-marks. The suggestion of consumption of meat on this basis seems premature. An extinct canid (*Dusicyon avus*) and a large deer were also recovered, all with cut-marks and anthropic fractures. Remains of huemul (*Hippocamelus bisulcus*), guanaco, red fox, other small mammals, birds, and even freshwater mollusks complete the faunal list. One flake, one end scraper, one side scraper, and two fragments of bone awls, together with lithic debris, including evidence of bifacial work, were found physically associated with the bones. The environment was already an open *Nothofagus* sp. forest (Whitlock et al. 2006). The upper layers include hearths, but sloth osteoderms continue to appear, which is another reason to

The Early Peopling 137

be cautious about their significance (for similar cases, see also Bellelli 1991; López Mendoza and Mena Larraín 2011).

Important cultural changes occurred after the initial low-intensity occupations of Northwest Patagonia, probably as adjustments to a changing environment. The forest was increasingly more important at the headwaters of the Limay River, an area that was intensively used during the Holocene (Hajduk and Albornoz 1999). Water availability near Cueva Epullán Grande was higher than today between approximately 10,000 and 7000 BP (Prieto and Stutz 1996), which is crucial in an area where human adaptations are tethered to water sources. The settlement pattern for most of the Holocene is effectively concentrated near water sources (Borrero 1982).

Beyond this northwestern cluster, no more early sites exist in North Patagonia. Excepting the Casa de Piedra site, near the middle Colorado River where the lower occupations were dated ca. 8600–7560 BP (Gradin 1984, see above), we have to move several hundreds of kilometers to the east to find evidence worth considering for a discussion of early settlement. On the top of Amigo Oeste, a small hill on the Somuncura plateau, over 100 complete and fragmented Fishtail projectile points were found together with discoidal stones, bifaces, and knives (Hermo et al. 2013; Miotti et al. 2010). This is a pattern that replicates the case of the Late Pleistocene Cerro Sombrero Cima (CoSC) site in the Pampas (Flegenheimer 2003) and clearly implicates the possibility of Late Pleistocene presence in Northeast Patagonia (Miotti and Terranova 2015). Even when this is for the moment sustained only on settlement and typological grounds, the combination of Fishtails and discoidal stones is a strong marker of an early assemblage (Flegenheimer et al. 2013a; Miotti et al. 2010). Unfortunately, there is no datable stratigraphic material.

Chronological evidence for the presence of Pleistocene megafauna before the arrival of humans was found at several sites in Northwest Patagonia. Only the ambiguous claims from Gruta del Indio, El Trébol, and Arroyo Corral I and II can be used to sustain human associations with megafauna, but the four cases still require more detailed discussions and publication. Interestingly, the initial occupations of the best published early sites in North Patagonia, both west and east of the Andes, show that guanaco, the most abundant vertebrate today, was not necessarily the main prey. This role was sometimes reserved for foxes, small mammals, or even plants. The sample of sites is too small and spatially dispersed to claim that the adaptive pattern is already clear, and it is entirely possible that we are simply looking at some aspects of a more complex organization. However, Early Holocene evidence from Marifilo shelter in south-central Chile indicates a good knowledge of the resources offered by the lower forests (Adán et al. 2004; Velásquez and Adán 2002), and plants, perhaps foxes, and other small mammals appear to be dominant. Suppose the presence of foxes can be attributed to human activities in all the mentioned sites. In that case, this evidence informs us about an important resource for the

Figure 4.12 View of Cueva de la Vieja, Chile. Photo courtesy César Méndez.

early explorers, a resource that later was to become secondary or ignored. As a corollary, we should consider the possibility of adaptations that were not centered on large vertebrates during transition times in North Patagonia.

Central-Western Patagonia: Aisén and West Chubut

Aisén is an area relatively close to the Western Archipelagos, characterized by a variety of habitats. Seasonality and a rugged topography probably conditioned the colonization of the habitats above 700 masl (Méndez and Reyes 2008; Reyes et al. 2006), but there is abundant evidence at lower altitudes. The older evidence comes from sites El Chueco 1, Cueva de La Vieja, and Baño Nuevo, all with brief occupations dated ca. 11,000–10,000 BP (López 2009; Mena and Stafford 2006; Mena et al. 2003; Méndez et al. 2019; Reyes et al. 2007b) (Figure 4.12).

The basal levels at Cueva de La Vieja, a briefly occupied location in Aisén, yielded debitage and one bifacial fragment manufactured on a nonlocal siliceous rock. The selected raw material for this basal deposit is a mid- to coarse-grained basalt (Méndez et al. 2019) (Figure 4.13). At El Chueco 1, only one multifunctional coarse-grained andesite tool was recovered at the lower layers

The Early Peopling

Figure 4.13 Excavations at Cueva de la Vieja. Lower layers. Photo courtesy César Méndez.

(Reyes et al. 2007b). In both cases, poor raw materials were used. The early component of Baño Nuevo 1, occupied a few hundred years later, displayed higher raw material diversity, including fine-grained siliceous tool stones (Méndez et al. 2019). A wider variety of stone raw materials was exploited later in the Early Holocene of Aisén.

The archaeofauna of these early sites include guanaco subadults accompanied by charred seeds and fruits (Belmar 2019; Belmar et al. 2017; Méndez et al. 2011, 2019), which are summer indicators. Very few artifacts associated with charcoal and hearth features characterize these early occupations. Relatively more intensive occupations occur throughout the Early Holocene, including the deposition of the remains of 10 individuals at Baño Nuevo 1. The earlier archaeological levels at Baño Nuevo produced only modern fauna, primarily guanacos (López 2009) and foxes (Trejo and Jackson 1998), reminding us of its importance for the older occupations at Traful or Marifilo. An association with red fox remains was observed in at least three of the burials of Baño Nuevo. The remains of three human newborns and two adults are associated with several radiocarbon dates of ca. 8000 BP, two of which were run on the bones of one of the adults. The individuals were deposited in a flexed position against the back wall of the cave and covered with stones, a feature that is reminiscent of the *chenques* – large burial mounds made with rocks – that characterize the Late Holocene of the region (Mena and Reyes 2001; Mena et al. 2003). Recent molecular studies of the human bones at Baño Nuevo identified the presence of haplogroup B (Reyes et al. 2012), correcting the view about its absence in Fuegian and Patagonian populations (Garcia Bour et al. 1998; Lalueza Fox 1995). This marker was later found in human remains recovered at two sites dated ca. 3500–4000 BP south of the Argentino Lake (Franco et al. 2010b; L'Heureux 2008; Moraga et al. 2009). Again, Pleistocene fauna were found only below the human occupations at Baño Nuevo, including abundant ground sloth osteoderms (López 2009; López and Mena 2011; Mena et al. 2003). Small quantities of lithics and fragments of an atlatl were found in the Early Holocene levels (Mena and Reyes 2001; Velasquez 1998).

On the steppes at the foot of the Andes, the Casa de Piedra de Roselló site at the forest-steppe ecotone was occupied around 8000 BP, and the Alero Dásovich site around 10,600–10,000 BP (Aguerre et al. 2017; Castro Esnal et al. 2017). In the southern part of central-western Patagonia, the earliest reliable date is around 9600 BP at the Casa de Piedra 7 (CCP7) site in Perito Moreno National Park (Civalero and Aschero 2003). Together with the sites found in Aisén, they comprise some of the best records to understand the colonization process of western Patagonia.

The occupation of Aisén reflects a process of increasing familiarization with the new habitats of that region, always within a framework of low human population density. Importantly, the Pleistocene faunal remains from Baño Nuevo 1 and Las Guanacas (Labarca et al. 2008) show that viable environments for humans existed well before the arrival of humans to central-western Patagonia (Borrero et al. 2019a).

Given the human pulses observed by Méndez et al. (2016a, 2019), the case of central-western Patagonia demonstrates that colonization is not necessarily a rapid or continuous event but rather a complex process involving potential lags or even failures (Méndez 2013). The punctuated presence of humans north of Pueyrredón lake and the Perito Moreno Park confirms this pattern (Aschero et al. 2007, 2019a).

Deseado Massif

The most important early cluster of sites is located at the Deseado Massif. Some classic sites, like Los Toldos 3 and many more, are found there. Los Toldos 3 is a potentially important site usually mentioned in discussions about the early peopling of South America (Cardich et al. 1973; Menghin 1952a), but the evidence is unclear. The lower level is associated with a single standard radiocarbon date of 12,600 ± 500 BP and is used to define what was called

The Early Peopling

the "Level 11 Industry" (Borrero 1989). This "industry" was characterized by unifacially marginal retouched tools, most of which are side scrapers. These tools were physically associated with remains of extinct horse, *Lama (Vicugna) gracilis*, and guanaco (Cardich and Flegenheimer 1978; Cardich and Miotti 1983; Mansur-Franchomme 1983). The anthropic evidence is robust; however, not only is the dating inconclusive but the association with extinct mammals cannot be trusted. A level immediately above was also dated with a single radiocarbon date of 8750 BP, apparently related to the butchered remains of *Lama (Vicugna) gracilis*, extinct horse, and guanaco in association with triangular projectile points and large end scrapers. At Cueva El Ceibo 7, some 150 km south, also in the Deseado Massif, an assemblage attributed to the "Level 11 industry" was recovered. Bones of an extinct horse, *Lama (Vicugna) gracilis*, *Felis concolor*, and probably guanaco were found (Cardich 1987; Cardich et al. 1981–1982). The excavators published no radiocarbon dates, but a date of ca. 9500 BP is mentioned by Miotti and Salemme (1999). On this poor basis, it can only be said that there is no evidence for the supposed Late Pleistocene age of the "Level 11 Industry" at El Ceibo. Below we will review another pertinent piece of information at the Arroyo Feo site for this elusive "industry." Summing up, the whole cultural and chronological sequences of Los Toldos 3 and El Ceibo need reassessment.

The really important sites in the Deseado Massif are those that are well studied and published. One is Piedra Museo, whose oldest layers are securely dated between 11,000 and 10,390 BP (Miotti et al. 1999, 2003; Ramirez Rozzi et al. 2000). Two stratigraphic units at Piedra Museo yielded Late Pleistocene human occupations (Miotti and Salemme 1999; Miotti et al. 1999). The remains of *Hippidion*, *Lama gracilis*, and guanaco were recovered. Of note is the finding of *Rhea americana* and *Rhea pennata* bones in the same stratum, two genera of flightless birds that today are allopatric. Cut-marks were observed on a *Mylodon* bone (Marchionni and Vázquez 2012), which is among the few cases in Patagonia, together with Fell Cave (Martin 2012) and the osteoderms of El Trebol. Two Fishtail projectile points and end and side scrapers made of large flakes were recovered (Cattáneo 2005; Miotti 1998). During the first occupation of Piedra Museo, exotic good-quality rocks arrived as bifaces, while later occupations were more focused on local and lower-quality rocks (Cattáneo 2004: 115).

Another important multicomponent site is Cerro Tres Tetas at 450 masl, some 55 km north of El Ceibo in the central Deseado Massif (Paunero 1993–1994). The oldest occupations with a good archaeological context were recorded between 11,087 and 10,260 BP, with end scrapers, side scrapers, knives, and retouched flakes. The lithic technology is basically unifacial, but the presence of bifacial debitage was recorded. Guanaco bones dominate the faunal remains. One characteristic of this site is that no Pleistocene faunal remains were found, which is not surprising from an organizational

Figure 4.14 View of Casa del Minero 1, Deseado Massif, Argentina. Photo courtesy Rafael Paunero.

perspective. There are also occupations around 10,260 BP, again dominated by heavily broken guanaco bones.

Not too far from Cerro Tres Tetas, at the La María locality, there is a concentration of sites (Paunero 2003a). The earlier evidence was obtained at the Casa del Minero site, dated 10,999 and 10,967 BP, and Cueva Túnel was occupied ca. 10,500 BP (Paunero et al. 2015, 2020) (Figures 4.14 and 4.15). Remains attributed to *Hemiauchenia paradoxa*, *Lama gracilis*, guanaco, and Rheidae were recovered at Casa del Minero and Camelidae and horse at Cueva Túnel, in both cases with hearths and lithic tools (Paunero 2000, 2003b; Paunero et al. 2017, 2020). The area is rich in lithic raw materials (Skarbun et al. 2019). Further south is La Gruta, dated between ca. 10,800 and 8000 BP (Franco et al. 2010a), in a sector where surface findings attributable to the early occupations are abundant (Vetrisano and Franco 2019).

There is some evidence of regional continuity in the Deseado Massif during the transition toward the full Holocene climatic conditions. The evidence consists of a largely repetitive pattern of deposition of tool assemblages with minimal bifaciality, some blades, bolas, and heavily processed guanaco bones. Several Early Holocene occupations at the Deseado Massif (Aguerre 1997b; Durán 1986–1987; Marchionni et al. 2010; Paunero et al. 2007) show a focus on the exploitation of guanaco, in some cases using triangular projectile points similar to those found at the earlier levels of the Río Pinturas sites. Few sites

Figure 4.15 Excavations at Cueva Túnel, Deseado Massif, Argentina Photo courtesy Rafael Paunero.

corresponding to this period were as intensively studied as Cueva Maripé, at 562 masl (Figure 4.16). This site produced important evidence of the Early Holocene occupation of the region (Carden et al. 2014; Magnin 2015; Miotti 2012; Miotti et al. 2007). What have we learned at Cueva Maripé? In the first place, that the evidence was obtained from two separate chambers, recording redundant occupations up to the Late Holocene (Carden 2008; Miotti et al. 2014). Importantly, both chambers differ: in their mode of use, paintings, sedimentation rates, and occupational chronology. We also learned that there are compromised sections of the stratigraphies, which were carefully isolated. This is a situation to be expected in caves and rock shelters, but it is rarely recognized. The earlier occupations occur approximately between 9500 and 7200 BP. Both chambers appear to have been used alternatively, with important gaps in between as in many other contemporary sites. Guanacos were the focus for subsistence, with a minimal representation of Rheidae. Another two sites in the plateau, El Verano and La Martita, can be used to evaluate the importance of Early Holocene human settlement on the basis of clear records of butchered guanaco remains found in association with triangular points, large end scrapers, and other edge-trimmed tools (Aguerre 1987; Duran 1986–1987).

Figure 4.16 View of Cueva Maripé, Deseado Massif, Argentina. Photo courtesy Laura Miotti.

Given its location within the core of the Massif, the excavators were expecting older occupations at Maripé (Miotti et al. 2007, 2014). However, the site makes sense as a station en route to the west. New weapons systems appeared, which, together with the production of blades, suggested important organizational changes compared with the Late Pleistocene (Hermo 2009; Hermo and Magnin 2012; Hermo and Miotti 2011).

In sum, the evidence from several sites in the Deseado Massif presents early occupations between 11,100 and 9230 BP and attests to the existence of an important node, perhaps a staging area, during the process of colonization (Miotti et al. 2003; Paunero 2009; Steele and Politis 2009). These were places where populations remained for several generations, establishing some regional continuity. This is expected in an area with widely available good lithic raw materials, abundant natural shelters, freshwater, and fuel, and which is well stocked with varied mammals. The Massif probably ranked high compared with many other locations in central Patagonia. The spatial distribution of the early sites makes great sense in terms of interacting hubs used by hunter-gatherers taking advantage of the relative continuity of abundant resources (Franco et al. 2019). Several localities were redundantly used, and some of them are placed near the borders of the Massif, like Cueva de la Gruta, and can be considered as part of a process of exploration toward the fringes of the western steppes (Civalero and Aschero 2003; Franco et al. 2012b).

The Early Peopling

145

The older western occupations are slightly younger than those recorded at the Deseado Massif. Near the headwaters of the Deseado basin, some 100 km west of the Massif, there is a concentration of Early Holocene archaeological sites. One of the most important is Cueva de las Manos, located at the base of a stepped cliff above the Pinturas River (Alonso et al. 1984–1985; Gradin et al. 1976, 1979; Mengoni Goñalons and Silveira 1976). Wall paintings that include hand negatives and depictions of guanacos have made this site world famous. Similar paintings were found at other sites, always north of the Santa Cruz River, forming part of the older rock art styles defined in Patagonia (Aschero et al. 2019b; Fiore 1999; Gradin 1987). Effectively, the lower occupations at Cueva de las Manos are dated between 9320 and 9300 BP, and some of the paintings may be of similar age based on the stratigraphic position of painted rock fragments fallen from the roof of the cave, providing minimum ages for the paintings (Gradin et al. 1976: 224). The lower layer of the cave is characterized by triangular projectile points and large side scrapers, which are associated with the remains of modern fauna, mainly guanaco.

Arroyo Feo, at 600 masl, is a cave located not too far from Cueva de las Manos, near the border of the high plateau (Aguerre 1981–1982; Gradin et al. 1979; Silveira 1979). The lithic inventory of the lower levels, dated between 9410 and 8410 BP, is similar to the "Level 11 Industry" of the lower layer of Los Toldos 3 (Gradin et al. 1987: 122). The absence of projectile points is the main reason for the overall similarity, but the chronology, slightly older than 9000 BP, is the same as that recorded at occupations characterized by projectile points nearby (Aguerre 1997b). Also similar is the faunal assemblages dominated by guanaco, without any evidence of extinct fauna. The excavators of Arroyo Feo were disappointed when an Early Holocene date was confirmed for their potential Late Pleistocene occupation. However, this result highlights that the absence of projectile points is not really unexpected from an organizational perspective. One corollary is that reading the content of the relatively ephemeral occupations of the early sites of South America in terms of the absence of tools, or even technologies, is an invitation to error. Once again, the ascription of a supposed "Level 11 Industry" to the Late Pleistocene was unsuccessful.

Sites located further south, like CCP7 and CCP5 at the Perito Moreno Park, 800 masl, also appear to represent forager incursions from the eastern steppes (Aschero et al. 2007; Civalero and Aschero 2003). Again, in this case, the megafauna disappeared before the arrival of humans, and guanacos dominate the bone assemblages (De Nigris 2004). All these sites in the Pinturas River and the Perito Moreno National Park consistently display traces of human occupation around 9000 BP or slightly before (usually characterized by triangular projectile points and large side scrapers), are not associated with megafauna, and use the obsidian source at Pampa del Asador.

Alero de la Oquedad in the San Martin basin, Chorrillo Malo 2 in the Lago Argentino basin, and Cerro León 3 in the eastern extreme of the Baguales

Figure 4.17 Location of Bloque Oquedad, Campo de Bloques 1. Cach Aike Hill in the background, Argentina. Photo courtesy Juan Bautista Belardi.

range are relatively isolated sites with Early Holocene occupations near the Andes (Figure 4.17). They probably indicate the initial human explorations of lake basins limited by western ice fields or mountainous ranges (Belardi et al. 2010; Borrazzo 2008; Franco and Borrero 2003) (Figure 1.6). In all three cases, guanaco is the dominant resource, and cases of large lithic tools with active edges, sometimes on blades extracted from prepared cores, are recorded. Looking further south, into the world of channels and interior seas, we found a similar situation at Ponsonby, one of the key places to understand the interaction between populations of the steppes and the channels (Legoupil 2003). Tools made of rocks available on the steppes east of the site were recovered. All these locations have represented the late exploration of the western lands between 44° and 51° S, perhaps summarizing the history of adaptations required to colonize those new habitats (Borrero and Martin 2018). All these cases coincide in showing the complexity of the process of colonization, with expected lags and failures (Borrero et al. 2019a; Méndez 2013). Only at the southern extreme of Última Esperanza did humans arrive before 10,000 BP and interact with extinct fauna during very short visits.

Summing up, conditions for the colonization of most of the Patagonian ecosystems during the Early Holocene were generally good. Paleoenvironmental

The Early Peopling

archives indicate a warming trend identified on the steppes and near the Andes (Mancini et al. 2011; Markgraf 1993). Low population density probably was part of the explanation for the discontinuous archaeological record (Pérez et al. 2016). However, access to some western areas surely was costly compared with previous times due to the expansion of forests near the Andes. Indeed, human circulation was relatively facilitated during the cold spells of the Pleistocene, with the large rivers seasonally frozen, but during the Early Holocene, the situation changed. Access to Última Esperanza became difficult, with forests expanding above the peat lowlands of Llanuras de Diana after ca. 10,000 BP. Indeed, radiocarbon dating indicates there is a period of nearly 2,000 years during which no human presence is recorded in Cerro Benitez. Human visits were reestablished during a late process of recolonization of the area around 8000 BP (Borrero and Martin 2018). Also, communication with Tierra del Fuego and the rest of the islands at that time was possible only by crossing water barriers. Evidence supports the existence of slightly higher populations in the continent during the Early Holocene, including the relative increase in the number of radiocarbon dates, the number of sites with occupations dated within that period, and the depositional rates of artifacts (Borrero 1994–1995). None of these measures is enough to demonstrate that populations increased, but they are consistent with that notion and somehow support the dispersal of demes into uninhabited land during that time.

Pali Aike Volcanic Field (PAVF)

The Pali Aike Volcanic Field is a large region impacted by successive volcanic episodes that dotted the landscape with craters, maars, and lava fields (D'Orazio et al., 2000) (Figure 4.18). This rugged region is full of tubes, caves, and rock shelters, many of which were used by hunter-gatherers in the past (Martin et al. 2011). Fell Cave is the most famous of these sites, a classic reference for the early peopling of South America, located near the Chico River (Bird 1938, 1988; Emperaire et al. 1963; Poulain-Josien 1963) (Figure 1.13). It is a relatively small rock shelter excavated by Junius Bird in the 1930s that was occupied between ca. 10,800 and 10,300 BP (Figure 2.9). The lower layers showed the association of extinct and modern faunal remains with hearths, several Fishtail or Fell Cave projectile points, discoidal stones, and an abundant lithic industry (Bird 1988; Flegenheimer and Cattáneo 2013; Martin 2013; Politis 1991; Waters et al. 2015). Recent work at the cave demonstrated that extinct faunal bones include evidence for both human and carnivore activities and suggest humans scavenging felid kills (Martin 2012). The evidence of cut-marks on *Mylodon* bones is important since, together with Piedra Museo, they constitute the only basis to discuss its exploitation in South Patagonia (Marchionni and Vázquez 2012; Martin 2013). The evidence from Fell Cave is reliable, but it

Figure 4.18 View of Pali Aike Volcanic Field, Argentina, and Chile.

was basically obtained between the 1930s and 1950s. Stratigraphic detail is not always present, and only recently a detailed study of the faunal remains recovered by Bird was completed. Among other things, this study demonstrated an unexpected dominance of *Hippidion* bones over those of camelids (Martin 2021). Fell Cave is the only site in Fuego-Patagonia showing this pattern since camelids are the most abundant species almost everywhere. In the end, this cave displays solid evidence for early human presence associated with extinct fauna. The predominance of a treeless herbaceous steppe prior to 11,000 BP, followed by xeric taxa between 11,000 and 10,000 BP, was indicated by pollen analysis (Markgraf 1988). Recent work is beginning to produce relevant information about the local environment at the time of the transition. A peat layer at the alluvial plain of the Chico River, not too far from Fell Cave, was dated ca. 8100 BP, while another two buried peat layers dated to ca. 12,800 and 14,100 BP were identified at Juni Aike (Martin and San Román 2010; Prieto 1997). The 12,600 BP R1 tephra from an eruption of the Reclus volcano was identified immediately above the upper peat layer. Charles Stern describes this eruption as "closer in size if not bigger than the 1932 Quizapu" (Stern 1990: 122), a comparison that clearly establishes the potential impact of the eruption for Patagonian ecosystems, including its herbivores.

The Early Peopling   149

This impact was undoubtedly more important in Última Esperanza, where the Reclús is located, an area that animals rapidly recolonized.

Other Patagonian sites excavated by Junius Bird during his pioneer expeditions present some chronological problems. Human remains from Cerro Sota and Pali Aike were for decades considered representative of Late Pleistocene populations (Bird 1938; Turner 1992), but three samples of human bone from Cerro Sota have been dated to ca. 3700 BP (Hedges et al. 1992) and a single radiocarbon date on a badly preserved human bone provides a minimum age of ca. 7800 BP for Pali Aike (Neves et al. 1999: 261). Interestingly, the human remains at Cerro Sota were averaged in the same layers with abundant remains of Pleistocene fauna. Bird defended the association between these animals and human burials, a position that was repeated in the literature (Turner 1992). Only recently were these human bones and those from Cañadón Leona the subject of modern taphonomic studies (L'Heureux and Amorosi 2009, 2010, 2012). The Pali Aike cave presents thick archaeological layers that cover most of the Holocene, with a rich paleontological layer at the base of the sequence (Borrero 2005; Martin 2013).

Other sites in the PAVF offer important evidence for the early peopling of the area. Cueva de los Chingues presents an important Pleistocene faunal assemblage (San Román et al. 2000), where the presence of *Arctotherium* was recorded (Prevosti et al. 2003). Fleeting human occupations were recorded, followed by a stronger Holocene occupation (Martin 2008, 2013). A previous claim of Late Pleistocene human occupation at Las Buitreras cave, Argentina (Sanguinetti de Bórmida 1976), was recently dismissed on the basis of a restudy of the stratigraphy, the chronology, and the faunal associations (Borrero and Martin 2008).

Última Esperanza Sound

There are three sites with Late Pleistocene human occupations in the south of Última Esperanza, only two of which offer substantial evidence. Cueva del Medio is a large cave with evidence of low-intensive early occupations dated between 10,930 and 10,410 BP (Martin 2013; Martin et al. 2015; Nami and Nakamura 1995). Fishtail projectile points, side scrapers, and other lithic tools were found in association with several hearths and the remains of Pleistocene and modern fauna (Huidobro 2016). Excavations by Hugo Nami in the 1980s and 1990s demonstrated repeated use of the cave near the end of the Pleistocene by hunters of guanacos and American horses (Nami and Menegaz 1991). Nami recognized two different occupation layers, but it was difficult to separate them chronologically (Martin et al. 2019). A recent excavation showed that some of the bones recovered at the Late Pleistocene layers resulted from natural deaths of animals using the cave before the arrival of humans, including ground sloths and hypercarnivores (*Smilodon* sp., *Panthera onca mesembrina*) (Martin et al. 2015). The fauna associated with human occupations are mainly restricted to *Hippidion* and an extinct clade of guanaco (Metcalf et al. 2016). These initial occupations were followed by a long gap of over 6,000 years before the cave was inhabited again.

Cueva Lago Sofía 1 is a narrow rock shelter with deposits containing broken horse and camelid bones associated with a hearth, and dates to between 10,700 and 10,140 BP (Prieto 1991; Steele and Politis 2009). Before the arrival of humans, the cave was occupied by Pleistocene mammals, particularly ground sloths. Pollen information indicates an open environment with scattered *Nothofagus* trees at the time of occupation of the rock shelter. Human remains recovered at Cueva Lago Sofía 1 were considered Late Pleistocene by some (Soto-Heim 1994), ignoring already published Late Holocene dates (Prieto 1991).

Finally, the evidence for Late Pleistocene occupations at Cueva del Milodón consists only of extinct horse bones with cut-marks recovered during some of the earlier excavations (Martin 2013). Recent excavations at different loci within the cave obtained detailed paleobiological and paleoenvironmental information but failed to uncover more bones with cut-marks. This situation suggests that human use of the cave at the end of the Pleistocene was probably limited. Cueva del Milodón began to be occupied by ground sloths around 14,000 BP and was discontinuously used as a ground sloth den up to ca. 10,000 BP (Borrero and Martin 2012). It is also possible that hypercarnivores occupied the cave during brief periods, as indicated by the evidence of intensive carnivore damage on sloth remains.

Geoarchaeological studies of the caves in Última Esperanza suggested that they were formed by a pseudokarstic process, and were available for use immediately after deglaciation, probably around 20,000 BP (Todisco et al. 2018). A long palynological column at Cerro Benitez showed that the deposition of pollen began ca. 14,900 BP (McCulloch et al. 2021). Then, there was a lapse of several thousand years after the retreat of the ice before the biological colonization of the area began. This lapse was interrupted only by the deposition of the R1 tephra produced by the Reclus volcano around 12,600 BP (Stern 1990). Potent deposits of this same tephra were also identified at several of the sites, particularly at Cueva del Medio and several paleontological sites on the West side of Cerro Benitez. The oldest recorded mammal is *Lama gracilis* at Cueva Chica, dated to ca. 15,000 BP (Martin et al. 2013). Megamammals and large mammals began to be recurrent inhabitants of the caves around 14,000 BP, with camelids, horses, and ground sloths defining an adequate environment for humans (Martin et al. 2013, 2015). All our evidence shows that the human arrival – just fleeting visits – occurred around 11,000 BP. Beyond these three sites, there are a number of Late Pleistocene assemblages recovered at caves and rock shelters, dated between 15,000 and 10,000 BP, with the

The Early Peopling

presence of American horses, ground sloths, extinct camelids, and several species of carnivores. All these sites are placed within a radius of about 5 km from each of the mentioned archaeological sites, indicating the availability of a diversity of extinct mammals for the first human settlers of the area. The existence of a freshwater lake near the caves probably made the place attractive for both prey and humans (Sagredo et al. 2011). It was suggested that these early human occupations resulted from short-term logistical use of a particular patch initiated at Pali Aike (Martin and Borrero 2017). However, the human presence was short-lived, with evidence of an occupational gap immediately after the Late Pleistocene incursions (Borrero and Martin 2018). Only around 8000 BP did hunter-gatherers reoccupy the zone, using a different technology focused on a diversity of modern species.

Tierra del Fuego

There is only one Late Pleistocene site in Tierra del Fuego, the Tres Arroyos 1 (TA 1) rock shelter at Cerro de los Onas. The older occupations at this site are dated between 10,685 and 9960 BP, implying that Tierra del Fuego was populated before it became an island. Five hearths indicate repeated visits by foragers preying on *Hippidion* and camelids (Borrero 2003; Massone 1987, 2004, 2009). The recovery of Rheidae bones dated 9960 BP was the first evidence for the presence of this flightless bird on the island (Martin et al. 2009). The TA 1 occupations are similar in content and age to those registered in the southern mainland at Fell Cave, Cueva del Medio, and Cueva Lago Sofía 1. Two fragments of projectile points found at TA 1 were considered similar to Fishtails (Jackson 2002). No more archaeological evidence was recovered on the island until the Middle Holocene when the first occupations of the coasts of the Beagle Channel occurred (Orquera and Piana 1999; Zangrando et al. 2018). They were followed by ephemeral occupations on the coasts of the Strait of Magellan and the Atlantic (Morello et al. 2012a; Salemme et al. 2007a). All this Holocene evidence was recovered at small, open-air sites.

FINAL REMARKS

During the Late Pleistocene the Pampas, the Campos of Uruguay and Patagonia shared some common features, such as the Fishtail projectile points, discoidal stones, and some technological traits (e.g., reduction sequence; see Flegenheimer et al. 2003; Nami 2021), which suggest a common origin and the maintenance of some kind of link or shared knowledge between these regions. Efforts are made to understand the processes and reasons behind the human selection of places for human inhabitation (Borrero and Franco 1997; Salemme and Miotti 2008). The evidence for the earlier human presence in the

Pampas and Patagonia is discontinuous, but the chronology for all the site clusters between 11,000 and 10,000 BP is tight. This supra-regional pattern speaks about a widespread human presence in a variety of habitats since the end of the Late Pleistocene.

On this basis, it is possible to maintain that the peopling of South Patagonia is older than of the northern. Early occupations were discontinued for varied periods in some places, but in others – like the Deseado Massif or the Pali Aike Volcanic Field – full colonization followed. Then, only a few regions appear to have been colonized during the initial period of human dispersal into Fuego-Patagonia. It is likely that not all the regions were equally productive, and some were probably well below the levels necessary to sustain or attract human populations during the Late Pleistocene. Nevertheless, this information about repeated successful inhabitation in separate places suggests that previous occupations must surely exist.

The summarized evidence suggests that the two Late Pleistocene clusters of sites in the Pampas, one in the Interserrana area and the other in central and southeastern Tandilia, would have been generated by the same populations who were occupying different ecosystems year round. The sites in the Interserrana area would represent kill/scavenging sites (Campo Laborde and La Moderna), or field processing camps (Arroyo Seco 2 and Paso Otero 5) generated during a period of band fusion to perform cooperative activities such as the hunting of megamammals. Complementarily, the rock shelter sites would be used by smaller groups (one band or even parts of bands) during a time of separation when visiting the hills to perform specific tasks such as gathering toolstones (Politis and Madrid 2001) or getting wood and water during droughts.

The presence of Queguay silicified limestone (>400 km from the Tandilia sites and Paso Otero 5) in several Pampean early sites calls attention to very extended mobility ranges if direct procurement is favored. The alternative explanation, a long-distance exchange, which allowed the transport of toolstones, could also be operating (Flegenheimer et al. 2015a). However, it has to be noted that this limestone is associated with Fishtail points and is registered in levels younger than 10,800 BP (Paso Otero 5, LCH1, LCH3, CoSA1, La Amalia S2, etc.), while in older levels (Arroyo Seco 2) and sites without Fishtail points (Campo Laborde and La Moderna) this raw material is absent. This suggests some spatial or temporal variations in the mobility circuits and in the network exchange within the Late Pleistocene periods.

In any case, the archaeological record suggests that hunter-gatherers occupied the region at low population densities and that they routinely traveled (the whole group [residential mobility] or specialized parties [logistical mobility]) extensively during annual rounds at scales not matched by later Holocene populations. How and why they obtained long-distance toolstones, basically the Queguay limestone, the metaquartzite from Ventania, and a red silica rock

The Early Peopling 153

of possible Patagonian origin in Cueva Zoro (Mazzia 2011), while they had plenty of good-quality material in the Tandilia range is a subject of discussion (Nami 2017). Flegenheimer and collaborators (2003) proposed a scenario in which various small groups inhabited different territories in the Campos and the Pampas but shared technical and nontechnical information and goods (see also Suárez et al. 2018). They postulated that this long-distance transport should be considered in a social interaction network framework. In this sense, the circulation of this raw material would be linked to social ties between bands that shared common ancestors and had large territories. Queguay limestone would materialize this social bond in a context of sparse populations with the need to keep intermarriage possibilities active. Some kinship patterns (exogamic bands, cross-cousin marriages, etc.; see Ives 2015) would promote the exchange of people between both areas to keep the social interaction fluid.

The presence of the Ventania metaquartzite seems to have a different explanation. This raw material is lower quality than the SBG orthoquartzite, but Ventania is closer than the Queguay limestone outcrops. The most parsimonious hypothesis is that the provisioning and transport of metaquartzite would have occurred during the annual round when bands were close to the outcrops or to secondary deposits of metaquartzite in Ventania. It then was transported across the Interserrana area, had a low reduction rate, and was discarded in low quantities en route.

Some unusual traits made CoSC and Cerro Amigo Oeste exceptional sites. Both hilltops were lookouts and should have had some advantages over other similar places, such as visibility, being the highest location in the area, convenient access, or a strategic location, which made them used preferentially (Flegenheimer et al. 2015b; Miotti and Terranova 2015). Both sites were used for refurbishing and replacement of Fishtail projectile points. These sites must have had an economic as well as a social function, probably linked to interband cohesion and information flow. Beyond this social value, Flegenheimer et al. (2015b) have added another layer of significance, proposing that CoSC was a "special place," imbued with meanings and operating in the symbolic and ideational dimension. In the same vein, Miotti and Terranova (2015) proposed that Cerro Amigo Oeste was a place for ceremonies, including offerings of special materials such as the Fishtail points. For them, these artifacts, as well as the discoidal stones, "could be items of social and symbolic communication like the female figurines (Venus) of the Upper Paleolithic of Eurasia" (Miotti and Terranova 2015: 191). It has been routinely stated that landscapes become heavily invested with symbolic and ideational meanings through their use by people and that people engage with landscapes through both bodily experience and perception, reproducing cultural meanings through these interactions (e.g., Bender 1993; Tilley 1994, 2004). However, there is very little in the archaeological assemblage of CoSC or Cerro Amigo Oeste that could be interpreted as primarily representing an ideational/sacred/

symbolic locus, and therefore the phenomenological interpretation appears to be more speculative. Although objects are indeed polysemic, and, therefore, the artifacts can have different meanings and functions simultaneously, which in turn are also dynamic, none of the Fishtail projectile points found at the top of the hills can be detached from their primary utilitarian function. Why are these artifacts linked to the worldview of hunter-gatherers (Flegenheimer et al. 2013b) or a function like the Paleolithic Venus? Why do not all the other artifacts such as the bifaces, the end scrapers, the side scrapers, and so on found at the top of the hills have the same symbolic status? All these questions have to be answered to assess the primary ideational condition of the Fishtail projectile points.

On the other hand, despite not having been dated, it seems that both hilltops were visited in the Late Pleistocene (Flegenheimer and Mazzia 2013; Miotti and Terranova 2015), maybe for only a few generations. However, we cannot deny that part of the surface assemblage – beyond the Fishtail points and the discoidal stones – could have been deposited during the Holocene. What would have caused the potential abandonment of the CoSC and Cerro Amigo Oeste? One reason could be the loss of their special meaning or their sacred status (if they ever had any). This answer is difficult to verify. Another alternative could be that in different ecological scenarios, the tops of the hills lost their advantages. To discuss this alternative, we will concentrate fundamentally on a landscape's physical attributes and how hunter-gatherers relate to those attributes.

What we know is that the hilltops had some advantages, such as better visibility (Miotti and Terranova 2015). From CoSC, the close hills and the neighboring plains can be seen up to 40 km, while from the Cerro Amigo Oeste, the range of visibility is between 40 and 60 km. Given these qualities, it has been proposed that both places could have functioned as lookouts to spot prey and other humans (Flegenheimer and Mazzia 2013; Miotti and Terranova 2015). Also, it would be a convenient location for communication by smoke signal (Mazzia 2010–2011). The abundance of *currumamuel* in Tandilia could have been greatly beneficial in this regard since this bush burns quickly and produces big flames and smoke.

What change(s) during the Holocene could have made these locations no longer attractive? At the end of the Pleistocene, environmental conditions shifted, and a great faunal extinction occurred in South America: megamammals disappeared, and the largest prey to survive was guanaco. Due to the lack of large consumers when megamammals became extinct, the changes in the grassland coverage also produced a deep transformation in the Pampean landscape. Therefore, if the tops of the hills were effective to scout large and medium-sized slow herbivores such as ground sloths and glyptodonts or herds of horses, during the Holocene it might not be as useful to spot medium-sized, agile guanaco or small Pampas deer. Another factor could be the partial

The Early Peopling

population replacement proposed for South America at ~ 9000 cal BP based on ancient nuclear DNA analysis (Posth et al. 2018). New people might have brought new technologies and new hunting strategies, and occupied other places. However, the latter factor is still based on a small sample that needs to be confirmed with more robust data.

The age, rhythm, and causes of the extinction of Pleistocene megamammals have been a subject of vivid discussion (among many others, Barnosky et al. 2015; Borrero 2009; Cione et al. 2009; Politis et al. 1995; Prado et al. 2015). After deglaciation and the short-term climatic changes of the Pleistocene to Holocene transition – including the cold spell of the Antarctic Cold Reversal – there was a climatic amelioration marked by rising temperatures (McCulloch et al. 2005). Beyond this warming trend, there were important environmental changes with consequences for humans. The rising of the sea and the extensive reforestation of the Andean area completely altered the available land for humans and its productivity. The extinction of the Late Pleistocene megafauna ca. 10,000 BP was another important change that presented geographic variants and peculiarities for the different species involved. In Patagonia, one observation is that very few of the disappearing animals are well dated, and even fewer are well represented at archaeological sites. The role of humans, climate, or ecology in the extinctions is not clear, but the process disrupted the Pleistocene trophic chains and affected human populations. Judging from the archaeological record, the direct impact of human activities does not appear to be important since there is minimal evidence of exploitation of extinct mammals (Borrero 2009b; Martin 2013; Martínez et al. 2016; Miotti et al. 2018; Paunero et al. 2017). Moreover, Patagonia's dominant animals in the earliest archaeological bone assemblages are usually medium-sized mammals like camelids or even smaller extant mammals. The most critical change produced by the extinctions was the almost exclusive subsistence focus on camelids during the Holocene, related to the general pattern of decreased faunal diversity (Miotti and Salemme 1999). One difficulty in assessing which fauna are associated with the earliest human occupations was that many relevant deposits are characterized by averaged faunas (Borrero 2005). Accordingly, only when taphonomic analyses were integrated into the studies of the early bone assemblages was it possible to clarify the panorama. These analyses worked both ways, changing the status of both archaeological and paleontological assemblages (Martin 2013).

Some changes were also identified after the extinctions. For example, the shift to hunting modern fauna was associated with the replacement of Fishtails by triangular projectile points (Flores Coni et al. 2020). Many questions follow from this fact. Were the Fishtails appropriate only for large mammals, as suspected by some (Morrow and Morrow 1999), or were they only useful during a process of exploration, as suggested by others (Maggard and Dillehay 2011)? Fishtail projectile points are truly diverse in morphology, technology, and function, which, together with their wide distribution, suggest that there is no single answer (Flegenheimer and Weitzel 2017). Anyhow, it is firmly established that this projectile point is the oldest model currently known in the Pampas, the Campos, and Patagonia. A strong correlation between Late Pleistocene species and Fishtail projectile points was recently used to suggest a causal role for humans in the extinction of megafauna in South America (Prates and Pérez 2021), affirmation for which Patagonia does not offer much support in the form of archaeological evidence.

The Pampas has been proposed as one of the few regions where some Pleistocene mammals survived well into the Holocene (Miotti et al. 2018; Politis et al. 1995; Prado et al. 2015). The region would have served as an ecological refugium during the Early Holocene, maintaining some favorable ecological conditions that allowed megamammals to survive there, while in most regions of America they became extinct (Politis et al. 2003). The evidence that would support this would come from AS2, La Moderna, and Paso Otero 4, as well as the paleontological deposits of Arroyo Tapalqué, Centinela del Mar, and Río Cuarto. Many of these Holocene dates have been rejected by authors due to diagenetic concerns or failure to replicate dates, or are otherwise suspect because the material dated is considered less reliable than bone collagen (e.g., tooth enamel bioapatite carbonate) (Messineo et al. 2021a). None of these Holocene dates were pretreated using an amino acid-based method or ultrafiltration. Therefore, the late ages may be due to contamination by fulvic and humic acids or other exogenous compounds. The case for Holocene survival of megafauna in Patagonia was restricted to Cueva del Milodón, which was rejected based on new excavations showing redeposition of sediments (Borrero et al. 1991), and Cerro Bombero (Paunero 2008) where *Hippidion saldiasi* bones were associated with a single standard Early Holocene radiocarbon date. Accordingly, Patagonia does not offer strong support for the hypothesis. The Holocene survival of Pleistocene megamammals and American horses in the Pampas and Patagonia is a hypothesis that needs to be tested with more high-quality radiocarbon data, and so far, it is currently under debate.

CHAPTER 5

THE MIDDLE HOLOCENE (~ 8200–4200 CAL BP; ~ 7500–3800 BP)

The Middle Holocene was a time of change in both the Pampas and Patagonia. In some way, these changes were the prelude to the demographic expansion, regional diversification, economic intensification, and social complexity that characterized the following period, the Late Holocene. During the Middle Holocene times, archaeological evidence in the Pampas was scarce until a decade ago or so, but recent research increased information significantly (e.g., Ávila 2011; Ávila et al. 2011; Bonomo et al. 2013; Donadei Corada 2020; Gutiérrez et al. 2010; Mazzanti et al. 2015; Messineo et al. 2019a, b, c; Politis et al. 2012; Scheifler 2019). This period is characterized by global warming, known as the Hypsitermal or Holocene Thermal Maximum (Renssen et al. 2012). As a result, in the Pampas, the sea level raised above the current level at around 7000 BP. However, there is no agreement about the magnitude of this raising (between 2.2 to 6 masl depending on the author) and the chronology of the maximum ingression (see revisions in Aguirre and Whatley 1995; Melo et al. 2003). For Isla and Espinosa (1995), it began at the onset of the Holocene, reaching its maximum height (around 2 masl) around 6500–6000 BP. This resulted in the coast having sometimes a transgressive position, such as in the east of the Salado Depression and the Paraná Delta (Cavallotto et al. 2004, 2005; Iriondo and Kröhling 2008), while in other cases, it was very close to the present according to the variations of the littoral morphology.

After ~ 6000 BP the regressive phase began, and with the sea's withdrawal, shallow estuary lagoons were formed with a local connection to the sea (Espinosa et al. 2013; Ferrero et al. 2005; Vilanova et al. 2006). Climate conditions were warmer and probably humid during this time, although cycles of aridity might have occurred during this interval in different areas at different times. In the Central Pampean Dunefield (CPD), several paleoclimatic proxies indicate that between 7000 to 4000 BP environmental conditions were arider than today with active dunes with low vegetation coverage (Messineo et al. 2019c). However, in the southeast of the Pampas, the environmental conditions in the Early to Middle Holocene indicate greater humidity, as well as an increase in the phreatic level, which favored the formation of pools in the fluvial valleys and in coastal interdunes (Quattrocchio et al. 2008). Different proxies set climatic changes for different intervals, while areal variations were also present, preventing a fine-grained reconstruction of the Pampean palaeoenvironments during this period.

The beginning of the Holocene saw a completely changed Patagonia in comparison with that of the Late Pleistocene. The deglaciation process and the subsequent rise of the sea level inundated a large portion of the continental shelf and created new maritime barriers, like the Strait of Magellan and the Beagle Channel (Bujalesky 2011; Clapperton et al. 1995; McCulloch et al. 2005). The environment was also drastically changing. Abundant palynological information shows an increase in temperature and the gradual dispersal of the forests from their Pleistocene refugia (Mansilla et al. 2018; Markgraf 1993; McCulloch et al. 2005; Moreno et al. 2012). With pollen evidence from sites Bloque 1-Oquedad, Chorrillo Malo 2, and Cerro León 3, all places near the Andes, this information shows significant floral changes during the Holocene. Steppe communities dominated by cold-resistant herbs and grasses covered the eastern plains (Mancini 1998; Mancini et al. 2011; Moreno et al. 2012), while *Nothofagus* forests were slowly replacing the tundra environments of the Andes, creating barriers to human circulation, like the Llanuras de Diana separating Última Esperanza from the headwaters of the Gallegos River, or the Brunswick isthmus, between the Otway Sea and the Strait of Magellan. Also, substantial temperature changes were accompanied by the proliferation of shrub patches along the plains. All these processes contributed to creating a diversity of habitats that became available for expanding human populations. The later dispersal process was initiated only during the Early Holocene and reached most of the available land during the Middle Holocene.

THE PAMPAS

Several significant transformations occurred in the Pampas during the Middle Holocene. The archaeological record in most areas there revealed diversification in both technology and economy. It is also during this period when the first direct evidence of marine resource consumption shows up. Moreover, concentrations of human burials suggest the existence of persistent inhumation places as well as complex mortuary rituals. Finally, at the end of the Middle Holocene, surprising data indicate a process of early stages of plant domestication and mound construction in the Campos of Uruguay (Iriarte et al. 2004; López 2001). These changes create a new cultural scenario, quite different from the Pleistocene to Early Holocene period.

The Middle Holocene 159

Middle Holocene populations, who still occupied permanently only some areas of the Pampas, set the conditions for a series of changes in the following period. No local extinctions or cultural disruptions have been detected, and therefore, we assume that it was a cultural and biological continuity between the Middle to Late Holocene times (see discussion in Chapter 7). However, as discussed in Chapter 6, technological innovations and new adaptive patterns emerged, creating a more diverse cultural scenario with distinct historical trajectories.

Since there are no significant topographic barriers, such as high mountain ranges, the differences in demographies of Pampean areas have to be the result of other factors. The two main rivers, the Paraná and Uruguay, have wide valleys, which would act as barriers, but the abundant islands and the delta make crossing both streams relatively easy. They do not seem to be an obstacle to hunter-gatherers' mobility. Therefore, the ecological limiting factors have to be sought in water availability and the related biomass (which in turn influence the food resources) and in the toolstone outcrops. While the first factor seems to determine the low-density occupations in the western areas and their concentration in the river valleys (e.g., the Salado-Chadileuvú-Curacó and the Colorado Rivers), the lack of raw material would explain the almost null population of the Salado River Depression and the Rolling Pampa areas. However, other factors, such as historical trajectories and cultural patterns, would be also operating since the CPD was occupied – at least temporarily – despite the lack of toolstone and the limited water supplies. Ethnic frontiers, hostile neighbors, and/or restrictions to access to the resources would influence the uneven demographic scenario in the Pampas during the Middle Holocene.

In the Interserrana area, the primary evidence for the Pampean hunter-gatherers' lifeway comes from the multicomponent sites of Fortín Necochea and Arroyo Seco 2 (AS2) (Figure 5.1), both interpreted as open-air campsites representing residential bases of hunter-gatherers (Crivelli Montero et al. 1987–1988, 1994; Politis et al. 2014; Rafuse 2017). There is a good record dated between 6010 and 3630 BP in the former site, while in the latter, the site functioned as a base camp, where human burials were frequently carried out between 7819 and 4487 BP (see Supplementary Tables 1 and 2). The archaeological sequences of Fortín Necochea and AS2 indicate a similar settlement pattern: redundant occupation events on borders of lakes or ponds of the same localities throughout the Middle Holocene. This suggests a technological continuity, including unifacial artifacts made from SBG orthoquartzite and secondarily from phtanite and silicified dolomite – basically double-sided and end scrapers and stemless triangular mid-sized projectile points with straight or slightly convex base (only in AS2; Figure 5.2), mortars, pestles, and bola stones. These sites show a comparable economy based on guanaco as a principal resource and Pampas deer, greater rhea, rodents, and armadillos as secondary or complementary resources. In both sites, marine shells (*Adelomedon* spp. and

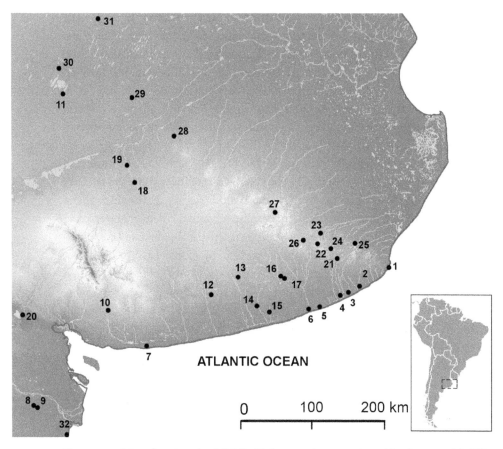

Figure 5.1 Map showing the Middle Holocene sites mentioned in the text. (1) Alfar; (2) La Tigra; (3) Chocorí; (4) Meseta del Chocorí; (5) Arroyo del Moro; (6) Necochea; (7) Barrio Las Dunas, La Olla and Monte Hermoso 1; (8) La Modesta; (9) Loma de Los Morteros; (10) Paso Mayor; (11) Laguna Chica; (12) Arroyo Seco 2; (13) Las Brusquillas; (14) Las Toscas; (15) El Guanaco; (16) Paso Otero 3; (17) Paso Otero 4; (18) Fortín Necochea; (19) Laguna Muscar 2; (20) Laguna de Chasicó S7; (21) Amalia site 2; (22) Lobería sitio 1; (23) La Cautiva; (24) Cueva El Abra, Abrigo La Grieta, Cueva Alí Mustafá, Abrigo Los Pinos, Alero El Mirador, Cueva Tixi; (25) Rincón Grande; (26) La China 2; (27) El Picadero and La Esperanza; (28) El Puente; (29) Laguna Cabeza de Buey; (30) La Susana 1; (31) Laguna de Los Pampas; (32) Cantera de Rodados Villalonga and Tres Bonetes 1-colección Donnay.

Amiantis purpurata) were recorded, suggesting connections with the seashore via direct access or exchange networks. In AS2, the zooarchaeological record indicates that hunter-gatherers gradually shifted their generalist diet, which included extinct mega- and large-sized mammals, during the Late Pleistocene to medium-sized prey in the following periods (Rafuse 2017; Salemme 2014).

One of the best records for the Early to Middle Holocene transition is the human burials from AS2. To date, 50 human skeletons (and counting) have been uncovered and dated ($n = 26$ dates), from ~ 7800 to 4500 BP (Barrientos

The Middle Holocene

Figure 5.2 Artifacts from the Middle Holocene levels of Arroyo Seco 2. (a–c) End-scrapers; (d and e) side scrapers; (f–I) triangular projectile points.

1997; Politis et al. 2014; Scabuzzo and Politis 2019; see Supplementary Tables 1 and 2). The burials occur as both single and multiple individuals, including adults, subadults, children, and infants. The earliest level of inhumation, dated between 7819 and 7615 BP, is represented by five skeletons with bifacial triangular stemless projectile points within the bodies (Escola 2014; Politis et al. 2014; Scabuzzo and Politis 2019) (Figure 5.3). The origin of these violent events is still subject to debate. Intragroup conflicts, violence between bands, or ritual sacrifices are among the most likely causes. Grave goods consisting of marine shell beads, necklaces of perforated canid canines, and powdered red

Figure 5.3 Lanceolate/triangular projectile points from the earliest human burials of AS2.

ochre occurred in 13 individuals (not the ones with the projectile points within), indicating an early and complex funerary treatment of the deaths. Moreover, the abundance of canid canines in a funerary context and the absence of other skeletal parts of canids in the site suggest that these animals would have a strong symbolic connotation, perhaps to mediate the relation between human and supernatural spirits or beings or to protect humans (see below).

Two secondary burials were recovered: one is simple (Burial 30) and dated to 6823 BP, while the other (Burial 33) contained the remains of four individuals and was dated to 7636 and 7602 BP (Scabuzzo and Politis 2011). In a sector of the site, burials are composed of infant and children skeletons dated between 4793 and 4487 BP, indicating a shift through time in the funerary place (Politis et al. 2014; Scabuzzo and Politis 2019). Although previous interpretations proposed the existence of three burial pulses (Barrientos 1997; Politis et al. 2014), the new data suggest a relatively continual process at different rhythms over ~ 3,300 years (Scabuzzo and Politis 2019). The rich and complex burial records in a specific redundant place indicate that certain parts of the landscape were selected for ceremonial and sacred purposes during millennia, which was a novel behavior in the Pampas.

Other sites in the Interserrana area show evidence of the consolidation of a lifeway based on guanaco, Pampas deer, and greater rhea, as well as a variety of

The Middle Holocene 163

smaller animals. This group includes Paso Otero 3 (dated ~ 4700 to 3000 BP) and Paso Otero 4 (dated between ~ 7700 and 4600 BP; Alvarez et al. 2013; Barros et al. 2014; Gutiérrez et al. 2011; Martínez 1999, 2006), Laguna Muscar 2 (dated to 4913 BP; Barros et al. 2018), Laguna Las Toscas (dated to ~ 4640 BP; Massigoge et al. 2021; Torino 2020), Paso Mayor (dated to between 5877 and 3820 BP; Bayón et al. 2010). These sites contain the characteristic assemblage of the other sites of the Interserrana area, composed of unifacial marginally retouched artifacts made of SBG orthoquartzite, a lesser percentage of phtanite artifacts, and a few bipolar cores from seashore cobbles. In Paso Mayor, immediately available rounded river cobbles, basically metaquartzite, quartz, and subarkose, predominate as raw material, but ortho-quartzite from Tandilia was present in regular percentages, despite the distance from the outcrops and the abundance of toolstones from Ventania (Barrientos et al. 2014). The differences in the quality of rocks from the two hill ranges do not fully explain this phenomenon and suggest the centrality of Tandilia in the territorial behavior of Middle Holocene hunter-gatherers.

In the Interserrana area, the coastal seashore conforms to an ecological and geomorphological zone with distinct characteristics. It has had its own research dynamic since the very beginning of archaeology in Argentina and has attracted the attention of both amateurs and professional archaeologists, mainly focused on surface lithic assemblages in the inter-dune blowouts (Chapter 2). In the seashore, a continuous field of active sand dunes up to 5 km wide runs parallel to the coast (Monserrat 2010). This continuous range of dunes, now partially fixed due to anthropic forestation, formed the Southern Dune Barrier, extending from Miramar to Pehuen Co (Isla et al. 2001). Despite long-term research, only at the very end of the twentieth century did systematic surveys and excavations occur (Bayón and Politis 1996, 2014; Bayón et al. 2012; Bonomo 2005; Bonomo and Leon 2010). Among the new data, the strati-graphic site of La Olla (LO), the Monte Hermoso 1 (MH1) human footprints, and the surface site of Barrio Las Dunas (BLD) stand out. These sites, close to each other (Figure 5.1), were discovered by chance and completely changed the models of seashore human occupation since they contained exceptional and unexpected archaeological contexts. Several paleoecological studies indi-cate that during the transition from the Early to the Middle Holocene, it was an estuary possessing different microenvironments, among which there were marine marshes, crab beds, and interdune lakes and lagoons (Aramayo et al. 2005; Blasi et al. 2013; Quattrocchio et al. 2008). This patchy environ-ment creates a scenario favorable for hunter-gatherer inhabitation at least on a temporal basis.

The LO site is submerged most of the time since it is placed at the limit of the lowest tide; it remains almost permanently covered by a water-saturated sand beach. The most remarkable characteristic is the integrity and resolution of the archaeological deposits and the exceptional preservation of organic

Figure 5.4 (a) View of La Olla 4; (b) wood point recovered at LO4.

remains, mainly wood and bones (Bayón and Politis 2014; Blasi et al. 2013; Leon et al. 2017). The LO site has four sectors (LO1, LO2, LO3, and LO4) and an extension of approximately 150 m. They are infilling pools or depressions some 40 or 50 m distant from each other and are similar in their areal development. They show a sub-oval shape and maximum diameters of ~ 17 m (Figure 5.4a). Sixteen radiocarbon dates were carried out for the LO site, ranging from ~ 7400 to 6480 BP, although human occupation would be more restricted, at least at LO3 and LO4, at ~ 7000 BP (Bayón and Politis 2014).

The evidence recovered in these infilling pools is made up of informal lithic tools, including a few hammerstones, wood artifacts, and abundant bone remains. Raw material comprises primarily local rocks, as in the case of fluvial metaquartzite cobbles and seashore rounded pebbles (Bayón and Zavala 1997). Less frequently, toolstones show broader supply radii, such as the muddy sandstone from the Ventania area (~ 100 km away north) and the SBG and Balcarce Formation orthoquartzites from Tandilia (~ 260 km away northeast).

The wooden tools from the LO site make up an extraordinary record for the region. Among the artifacts, there are three complete wooden points and two medial fragments (Figure 5.4b). A second group consists of artifacts with a cylindrical bodies and blunt, broad, thick ends, resembling wooden clubs. Two exceptional items stand out: a handle with the stone head still tied on and a spatula-like decorated piece (Bayón and Politis 1996, 2014). Also, an expedient

The Middle Holocene

tool of sea lion bone (Johnson et al. 2000) and three guanaco-bone artifacts were recorded (Leon et al. 2017). While expedient bone tools were recorded in the Pampas at the end of the Pleistocene (in Campo Laborde, see Chapter 4), wood artifacts were documented for the first time in the region. Were they in the technological repertory of the Pampean hunter-gatherers before but not detected due to preservation conditions? Although a definitive answer cannot be given, the unique micro-environmental conditions at LO, including the development of algal mats (Blasi et al. 2013), were responsible for the conservation of wood technology, which was probably in use in previous times. Luckily, the LO record provides a glimpse of this ghost technology.

Two species of sea lions were identified (*Arctocephalus australis* and *Otaria flavescens*). According to age (litters, juveniles, and adults) and sex determined based on the bone recovered, nonselective exploitation of sea mammals, a complete transport of the animals, and an in situ consumption of low- to middle-yield anatomical units were proposed (Leon et al. 2017). In addition to the Otaridae, both sea and land species (whales, dolphins, and guanaco) were consumed, although in much lower percentages. The site is interpreted as a succession of field processing camps of sea mammals, during a short period, in a mixohaline marsh developed in the upper intertidal to lower supra-tidal zone occupied intensively between 6960 and 6885 BP (Blasi et al. 2013).

MH1 was located near a freshwater paleo lake between the dunes near the ocean, surrounded by the typical humid interdune vegetation with slight marine influence (Zavala et al. 1992) or in the upper borders of the mixohaline marsh where LO was located (Blasi et al. 2013). The site comprises hundreds of human footprints in different layers in the upper sector of the current beach (Bayón and Politis 1996, 2014).

The several layers with footprints indicate that hunter-gatherers periodically visited the place for a few hundreds of years. On the eastern sector of the site, there are hundreds of footprints (~ 472) of children, youths, and probably women, who wandered around the littoral lagoon or marsh while they were probably gathering. Almost no artifacts have been found in this sector. In contrast, other activities are recorded in the western sector, and faunal remains and lithic and wooden artifacts were found scattered in very low density, suggesting an area surrounding a camp. The footprints found in this sector belong to adults with a predominantly southeast to northwest direction, prompting a transit path (Figure 5.5). The human footprints' layers have been dated between 7125 and 6795 BP (Bayón and Politis 2014). Also, human bones of two adult individuals dated 7886 and 6606 BP were found very close to the footprints, redeposited on the surface at the back of the beach, at the base of the dune range (Bayón and Politis 2014).

The third related site is BLD, located in the interdune close to the sea. Bones of black sea bass (*Pogonias cromis*) and sea lions with evidence of human modifications have been recorded. The assemblage includes hundreds of stone

Figure 5.5 Western sector of the Monte Hermoso 1 human footprints. (a) Tracks with a southeast-northwest direction; (b) detail of a footprint.

artifacts, including a few bifacial tools, made of immediately available basalt, followed by quartzite and subarkose (Bayón et al. 2012). The site is dated at 6924 BP, the same age as LO. It is similar to many other surface sites between dunes, but in this case, the association with fish and sea lion bones, as well as the potential link with LO and MH1, make it more significant.

In sum, LO, MH1, and BLD sites seem to be part of the same settlement system at the onset of the Middle Holocene and show the earliest adaptation to the Atlantic maritime littoral in the Pampas. The dating of human bones from MH1 at 7866 BP marks the beginning of human occupation on this part of the coast. Whereas LO can be interpreted as a temporary camp or a locus for processing mostly sea lions on the edges of a mixohaline marsh, the nearby contemporaneous site BLD may have functioned as a more stable camp, with multiple activities, in the higher sectors on the interdune. MH1 would have been a transit/wandering area from or to campsites on the edges of some littoral lagoon or marsh.

The other bulk of information comes from the eastern sector of the Atlantic coast, between Cabo Corrientes and the Quequén Salado River. In this sector, several primary human burials were discovered at the beginning of the twentieth century (see Chapter 2). As we summarized before, some of these skeletons have been dated to Middle Holocene times, between 6620 and 7270 BP, a surprisingly narrow time frame, considering the disparate finding

The Middle Holocene

circumstances (Politis et al. 2011a; Toledo et al. 2010; see Chapter 2 and Supplementary Table 2). They would represent a population pulse of the coastal environments during this period, which can also be supported by the chronology of LO, MH1, and BLD. It is not clear yet if there were some ecological conditions, such as the abundance of sea mammals, during this time that made this zone more attractive for human occupation.

The El Alfar site, on the right margin of the Corrientes creek, provided stratigraphic information from this sector of the seashore, which was plagued by surface sites heavily looted (Bonomo and Leon 2010; Bonomo et al. 2013). The archaeological context lay on the edge of an extinct water body between the dunes. Rounded seashore cobbles reduced by bipolar technique predominate among lithic material, and faunal association includes abundant remains from sea mammals (Otaridae) and, to a lesser extent, other marine resources such as *Amiantis purpurata*, *Mesoderma mactroides*, *Spheniscus* sp., and Cetacea. Inland species were also recorded: guanaco, Pampas deer, armadillos, plains viscacha, greater rhea, and other species. This site, dated to 5700 BP, has been interpreted as a residential camp close to the seashore, where sea lions were the main exploited resource, and the immediately available rounded cobbles were used for expedient tools (Bonomo et al. 2013).

Most Middle Holocene sites in Tandilia are caves or rock shelters that also contained components dated to the Pleistocene to Holocene transition and the Late Holocene, which indicates redundancy in the occupations of these sites, although discontinuously. One of the characteristics of most levels is the lack of bone remains, as also observed in the Late Pleistocene to Holocene transition layers (see Chapter 4). This absence is being interpreted as the consequence of the taphonomic process (Mazzanti et al. 2015). Lobería 1 contains two Middle Holocene components, one dated to ~ 7900 BP and the other to ~ 5350 BP. Both included undifferentiated lithic artifacts (mostly on SBG orthoquartzite), pigments, and charcoal. In Cueva Tixi, archaeological level 2, dated to 4865 BP, shows the greatest variety of consumed fauna remains in the area: guanaco, Pampas deer, three species of armadillos (*Zaedyus pichiy*, *Chaetophractus villosus*, and *Dasypus hybridus*), plains viscacha, coypu, and greater rhea. This layer would have functioned as a site close to a hunting place where carcass processing was performed. Notably, in a central place in the cave, there was a pile of bone from guanaco and Pampas deer represented by all skeletal parts (see Mazzanti et al. 2015: figure 3). Inside the pile, a fragment of a human mandible was recovered, interpreted as a part of a secondary burial (Mazzanti et al. 2015). This is one of the few human remains found in Tandilia, which is odd given the density of occupation in the area since the Late Pleistocene. The scarcity of human burials has several explanations. Were the Pampean hunter-gatherers not buried in the hills, as AS2 would suggest, or were they buried in other sectors outside the caves, not yet detected or destroyed by taphonomic processes? Funerary practices in Tandilia are almost unknown and remain one of the key unsolved issues in Pampean archaeology.

Other sites from the same period include Los Pinos and Alero El Mirador (dated between 5247 and 5089 BP), Alero El Abra (6654 BP), Rincon Grande Site 1 (3932 BP), and La Cautiva S2 (5068 BP) (Donadei Corada 2020). In terms of raw material management, the most frequently used is the immediately available rock, the coarse and medium-grained Balcarce Formation orthoquartzite (>60%), which was registered in three sites in the la Vigilancia valley (Abrigo La Grieta, Alero El Mirador, and Abrigo Los Pinos) and in relation with short-term occupations (Donadei 2019; Donadei and Bonnat 2016). In these other sites, there was a higher frequency in all artifact categories of the SBG orthoquartize, despite the fact that it outcrops between 60 and 120 km away. They have been interpreted as the result of strategic stops during daily foraging trips (stations, sensu Binford 1980) using expedient technology during short occupations (Donadei Corada 2021).

Other sites in Tandilia include El Puente, at the head of the Tapalqué creek dated to 5691 and 4500 BP (Messineo et al. 2014), and La China 2, which has triangular stemless projectile points and dated by thermoluminescence to 4540 BP (Zárate and Flegenheimer 1991). All of these sites indicate that Tandilia was fully inhabited during the Middle Holocene and, in some cases, using the same rock shelters and caves occupied in previous periods.

Also, in the central Tandilia area, there are several quarries and workshops of high-quality raw material (SBG orthoquartzite and silicified dolomite) whose earliest dates fall into the Middle Holocene: Arroyo Diamante (~ 4000 BP), El Picadero (~ 4600 BP), and La Esperanza (~ 5100 BP) (Colombo 2011, 2013; Flegenheimer et al. 1999; see Chapter 3).

In Ventania, there is extremely little archaeological evidence for this period, which contrasts with the relative abundance of sites in the neighboring areas. This is unexpected since Ventania has a variety of good-quality toolstones and permanent watercourses, while faunal and floral resources should not have been in short supply during the Holocene. Actually, only one site reported for the area, Caverna El Abra, was preliminarily published. There is a date of 6230 BP for the site (Castro 1983), which is doubtful since the charcoal samples were collected in three different levels from three different excavation units. The scarcity of sites in Ventania dated to the Middle Holocene, as well as to previous periods, seems to be related to sampling bias more than being the result of the lack of human occupation. More research is needed in the area to contrast both alternatives.

The first human signal occurred in the southern area in the Middle Holocene (Catella 2014; Martínez 2017; Oliva et al. 1991). It is unclear whether the area was occupied during the Late Pleistocene and Early Holocene or whether geomorphic factors and/or archaeological visibility problems occurred for early deposits (see discussion in Martínez and Martínez 2011). Catella (2014) also notes that the current fluvial system formed at 3000 BP produced significant changes in the geomorphology of the southern plains of Ventania, which in turn

The Middle Holocene

would affect the visibility of the archaeological record of the area. Moreover, if pre-hypsithermal coastal sites existed, they should be under sea level or have been destroyed by marine erosion.

Currently, there are five archaeological sites for this period, four of them associated with the paleo delta of the Colorado River: La Modesta (5890 and 5904 BP), Loma de Los Morteros (4454 BP), Tres Bonetes 1-colección Donnay (5339–5182 BP), and Cantera de Rodados Villalonga (4889–4100 BP) (Martínez 2017; Martínez et al. 2012). The former two sites are located very close to each other, in an area of deflated dunes, some 60 km from the Atlantic seashore. Surface findings at blowouts include grinding stones, triangular projectile points, and lithic debris. Most are made of silex, basalt, and andesite, and their provisioning could have occurred in the Atlantic coastal rounded cobble deposits (Chapter 3). A low percentage of long-distance provenance rocks might have been obtained from southeastern and western Pampa and Northeast Patagonia and indicate wide mobility ranges (Santos Valero 2017). Faunal assemblages are formed by guanaco, coypu, armadillos, rodents, and birds (Alcaráz 2015, 2017; Stoessel 2015), while the use of nets was proposed for the massive capture of perch (*Percichthys* sp.) (Stoessel 2017). This is an exceptional trait for the Pampas and opens the possibility of an unrecorded technology for fish. Engraved Rheidae eggshells were recovered on the surface of the blowouts (Carden and Martínez 2014; Martínez 2017) as well as human remains in sites that were interpreted as residential settlements (Martínez 2017).

The other two sites, Cantera de Rodados Villalonga and Tres Bonetes 1-colección Donnay, are human burial settings along the Atlantic seashore (Martínez 2017; Martínez et al. 2012). Isotopic studies show that some individuals consumed marine resources (e.g., catfish, *Genidens barbus*, and white croaker *Micropogonias furnieri*) as well as sea lions (*Otaria flavescens*). Other individuals show a mixed diet based on both marine fish and terrestrial herbivores. Finally, the skeletons from the inland sites, Loma de Los Muertos and La Modesta, show the consumption of mainly terrestrial resources, with dominant proportions of C3 pathways (Flensborg et al. 2018). Abundant grinding stones were recovered from these sites, suggesting intense exploitation of plant resources (Santos Valero 2017), as is also indicated by isotopic results (preferably C3 vegetables). We should remember that this area is mostly in the Spinal forest, and, therefore, more trees with edible fruits occur compared with other close areas. Some coastal elements, such as *Adelomedon* gastropods and seashore rocks, were found in both sites. These elements could result from occasional visits to the seashore or items obtained through exchange with coastal people. They would belong to prestige technology and not as part of the diet.

The fifth site is Laguna de Chasicó S7, on the border of the homonymous lake. This surface site is formed by an assemblage of lithic materials (both knapped and grinding stones); a few bones remain, and a Pampas deer bone awl. A human tooth recovered on the surface within this assemblage was dated to 3925 BP (Catella 2014).

All these sites represent the initial peopling of the area and show a variety of strategies to exploit different environments (the seashore, the Colorado River delta, the Spinal forests, etc.) as well as a variety of toolstones from various provenances (Catella 2014; Santos Valero 2017). In general terms, a distinct adaptive pattern can be recognized in the area for this period (Martínez 2017).

Some areas of the western Pampa began to be occupied for the first time in the Middle Holocene, although with a low human signal. There are a couple of burials from this period. One is an adult individual from Casa de Piedra site 1, dated to 6080 BP (Gradin 1984; Vayá 1984), in the southwestern border of the region; the burial had ochre in the surrounding sediments, and funerary goods made by lithic instruments in different stages of manufacture, a stone retoucher, and fragments of a bivalve (*Diplodon* sp.). The other is the burial from Cerro de Los Viejos site 2 (CLV2), dated to 6000 BP (Lucero et al. 2020). This hill is a prominent physiographic feature in the Close Basins area (see Chapter 1), which was occupied recurrently, with different functions. The buried individual was an adult-mature man who enjoyed a good state of health since childhood, although he could have suffered some episode of metabolic stress during this stage (Lucero et al. 2020). It was covered and surrounded by slit stones, adding profuse and varied goods (lithic artifacts, bone tools, a shell bead, and red ochre). In conjunction with the absence of functional stress markers, these traits might suggest that the individual played a special role within his social group.

The burials of Casa de Piedra, CLV2, and AS2 in the Interserrana area reflect complex mortuary rituals, including the preparation of the burial space and the accompaniment of funerary goods. Canids seem to play a key role in the sacred realm and could embody strong spirits, whose power might protect or help individuals in their death transit. Also, red ochre was fully used in mortuary practices. Interestingly, secondary burial modalities emerged in this period, representing a sense of belonging or perhaps connecting ancestry with territory and landscape (Scabuzzo and Politis 2011).

The area of the Salado-Chadileuvú-Curacó shows a firm human signal in the Middle Holocene but with a clear axis in the river valley. Although most of the archaeological sites are superficial (Berón and Curtoni 2002), there is an extensive cultural sequence in the Tapera Moreira locality, ranging from 5000 BP to ~ 300 BP. This area seems to be the only one with records of relatively continued human occupation in the western Pampa, probably due to permanent water and higher biomass in the valley (Berón 2004, 2015).

The key place is Tapera Moreira locality (Berón 2004). It is situated on the western bank of the Curacó River and is formed by five sites, surrounded by a dense *chañar* forest (Figure 5.6). Site 1 is multicomponent, with occupations ranging from the middle until the final Late Holocene. The oldest component

The Middle Holocene

Figure 5.6 View of the excavation of Tapera Moreira locality. Photo courtesy Mónica Berón.

dated to 4550 BP is associated with an early stage of exploration of this area (Berón 2004). No projectile points have been recovered in these levels except for a preform of Fishtail point made of heat-treated silica, which would be collected from older sites (Berón and Carrera Aizpitarte 2014). Given that this is only isolated preform instrument, it is difficult to discuss this unusual finding in the regional and supra-regional context. Lithic assemblage is dominated by expedient instruments made of basalt and silex, although some small end scrapers are present. As in the rest of the Pampas, guanaco was the main prey along the sequence. Site 2 shows a similar context, but with a lesser density, while in site 3 human remains of two individuals were recovered, one of which (Burial 2) was dated to 2630 BP. Finally, site 5 is the result of a Late Holocene occupation, where the presence of Vergel-Valdivia pottery indicates long-distance – trans-cordilleran – contact at ~ 700 BP (see Chapter 7).

It was during the Middle Holocene that human signals became stronger in the Central Pampean Dunefield. Two outstanding localities show not only a varied archaeological record but also several human burials of different ages: Laguna de Los Pampas (LLP) (Messineo et al. 2018; Politis et al. 2012) and Laguna Chica (LCh) (Messineo et al. 2019c; Scheifler 2019). These localities are situated in the current margins of shallow lakes, with evidence of recurrent hunter-gatherer

Figure 5.7 Aerial view of Laguna Chica site, in the Central Pampean Dunefield (CPD), with the location of the human burials.

occupations through the Holocene. In LLP, eight burials were recovered in two sectors of a lake's beach, showing an unusual record for the area. Moreover, isolated human bone remains corresponding to eight other individuals were found along the beach in both sectors. Burial 1 is dated to the Early Holocene (~ 8900 BP, see Chapter 4), and burials 2 and 3, both simple and primary, are dated back to 5688 BP and 5819 BP, respectively. Bone remains of burials 4 and 5, dated to 5924 BP and 7089 BP, were found dispersed on the surface.

The Laguna Chica (LCh) locality is in the southeast of the Hinojo-Las Tunas Lake System. Seven burials were identified: four in the southern part of the lake and three in the western area (Figure 5.7). Burial 1 is dated back to 6870 BP and contained a decorated pendant made of a jaguar canine (*yaguareté*, *Panthera onca*), probably as a personal belonging. Burial 2 contained two individuals: a female adult dated to 5930 BP and a male adult dated back to 6080 BP. Burial 4 was an infant dated to 1750 BP. The other burials were simple and contained incomplete skeletons. Notably, Burial 7 has a fine bone tool made of a guanaco metapodial (Figure 5.8). The finding of a *yaguareté* tooth pendant could be related to the sacred character or the protective value this animal would hold. Similar pendants, but made of canid teeth as the found

The Middle Holocene

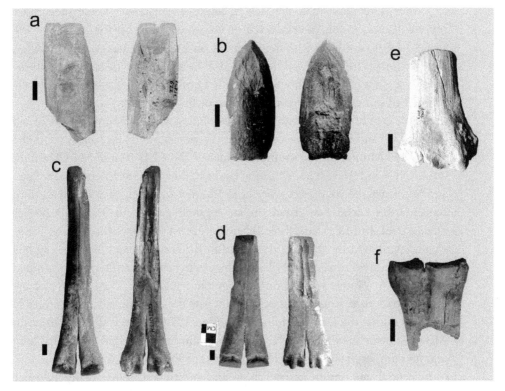

Figure 5.8 Bone artifacts from different sites of the CPD. (a) Bevel-ended tool made of guanaco tibia; (b) point made of artiodactyl long bone; (c and d) bevel-ended tools made of guanaco metapodial; (e) tibia waste with sawing and grinding marks; (f) metapodial waste with sawing and grinding marks. Photo courtesy Maria Clara Álvarez.

in AS2, indicate the symbolic importance that carnivores would have in Pampean cosmology since at least the Middle Holocene. This role was maintained and reinforced in the Late Holocene (Bonomo 2006; see Chapter 6).

Stratigraphic excavations have been performed in both localities (Messineo et al. 2019d). In LLP a date of 5684 BP was obtained from a guanaco bone tool found on the surface, while two dates from stratigraphy gave ages of 7024 and 5815 BP. The lithic materials are characterized by a predominance of SBG orthoquartzite and phtanite (>90%) from Tandilia. Other lithic raw materials, such as granite, silicified dolomite, metaquartzite, rhyolite, basalt, silex, micaceous schist, and obsidian, were present in low frequencies. Some of these rocks come from diverse areas of the Pampas (Ventania, Patagonian Shingle Mantle, and the West Pampa – possibly from El Fresco Plateau; see Chapter 3), and in the case of the obsidian, it would be extra-regional. Different from other sites, in LLP, local bone tool production was recorded (Figure 5.8). This standardized bone technology was centered on producing beveled tools and blunted points made of guanaco tibiae (Álvarez 2014a); it has to be understood as a strategy to cope with the lack of lithic raw material. These sites might represent a succession of residential or logistical camps on the border of the shallow lakes of hunter-gatherers focused on exploiting guanaco, armadillos, and greater rhea eggs. The different and distant locations of the raw material sources suggest high mobility and extended home ranges, although the development of some exchange networks cannot be ruled out.

Whole eggs of Rheidae with a small perforation at the minor pole were found in both LCh and LLP sites as well as in Las Gaviotas and the Pintado II site in the Laguna del Monte, on the southern border of the CPD (Carden and Martínez 2014; Oliva and Algrain 2004). In the last case, they have geometric engravings. In the former site, two eggs were found buried together, and a broken third remains; this cache was dated on an eggshell sample to 7230 BP (Politis et al. 2021a). In LLP, four whole Rheidae eggs were found; three were buried aligned, separated by 30 m. A date of 6620 BP was obtained from an eggshell sample (Messineo et al. 2021b). These holey eggs have been interpreted as liquid containers or canteens based on ethnographic analogies. They were possibly employed to store water as a strategy to mitigate the droughts that were probably frequent during the Middle Holocene in the CPD (Carden and Martinez 2014; Messineo et al. 2018). This behavior is common in hunter-gatherers inhabiting regions with water shortages (Hitchcock 2012; Silberbauer 1981).

In central and southeastern Pampa and North Patagonia, many Rheidae eggshell fragments have been found in archaeological deposits interpreted as food debris. However, some of them in the southern area, such as La Modesta and Loma de Los Morteros (Stoessel 2014), display engravings and perforations similar to those from LLP and LCh (Carden and Martínez 2014). These fragments are perceived as broken eggs that would have functioned as flasks in a scenario of relatively open social relations (Martínez 2010), while the macro-regional recurrence of the engraved motifs on Rheidae eggshells could be understood as reinforcing the hunter-gatherers' social networks (Carden and Martínez 2014). It seems that during the Middle Holocene, Rheidae eggs began to be used as liquid containers and as holders of images for symbolic or communication purposes. In the southern area, these uses continued until the Late Holocene, but at ~ 1000 BP, the eggshells stopped being decorated (Carden and Martínez 2014), which could probably be related to the cease of their function as flasks or canteens and/or changes in the system of visual representation or symbolic communication. However, only in the CPD have these eggs been found complete and intact, because they have been intentionally buried (in caches) for storing liquid, probably for delayed consumption during droughts.

Other localities situated in the CPD are the Cabeza de Buey lake and La Susana 1. The former was investigated by Marcelo Bórmida in the late 1950s, who analyzed a surface lithic collection and carried out some excavations (Bórmida n.d., 1960; see Chapter 2). This was a key site in Bormida's models and set the foundation for the definition of the "Bolivarense" industry, a landmark in

The Middle Holocene   175

the *kulturkreise* scheme. Recent excavations performed by Messineo at site 2 adjacent to the ancient dig made by Bórmida uncovered two Middle Holocene levels dated to 6801 BP and 4150 BP (Messineo and Scheifler 2016; Messineo et al. 2019d). In the La Susana 1 site (LS1), located on the southeastern border of the Las Tunas Chicas lake, the main component was dated to 7446 BP (Scheifler 2019). In both sites, fauna exploitation and lithic technology are similar to the Interserrana area with some nuances, such as the exploitation of the big armadillo *Tolypeutes matacus* in Cabeza de Buey. In this site, 95% of these lithic raw materials came from the Tandilia hill range (120–220 km from the site), but there is also one toolstone from the western Pampa (~ 400–500 km) (Messineo et al. 2019d).

Finally, the site Laguna El Doce shows a good record of human burials from the Early Holocene (see Chapter 4) up to the Late Holocene. Abundant lithic tools, faunal bones, and pottery found on the surface result from the erosion of several human occupation layers along the Holocene, as several radiocarbon dates indicate (Ávila 2011). Although it is virtually impossible to discriminate these surface assemblages chronologically, one ^{14}C date from a guanaco bone gave an age of 7026 BP. Guanaco and Pampas deer dominate the bone remains, while raw material shows two distinct origins: orthoquartzite, phtanite, and schists from the Tandilia and Ventania hills, and quartz, cherts, orthogneiss, and granites from the Central Hills region (Ávila et al. 2011). A remarkable finding is the marine gastropod *Adelomedon brasiliana* (Cornaglia Fernández 2009, 2011), since the Atlantic coast is at least 550 km away south. This is probably one of the larger distances that *Adelomedon* is registered in inland sites and suggests extended exchange networks. Marine shells must have had a prominent role as prestige items in the Pampas, which justified the effort and complexity required to transport them hundreds of kilometers.

In the Northwest area, there are no stratigraphic sites that could be assigned to the Middle Holocene. However, various bifacial lanceolate projectile points, some of them stemmed as the type known as Ayampitín (González 1960), have been recorded in the northern sector (Heider and Rivero 2018). About half of them are of quartz (a preferred raw material in the Central Hills region) and have been interpreted as a part of the atlatl weapon system (Heider and Rivero 2018). This type of projectile point was dated in the Central Hill at the end of the Early Holocene to Middle Holocene, an age that could be extended to the Pampean specimens. Except in the Northwest area, they have not been registered in the Pampas. Its presence in the northern sector of the area is related to the expansion of the hunter-gatherers from the Central Hills, a subject we discuss in Chapter 7.

Human Diet Based on Isotopic Studies

Although there is still an incomplete isotopic record for the Pampas during this period, some trends can be outlined. Isotopic studies on Middle Holocene human bone indicated variations in the sources of protein intake, including the consumption of terrestrial and marine resources in different proportions. Isotopic results from AS2 show that the diet of the Interserrana inland populations during the Early to Middle Holocene was based on the consumption of terrestrial herbivores, which in turn consumed C3 plants (Politis et al. 2009). The values from the sample Arroyo Chasicó S7 ($\delta\ ^{13}C_{col}$ = −17.90; Catella 2014) in the inland southern area shows the same kind of diet. The isotopic values obtained for these remains are consistent with the isotopic data available for the most representative fauna in the region (guanaco, Pampas deer, armadillos, rodents, etc.). There is only one exception, the individual AS36 from AS2, who presents the most enriched $\delta\ ^{13}C_{col}$ values ($\delta\ ^{13}C$ = −12.4‰) and a small range between both bone fractions, indicating that marine foods provided the basis of his diet (Politis et al. 2009).

Moreover, some individuals (75% men) added proteins of marine origin to their diet. These results are interesting because they constitute evidence of intra-population dietary differences. Whether the consumption of marine foods – obtained over 60 km away from the site – by some individuals implied the mobility of a band segment only or if the entire group moved to the coast is still an unresolved issue. One possibility is that AS2 men (eventually some women) regularly visited the beach during logistical trips and consumed marine resources there, while other band members, primarily women and children, remained in the inland residential camps. A second possibility is that some food taboos or dietary restrictions existed within the group. A third possibility is that men from coastal territories coupled with women from the inland followed a matrilocal postmarital residential pattern. In this sense, the strong marine resource consumption during part of their life may have left an isotopic trace that was still recognizable in their bones. This could be the case for individual AS36, a young man presenting an enriched $\delta\ ^{13}C_{col}$ value who was buried with a young female. This could be the case of a recently arrived young man who died shortly after coming (Politis et al. 2009).

In contrast, as in the southern area, the western coastal sites (MH1) show a different isotopic signature during the Middle Holocene. The two individuals recovered from MH1 show a diet based on marine resources ($\delta\ ^{13}C_{col}$ = −13.6 and −13.2; Politis et al. 2009). On the other hand, in the eastern sector of the seashore, mixed diets, like most of the men of AS2, are characterized by the consumption of C3 plant-eating herbivores – a continental diet – and the incorporation of some marine proteins in different amounts (Arroyo del Moro, Meseta del Chocorí, Necochea sites). This is also in concordance with the archaeofaunistic record (Bonomo et al. 2013).

In short, the evidence indicating marine diets of the Middle Holocene of the Pampean region comes from the coast of the southern area (Tres Bonetes 1 and Cantera de Rodados Villalonga), from the southern end of the coast of the Interserrana area (MH1), and a single individual of AS2. The different dietary

The Middle Holocene

patterns between coast and inland in the southern area have been interpreted as the result of possible territorial demarcations (Flensborg et al. 2018). On the other hand, from the Quequén Salado River to Corrientes Cape, the diets are mixed, indicating mobility that includes the consumption of inland resources as well as coastal resources (although in the coastal dunes, there are also some terrestrial resources available). In this sector, there do not appear to have been predominantly coastal band territories.

The only isotopic data for this period in western Pampa is in the Close Basins area in CLV2. The isotopic analysis (δ $^{13}C_{col}$) has a value of -16.27‰, indicating the contribution of an important component of terrestrial animal proteins in the diet. It is also supported by the value of δ ^{15}N (12.35). The total diet (δ $^{13}C_{apat}$) gave a value of -9.75‰, which is enriched given the known values in the area (-12.5‰) (Barberena et al. 2018; Berón et al. 2009). Besides, the analysis of δ ^{18}O = 1.32‰ (Lucero et al. 2020) suggests that the individual had a local residence and a terrestrial diet, perhaps with minimal consumption of cariogenic foods.

PATAGONIA

In contrast with the Pleistocene to Holocene transition, the beginning of the Holocene is characterized by a wider distribution of archaeological remains. This distribution indicates that most terrestrial barriers were permeable except for the Continental Ice Field (Borrero and Borrazzo 2011) (Figure 1.6). In contrast, the maritime barriers acted as more powerful filters. The maze of channels and islands of the southwestern archipelagos became more and more fragmented due to the gradual rise of the sea level. These channel and shoreline modifications, compounded by isostatic and tectonic processes, completely changed the available space for human settlement (Reyes 2020; Reyes et al. 2018). Changes included the final disappearance of a land bridge with Tierra del Fuego (McCulloch and Morello 2009).

Once the Strait of Magellan was formed, isolation of human populations on the island ensued, triggering founder effects and leading to technological innovations (Borrero 1989–1990). We already saw that the pioneer settlement in Tierra del Fuego, recovered at the site of Tres Arroyos 1, was similar to that present at the earliest occupations on the mainland. Effectively, similar hearths, projectile points, and prey remains are recorded at Fell Cave, Cueva del Medio, and Cueva Lago Sofía 1 sites. All these sites were located in treeless terrestrial habitats. Notably, the older Fuegian occupations after the abandonment of Tres Arroyos 1 ca. 10,200 BP were found hundreds of kilometers south, in a completely different habitat near the Beagle Channel. Among many differences, this habitat offered access to marine mammals, mollusks, and a greater variety of birds. The increasing availability of forests was another

Figure 5.9 Excavations at Site 11 at Bahía Valentín, Tierra del Fuego, Argentina. Photo courtesy Atilio F. Zangrando.

significant difference, which was key for the subsequent human adaptation to the lifeways of the channels (Orquera and Piana 1999). The earliest occupations recorded near the Beagle Channel are substantially different from all previous records (Zangrando et al. 2018). An extensive reconnaissance of some of the habitats existent on the island of Tierra del Fuego probably occurred before humans settled near the channel, a process that undoubtedly was accompanied by further cultural changes. This divergence within the island was probably important for the later appearance of the maritime occupations in the southwestern archipelagos, the Beagle Channel, and Mitre Peninsula (Figure 5.9). They resulted in the spread of navigational technology that helped to resume contact between human populations on both sides of the Strait of Magellan (Fiore 2006) and opened the colonization of the fragmented archipelagos. Accordingly, the lifeways of hunter-gatherer populations were fundamentally redirected in terms of subsistence, settlement, and organization.

At any rate, nondirectional change was the inevitable result of human geographic isolation in Tierra del Fuego. Using a large spatial scale, technological and morphological divergences were observed (Borrero 1989–1990; Charlin et al. 2013; Scheinsohn 2014), including that after ca. 6500 BP, navigation technology appeared in the southwestern channels. No canoes or

The Middle Holocene

parts of canoes were found, but the abundant evidence for the occupation of islands such as Englefield or Navarino clearly marks their existence. Sites located on islands such as Englefield, Bahía Colorada, Pizzulic, or Grandi not only are all dated around 6000–5000 BP, but their archaeological content clearly responds to a maritime lifeway (Emperaire and Laming 1961; Legoupil 1997; Legoupil and Fontugne 1997; San Román et al. 2013) (Figure 5.10). Whether this successful installation near the channels results from local innovation or human migration is still an open question (Orquera and Piana 1999; Orquera et al. 2011). Highly contrasted terrestrial and maritime lifeways are found among the oldest occupations near the Beagle Channel. These Middle Holocene terrestrial occupations at Túnel I, Imiwaia I, and Binushmuka I sites are characterized by their technology (Orquera and Piana 1999: 48; Piana et al. 2012; Zangrando 2009a; Zangrando et al. 2018) but include pinniped bones at Túnel I. After those initial occupations, shell midden formation and indications of maritime lifeways started around 6400 BP. Zangrando et al. (2018) proved that no major chronological discontinuity existed during these early occupations, only a short hiatus at the beginning of the Middle Holocene. Then, the strong cultural contrast between Early and Middle Holocene occupations is what matters. Can the contrast be understood as an internal transformation from terrestrial to maritime-oriented adaptations? Orquera and collaborators (2011: 65) claimed that changes were "too large to be a product of a local transformation process of fewer than three hundred years," and therefore, they suggest that it was a case of population replacement. The answer is not yet clear, but Zangrando and collaborators (2018) also noted that some of the earliest shell middens at the Beagle Channel occupy the same loci used by previous terrestrially oriented occupations, a situation they do not think as fortuitous. This is extremely important because it suggests that the inhabitants of that part of the island shared similar cultural geography despite the notorious differences observed in their technology and use of resources.

Importantly, green obsidian from the Otway Sound is present in all these sites. At Binushmuka, 146 out of 2,664 artifacts are made of green obsidian (Zangrando et al. 2018) (Figure 5.11). Those artifacts were seen as supporting social maritime trade routes or networks between the Beagle Channel and the Brunswick Peninsula (Alvarez 2004; Morello et al. 2012b), but the movement of people during the dispersal of the maritime lifeways also needs to be considered. Thus, we are now talking of a marine world. Is this new world the result of the opening of the Strait of Magellan? Prieto et al. (2013) dismiss it as the cause for the origin of a maritime adaptation, arguing that it occurred a long time before. This is hardly a reason to dismiss it as a factor. One problem is that this dismissal is focused on the opening of the Strait itself, but the actual motor for change was not necessarily that particular waterway. Instead, the change that precipitated the maritime adaptation was the slow drowning of peninsulas and islands caused by the Middle Holocene sea transgression that

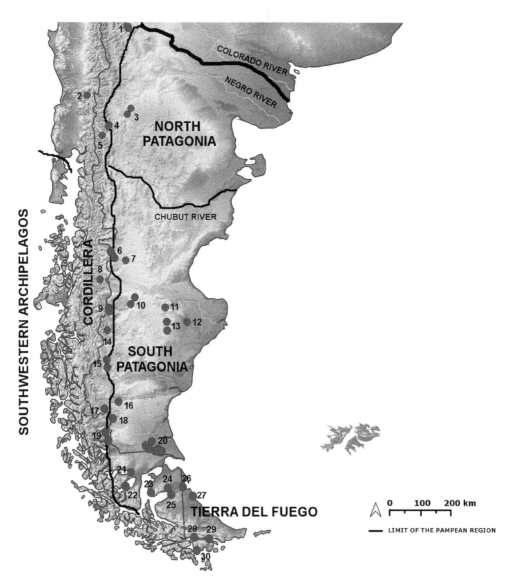

Figure 5.10 Map showing Middle Holocene sites mentioned in the text.
(1) Cueva Huenul; (2) Marifilo; (3) Cueva Epullán Grande, Piedra del Aguila 11; (4) Traful, Cuyín Manzano; (5) El Trébol; (6) Baño Nuevo, Casa de Piedra Roselló; (7) Alero Dásovich; (8) Alero Fontana; (9) Alero Entrada Baker, Milodón Norte 1, Cerro Cuadrado 3; (10) Arroyo Feo, Cueva de las Manos; (11) Los Toldos 3; (12) Piedra Museo; (13) Cerro Tres Tetas, Cueva Maripé; (14) Cerro Casa de Piedra 7; (15) Cueva del Paisano Desconocido, Alero del Paisano Desconocido, Bloque 1 Oquedad; (16) Río Bote 1; (17) Chorrillo Malo 2; (18) Cerro León 3; (19) Cerro Castillo, Alero Quemado, Alero Pedro Cárdenas, Alero del Diablo; (20) Las Buitreras, La Carlota 1, Don Ariel, Fell Cave, Pali Aike, Potrok Aike 11, Tom Gould, Cueva de los Chingues; (21) Ponsonby; (22) Englefield, Bahía Colorada, Pizzulic; (23) Cabo Monmouth; (24) Myren; (25) Marazzi; (26) Cerro Bandurrias; (27) La Arcillosa 2, Río Chico 1; (28) Túnel I; (29) Imiwaia I, Binushmuka I; (30) Grandi.

The Middle Holocene

Figure 5.11 Excavations at Binushmuka I, Beagle Channel, Tierra del Fuego, Argentina. Photo courtesy Atilio F. Zangrando.

culminated around 6000 BP (Isla and Bujalesky 2008; Rabassa et al. 2009). This event created a real obstacle for human connectivity. Alternatively, Prieto et al. (2013) favored an explanation centered on the ca. 6900 BP eruption of the Hudson volcano. They boldly maintain that "the H1 eruption may have killed all the terrestrial hunter-gatherer population on Tierra del Fuego" (Prieto et al. 2013: 9). In their view, the lack of terrestrial food was the trigger for maritime adaptation.

Nevertheless, they also suggest that the maritime way of life resulted from some survivors deciding to change habitat and resources. The argument becomes murky here. They remarked that very few sites were first occupied by terrestrial hunters and later by maritime hunters, mentioning Ponsonby on the mainland and Túnel I and Imiwaia 1 at the Beagle Channel. We have already observed that the latter two sites also constitute the older evidence for terrestrial hunters in Tierra del Fuego after the opening of the Strait of Magellan and that they show abrupt changes leading to littoral exploitation strategies (Prieto et al. 2013: 6), without evidence for any transitional process beyond the presence of pinniped bones at Túnel I (Bjerck et al. 2016; Zangrando et al. 2018). Prieto and collaborators mention the reason offered by Orquera and Piana (2009) for their population replacement interpretation. This basically is the identification of "atypical" industries at Túnel I and Imiwaia I, characterized by the presence of polished lithic wedges, a tranchet, a very long leaf-shaped blade, and a borer. One problem with this interpretation is that they are just comparing lists of tool types, which from an organizational perspective makes little sense since they also can be the result of divergence. The distance of close to 200 km between Tres Arroyos I and the sites in the Beagle Channel is sufficient to expect cultural changes, particularly given the important differences in habitat. There are no grounds to call these tools anomalous.

Regarding the older terrestrial sites on the Atlantic coast of Tierra del Fuego (Salemme et al. 2007a; Santiago 2013), Prieto and collaborators found it significant that they contain lithic repertoires that differ from those before the H1 eruption at Túnel I and Imiwaia 1. Again, this is not surprising from an organizational perspective, particularly with small samples (see also Zangrando et al. 2018). Most researchers agree that the older maritime occupations at Túnel I do not present signs of incipient adaptation to the sea but instead appear to be fully adapted (Orquera et al. 2011: 65). On this basis, Prieto et al. maintain that there was a radiation of people from the Otway Sound and another from the continent, which "independently repopulated a possibly totally unoccupied Tierra del Fuego inland area after the H1 event" (Prieto et al. 2013: 6). None of these movements is sustained by anything but thin air. Based on chronology and logic, it was repeatedly maintained that the origin of the maritime adaptation occurred in the area of the Otway Sea/Strait of Magellan, perhaps at places like Punta Santa Ana on the mainland (Morello et al. 2012b; Orquera et al. 2011; Ortiz Troncoso 1975; San Román 2013, 2016), which certainly makes sense without invoking a catastrophe.

The known utilization of the Patagonian coasts began at different places around 6000 BP or before with a relatively varied record that included different types of shell middens and concentrations of otolites (Borella and Cardillo 2011; Caracotche et al. 2017; Favier Dubois et al. 2008; Gómez Otero 2007; Gómez Otero et al. 2013; Scartascini 2012, 2020; Zubimendi 2010). Between 6000 and 3000 BP, the interest in coastal resources is recorded almost everywhere on the Atlantic coast. Not only are open-air sites recorded, but also rock shelters (Ambrústolo et al. 2011; Castro et al. 2003, 2007, 2008; Gómez Otero 1995; Gómez Otero et al. 1999; Hammond and Zubimendi 2013; Mansur et al. 2004; Moreno 2008; Muñoz et al. 2016; Salemme et al. 2007a). Most of these cases result from hunter-gatherers' complementary use of coastal resources for a diet that was mainly focused on terrestrial resources. Only rarely are marine resources dominant. There is a contrast with the already mentioned human use of the southwestern archipelagos, where a maritime way of life was fully developed since ca. 6500 BP and persisted with changes up to historical times everywhere. The evidence across this long chain of archipelagos is similar in chronology and mode of adaptation. These occupations were recorded in the north (Legoupil 2005; Reyes et al. 2020; Rivas et al. 1999), the south (Emperaire and Laming 1961; Legoupil 1997, 2000; Legoupil et al. 2011; Ortiz Troncoso 1979; San Román 2013, 2014, 2016; San Román et al. 2002, 2016), and the southeastern archipelagos (Legoupil and Fontugne 1997; Orquera 1987; Orquera and Piana 1999;

The Middle Holocene

Piana et al. 2004; Zangrando 2009a). This general similarity among archaeological assemblages separated by thousands of kilometers speaks to the general homogeneity of the environment and the necessity of using navigational technology to exploit them. Of course, there are many variations whose significance is not yet well understood. For example, in the northern extreme of the archipelagos, plants were more regularly consumed, and lithic tools were not abundant (Reyes 2021; Reyes et al. 2020). The main variant recorded in the southern and southeastern sequences is the interdigitation of periods in which either guanacos or sea mammals are the most important resources, sometimes accompanied by birds and fishes (San Román and Prieto 2004; Zangrando 2009a). One major process that still needs to be fully decoded concerns the changing relationship between the stability of pinniped populations and human hunting strategies (Zangrando 2009a).

The evidence for human occupation during the Middle Holocene in the northern steppes of Tierra del Fuego is not abundant, which is one reason why people like Borrero (1997) or Prieto et al. (2013) suggested the existence of an occupational gap. The evidence for coastal sites is restricted to minimal occupations recorded at the Marazzi, Cabo Monmouth, or Cerro Bandurrias sites (Favier Dubois and Borrero 2005; Laming-Emperaire et al. 1972; Morello et al. 1999, 2009, 2012a). In the inland, we have only the Myren site, where a guanaco bone bed dated ca. 4000 BP was discovered embedded in a peat layer (Prieto et al. 2007). Skeletal remains of at least nine individuals were found. Whereas anthropic fractures are abundant, and about 30% of the bones present cut-marks, guanaco skulls and several long bones were not broken. Bolas and side scrapers were also found, forming a peculiar lithic repertoire. All side scrapers – with evidence of use – were concentrated in a small sector of the site, leading to speculations of a cache. The plausible interpretation of scavenging of animals trapped in the mud was offered (Prieto et al. 2007: 101). The case is similar to that recorded at the lower layers of Ponsonby (Lefèvre et al. 2003).

Evidence for Middle Holocene occupations is clustered at the Chico River Basin. La Arcillosa 2, located on top of a high cliff, presented ephemeral occupations dated between ca. 5500 and 3700 BP. Bifaces, bolas, and other lithic tools were found. The organic remains include concentrations of mollusks, very few poorly preserved mammal bones (basically guanaco and rodents, but also the minimal presence of maritime mammals and fishes), and one human burial (Salemme et al. 2007a; Santiago 2013). The latter was dated to 5200 BP. The Río Chico 1 site is a shell midden located nearby and dated to 5800–4400 BP. One difference with La Arcillosa 2 is that better preservation of organic remains was detected. The midden is basically formed by *Mytilus edulis*, but many other species are also present. The abundance of fishes, particularly *Merluccius*, is to be noted. Guanaco, birds – including penguins – foxes, and pinnipeds are present in minor frequencies. A few dolphin bones and one

Balaenoptera borealis radius complete the image of hunter-gatherers with a strong interest in the products of the sea. More than 1,600 lithic remains were recovered, but only 11 are tools, including side scrapers and bolas (Santiago 2013)

Mainland Patagonia at the beginning of the Middle Holocene presents a completely different situation. Not only is the archaeological evidence more equitably distributed among the different ecosystems, but there is also evidence of a relatively more continuous regional occupation of most of those ecosystems. The Middle Holocene in Patagonia was a strange period of high cultural diversity but still routinely associated with the exploitation of guanacos. In other words, variable technologies are applied to the procurement and utilization of the same prey. In a very few cases, guanacos were not the basic resource during this period. The main exceptions occurred at coastal and forested habitats, where alternative resources were also incorporated. There are also some specialized sites, such as burials or places of exploitation of rocks, in which there are no guanaco remains.

As already mentioned, the extinction of the megafauna precipitated a sharper focus on guanacos. Even in the absence of intense exploitation of extinct mammals, the list of potential targets was dramatically reduced at the beginning of the Holocene (Miotti and Salemme 1999). Perhaps the guanaco's importance is partly the result of most of the Early Holocene sites being caves, while a more varied record lies buried in slumped slopes of aeolian sediments. However, the few known open-air sites are also focused on the consumption of guanaco (Massone 1989–1990). The frequency of open-air sites increased during the Middle Holocene, but they are concentrated in coastal environments, where the systematic use of maritime resources started. This is in sharp contrast with the Late Pleistocene and Early Holocene sites where, excepting isolated mollusks, there are no signs of any connection with the sea. However, it must be said that it is more than possible that evidence of previous acquaintance with marine resources now lies under the oceanic waters. The regular use of maritime habitats can be seen as the result of a process of continuous dispersal of human populations. This process was the result of the stabilization of the coast and its later biological colonization at a time of demographic growth. The coast was an attractive environment that offered combined access to both terrestrial and maritime resources. Mollusk colonies and pinniped rookeries probably were among the main coastal attractors, together with a huge diversity of lithic raw materials. The coasts were also a rich source of bones to make tools (Christensen 2016; Scheinsohn 1993–1994, 2010). Nevertheless, opening this new niche during the Middle Holocene in mainland Patagonia did not mean that guanacos were dropped from the diet. Guanacos were still important, at least on a seasonal basis.

The evidence from the Middle Holocene in Northwest Patagonia is limited, including sites like Huenul where it is practically absent, except for the rock

The Middle Holocene

paintings dated to that period (Romero Villanueva 2019). Excavations at Traful I and other sites produced evidence of redundant use of the cave by guanaco hunters using triangular projectile points (Cordero 2011). Sites like El Trébol contain incompletely published evidence for human presence (Hajduk et al. 2007), while other sites such as Cuyín Manzano or those tested by the Spanish team probably were also utilized at that time (Arias Cabal et al. 2012; Ceballos 1982). Since practically all the latter sites are still undated and unpublished, searching for patterns in this corner of Patagonia is useless.

The quality of the evidence improves in the steppes, where sites such as Epullán Grande and Piedra del Aguila 11 indicate recurrent utilization of places near the Limay River (Crivelli et al. 1996; Sanguinetti and Curzio 1996). Several relatively ephemeral occupations associated with abundant plant beds were recovered at these sites. In the case of Epullán Grande, several human burials were found. These sites are also characterized by incorporation of a diversity of subsistence resources, such as small animals and plants (Cordero 2009). We know very little about plant exploitation. The best evidence for the consumption of plants in Patagonia resulted from the extraordinary efforts of Carolina Belmar at Baño Nuevo, Aisén. In the first place, Belmar evaluated several alternative ways in which plants can be naturally introduced to the site. After that control, a variety of indicators, including residues on human teeth calculus and on the edge of lithic tools, demonstrated the use of plants throughout the Holocene (Belmar 2019). We must be open to the notion that plants were a more important resource than what we know so far (Ancibor and Pérez de Micou 1995; Belmar et al. 2017; Bernal et al. 2007; Ciampagna et al. 3020; Llano and Barberena 2013; López et al. 2020; Martinez Tosto and Burry 2019). Plants were used not only as food but also as fuel or as raw material for several tools and handicrafts. They were also used as bedding in the human living space.

Epullán Grande is among the few sites where Rheidae bones are relatively well represented in Patagonia. The presence of over 70 Rheidae bones is quite impressive, but they represent only a single individual (Cordero 2009). It must be mentioned that the elusive presence of Rheidae bones in Patagonian sites is paradoxical, given their abundance and palatability. This is especially true considering that the lesser rhea was the classical prey of Patagonian hunter-gatherers during historical times (Fernández 2000). Basically, lower leg bones are found, a pattern that can only partially be related to differential bone survival.

Baño Nuevo, Casa de Piedra de Roselló Cave, Alero Dásovich, and other sites in Aisén and Western Chubut present a highly discontinuous occupational record throughout the Holocene (Méndez et al. 2019). Evidence from the Cisnes Valley, Aisén, indicates at least two pulses of occupation during the Middle Holocene. The first pulse occurred around 6000 BP and shows short human occupations, where hearths, lithic tools, and prey bones were deposited. Evidence of blade technology

Figure 5.12 Location of Casa de Piedra de Rosello, Argentina. Photo courtesy Analía Castro Esnal.

and bifacial thinning flakes is present. Processing of guanacos and canids is well recorded, and the presence of *Dusicyon avus* ca. 6000 BP must be noted. This extinct canid is also present at Baño Nuevo, Aisén, ca. 6000 BP (Velásquez and Mena 2006). The second pulse, ca. 4500 BP, is interesting because tools are dominant over lithic debitage, indicating that the recovered evidence probably represents the use and discarding of transported tools. The high frequency of blades and the presence of a triangular projectile reused as an end scraper on obsidian from Pampa del Asador must be noted (Méndez et al. 2008–2009, 2011). Summing up, both occupations reiterate the coexistence of bifacial technology and blades. Importantly, the presence of *Berberis* sp. fruits and seeds at one hearth adds to our meager record of the use of plants in Patagonia (Méndez et al. 2011). Occupations at Casa de Piedra de Roselló Cave are intense between ca. 5600 and 7800 BP, and in addition to guanaco there is evidence of minimal exploitation of huemul, perhaps related to an eastern extension of the forest as a result of higher humidity (De Porras et al. 2012) (Figure 5.12). Some similarity between the evidence at Casa de Piedra de Roselló Cave and Baño Nuevo suggests the possible existence of mobility circuits and interaction among groups with good detailed knowledge of their environs (Castro Esnal et al. 2017) (Figure 5.13).

In the Chacabuco valley (Mena and Jackson 1991), Alero Entrada Baker, located in Chile at approximately the same latitude as the Pinturas Basin, was shortly occupied ca. 7600 BP (Mena and Jackson 1991). Even when it is not completely clear, later occupations displaying a diversity of projectile point shapes mainly belong in the Late Holocene. Cueva de las Manos, Cueva Arroyo Feo, and other sites in or near the Pinturas Basin continued to be occupied by guanaco hunters armed with triangular projectile points during the Middle Holocene (Gradin et al. 1976; Mengoni Goñalons et al. 2009). There are occupations with and without projectile points during this period in

The Middle Holocene

Figure 5.13 Excavations at Casa de Piedra de Roselló. Photo courtesy Analía Castro Esnal.

which the production of blades increased. Information from these sites was published in detail. Cueva de las Manos, located in a deep canyon, is difficult to access. In contrast, Cueva Arroyo Feo is located on a less steep canyon, with easy access to the upper plains (Gradin et al. 1979). Substantial portions of guanaco carcasses were transported to these sites (Mengoni Goñalons and Silveira 1976; Silveira 1979). The dominance of the appendicular skeleton was recorded, a pattern to be repeated almost everywhere in the Patagonian steppes. The faunal evidence from Arroyo Feo shows an increase in the number of guanacos deposited during the Middle Holocene (Silveira 1979), which probably resulted from a more redundant use of the cave (Borrero 1993). A similar panorama is offered by the basal occupations of Milodón Norte 1 and Cerro Cuadrado 3, north of the Pueyrredón Lake (Aschero et al. 2019a). Cerro Casa de Piedra 7, located in the Perito Moreno Park, presents relatively intense Middle Holocene occupations focused on guanaco hunting with the addition of the increasingly available huemul (Civalero and Aschero 2003; De Nigris 2004). Mariana De Nigris (2004) observed that the proportion of both species is relatively constant along the sequence. Alero Fontana in Aisén is one of the few sites indicating the intensive exploitation of huemul since ca. 4600 BP (Mena et al. 2003). More unusual is the importance of *Pseudalopex griseus* and *Pudu pudu* as subsistence resources during the Middle Holocene at Marifilo, located in the forest (García 2007).

Aschero and collaborators (2019a) recently considered that the absence of occupations after 6900 BP at sites near the Pueyrredón Lake and the Perito Moreno Park resulted from the catastrophic H1 eruption of the Hudson volcano. They claim strict chronological control at Cerro Casa de Piedra 7, which is difficult to accept judging from the numerous reversed chronologies in the stratigraphy (Aschero et al. 2007, 2019a). At any rate, the presence of a relatively important occupational discontinuity is an interesting possibility that helps us to make sense of many organizational changes recorded at this time. These changes include thinning of lithic tools, the appearance of blades with marginal retouch, and an increase in cut-marks on guanaco bones. Interestingly, the study by Aschero and others (2019a) differs from that of Prieto et al. (2013) in that they are proposing the abandonment of the area instead of the extinction of the local populations. This is significant given the fact that this area is closer to the Hudson volcano. Other occupational discontinuities attributed to volcanic activities were proposed for that general area in Santa Cruz, which were similarly interpreted as evidence for human abandonment of the area (Mengoni Goñalons et al. 2019). Like those near the Cardiel Lake, some places away from the Andes present minimal evidence pertaining to the Middle Holocene (Goñi et al. 2006). A discussion of the reality of these discontinuities is presented by Garvey (2021).

The concentration of sites at the Deseado Massif presents a strong Middle Holocene signal with occupations at Piedra Museo, Cerro Tres Tetas, and many other sites. Evidence of technological variation was present in these occupations. Diversification in lithic technology has been evident at least since the end of the Middle Holocene. One important change was the growing importance of blades within the so-called Casapedrense industry (Menghin 1952a). These sites are also characterized by an increase in the abundance of guanaco remains. For Augusto Cardich this industry disappeared because a volcanic eruption of the Hudson volcano caused people to move away from the region (Cardich 1984–1985). The chronologies of both the volcanic eruptions in Patagonia and the human occupations at the Los Toldos Cave were revised, and the sequence of the latter still needs to be reorganized (Stern 2008). Nevertheless, Hermo and Magnin (2012: 76) rightly believe that perhaps this interpretation must be replaced by "partial depopulation . . . due to changes in the mobility patterns at the regional level" (Hermo and Magnin 2012: 76). Beyond the presence of blades, the lack of projectile points was the main characteristic of this industry. It was defined as a techno-complex found at several sites in South Patagonia – particularly between the Chubut and Santa Cruz Rivers – that used only bolas as hunting weapons (Cardich et al. 1973; Menghin 1952a). The importance of blades began at a number of sites ca. 5000 BP or before (Bellelli 1987, 1988; Carballido Calatayud 2009; Méndez et al. 2011). However, their relationship with other archaeological assemblages characterized by projectile points was not completely explored (Borrero 1989;

The Middle Holocene

Mena 1991). We already saw that both blades and bifaciality coexist at the Cisnes valley, Aisén (Méndez et al. 2011). But even more important, there is definitive evidence from the very area where the "Casapedrense" was invented. The Middle Holocene occupations at Cerro Tres Tetas, Piedra Museo, and Maripé in the Deseado Massif are particularly informative. They represent intensive occupations and are characterized by abundant blades, triangular projectile points, bolas, and archaeofaunas dominated by guanaco bones (Castro et al. 2016; Cueto et al. 2020; Miotti et al. 2014, 2015). Indeed, information from these and other sites makes it increasingly clear that projectile points were important in several assemblages at this time (Borrero 1994–1995; Gradin et al. 1979; Hermo and Magnin 2012; Mena 1991; Méndez et al. 2011; Miotti et al. 2014), showing that the "Casapedrense" label is distracting at best, if not plain useless. A diversity of lithic assemblages with different combinations of blades and projectile points probably was a response to seasonal, functional, social, and other organizational differences among sites. A study by Cueto and others (2017: 8) concluded that the so-called Casapedrense can be considered a standardized technological system focused on maximizing functional edges, in which tools were used either hafted or unhafted, sometimes with multiple functions. Also, our knowledge of the importance of blades in other contexts, including some located south of the Santa Cruz River, is increasing (Hermo and Magnin 2012; Pallo et al. 2020; Vetrisano 2018).

During the 1990s it was even considered that the already mentioned proliferation of guanaco remains at Middle Holocene sites resulted from an experiment in pastoralism that was interrupted by the volcanic eruption (Cardich and Paunero 1994). It was an idea for which there is absolutely no supporting evidence. At any rate, since the dominant faunal association in all cases is with guanacos, the beginning of specialization in the consumption of guanaco was claimed (Cardich 1984–1985), but there are two obstacles to this interpretation. First, a specialization in guanaco was already in place at least since 9000 BP. Second, the only reason behind this supposed Middle Holocene specialization is the increased number of guanaco remains. This could simply have resulted from human demographic growth (Pérez et al. 2016) or more continuity in the use of sites, both factors rarely considered in the literature.

Other areas near the Andes, such as the Tar-San Martín or Argentino lakes and the Baguales range, were more discontinuously occupied (Borrazzo 2008; Borrero et al. 2006; Espinosa et al. 2013; L'Heureux and Borrazzo 2013) (Figure 5.14). Evidence from two sites at the San Martín Basin, Cueva del Paisano Desconocido and Alero del Paisano Desconocido, indicates the punctuated presence of hunter-gatherers during the Middle Holocene. These occupations are always ephemeral, focused on the exploitation of guanaco, and probably related to the use of mobility circuits that repeatedly visited the same places (Espinosa et al. 2013). Cerro León 3, Chorrillo Malo 2, Cerro Castillo, and other sites with Middle Holocene occupations located south of

Figure 5.14 View of Baguales Range, near Cerro León, Argentina. Photo courtesy Karen Borrazzo.

the Santa Cruz river present technological diversity, including different flaking procedures like the Levallois technique (Borrazzo 2008; Franco et al. 2019; Langlais and Morello 2009). All these sites are routinely associated with adaptations focused on guanacos using long-distance weapons like projectile points (Franco et al. 1999; Langlais and Morello 2009; Legoupil 2009). The importance of guanaco is confirmed even for sites where burial activities were privileged, like Río Bote 1 (Franco et al. 2017b). Evidence of the consumption of guanaco meat and marrow was identified at this site (Fiel 2019).

The Pali Aike Volcanic Field was extensively occupied during the Middle Holocene. A number of cave sites, such as Las Buitreras, Don Ariel, Cueva La Carlota 1, Fell Cave, Pali Aike, or Cueva de los Chingues, present a diversity of human activities, showing the operation of logistical systems, sometimes involving a few resources from the oceanic coast (Bird 1988; Campan et al. 2007; Martin 2013; Massone 1981; Nami 1999; Sanguinetti de Bórmida 1976). A diversity of projectile point shapes was identified, but stemmed points are the most abundant (Banegas et al. 2014; Bird 1988). Interestingly, not all these sites are located near water sources, suggesting either important changes in water availability through time or a complex settlement pattern. Open-air sites like Potrok Aike 11 and Tom Gould, located near

The Middle Holocene

lagoons, were also identified (Borrero et al. 2013; Massone 1989–1990). The importance of guanacos is reiterated at all these sites, complemented by the minimal presence of birds and rodents.

Ephemeral Middle Holocene occupations are recorded at several sites in the Última Esperanza area that are also focused on guanaco for subsistence but complemented with huemul and smaller resources like mollusks (Borrero and Martin 2018). Sites such as Alero Quemado, Alero del Diablo, and Alero Pedro Cárdenas indicate this particular subsistence mix, emphasizing terrestrial resources complemented by limited use of the coastal resources. Most of these Middle Holocene occupations occurred at new loci created as a result of a process of human recolonization of Última Esperanza and the near Andean southern zone in general. This process appears to be recorded at places such as Chorrillo Malo 2, Cerro León 3, and Ponsonby, all of them located very close to the forest-steppe ecotone. A long history of redundant use of rock shelter Chorrillo Malo 2 and nearby available resources attests to increasing knowledge of the region (Otaola and Franco 2008). At rock shelter Cerro León 3, a site located slightly above 400 masl, the earlier occupations occurred when a sub-arbustive steppe characterized the area (Mancini et al. 2011), and it also shows a history of increasing knowledge of the local resources (L'Heureux and Borrazzo 2013). In contrast, Ponsonby is an open-air site discovered by the French Mission in the 1960s (Laming-Emperaire 1968). Lithic projectile points led to alternative interpretations of terrestrial or littoral hunter-gatherers (Legoupil 2003; Piana and Orquera 2007). Notably, several thumbnail end scrapers made of chalcedony were recovered (Pigeot 2003: 149), which were interpreted as curated tools transported from the east (Schidlowsky 2003: 167–169). Thus, these three sites are somehow related to the dispersal of terrestrial hunter-gatherers from the east.

FINAL REMARKS

In general terms, the archaeological evidence in the Pampas region shows a cultural continuity between the Early to Middle Holocene population and intraregional differentiation. This would be the result of evolutionary and historical processes that during these periods produce different adaptive patterns. Most researchers (López Mazz 2001; Martínez et al. 2015; Mazzanti et al. 2015; Politis 2008; Politis and Madrid 2001) interpret the main changes that occurred in the Middle Holocene in the Pampas and the Campos as the result of transformation in several dimensions that occurred within the Early Holocene populations. However, not all areas of the Pampas were inhabited, at least not permanently. Although sampling bias and taphonomic factors might have affected the currently available information, the primary demographic densities are in the Interserrana and Tandilia areas, as in the Late Pleistocene and Early Holocene, and in second place the CPD, southern, and the Salado-Chadileuvú-Curacó areas. North of Tandilia (the Salado Depression, the Rolling Pampa, and the northeastern areas) human signal was almost null during this period. What we see during the Middle Holocene is a vector of human density, from east to west, with the Interserrana and Tandilia areas more densely populated and the western and southern areas with less density. The current information makes it difficult to assess if the lack of evidence north to Tandilia is a sampling bias or the result of very low population density.

The Middle Holocene archaeological record suggests an economy based on the guanaco and the Pampas deer, plains viscacha, and armadillos and rodents as secondary resources. Álvarez (2014b) suggests that for the Interserrana area, hunting was generalized during the Early Holocene but in the first part of the Middle Holocene became specialized in guanaco toward ~ 4500 BP. As in Patagonia, greater rhea remains are not abundant in the sites and are restricted to the lower bones, which, beyond taphonomic processes, suggests a limited consumption. A few species are found only in some sites: *Tolypeutes*, Pampean fox, jaguar, and other species, suggesting that their hunting was occasional or exceptional. Except for the freshwater fish (perch) consumed in the Colorado River delta, all diets from inland people are terrestrial, but some men of AS2 have a marine complement. Also, with the exception of one individual from AS2, only on the coast of the southern area and the southwestern extreme of the Interserrana seashore was a marine diet found.

Technology shows few chronological changes along this period but instead some intraregional variation. Medium-sized triangular stemless points, probably used in projectiles thrown by atlatl, bola stones, as well as grinding stones are the basic hunting and processing tools. The double-sided, amygdaloid, unifacial, plano-convex scrapers, most of them made of SBG orthoquartzite, seem to be the most popular and idiosyncratic artifact in this period and in the following. Experimental and micro-wear studies performed by Leipus (2004) in a large Pampean sample show that the edges are stable and last a long time, making it a very versatile, durable, and efficient tool. All these advantages transformed the double-sided scraper into a ubiquitous and characteristic artifact for the Pampean hunter-gatherers. Small scrapers with frontal and extended edges, made of both SBG orthoquartzite and phtanite, are also ubiquitous. Technology is unifacial and generates a variety of marginal retouched flakes. Bifacial technology is restricted almost exclusively for the mid-sized triangular projectile points, and only a few instruments, such as knives, show bifacial retouches. Bone tools were also used but to a much lesser extent and with more limited functions. However, in the CPD, these instruments seem to be more frequently used than in the rest of the Pampas (Álvarez 2014a), which would have been a strategy for coping with the lack of toolstones in the area. The wood artifacts recovered in exceptional condition at the La Olla site and the intensive use of lithic artifacts on wood (Leipus 2004, 2016) warn about the possibility of ghost technology, which formed a significant component of the artifact assemblages but did not survive due to preservation conditions.

There are four significant innovations that occurred in the Middle Holocene. First, although the SBG orthoquartzite quarries were probably exploited since the Late Pleistocene, it is just in this period when chronological data place them between 5100 and 4000 BP, suggesting the onset of a period of intense exploitation (Flegenheimer et al. 1999). As we have shown in this book, the SBG orthoquartzite was the most important toolstone in eastern Pampa and was widely circulated across the whole region. Second, it was during the Middle Holocene when coastal adaptation began. Although the exploitation of seashore cobbles was detected in the Late Pleistocene, it is in this period that the consumption of sea mammals and fishes is documented as well as their incidence in the diet of the southern coast populations. Third, a variety of burial practices emerged. This includes primary and secondary burials, redundant spaces for inhumations, and rich funerary goods. And fourth, in the ideational realm, carnivores' teeth (foxes, jaguar, smaller felids, etc.) started to be used for symbolic and ceremonial purposes, indicating the sacred or spiritual character of these animals.

Most of the recovered evidence in terrestrial or aquatic habitats in Patagonia displays a dynamic of changing adaptations, sometimes involving both habitats. Temporal variation in the utilization of resources is manifested everywhere (De Nigris 2004; Zangrando 2009a), which in some cases appears to be related to an increase in knowledge of the environment. The variability of procurement and exploitation of animals is high, with a repertoire of lithic weapons that goes from projectile points to bolas. There is even evidence of possible scavenging of guanacos at mires, peat bogs, and other places where animals can be trapped. Important variations in lithic technology were also observed in the extensive steppes of Patagonia. This variation goes from the widespread presence of blades to incorporating new flaking procedures (Charlin 2009b; Cueto et al. 2020; Franco 2002a; Hermo and Magnin 2012; Langlais and Morello 2009). In general terms, it can be defended that the intensity of occupation of many sites increased in comparison with the Early Holocene (Borrero 1993). Redundancy in the occupation of sites is one of the main reasons, giving the impression that special places were incorporated within long-range human circuits. Potential alternation in the use of extensive portions of land related to volcanic activity is inferred from occupational gaps. This dynamic panorama is probably related to demographic changes that resulted in exploring new niches near the Andean Cordillera and the oceanic coasts. It also resulted in increased demarcation of territories (Borrero 1994–1995; Miotti 2006a). Interestingly, most of these cultural trajectories are nonlinear and are often interrupted not only by climatic or ecological hazards but also by the social tensions created by the use of more and more restricted habitats. These tensions derived from a continuously renovated map of changing or even restricted access to known resources, the close presence of friendly or hostile neighbors, and changes in the abundance and availability of resources.

CHAPTER 6

THE LATE HOLOCENE DIVERSIFICATION (~ 4200 CAL BP TO ~ 400 CAL BP; ~ 3800 BP TO ~ 400 BP)

During the Late Holocene time, regional differentiation, which became visible during the Middle Holocene, produced a wide variety of historical trajectories and adaptive patterns in the Pampas and Patagonia. It is clear that around 4000 BP human populations were selectively using all the diverse, available habitats. In this period, the archaeological visibility increased significantly, a fact that also suggests a rise in the population density of both regions (see discussion in Chapter 7).

Based on different proxies, more humid conditions were established after ~ 3000 BP, although permanent fresh water sources were always scarce in the western Pampa. Several significant cultural changes occurred during this period in the Pampas, such as a reduction in residential mobility and the development of wide – supra-regional – interaction networks, which, along with some important innovations, such as pottery, bow and arrow, and, in the northeastern area, small-scale horticulture, suggest the development of a process of economic intensification in several areas (Berón 2004; Bonomo et al. 2011a; González 2005; Loponte et al. 2004; Martínez and Mackie 2003–2004; Politis et al. 2001). Also, an emergent social complexity occurred in the Middle and Lower Paraná and Lower Uruguay Rivers (Politis and Bonomo 2012, 2018).

In the Pampas (excluding the northeastern area), Martínez and Gutiérrez (2004) have defined a pattern of diversification and intensification of areal economies based on the zooarchaeological record. This record shows an important taxonomic diversity and richness, which may have changed around 1000 BP due to the establishment of the current ecosystems. Among 72 genera recorded in the faunal assemblages, 22 were exploited. This number has increased with new zooarchaeological research in the last decade (i.e., Álvarez and Salemme 2015; Day Pilaría 2018; Salemme et al. 2012, Scheifler 2019; Stoessel and Alcaráz 2017). During this time, the main subsistence strategies of hunter-gatherers in the Pampas vary from exploiting the

The Late Holocene Diversification

xerophytic forest in the west and the open grasslands plains in the central-east to the marine seashore and fluvial environments in the east.

Also, another economic pattern emerged in the northeast: the cultivation of some species (mainly maize, bean, and squash) in the Paraná and Uruguay River areas at least some 1500 years ago (Bonomo et al. 2011b; Colobig et al. 2018). Finally, the expansion of the Guaraní into the northeastern part of the region introduced a new socioeconomic form a few centuries before the European conquest (Brochado 1984; Bonomo et al. 2015; Loponte et al. 2011). Except for some archaeological entities proposed for the northeastern area, such as Goya-Malabrigo (also called Ribereños Plásticos by Serrano 1972) and the Guaraní, no other "archaeological cultures" are under consideration in the region.

There was a strong environmental contrast between habitats near the Andes and those located in the eastern steppes in Patagonia. This contrast was critical in molding human adaptations on the southern part of the continent and was accentuated by changes in the position and intensity of the westerlies (Mancini et al. 2011; Moreno et al. 2012). Models of winter stress showed an important increase in seasonality near the Andes, a situation that hindered human exploitation during winters (Pallo 2012). It is possible that cold winters were behind the patterns of late human dispersal toward the Andes (Borrero 2004), resulting in the punctuated use of those relatively harsher environments (Méndez et al. 2019). On the other hand, low annual rainfall and few sources of year-round water in the eastern steppes tethered human groups to the river valleys (Mayr et al. 2007; Pérez et al. 2016). This shortage of water limited connectivity between populations occupying different hydrological basins and, as the warmer Holocene unfolded, probably pushed populations toward the more humid western environments. This process could have been behind the early exploration of Última Esperanza near the end of the Pleistocene when the eastern plains were beginning to become dryer and warmer. Human western dispersal culminated with the occupation of places above 600 masl in Aisén, the Perito Moreno Park, the Baguales range, and some plateaus (Aschero et al. 2007; Belardi and Goñi 2006; Borrazzo 2008; Franco and Borrero 2000; Franco et al. 1999; Goñi et al. 2011–2012; Méndez et al. 2019). Indeed, some of these places have been seasonally exploited since the Early Holocene, but most of them were regularly visited only during the Late Holocene (Dellepiane and Cassiodoro 2019; Goñi et al. 2014a; Morano Büchner et al. 2009). The human settlement of mountains and plateaus resulted from a gradual process of advance and retreat that began during the Early Holocene and gained momentum during the Late Holocene. The Strobel plateau case is key to understanding the use of these high-altitude places since it was convincingly argued that it was the locus for the aggregation of populations (Belardi and Goñi 2006). Similarly, in the highlands of Northwest Patagonia, there is another probable case of convergence of human populations (Romero Villanueva 2019; Romero Villanueva et al. 2020). Both cases have in common the use of rock paintings or engravings to recognize the presence of people from different places.

Growing populations during the Late Holocene were not using the interior fluvial basins homogeneously (Pérez et al. 2016). How real the increase was in the frequency and diversity of archaeological materials during this period is not yet thoroughly studied, and the possibility remains that it only reflects the age of the surfaces on which the materials rest or other biases (Holdaway et al. 2008). Slow dispersal of people was suggested for south-central Patagonia, including the circulation across the plateaus, a process necessarily tethered to water sources (Goñi et al. 2004; Goñi et al. 2014a; Stine 1994), although this relationship was not confirmed by a recent study (Lange and Tchilinguirian 2019). However, the concentration of people near lake basins such as Posadas/Pueyrredón, Cardiel, San Martín or Argentino during the Late Holocene is well attested (Carballo Marina and Ercolano 2003; Cassiodoro et al. 2013; Espinosa et al. 2013; Franco et al. 1999; Guráieb 2004). These occupational sequences are almost always discontinuous. The area of Lago Argentino was totally or partially abandoned ca. 1000 BP (Franco and Borrero 2001). Was this a result of disinterest in using places far from eastern occupational nodes? Interestingly, the few known sites younger than 1000 BP were located mainly in new places, for example, in the plateau between Lago Argentino and Lago Viedma (Franco and Borrero 1996). There is simply no pattern of reuse of previously occupied sites, which is an important mark of discontinuity in the human occupation of the land. Similarly, complex occupational histories are recorded in other western lake basins (Belardi et al. 2009; Espinosa et al. 2013). This diverse panorama indicates that a number of cultural trajectories were interwoven on the Patagonian steppes.

THE PAMPAS

The hunter-gatherers of the xerophytic forest are well represented in the upper level of the Casa de Piedra site, the Tapera Moreira locality, and several localities of the Lower Río Colorado River (Figure 6.1). Faunal assemblages indicate that guanaco was the main prey, while Pampas deer, armadillos, and greater rhea were secondary resources. These prey are well distributed along the region, although there are areal nuances; they are basically the same as in the Middle Holocene, which shows a continuity in the exploitation of the faunal resources. The abundance of grinding stones suggests that fruits of the xerophytic forest (*caldén* [*Prosopis caldenia*], *chañar* [*Geoffrea decorticans*], and *algarrobo* [*Prosopis flexuosa*]) might have been consumed intensively. The upper level of Casa de Piedra indicates stronger similarities with the North Patagonian forages during the Late Holocene time (Gradin 1984). Close to

The Late Holocene Diversification

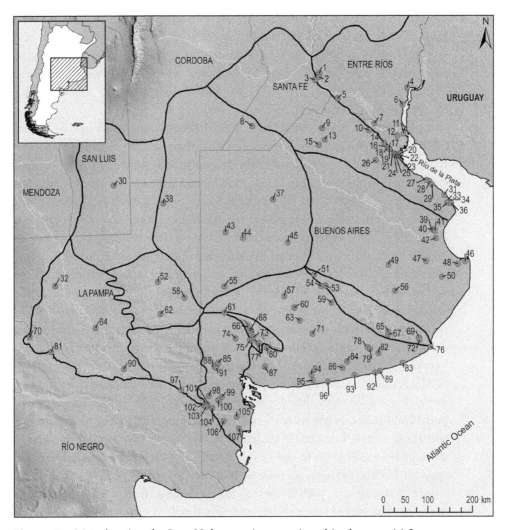

Figure 6.1 Map showing the Late Holocene sites mentioned in the text. (1) Los Tres Cerros; (2) Cerro Isla Grande de Los Marinos; (3) Playa Mansa; (4) Cerro Boaris; (5) Cerro Grande del Paraná Pavón; (6) Puerto Landa; (7) Isla Lechiguanas; (8) Laguna del Doce; (9) Fontezuelas; (10) Cañada Honda; (11) Túmulo II del Brazo Largo; (12) Túmulo 1 and 3 of Paraná Guazú; (13) Meguay; (14) Túmulo de Campana; (15) Hunter; (16) Río Luján; (17) Las Vizcacheras; (18) Anahí; (19) Laguna Grande; (20) Arroyo Fredes; (21) Garín; (22) Arroyo Guazunambí; (23) La Bellaca 2; (24) La Bellaca 1; (25) Arroyo Sarandí; (26) Cañada de Rocha; (27) La Higuera; (28) La Norma; (29) La Maza I; (30) Loma de los Pedernales; (31) Las Marías; (32) Poitahue; (33) San Clemente II; (34) San Clemente III; (35) San Clemente I; (36) San Clemente IV; (37) Laguna de Los Pampas; (38) Chadilauquen; (39) La Guillerma 1; (40) La Guillerma 2; (41) La Guillerma 3; (42) La Salada; (43) Huencú Nazar; (44) Laguna Chica; (45) Laguna Cabeza de Buey; (46) Divisadero; (47) San Lorenzo; (48) La Loma; (49) La Colorada; (50) Los Molles; (51) Cerro Curico; (52) Cueva Salamanca; (53) Calera; (54) Empalme Querandíes; (55) El Venado; (56) Pessi; (57) Escuela Agrícola; (58) Laguna Chilihué; (59) Laguna La Barrancosa; (60) Fortín Necochea; (61) Laguna de Puan; (62) La Tigra; (63) Laguna del Trompa;

this site, in the limit of the Pampas region, pottery of the Vergel-Valdivia type from Central-South Chile was recovered at the Rinconda Giles site (~ 700–300 BP) (Berón 2004). In addition, burial practices were registered in two neighboring sites, Puesto Hernández (~ 900 BP) and Médano Petroquímica (between 419 and 363 BP) (Bernardi et al. 2020; Bottini et al. 2020; Mendonça et al. 2010).

In the Salado-Chadileuvú-Curacó area, the multicomponent sites of Tapera Moreira are representative of the cultural sequence of the area. The Cumbre subcomponent (~ 3500–3000 BP) contains end scrapers, cores, a few unstemmed projectile points, and burnt guanaco bones, while the medium component (~ 2100–1800 BP) includes bone tools as well as abundant end scrapers and unstemmed triangular projectile points (Berón 2004; Salemme and Berón 2004). The upper component (~ 1200–500 BP) reveals a multiplicity of pottery types, the coexistence of medium and thicker stemless projectile points with thin and small projectile points, and engraved plates. Obsidians from distant sources such as El Maule, Cerro Huenul, and Portada Covunco (Neuquén province) were recorded in all levels. The exploitation of these rocks, together with the eastern Pampa orthoquartzites, indicates interaction networks that connected the area with distant regions (Berón et al. 2018; Giesso et al. 2008; Stern and Aguerre 2013).

Also located in this area is the outstanding burial site Chenque 1. A complex stone elliptical structure, known as Chenque 1 site, with at least two levels of burials inhumated between 1030 and 370 BP, is an outstanding record for the area (Berón 2018; Luna 2008). At least 216 individuals have been unearthed in the Upper Level and 89 in the Lower Level. The structure is formed of three types of burials: primary, secondary, and a type called *disposition*. The latter consisted of skeletons, partially articulated, with the anatomic units reorganized (e.g., the skull placed inside the thoracic cavity). This strongly structured place for inhumation has been interpreted as the result of the intensive reuse of a particular locus to enforce its sacredness. The use of this place as a cemetery

---

Figure 6.1 (*cont.*) (64) Chenque 1; (65) El Aljarafe; (66) La Sofía; (67) Cerro La China; (68) Santa Marta; (69) Cueva Tixi; (70) Médano Petroquímica; (71) Laguna Tres Reyes; (72) La Amalia 4, Lobería 1, Cueva el Abra y Abrigo la Grieta; (73) Alero Corpus Christi; (74) Laguna Los Chilenos; (75) Cueva Cerro Manitoba; (76) Alfar; (77) Cueva Florencio; (78) Zanjón Seco; (79) Paso Otero; (80) La Toma; (81) Casa de Piedra; (82) La Horqueta; (83) Túmulo de Malacara y Nutria Mansa 1; (84) Cortaderas; (85) San Martín 1; (86) Laguna Las Toscas; (87) Paso Mayor; (88) Laguna Chasicó; (89) Punta Negra; (90) Tapera Moreira; (91) Arroyo Chasicó 1; (92) Punta Florida; (93) El Guanaco; (94) La Represa; (95) Quequén Salado 1; (96) El Caracolero; (97) La Enriqueta; (98) El Caldén; (99) Loma Ruiz; (100) Campo Monaldi; (101) El Puma; (102) Paso Alsina 1; (103) Zoko Andi; (104) La Petrona; (105) La Primavera; (106) Loma de Los Morteros; (107) El Tigre.

The Late Holocene Diversification

also would have functioned as a strategy to legitimate access to certain area resources (Berón 2004). Various funerary goods, including shell beads and metal objects, were deposited in the burials. Interestingly, the early burials with signs of violence (e.g., projectile points in the skeleton) have oxygen isotope values and artifacts that suggest a trans-cordilleran origin (Barberena et al. 2015; Berón 2018; Berón and Carrera Aizpitarte 2019), while the burials with signals of violence from the later period show oxygen isotopic values related to local environment ranges, including the western Pampa, the southern end of Mendoza, and northern and eastern Neuquén (Berón 2018)

In the Transversal Valleys, the archaeological record is similar to the CPD and Interserrana areas (Berón et al. 2015; Curtoni 2007) but with some particularities. For example, artificial cranial deformation was recovered in the Chillihué lake in a human skeleton, dated to 1930 BP with a tabular-erect (*planolambdica*) variety (Berón et al. 2015). In the center-east fringe, sites are mostly surficial in the border of lakes or in dunes, with few human burials and significant use of orthoquartzite and phtanite (e.g., the La Tigra, Bajo de Atreucó, and El Carmel sites), to make characteristic instruments similar to the CPD, Interserrana, and Tandilia areas. The typical double-sided amygdaloid scrapers on orthoquartzite are frequent (e.g., Phagouapé collection). In a few sites (e.g., Laguna del Fondo), the use of rocks from the western areas, such as the chert from the El Fresco Plateau, predominates. Regarding this area, Berón (2004) has proposed that these would have functioned as corridors of social communication between the populations settled in the eastern and western Pampa.

In the Close Basin area at the middle course of the Colorado River, La Enriqueta and Don Aldo 1 sites were excavated. The former contains human burials (MNI [minimum number of individuals] = 9) dated to 1005 BP (Carrera Aizpitarte et al. 2013), while the latter has been interpreted as a residential camp where one individual was buried (Prates et al. 2006). A notable finding is the fixed mortars of Cerro de Los Viejos. The set of artifacts detected in these hills comprises 11 mortars, two grinders, and some associated features (Paez et al. 2020). Some mortars are interconnected with channels carved in the rock, which suggests that they also could have been used for managing and storing liquids. These mortars are interpreted as part of a transgenerational enterprise that could encourage the continued occupation of this place over time by promoting feelings of appropriation of space. Although the mortars have not been dated, most cultural manifestations recorded in their surroundings are placed in the Late Holocene, including a human skeleton (Cerro de los Viejos 1 [CDV1]) dated to 3035 BP (Paez et al. 2020).

In the southern area, the bulk of information comes from the Lower Colorado River. Several sites were dated to the early Late Holocene (~ 2900–1100 BP): La Primavera, Loma Ruiz 1, Zoko Andi 1 (lower component), El Caldén, and El Puma (Martínez 2017). In all these sites, subsistence was based on the typical Pampean prey plus tinamids (Alcaráz 2017; Stoessel and Alcaráz 2017). Also, a particular type of decoration, an incised diagonal-line design, is characteristic of this area as well as of the Salado-Chadiluevú-Curacó and the Close Basins (Borges Vaz 2017). At around 1000 BP, some significant changes occurred in the area. The diversity of the exploited species is much greater than previously, and some rodents, perch, and bivalves are incorporated into the diet (Alcaráz 2017; Stoessel and Alcaraz 2017), which would be the result of an intensification process (Stoessel and Martínez 2014). Main sites of this second period are El Tigre, Zoko Andi 1 (upper component), San Antonio, La Petrona, and Paso Alsina 1. Settlements become much more redundantly occupied, and between ~ 1400 and 250 BP, there was great variability in the mortuary practices performed (Flensborg et al. 2017). In this sense, secondary modalities were registered in reoccupied residential camps (Zoko Andi 1 and La Petrona) in formal burial areas (Paso Alsina 1, Martínez et al. 2012).

These sites, as well as other sites, such as El Túmulo de Malacara (Politis et al. 2011; Vignati 1960), El Guanaco 1 (Mazzia et al. 2004), and Laguna Tres Reyes (Madrid and Barrientos 2000), show the great variability in mortuary practices in the Pampas during the Late Holocene and the existence of well-defined formal inhumation areas. In this period, multiple primary and secondary burials, formed by tens of individuals with intense skeletal manipulation (e.g., Paso Alsina, Chenque 1, Médano Petroquímica), appeared for the first time.

Other Late Holocene sites, recorded in the southern area, are located in blowouts in eolian corridors such as Campo Monaldi 1 and 2 (1602 BP, Martínez 2017), in the borders of the Chasicó Creek (Catella 2014) such as San Martín 1 (2890 and 2526 BP, Oliva et al. 1991, 2010), or in the beaches of lakes such as Laguna Chasicó 1 to 9 (Catella 2014), Villa Iris S1 (Oliva et al. 2006), and Los Chilenos 1 and 2 (dated to 606 and 2323 BP, respectively). This variety of environments indicates a more flexible pattern of occupation and a denser population compared with the previous period.

The Ventania hill range was the second most important source of toolstone after Tandilia (see Chapter 3). However, a few quarries have been detected: Laguna de Puán (Oliva and Barrientos 1988), the headwaters of the Naposta creek (Oliva 2000), and the outskirts of the Abra de Saavedra (Oliva and Moirano 1997). The main procurement places were probably the secondary deposits in the foothills and the heads of the creeks, where a variety of pebbles are readily available. Some potential sources were identified, such as the Arroyo Saudade (Catella 2014) and the conglomerates of the La Lola Formation (Catella et al. 2017). Metaquartzite, orthoquartzite, and rhyolite were the most exploited toolstones, although the first two predominate only locally and are scarce in most other areas of the Pampas. On the contrary, rhyolite traveled longer distances and has been detected in many areas: in the south, Interserrana, Tandilia, CPD, and probably in the western Pampa.

The Late Holocene Diversification 201

Systematic excavations are limited to La Sofia S1 (1595 BP), La Montaña S1 (700 and 385 BP), and Laguna de Púan (Catella 2014; Oliva 1991, 2000; Oliva and Moirano 2001). A core of rhyolite and large bifacial artifacts in a small area in La Montaña S1 suggests that they could be part of a cache. Another cache of rhyolite was recovered at the Laguna de Púan site 1. It was formed by one core (9 kg), four nodules, and eight artifacts. There is only one date, 3330 BP, for the locality, obtained from a secondary human burial found on the lake beach. It is not clear yet if there is a relationship between both kinds of findings.

A remarkable record in Ventania is the presence of paintings in caves and rock shelters where some 40 sites have been detected in the western ranges of the system, in the Sierra de La Ventana and Sierra de Curamalal (e.g., Gruta de Los Espíritus, Cerro Manitoba, Cueva Florencio, Santa Marta; Consens and Oliva 1999; Madrid and Oliva 1994; Perez Amat et al. 1985). More than 90% are abstract motifs, with a high proportion of red geometric-rectilinear designs (Consens and Oliva 1999; Oliva 2000; Oliva and Algrain 2005). The few figurative motifs recorded were mainly schematic representations of anthropomorphs, human faces (Holmberg 1884) or masks (Oliva 2013), and greater rhea footprints. This rock art has been interpreted in different ways. First, it was assigned to a "stylistic modality": abstract-geometric, simple related to the "grecas" (frets) style of Patagonia (Madrid and Oliva 1994). Styles named A, B, C, D, and E were defined and compared with neighboring areas (Consens and Oliva 1999). Later, from a semiotic perspective, this rock was explained as a way for encoded communication, a sort of "vocabulary" for the transmission of certain messages (Panizza et al. 2010). On the other hand, some motifs have been interpreted from a "neuropsychiatric" perspective (Lewis Williams and Dowson 1988) and were considered "shamanic art" resulting from altered stages of consciousness produced by psychotropic drugs (Oliva and Algrain 2004). Although not clearly supported, these authors also proposed that this "shamanic art" functioned as territorial markers (Oliva and Algrain 2004: 59). There are two exceptional motifs. One is the three human handprints in the Santa Marta locality (Perez Amat et al. 1985), while the other is a figurative/schematic representation found in Cueva Florencio interpreted by Madrid and Oliva (1994) as a European ship and later and more specifically as a corvette (Oliva and Panizza 2016). Although this interpretation cannot be ruled out, it remains highly speculative. There is not any date clearly associated with the Ventania paintings, but based on stylistic similarities with the rock art of Patagonia and with other decorated elements (such as engraved eggshells and plaquettes), they have been broadly placed in the Late Holocene (Curtoni 2006), and more specifically in the last 1,500 years (Oliva 2000, 2006).

In the southeastern sector of Tandilia, several paintings display abstract and geometric designs similar to those at Ventania (Mazzanti 1993; Mazzanti and Valverde 2003). Main sites includes Haras Los Robles, Lobería 1, Los Difuntos 1 and 2, La Cautiva S1, Pancha, Antú, and Cueva El Abra. There are some

Figure 6.2 Cerro Curicó rock art. Complex design, related to the ones painted on *quillangos*, the traditional blanket made with guanaco skins by Patagonian Indians. The photo has been processed with DStretch by Augusto Oliván.

anthropomorphic motifs, including a schematic human figure throwing a bola stone and greater rhea footprints (Mazzanti 1993). For Mazzanti and Valverde (2003: 313), most of this rock art is placed in strategic locations, close to critical resources, and would function as territorial control. In the northwestern extreme of Tandilia, in the Curicó hill, a complex design related to the ones painted on *quillangos* (the traditional blanket made with guanaco skins by Patagonian Indians) was recorded (Madrid et al. 2000) (Figure 6.2). This diversity indicates the complexity and the diachronicity of the rock art in the Pampas, some of which were probably made in very late pre-Hispanic times or even early colonial periods.

In western Pampa, there are only two groups of rock paintings: one is Salamanca Cave in the Transversal Valleys (Curtoni 2007; Gradin 1975), and the other is the Lihué Calel hills (Berón 2004; Gradin 1975; Zetti and Casamiquela 1967). Both places have abstract motifs painted in red, white, and black. Some of these motifs differ from those in Tandilia and Ventania and display geometric figures, including staggered, comb-like designs and curves in a C form. In Lihué Calel, there are few anthropomorphs and stylized zoomorphic figures. Some of these motifs have been interpreted as the representation of shamanic spiritual trips (Llamazares 2004). For Curtoni (2006), these sites are related to Tandilia and Ventania and are the result of a shared cosmovision. They are also placed in the Late Holocene.

Although with local nuances, many sites testified to the population increase and the occupation of all Pampean environments. One key sector was the Quequén Grande River, where several sites has been recorded: Paso Otero 3; Zanjón Seco 1 and 2, La Horqueta 1 and 2, and others. Paso Otero 1, a site repeatedly mentioned as having anthropogenic piles of guanaco bones (Johnson et al. 1997; Politis et al. 1991), is now interpreted as a natural bone accumulation due to water transport (Gutiérrez and Kaufmann 2004).

The Zanjón Seco locality is formed by a series of residential campsites located on the border of the Quequén Grande River. In site 2, the oldest Pampean pottery, dated to ~ 3000 BP, was recovered (Figure 6.3). Sherds are decorated with incised complex geometric motifs, indicating that decoration was present at the beginning of pottery in the region (Di Prado 2015; Politis et al. 2001). In the Zanjón Seco 3 (1440 BP), a formal disposal structure made almost exclusively of hundreds of guanaco bones was recorded (Tonni and Politis 1986). These types of features are exceptional in the Pampas and are

Figure 6.3 Incised pottery from Zanjón Seco 2. This is the earliest pottery in the Pampas, dated ~ 3000 BP.

interpreted as part of the residential camps, in the context of more planned and more prolonged occupation, with an economy oriented toward the intense exploitation of guanaco.

Other interesting features are the combustion structures, which became more abundant in the Late Holocene. Hearths are rare in Pampas and were found only in caves in Tandilia (Mazzanti et al. 2015) and in few Late Holocene open-air sites such as Laguna XX, La Barracuda, Laguna el Trompa (Crivelli Montero et al. 1994), and Laguna El Venado (dated to 2700 BP; Oliva and Solomita Banfi 2017). Bones of guanaco and Pampas deer were used as fuel, which could be the result of the lack or scarcity of wood (Crivelli Montero 1994; Joly et al. 2005).

The Huencú Nazar site, in the CPD, contains a high density of hearths, some of them probably functioning simultaneously, which were fueled with guanaco bones (Scheifler 2020). These hearths, dated to ~ 3000 BP, are associated with abundant grinding stones, bola stones, a few small-sized triangular projectile points, and a great variation of flaked artifacts. Two caches of orthoquartzite were also detected on the site. All evidence suggests the planning of the settlement and longer stays, as in the Quequén Grande Basin (Martínez 1999).

Most sites are located on the borders of lakes, rivers, and creeks. In the Interserrana area they share the same basic bone and lithic assemblages, showing a common adaptive pattern and technological organization: La Represa (3430 and 2110 BP; March et al. 2011); Las Brusquillas 1 (~ 3300 BP), 2 (~ 1800 BP), and 3 (2830 BP; Massigoge 2011, 2012; Massigoge et al. 2018); Cortaderas (Massigoge 2009); Puente de Fierro (Frontini 2012); Fortín Necochea (Units A and B) and Laguna del Trompa (Crivelli Montero et al. 1994); Quequén Salado 2 (1720 BP; Madrid et al. 2002); Laguna Tres Reyes (dated between ~ 2500 and 1800 BP; Madrid et al. 1991, 2002; Salemme and Madrid 2007); Laguna La Barrancosa 1 (dated 1670 BP; Messineo 2011); Empalme Querandíes 1 (Messineo et al. 2013); Hangar (Álvarez 2020); La Toma (dated between 3523 and 995 BP; Álvarez and Salemme 2015; Madrid and Politis 1991; Politis 1984); and Laguna La Larga (Madrid et al. 2002).

During the Late Holocene, guanaco was the primary food resource in all areas, except in the northeast and the Salado Depression (Politis and Salemme 1989). Pampas deer, armadillos, rodents, and greater rhea were consumed as secondary resources in these areas. The guanaco population started a retraction toward the west and became scarce in the east at around 1000 BP due to the environmental change derived from the Medieval Thermal Maximum (Politis and Pedrotta 2006; Politis et al. 2011). When Europeans arrived, guanaco inhabited only Ventania (Figure 1.4), the south, and the western Pampas.

At the same time, after ca. 1500 BP there was a southern expansion into the Pampas region of subtropical fauna, such as the wild cavy (*Cavia aperea*) and the armadillo (*Chaetophractus villosus*) (Quintana and Mazzanti 2001; Tonni

The Late Holocene Diversification

et al. 2001; Vizcaíno et al. 1995). In this period, subsistence was regionally diverse. For example, in the Tandilia hills, lizards (*Tupinambis* cf. *merianae*), coypu, and some rodents (Cavidae) became important resources, along with the occasional consumption of catfish (*Rhamdia* cf. *sapo* and *Corydoras* cf. *paleatus*) (Quintana at al. 2002). Quintana and Mazzanti (2001) proposed that the intensification process involved changing the use, selection, and incorporation of small animals with shorter reproductive cycles and high birth rates, such as lizards and wild cavies. For these authors, the amplification in the diet would be related to the decline of the guanaco populations. On the other hand, both marine and freshwater fish (perch) were exploited in the Colorado River delta (Stoesel and Alcaráz 2017)

The lithic technology is represented in a basic unifacial tool kit made of quartzite, phtanite, and chert. The main types included the typical double-sided amygdaloid scrapers, short-ended scrapers, bola stones, and ground stones. However, some new artifacts began to be used. Finely made small to very small triangular stemless projectile points showed up in this period, suggesting the spread of bows and arrows after 3000 BP. This date is associated in the Calera site (Politis et al. 2007; Figure 6.4) with a projectile point interpreted as being an arrowhead (Kaufmann et al. 2021). Although there is a close association between the point and the dated sample, this age has to be taken with caution because it is earlier than the dispersion of bows and arrows in South America and it is still unique. The solid record of arrowheads appeared later and had a strong signal after 1200 BP (Barros et al. 2018). In three rock shelters, Alero Curicó (412 and 385 BP; Pedrotta et al. 2009), Lobería 1 (883 BP and 158 BP; Mazzanti 2006), and El Abra-Upper Component (958 BP; Mazzanti 2006), many arrow points, complete and broken, appeared concentrated in restricted spaces. The latter two sites contained approximately 300 points each (Diana Mazzanti, pers. comm.)

One exceptional site, Calera, in northwestern Tandilia, is formed by the purportedly filling of four pits with a great variety of materials. These elements include marine shells, a variety of rocks from many different sources, incised pottery with anthropomorphic schematic designs, as well as prestige technology (carved stone plaquettes, a bezoar shaped like a phallus, shell beads, etc.; Figure 6.4). The bone remains recovered in the infill of the pits suggest that feast food remains would have been intentionally buried, a frequent practice among the Mapuche Indians in the Pampas. The deposit is interpreted as being formed as the result of rituals carried out between 3390 and 1748 BP. These ceremonies and feasts included items and decorative motifs from different places, suggesting several events of band aggregation during the Late Holocene (Álvarez 2008; Di Prado 2013; Politis et al. 2005).

Plain and incised pottery is also present south of the Salado River Depression after ~ 3000 BP, although in low frequencies (Di Prado 2018; Politis 2005). The origin of this technological innovation is not clear, although

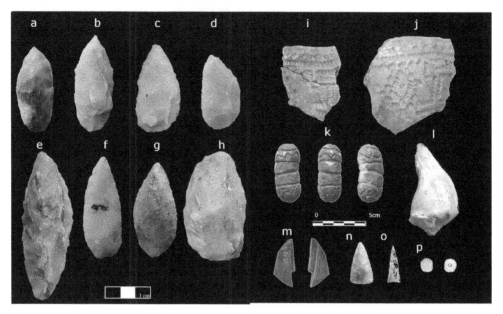

Figure 6.4 Artifacts from the Calera site. (a–h) Double-sided scrapers; (i and j) decorated pottery with anthropomorphic schematic designs made with drag and jab technique; (k) phallus-like bezoar; (l) *Adelomedon* shell; (m) carved stone plaquette; (n and o) projectile points; (p) shell beads.

there is some agreement about an eastern lowland source following a north-to-south vector (Eugenio and Aldazabal 1988; Politis et al. 2001; Sanguinetti de Bórmida 1970; but see Di Prado 2018). Grog tempered addition is rare, and decoration is primarily made with various incised techniques (linear, punctuated, zig-zags, etc.). Drag and jab technique, including typical continuous sub-rectangular imprints, known as *banderitas* ("small flags"; González 2005), is also present. This element would have functioned as a diacritic for social interaction among the eastern Pampa and northeastern Patagonia (Di Prado 2018). Pottery was made with local clays, but motifs were shared by people from different regions and probably from different ethnic groups.

Since the beginning of the archaeological research in the Atlantic seashore, two models have been competing. One interpreted the coastal lithic surface assemblages as a result of local adaptations, as a sort of material expression of a distinctive ethnicity (e.g., Austral 1965; Bórmida 1969; Menghin 1957), while the other proposed that these assemblages were the product of the inland hunter-gatherers during periodical, seasonal visits to the coast (Aparicio 1932; Hrdlička 1912; Politis 1984). After complete and systematic research Bonomo (2005) proposed a model that articulates the site function and the settlement pattern (Figure 6.5). On the beach, hunter-gatherers might have exploited seals and collected rounded pebbles, cobbles, and shells; the tide and the marine erosion washed out the by-products of these activities. In the blowouts

The Late Holocene Diversification

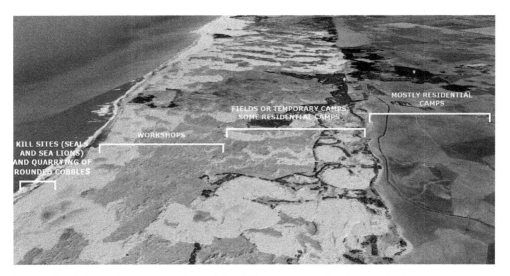

Figure 6.5 Schematic representation of the different types of settlement in the seashore. Based on Bonomo 2005.

in between the mobile dunes, at <0.5 km from the coast, the lithic assemblages, in the great majority surficial (e.g., Arenas Verdes, Caracolero, Mar del Sur, Punta Negra, Punta Florida), were composed mainly of seashore pebbles and cobbles (bipolar cores and flakes) and are interpreted as the result of short-term workshops. The fixed dunes, located further from the seashore, were occupied for more extended periods and functioned as temporary or residential camps. Seashore cobbles decrease, and raw material from the hill areas (SBG orthoquartzite, phtanite) increases. Finally, the sites beyond the dune ranges, around the inland lakes (El Guanaco Upper levels) or in the borders of rivers (Cueva del Tigre, Quequén Salado 1) or creeks (Nutria Mansa 1, La Ballenera, etc.), functioned as large residential camps. In these sites, the percentage of seashore cobbles falls dramatically (<30%), and the SBG orthoquartzite increases significantly. The transport of large cores of this raw material as well as the abundance of grinding stones in sites such as Nutria Mansa 1 (dated between 2705 and 3080 BP), 3.5 km from the coast, are interpreted as site furniture, the outcome of a strategy of provisioning places (Bonomo 2005; Matarrese 2015). A concentration of guanaco bones in this site, similar to some areas of the middle basin of the Quequén Grande River, suggest longer stays and more structured camps. The fall-off curve of rounded seashore cobble shows a steep fall-off after 13 km from the coast and remained <3% in the eastern Pampa inland sites. Based on several lines of evidence, Bonomo (2005) proposed that during the Middle and Late Holocene, the inland eastern Pampean foragers visited the coast seasonally for specific purposes, generating the coastal lithic assemblages.

Interestingly, there are no shell middens on the Pampas, which are relatively abundant in the seashore of southern Brazil and North Patagonia. The southern shell middens in the Campos of Uruguay are at La Esmeralda on the northeastern coast, dated between 3000 and 1000 BP (López Mazz and Villamarzo 2009). It is unclear if this gap in the Atlantic coast is cultural or if there were some ecological constraints in the abundance and availability of bivalves (see discussion in Bonomo and Aguirre 2009). No evidence of fishing has been detected in the Pampas Atlantic coast, except in the area of the Colorado River mouth, where sea catfish (*Genidens barbus*) and whitemouth croaker (*Micropogonias furnieri*) were seasonally captured (Avigliano et al. 2020; Stoessel and Alcaraz 2017). The captive Teófilo Gomila mentioned at the end of the nineteenth century that the low tide left abundant fishes in the ponds and streams at the mouth of the Colorado River, which were easy to catch without any gear.

A few sites from the northern part of the CPD shared the same characteristics as the southeastern areas, suggesting a similar adaptive pattern and technological traits: Laguna El Doce (2350 BP and 1555 BP) and Las Marías (excavated by Carlos Ceruti and dated to 1880 and 2140 BP; Ávila 2011). In the Chadilauquen site, redeposited human bones were dated to ~ 3700 BP (Mendonça et al. 2013), and the presence of pottery with basket imprints suggests a link with the Central Hills (Aguerre 1996; Tapia et al. 2020).

In the Rolling Pampa, the archaeological record is extremely scarce. It is restricted to sites discovered at the end of the nineteenth century: the Fontezuelas human skeleton, dated to ~ 2000 BP, and Cañada Rocha, excavated by F. Ameghino in the 1870s (see Chapter 2). The latter is a palimpsest of pottery, lithics, and bones from a variety of Pampean fauna (some allopatric; Salemme 1987) deposited in the alluvial plain of a creek. Five radiocarbon dates on bone gave anomalous recent ages between 560 and 260 BP (Acosta et al. 2020; Toledo 2011) due to heavy contamination probably with organic preservatives during storage and manipulation for more than 140 years (Politis et al. 2019). The other two sites in the area – Hunter (1990 BP) and Meguay (1120 BP) – show the typical association of the southern areas: guanaco and Pampas deer bones and artifacts made of SBG orthoquartzite and phtanite (Loponte et al. 2010). In the upper sector (above 10 masl) of the Salado River Depression, the sites Pessi (~ 3000 and 2000 BP; Aldazabal 2002) and La Colorada (Aldazabal 2002) exhibit roughly the same context.

The guanaco bones on the sites in the Paraná-Plata riversides are scarce and always represent an extremely low proportion of the faunal assemblages (<0.1 of the total taxonomically determined remains of these sites; Politis and León 2010). The low frequency of guanaco bones and their anatomical assignation to metapodium and phalanges have been interpreted mainly as attached to hides transported from other areas (Loponte 2008; Politis 2005). In support of this hypothesis, it is important to mention that, until recent times, the Aónikenk of Patagonia, during the guanaco skinning, kept the metapodium and basipodium elements attached to the skin to be able to tie it to the supporting poles of the tents (*toldos*) (Aguerre 2000).

The hunter-gatherer-fishers of rivers and lakes are well represented in the lower sector of the Salado River Depression, mostly below 10 masl (Aldazabal 2002; Frère 2015; González 2005; González and Frère 2009; González et al. 2007) and in the shores of the lower Paraná-La Plata Rivers (Acosta 2005; Loponte 2008; Paleo and Perez Meroni 2004, 2007; Paleo et al. 2002). These sites indicated diversification in the faunal exploitation, with a predominance of fish (Doradidae and Pimelodidae) and rodents (mostly coypu and wild cavy) and complemented with Pampas deer, marsh deer, and, in same places, freshwater shells. The coypu, an aquatic rodent with high reproductive rates, seems to be a key resource since it provides meat, fat, and skin (Escoteguy et al. 2012). In terms of raw materials, since suitable rocks are entirely absent in both areas, bones, and possibly wood, became the preferred raw material for making tools (Buc 2012, 2019; Escosteguy et al. 2017; Salemme 1987). Small artifacts, including triangular stemless projectile points made from SBG orthoquartzite and phtanite, are always present in low quantities. This raw material was obtained in Tandilia, although it is unclear if it was by exchange or direct procurement (Frère 2015: 194). Pottery is abundant, and pottery types include both plain and decorated with geometric incisions, with drag and jab predominant. Motifs are lines, zig-zag, and bands of the "small flag" design (Di Prado 2018; Frère 2015). Zoomorphic appendages are absent, but one particular pottery, called "tubular" (a sort of tube with one everted rim), which would be used as funnels to transfer liquids, are frequent (Giani Etchenique et al. 2013). Most incised techniques and designs are common in eastern Pampa areas, although with local variations (Di Prado 2015).

In the lower sector of the Salado River Depression, subsistence was complemented by fruits from *tala* woodlands, which formed dense forests parallel to the La Plata River and estuary. Several radiocarbon dates place the occupation of this environment between ~ 2400 and 370 BP, although there is a strong human signal after ~ 1700 BP. The most representative sites are La Guillerma 1 (~ 1200– 600 BP), La Guillerma 4 (1730 BP), La Guillerma 5 (~ 1700–400 BP), San Ramón 7 (2433–839 BP) (González 2005), Techo Colorado (1934 BP), San Genaro (1770 BP), Los Paraisos (1539 BP), Los Teros (1103 BP), La Cuña (550 BP) (Frère et al. 2016), La Salada (1470 BP; Aldazabal 2002), El Divisadero (540 and 510 BP; Aldazabal and Vázquez 2015) and La Loma (Aldazabal 2002).

Interestingly, the foragers of the western shore of the La Plata River between 1800 and 800 BP consumed, with a certain abundance, black drum (*Pogonia cromis*; Day Pilaría 2018), a saltwater fish that lives in estuary waters now 30–40 km south of the sites (Politis and León 2010). The San Clemente Locality (Paleo et al. 2002) and the Las Marías site (Paleo and Perez Meroni 2007) are representative of these adaptations. However, Los Tres Ombúes site, dated to 1110 BP, does not show an intense fish and coypu consumption (Ghiani Echenique and Paleo 2018). On the contrary, Pampas deer and marsh deer seem to be the primary prey, suggesting some (seasonal) variation in the local resource exploitation.

The first record of human occupation in the delta and the lower Paraná River is linked with exploiting fluvial resources. These sites are the level IV of Lechiguana 1 (dated to ~ 2300 BP; Caggiano 1977; Loponte et al. 2012), Playa Mansa (2400 BP; Acosta et al. 2010; Sartori and Colasurdo 2011), and Cañada Honda (2130 BP and 2030 BP; Lanzelotti et al. 2011). Since 1700 BP several sites in the western shore of the Lower Paraná floodplain (the Bajíos Rivereños Meridionales), such as La Bellaca 1 and 2, Anahí, Garín, Arroyo Guazúnambí, Laguna Grande, and Arroyo Sarandí, indicate adaptation to the riverside environment (Acosta 2005; Lafon 1971; Loponte 2008). Loponte and Acosta (Acosta et al. 2013; Loponte et al. 2012) proposed for this micro-region two "archaeological lineages" defined by the covariation of "packages of traits." Among them, they considered relevant the incidence of fish in the diet, the degree of carcass fragmentation, the shape of the *tembetás* (lip plugs), the use of lithic material, and the presence/absence of incised pottery. These traits co-occur differently outside this micro-region, and therefore, the lineages proposed by Acosta and Loponte are difficult to recognize in the rest of the Paraná Delta (Politis et al. 2017).

During Late Holocene in the Pampas the interaction network amplified and there is much evidence of exotic material with highly symbolic value circulating in the different areas (Acosta et al. 2015; Aldazabal and Cáceres 1999; Berón 2004; Bonomo et al. 2017; González et al. 2007; Martínez et al. 2017; Politis and Madrid 2001). For example, in the Tapera Moreira locality, the Chilean pottery type "Vergel-Valdivia" coexisted with the local pottery; in the lower Colorado River, lips and earplugs are present in several sites; in the Salado River Depression, several beads made of chrysocolla and semi-precious extra-regional rocks have been found (González 2005), while the typical Patagonian engraved stone plates were recovered in a few sites (Aldazabal 2002; Curtoni 2006; Politis et al. 2007; Scheifler 2019). Small obsidian flakes and instruments from different Andean sources were found in most areas (Berón et al. 2018; Santos Valero 2017; Stern and Aguerre 2013). Objects made of copper from the Andes were recovered in human burials at the Paraná Delta (Bonomo et al. 2017). For some authors (e.g., González 2005; Politis and Bonomo 2018), these exotic items would have played a central role in the economic organization and would suggest some kind of social hierarchy.

The Goya-Malabrigo Archaeological Entity

In the Middle and Lower Paraná–Lower Uruguay Rivers, a distinctive archaeological entity, known as the Goya-Malabrigo (Ceruti 2003; González 1977), is registered at about 2400 BP (Cornero 2021). Rodríguez (1992, 2001) included it in what he defined as the Tradición Ribereña Paranaense. This archaeological entity was recently redefined based on new findings and

The Late Holocene Diversification 211

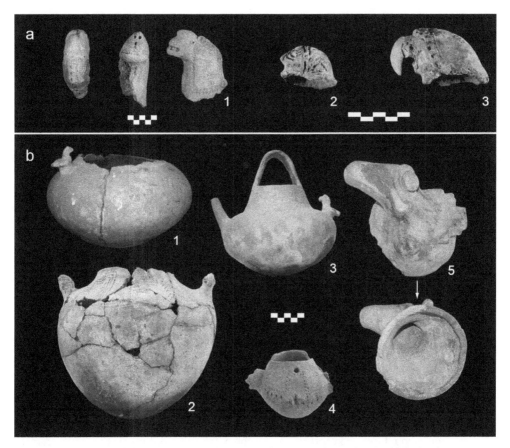

Figure 6.6 Goya-Malabrigo pottery. (a) Biomorphic appendages, heads: (1) hybrid being, (2) bird, (3) parrot. (b) (1, 2, and 4) Appendages attached to globular vessels, (3) "pava" (kettle), (5) two views of a *campana* (bell). Modified from Bonomo et al. 2021.

interpretations (Politis and Bonomo 2012, 2018). It is characterized by distinctive pottery with incised decorative designs made by drag and jab technique, zoomorphic appendages (especially bird's heads but also mammals, reptiles, and mollusks), closed-mouth vessels, "kettles," and spouted spoons. Truncated cone-shaped pottery pieces modeled with bird head appendages called *campanas* (bells) are diacritical for this entity (Figure 6.6). For Ottalagano (2009), this set of designs and modelings functioned as an emblematic style, while for Bonomo and collaborators (2021: 439; but see Bastourre 2021), the biomorphic representations "are concrete evidence of the belief system and ontology of the indigenous societies of the Paraná River, showing not only the cultural appropriation of nature but also the domestication of the landscape." Goya-Malabrigo had a mixed economy that combined the provisioning of wild resources through hunting (coypu, marsh deer, and brocket deer [*Mazama* sp.]; Bastourre 2014; Ceruti 2003), river fishing (Bastourre and

Azpelicueta 2020), and gathering shellfish, fruit, and plant seeds (*algarrobo*, and eventually palms and wild rice). This wild resource–based diet was supplemented with food production by practicing small-scale horticulture of the maize-squash-beans triad, probably in house gardens. In these plots, several domestic plants (C3 and C4) could have been cultivated. However, the consumption of maize (C4) was not strong enough to leave a clear isotopic signal (Bonomo et al. 2017; Ottalagano and Loponte 2016), suggesting a marginal contribution role in the diet or ritual consumption (Bonomo et al. 2017). As proposed by Hastorf (1994) for other regions, rather than satisfying a need for daily food intake, the presence of maize in Goya-Malabrigo sites might be better associated with the social and symbolic uses of food or stimulant drinks (chicha beer) consumed on special occasions such as rituals, ceremonies, and feasts. The record of some skeletons in the Goya-Malabrigo context with enriched δ ^{13}C values could be attributed to some individuals with specific spiritual functions who consumed more maize than the rest of the population (Bonomo et al. 2017).

Traditionally, it has been proposed that Guaraní people introduced horticulture into the region (Rodríguez 2004; Schmitz 1991). According to this hypothesis, once the Guaraní arrived, the local populations adopted cultivated plants into their economies or obtained crops by exchanging with them. Some researchers (Loponte and Acosta 2007; Loponte et al. 2011; Ottalagano and Loponte 2016) are still influenced by this idea and, based on the isotopic results of individuals who do not show enriched δ ^{13}C, regard all non-Guaraní groups (including Goya-Malabrigo) from the Middle and Lower Paraná Rivers as complex hunter-gatherers. However, the evidence obtained in the last 10 years clearly shows that cultivation was widespread among the Goya-Malabrigo populations at least since 1200 BP and probably by 1700 BP (Bonomo et al. 2017; Colobig et al. 2015, 2018; Cornero and Rangone 2013), centuries before the arrival of the Guaraní people into the area (Bonomo et al. 2015).

One of the relevant characteristics from Goya-Malabrigo was the construction of earth mounds, locally known as *cerritos*, in the flood plain of the Middle and Lower Paraná Rivers (Bonomo and Politis 2018; Castiñeira et al. 2013, 2017; Ceruti 2003), as well as in the Lower Uruguay (Capdepont Caffa 2018; Castro 2018). Mounds in the Paraná River Delta are generally found isolated or in clusters of two or three. Their height ranges between 1.0 and 2.5 m, and their morphology is elliptical, with maximum diameters ranging from 35 to 80 m (Bonomo et al. 2011a; Figure 6.7). However, in the Lower Uruguay River, there are some higher mounds associated with Goya-Malabrigo (Castro 2018).

Since the recognition of these earth mounds at the end of the nineteenth century, their natural versus cultural origin has been discussed (see summary in Castiñeira et al. 2013). Most of these mounds were also places to bury the dead throughout generations (Kozameh et al. 2018; Mazza 2015; Scabuzzo and Ramos Van Rapp 2017; Scabuzzo et al. 2015). Based on the detailed study

The Late Holocene Diversification

Figure 6.7 View of Los Tres Cerros 1, an earth mound located in the Upper Delta of the Paraná River.

of the Los Tres Cerros 1 (LTC1) site in the Upper Delta of the Paraná River dated between 1227 and 507 BP (Castro and Castiñeira 2018; Politis et al. 2011, 2021b), Castiñeira and collaborators (2014) propose that mound-building was carried out using a selection of local and allochthonous sediments. These sediments were mixed with pottery, thermo-altered sediments, and organic materials to obtain an optimal building mixture for the accretion and consolidation of earthworks. These construction techniques were also used in other mounds of the Upper Delta. The origin of ones of the Paraná River Delta seems to be later (~ 1900 BP; Castiñeira et al. 2017) than eastern Uruguay and it is probably linked to the southern Arawak expansion (Politis and Bonomo 2018). However, in both regions, the *cerritos* became transgenerational, long-term structures that, besides their functional advantages in the flooded areas, connected the past and the ancestors with the living people (Gianotti and Bonomo 2013). The Arawak would have contributed to the spread of horticulture, the hydrocentrality, and the emergence of a ranked sociopolitical organization (Politis and Bonomo 2012).

The Guaraní Archaeological Tradition

The Guaraní ethnic/linguistic group belongs to the Tupí stock and has a very distinctive material culture, burial practices, and adaptive patterns, which allow its identification in the archaeological record (Brochado 1984; Noelli 1999–2000). Its origin would be in the Madeira-Guapore basin, in Amazonia, and in the process of continuous demographic growth and territorial expansion, they spread through several regions of southeastern South America and reached their southern limit, the Lower Paraná Delta, at ~ 700 BP (the Arroyo Fredes site; Bonomo et al. 2015; Loponte et al. 2004). However, the Guaraní presence in the Lower Uruguay River concentrates in a slightly younger period, between 600 and 300 BP (López Mazz and López Cabral 2020).

In other sectors of the Middle and Lower Paraná, several sites contain Guaraní pottery in a Goya-Malabrigo matrix. Except for the Pajas Blancas site (Badano 1940), where a burial urn suggests the inhumation of a Guaraní individual, all the others contain only a few Guaraní sherds (corrugated, brushed, etc.). This would indicate that this pottery was circulating among local groups, not implicating an effective Guaraní territorial control (Politis et al. 2018). The same happened with several sites in the littoral of the Salado River Depression (i.e., Los Molles, Aspiroz, etc.) that represent the southernmost expansion of this pottery (Aldazabal and Eugenio 2013; González and Frère 2010). It has been interpreted as the result of an exchange or interethnic marriages, which included Guaraní woman potters (Aldazabal and Eugenio 2013).

Guaraní's presence is well defined based on characteristics of the material culture, burial practices, and settlement patterns. Polychrome, corrugated, and brushed pottery, completely different from the other, local, types in the Lower Paraná and Uruguay Rivers, as well as polished stone axes are defining material traits of the Guaraní people (Bonomo et al. 2015; Loponte et al. 2011; Noelli 1998, 2004). Some vessels were used for human inhumation, a practice completely absent in the Pampas and Northeast Argentina before the Guaraní's arrival.

Beyond Goya-Malabrigo and Guaraní, there are some archaeological contexts in the Lower Paraná Delta (Caggiano 1984; Loponte et al. 2016; Politis et al. 2017; Torres 1911) and the Lower Uruguay River (Capdepont Caffa 2012; Castro 2018; Rodriguez 1992) that do not fit well in any of these two entities. Some are earth mounds, up to 6 m high, used for living and funerary purposes, but the typical Goya-Malabrigo biomorphic appendages are absent (Castro 2018; Greslebin 1931; Loponte et al. 2016). Also, it is not yet clear to what extent horticulture was practiced (Bonomo et al. 2011a), but an intense use of palm fruits (*Butia yatay* and *Syagrus rommanzoffiana*) was recorded (Acosta and Ríos Roman 2013; Caggiano 1984; Torres 1911). These peculiarities were noticed early (Aparicio 1948), and in consequence, several archaeological entities were proposed to account for these properties of the archaeological record: the Ibicuy or Ibicueña Phase of the "Cultura Entrerriana" (Caggiano 1984: 42–43; Serrano 1972: 22–27) and the Ibicueño complex (Rodríguez

The Late Holocene Diversification

2001). These contexts also indicate an intense exploitation of aquatic resources (fish, coypu, freshwater shells, marsh deer, etc.) and a marked consumption of palm fruits. Except for the biomorphic appendages and a few vessel shapes, the pottery is similar to Goya-Malabrigo.

PATAGONIA

One of the forms of archaeological diversification is the appearance of complex settlement patterns in a variety of habitats (Figure 6.8). In Patagonia, there is a marked distinction between habitats available all year long and those just used during the warm season, particularly near the Andes, where the threshold between winter and summer areas is around 400 masl in the south (Belardi et al. 2019) and much higher in the north (Barberena et al. 2011). Large concentrations of rock structures, probably hunting blinds, were found in several regions, particularly in the high plateaus (Belardi et al. 2017; Franco et al. 2021; Goñi et al. 2006; Miotti et al. 2016; Vargas Gariglio et al. 2019). Many of those plateaus were rarely used before the late Holocene (Goñi et al. 2011–2012: 22), suggesting they were obstacles for human dispersal before that time. Indeed, the archaeological record of many of those high-altitude habitats can be described as the result of a late exploration phase (Borrero 1989; Franco 2002b), and appears to result from hunting or circulation and, in cases like Cerro Pampa, lithic provisioning (Goñi et al. 2011–2012). Dellepiane and Cassiodoro (2019) suggest caution in the interpretation of rock structures, given the presence of habitational evidence. This was already known for similar structures in Somuncurá since the 1970s (García and Pérez de Micou 1980), but independently of the range of activities inferred for a site, the reason for the visits is still focused on hunting. Certainly, camps were expected since hunting, and the associated butchering and processing require more than a fleeting visit. Re et al. (2017) distinguish between logistic and seasonal movements, with the latter implying longer stays at the plateaus. This difference indicates that stays need not be ephemeral, but the concept remains that hunting is the reason for the visits. Fauna dominated by guanacos (especially subadults), evidence of tool repair, and many projectile points – including evidence of replacement – constitute unequivocal proof (Dellepiane and Cassiodoro 2019; Re et al. 2017). Evidence of fuel transport from the lower lands surrounding the plateaus is confirmatory of the logistic status of those findings (Pasqualini et al. 2016). People geared up with tools and fuel before moving up the plateau, in what Lovis et al. (2005) called long-distance logistical exploitation. These visits to the plateau probably occurred during the warm months of the year (Belardi et al. 2017; Cassiodoro et al. 2014; Franco et al. 2021; Goñi et al. 2014b; Miotti et al. 2016), which suggests the possibility of temporal stress on the fabrication of tools (Franco and Borrero

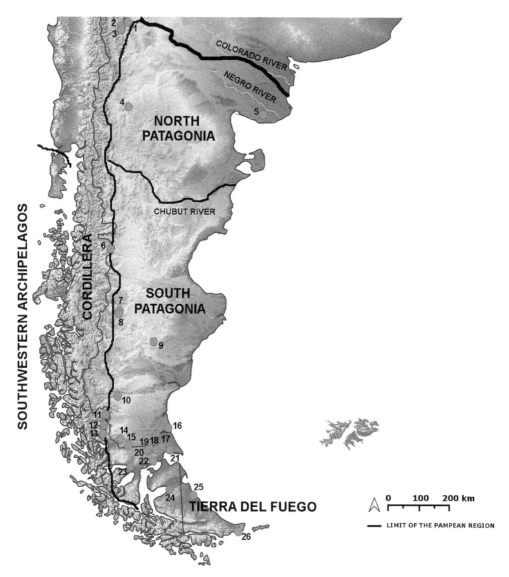

Figure 6.8 Map showing Late Holocene sites mentioned in the text. (1) Cueva Huenul; (2) Aquihuecó; (3) Caepe Malal I; (4) Epullán Grande; (5) Laguna del Juncal; (6) Baño Nuevo; (7) Lake Salitroso; (8) Cerro de los Indios; (9) Viuda Quenzana; (10) Río Bote; (11) Cerro Guido; (12) Cerro Castillo; (13) Cueva Lago Sofía 1; (14) Laguna Cóndor; (15) Penitente Basin; (16) Punta Bustamante; (17) Orejas de Burro; (18) Pali Aike Cave; (19) Fell Cave; (20) Cerro Sota; (21) Cañadón Cóndor; (22) San Gregorio; (23) Ponsonby; (24) Marazzi; (25) Las Vueltas; (26) Site BVS1.

1996). Like activities related to inscribing places with rock art, many other activities were undoubtedly attached to those visits. It is indeed possible that once the land was inscribed in that way, more complex meanings and activities attracted human attention, but for now, our way to understand them is based

The Late Holocene Diversification

on evidence for hunting and circulation. The realization of hunting rituals, the construction of landscape markers to navigate the plateau, and other interpretations are certainly plausible, but we are still a long way from finding support for them. The use of ethnographic analogies, for example, the evidence for hunting rituals based on the placement of guanaco skulls above rock structures, is compelling, but the fact remains that the only findings of archaeological accumulations of guanaco skulls were not related to rock structures (Moreno 1879).

Última Esperanza is one relatively strange area, which despite being occupied since the end of the Pleistocene, does not appear to have been intensively used (Borrero and Martin 2018; Prieto 1991; Sierpe et al. 2009). The reasons for this difference from other areas with evidence of early colonization are not evident and might include the relative isolation offered by the Baguales and Oriental Cordilleras, which in combination with an increasingly wooded landscape limited human connectivity with eastern Patagonia. Alternatively, it might be simply a question of low human population density. After the ephemeral occupations during the Early and Middle Holocene, the signal for human presence intensified (Pérez et al. 2016), although a preservational bias cannot be completely excluded. During the Late Holocene, human subsistence diversified, including the consumption of mollusks and evidence of long-distance interactions. Since archaeological visibility is very low in this area, inferences were derived from a variety of stratigraphic locations (Borrero and Martin 2018).

The South Patagonian hinterland was systematically used by guanaco hunters with a variety of hunting weapons, from bolas to projectiles with stone heads propelled by spearthrowers or bows (Banegas et al. 2014; Ratto 1994). Similar adaptive patterns were slowly emerging in the different regions of Patagonia. The huemul and even the pudu were also hunted, but they never attained the importance of the guanaco in the human diet (De Nigris 2007; García 2007; Mena and Jackson 1991). Pérez and Batres (2008) maintain that the importance given to guanacos in the Patagonian diet resulted from misinformation about the forest's resources, and they present evidence about their importance in some North Patagonian sites. Nevertheless, their exploitation is still restricted to the forested fringe near the Andes, and guanacos were the main prey in most of Patagonia.

It was argued that costly adaptations focusing subsistence on diverse and sometimes scattered resources characterized the Holocene in South America (Stahl 1996). However, the importance of small-package, low-ranked resources in Patagonia was recorded only in North Patagonia, with evidence of both plants and small animals significantly added to the diet (Belmar et al. 2017; Borrero 1981; Martínez et al. 2017; Neme 2007; Neme et al. 2015; Prates 2008). We saw that even small-package, low-ranked resources like birds or fishes could also be exploited using low-cost tactics along the continuum between scavenging and collecting. Of course, our knowledge of these adaptations is partial. For example, we know next to nothing about trapping technologies, although they were plausibly used for birds and fishes (López et al. 2020; Tivoli 2010; Torres Elgueta 2016), and we are just beginning to explore the role of plants (Ancibor and Pérez de Micou 1995; Belmar 2019; Martínez Tosto and Burry 2019). *Prosopis* sp. was one important plant resource consumed in North Patagonia (Bernal et al. 2007; Capparelli and Prates 2015; Lema et al. 2012; Llano and Barberena 2013; Prates et al. 2019), including the western archipelagos (Reyes et al. 2020) and the Atlantic coast (Ciampagna 2016; Ciampagna et al. 2020). *Araucaria araucana* was seasonally exploited in Northwest Patagonia. Notably, Cactaceae were stored in numbers at Epullán Grande (Crivelli et al. 1996: 205–208), demonstrating its importance within the annual cycle. The possible role of *Oxalis* sp. as a famine food also needs to be mentioned (López et al. 2020). The presence of *Zea mays* was detected in some northern locations, but never in a context suggesting cultivation (Gil et al. 2020; Pérez and Erra 2011; Prates et al. 2019). It also needs to be said that anthracological studies show highly selective choices of woods for hearths, indicating good knowledge of the available resources (Caruso Fermé et al. 2011; Pasqualini 2015).

Contrary to the situation in North Patagonia, evidence for the exploitation of small-package resources, like birds, plants, or rodents, played only a minimal role in South Patagonia (Belmar 2019; Cruz 2000, 2007; Pardiñas 1999). The case of the archipelagos is different with a subsistence in general based on large mammals, but complemented by birds, fishes, and mollusks (Bahamondes 2004; Orquera and Piana 1999; Tivoli 2010; Torres 2009; Zangrando 2003). Clearly, the panorama is more complex than initially envisioned when we characterized Patagonian adaptations as routinely focused on guanacos, and now processes like intensification and regionalization need to be considered (Tivoli and Zangrando 2011).

As already mentioned, the availability of water played a crucial role in organizing the settlement pattern in Patagonia. In the Limay and Negro basins, it was concentrated in the main valleys or not too far away (Crivelli et al. 2009; Fisher and Nacuzzi 1992; Prates 2008; Serna et al. 2019). Sites are found near oxbow lagoons or abandoned arms of the river, which are places of high biological richness where animals, plants, and rocks are concentrated (Borrero 1981, 1986b; Prates 2008; Prates et al. 2010). However, research at nearby plateaus suggests the logistical hunting of guanacos (Prates 2008). Extensive dry lowlands constitute harsh and low-ranked habitats in North Patagonia, which were probably used as transit zones between the Limay-Negro basins and the Somuncurá plateau (Prates and Mange 2016). Faunal resources are homogeneously distributed in these lowlands, but very few places present adequate conditions for continuous human occupation (Serna et al. 2019).

Relatively high-altitude places occupy an important place in the organization of human settlement. Belardi recorded Late Holocene occupations during

The Late Holocene Diversification

the warm months at Cerro Castillo, above 1250 masl, and contrasted it with the use of places available year long like the Piedra Parada valley, some 100 km away. He suggested the existence of a wide mobility circuit that includes both locations (Belardi 1996). The rich evidence obtained at several sites in Piedra Parada indicates several occupational variants used during the end of the Middle Holocene and the Late Holocene (Aschero 1983; Bellelli 1988, 1991; Bellelli and Guráieb 2019), but certainly, the annual range of those hunter-gatherers was larger, no doubt including areas north and south of the valley.

A number of archaeological projects in places such as Lago San Martín, Lago Cardiel, Perito Moreno National Park, Lago Viedma, Lago Argentino, Cabo Vírgenes, and Piedra Parada, among many others (Aschero 1983; Belardi et al 2010, 2019; Borrero et al. 2008a; Carballo Marina and Ercolano 2003; Goñi et al. 2014a; Prates 2008), produced a rich Late Holocene record. As a result of this evidence of human dispersal throughout Patagonia, there was a multiplication of large and small archaeological loci. Places such as Cerro de los Indios in the steppes (Aschero et al. 1992, 1999; Guráieb 2004; Mengoni Goñalons 1999) or Punta Bustamante at the mouth of the Gallegos River (Mansur et al. 2004) probably were important habitational nodes around which many satellite sites with shorter occupations are recorded. In comparison with previous periods, this is a world with neighbors, where humans are present almost everywhere. Abundant small lithic and bone assemblages are found all around the large lake basins and scattered along the river basins. Only rarely were those small sites studied, dated, and published, but the few available reports describe varied Late Holocene activities away from the main habitational sites (Belardi et al. 2006; Carballo Marina et al. 2008; Castro et al. 2003; Espinosa 2000; Franco et al. 1999, 2004; Garibotti et al. 2011; Goñi et al. 2014a; Leonardt et al. 2015; Marchionni et al. 2020; Rindel 2009; Rindel et al. 2007, 2011; Sierpe 2020) (Figure 6.9). Open-air sites were recorded for this period, particularly on the Atlantic coast, and can be considered in the discussion of complementary use of space (Hammond and Zubimendi 2013; Hammond et al. 2019). An important distinction was made between open-air sites characterized by the initial butchering of guanacos and rock shelters where final processing of carcasses occurred (Rindel et al. 2011). Other situational distinctions between open-air and cave sites were discovered near the Andes (Carballo Marina et al. 2008; Franco et al. 1999). Repetitive use of rock shelters during thousands of years was increasingly recorded (Aschero et al. 1992, 2005; Barberena et al. 2007; Civalero and Aschero 2003; De Nigris 2004, 2007; Durán 1986–1987; Durán et al. 2003; Fernández 2017; Goñi et al. 2014a; Gradin et al. 1979; Otaola and Franco 2008; Sanguinetti 1976). And these redundant occupations show not only site fidelity but a world with restrictions in access to places. Indeed, processes of regionalization appeared during the Late Holocene.

The archaeological record of the middle Rio Negro basin in the north is restricted to relatively late occupations, probably as a result of visibility

Figure 6.9 Rock structures of unknown function. Lago Argentino. Photo courtesy Karen Borrazzo.

problems (Prates 2008), but a clear pattern of alternance in the shape of small triangular projectile points was recorded, perhaps related to some differentiation of populations (Prates 2008: 259). Local lithic raw materials were predominantly used to make informal tools, with small triangular projectile points among the few that were curated. Similar visibility problems occur at the Lower Colorado Basin, where even evidence of Middle Holocene occupations was found. These occupations reflect the activities of open cultural systems, where access to neighboring places appears to be unrestricted. In contrast, Late Holocene occupations initiated a transformation to relatively closed social networks (Martinez et al. 2017). A reduction of human ranges and increasing intensity of occupation, accompanied by complex funerary practices, are strong markers of this regionalization since ca. 1000 BP (Flensborg et al. 2017). In spite of this regionalization, the wide circulation of individuals, ideas, and special objects – particularly those called "ceremonial axes" – was also proposed for this final period (Fisher 2009).

Settlement at the Lago San Martin area started ca. 9700 BP with relatively isolated occupations. After a relatively long temporal gap, Late Holocene occupations are identified along the coasts, displaying a pattern of decreasing intensity of use toward the Andes. The only exception is the Maipú península in the west, probably logistically occupied on a seasonal basis during the Late Holocene (Belardi et al. 2010, 2019; Espinosa et al. 2009, 2013) (Figure 6.10).

Figure 6.10 Isthmus Península Maipú, Argentina. Photo courtesy Patricia Campan and Juan Bautista Belardi.

The cultural geography of this region is clearly related to the limit imposed by the Continental Ice Field (Belardi et al. 2009, 2010), and these patterns were elucidated because a distributional approach informed by both stratigraphic and surface evidence was used. Similar discontinuous patterns are recognized in other areas. Sometimes it is possible to discuss the Late Holocene human settlement using tools discarded outside caves (Belardi and Borrero 1999; Belardi et al. 2015; Hermo and Magnin 2012; Marchionni et al. 2020), an excellent addition to information that was mostly obtained at caves.

In general, relatively continuous human occupations and increases in tool depositional rates are recorded during the Late Holocene (Borrero 1993), while occupational gaps persisted in Tierra del Fuego well into the Late Holocene. For example, most of the Holocene is not represented at Tres Arroyos 1, with humans returning ca. 1400 BP after a gap of about 9,000 years.

Regionalization and growing population density precipitated the active incorporation of most of the Patagonian ecosystems within the human domain. Caridi and Scheinsohn (2016) discussed Late Holocene connectivity between areas in Central Patagonia based on the distribution of rock art that, using other methodologies, was also discussed for other regions (Carden 2008; Re et al. 2009; Romero Villanueva 2019). Stable isotopes of human bones highlighted the importance of the forest and its resources for specific populations during the last millennium (Fernández and Tessone 2014; Méndez et al. 2014; Pérez et al. 2019), supporting models of regular use of the forest and its resources in the eastern Andean region of Patagonia (Belardi et al. 2019; Bellelli et al. 2003; Fernández et al. 2011; Pallo and Borrazzo 2017). With the full occupation of forests, human populations in North Patagonia were in a position to establish contact with the western channels. However, the evidence for such contacts is limited. The forests and ecotone of the Cisnes basin in Aisén are located between the eastern steppes and the channels of the Pacific coasts, but no evidence of contact was recorded (Méndez and Reyes 2008). In sum, connections between both sides of the Andes are elusive. Further north, in a different kind of forest, some connections are indicated by rock art (Bellelli et al. 2008; Podestá et al. 2008). Also, in the far south there is evidence of contacts across the low-altitude Cordillera Oriental, particularly at the forests of Cancha Carrera (Pallo and Borrero 2015b), an area fully integrated with the headwaters of the Gallegos River (Borrero and Borrazzo 2011; Carballo Marina et al. 2016; Charlin 2012; Charlin et al. 2011). Interactions between maritime and terrestrial populations also occurred at places away from the Andes, such as the Ponsonby site at Isla Riesco.

East of this region, we enter the area of influence of the Pali Aike Volcanic Field, with its own dynamics at least since the Middle Holocene (Barberena 2008; Barberena et al. 2007; Carballo Marina 2007; Charlin 2009b). Fell Cave, Pali Aike Cave, and several other sites attest to the intensive Holocene use of the volcanic field (Massone 1981), which was fully confirmed by recent explorations of the interfluve of the Gallegos and Chico Rivers (Borrazzo and Cirigliano 2020; Borrazzo et al. 2019) (Figure 6.11). Excavations at Cañadón Cóndor, San Gregorio, and many other localities near the Strait of Magellan indicate transient occupations by terrestrial hunter-gatherers (Laming-Emperaire 1968, 1972; Massone 1979). The consumption of guanaco, sometimes complemented with resources from the sea, is the pattern at most of these sites.

However, archaeological evidence is not abundant everywhere. The area west of the Pali Aike Volcanic Field is among the most notable examples of a low-density archaeological record (Gómez Otero 1991). Only recently, after years of research, we are beginning to understand the very late human use of that partially forested zone (Charlin 2012). Late archaeological manifestations found at Laguna Cóndor and the Penitente Basin indicate two things. First, they demonstrate the interdependence between that intermediate zone and the PAVF since ca. 500 BP. Second, they show its importance in connecting the middle Gallegos River with the Strait of Magellan (Belardi et al. 2020; Cirigliano et al. 2020; L'Heureux and Borrero 2016).

In general, there were changes in the mode of use of places. Biological and cultural continuity associated with a reduction in residential mobility that probably favored population growth was proposed for the Late Holocene at Lake Salitroso (García Guraieb et al. 2015; Tessone et al. 2008). If this increase

The Late Holocene Diversification 223

Figure 6.11 Transects at the interfluve between the Gallegos and Chico Rivers, Argentina. Photo courtesy Karen Borrazzo.

in population is accepted, then we can also probably accept a diminution of the size of home ranges. The size of the home range is a measure of the quantity and distribution of resources and the effectiveness of the selected exploitation strategies. This situation can be extended to other regions as well. It was only during historical times that this trend was reversed when relative sedentarism was associated with an increase in logistical movements (Goñi 2010).

The use of the best locally available rocks indicates intimate knowledge of Patagonian resources that drastically differs from the situation during the Late Pleistocene. It is also the time for the full incorporation of rocks from highly localized sources, like the black obsidian from Pampa del Asador (Espinosa and Goñi 1999), the green obsidian from the Otway Sea (Morello et al. 2001) or other obsidians (Stern and Franco 2000; Stern et al. 2012), which began to be used at different times during the Holocene. Pampa del Asador obsidian frequencies recovered far away from the source, for example, at Fell Cave or in North Tierra del Fuego (Morello et al. 2012a; Stern 1999, 2000, 2004), initially suggested the existence of large networks. However, when the number of recovered obsidian fragments and the shape of their distributions were inspected, any evidence of long-distance trade of black obsidian disappeared (Pallo and Borrero 2015a). An illustrative example of the size of the obsidian samples is presented by Morello and collaborators (2001: 131), showing that the 1.3% obsidian published by Stern (2000) for Fell Cave sums up values for green, black, and banded gray obsidians and that only 0.02% corresponds to green obsidian. Other relatively restricted rock sources also began to be intensively used. For example, in the Late Holocene there was an increase in the number of artifacts of translucent chalcedony from the Somuncurá Plateau found in the San Matías Gulf (Alberti et al. 2015; Favier Dubois et al. 2009a) or red silex at Oso Marino Bay (Ambrústolo and Zubimendi 2019).

The archaeology of Late Holocene Tierra del Fuego and the southern channels present some peculiarities. Sites multiply during the Late Holocene in North Tierra del Fuego. For example, occupations at Tres Arroyos 1 immediately above the late Pleistocene levels consist of thick layers of butchered guanaco remains dated between 1400 and 700 BP (Massone 2004; Muñoz 1997). Huge gaps like this undoubtedly played a role in producing interpretations of local human extinction by isolation (Borrero 1997) or by catastrophe (Prieto et al. 2013). In fact, beyond the case of Marazzi (Calás 2014; Morello et al. 1999) and a few other Middle Holocene sites, most of the known archaeological sites of the north of the island are dated within the last 2,000 radiocarbon years (Borrero and Barberena 2004; Calás and Lucero 2009; Massone et al. 1993; Morello et al. 2012a; Oría and Mari 2019; Salemme et al. 2007b). Excepting a few concentrations on the coast, these are all extremely ephemeral occupations by people focused on terrestrial resources, complemented by minimal use of maritime foods (Barberena 2004). Claims of large human aggregations in the isthmus between Inútil and San Sebastián Bays were made on the basis of concentrations of potential living structures (Massone et al. 1993). However, this hypothesis was recently revised (Ozán and Borrero 2018), as it was found that several of the structures resulted from animal activities. Moreover, the Late Holocene archaeological evidence recorded across Cerro de los Onas was not synchronic. In the end, the explanation for this concentration was the redundant use of the hill. Ephemeral occupations in the mudflat fields and clay dunes of San Sebastián Bay are found above the few Tertiary outcrops (Borrazzo 2009) (Figure 6.12). The detailed study of the talus of one of these Tertiary outcrops showed additional short-time occupations in the periphery (Ozán et al. 2015). Limited stratigraphic and abundant surface information from the seasonal lagoons between clay dunes displays concentrations of averaged materials (Borrazzo 2010; Borrero et al. 2008b; Oría and Salemme 2019; Oría et al. 2020). All this evidence is consistent with a highly mobile population. This notion is reinforced by peculiar findings like a projectile point made of green obsidian (Oría et al. 2010) or nonlocal quartz crystals interpreted as amulets or ornaments (Mansur et al. 2021), cases that attest to the high mobility of individuals. Occupation of the Fuegian forests south of the San Sebastián-

The Late Holocene Diversification

Figure 6.12 Clay dunes at San Sebastián Bay, Argentina. Photo courtesy Karen Borrazzo.

Inútil isthmus was identified near the Fagnano Lake (De Angelis 2015; Mansur and De Angelis 2016; Mansur and Piqué 2009) and on the Atlantic coasts since 3000 BP (Borrero et al. 2017), and even before on the Beagle Channel (Estévez and Vila 1995, 2006; Orquera and Piana 1999, 2009; Zangrando 2009a; Zangrando et al. 2018).

Combined information from middens and habitational sites together with isotopic studies displays a mosaic of human adaptations. It indicates the consumption of terrestrial resources ca. 3600–3200 BP at the lower valley of the Río Negro (Flensborg et al. 2019), while on the coasts of Golfo San Matías (Figures 6.13 and 6.14), there is a change from a focus on marine resources ca. 3100–2200 BP to one on mixed-terrestrial diets ca. 1500–420 BP (Favier Dubois et al. 2009b). In most cases, the exploitation of coastal resources appears to be complementary, confirming that human populations relied mostly on terrestrial resources (Barberena 2002; Borrero and Barberena 2006; Mansur et al. 2004; Massone 1979; Miotti 1998). Hinterland hunter-gatherers regularly focused on the consumption of terrestrial protein in North Tierra del Fuego, but a maritime component is always present (Barberena 2002, 2004; Barberena et al. 2007; Borrero et al. 2009; Pérez et al. 2019). On the other hand, samples from the Strait of Magellan and the mainland coast indicate a combination of

Figure 6.13 View of islote Lobos, west coast of Golfo San Matías, Argentina. Photo courtesy Florencia Borella.

terrestrial and maritime protein (Borrero et al. 2001; Moreno et al. 2011), with cases of full maritime signal (Zilio et al. 2018). Of course, all these isotopic patterns are in correspondence with highly contrasted archaeological records showing the whole continua from purely terrestrial to maritime adaptations, usually interpreted in binary terms (Borrero 1997). However, starting with the unexpected discovery of full marine signals on the Atlantic coast of the mainland, that picture is changing.

Isotopic evidence from sites in the archipelagos shows that a fully maritime signal generally agrees with the content of the middens (Kochi 2017; Reyes et al. 2012, 2015, 2019). Effectively, even the limited published information for Chiloé shows some continuity of marine hunting and gathering through time (Reyes et al. 2016, 2020), with the addition of the pudu, a small terrestrial mammal. Hunting of *Arctocephalus australis* dominates the southern early bone assemblages from the Sea of Otway, the Strait of Magellan, and the Beagle Channel, with the complement of pelagic birds – particularly shags (*Phalacrocorax* sp.) – and fishes (Kochi 2017; Lefèvre et al. 2003; Mardones 2019; San Román 2016; Tessone et al. 2003; Tivoli 2010; Torres Elgueta 2016; Zangrando 2003, 2009). The panorama is more complex at the Mitre Peninsula, east of the Beagle Channel. Site BVS1 was briefly occupied during

Figure 6.14 Faro San Matías, north of Golfo San Matías, Argentina. Photo courtesy Florencia Borella.

the Middle Holocene with an adaptation similar to the central Beagle Channel, while later occupations show more variation, perhaps explainable as an interdigitation between terrestrial and maritime occupations (Vázquez et al. 2011; Zangrando et al. 2009) (Figures 6.15 and 6.16). The archaeology of this peninsula is further complicated by several contrasts between the habitats and sites on the northern and southern coasts (Muñoz and Belardi 2011; Vázquez 2019) and also by the archaeological evidence recovered at the Isla de los Estados (Horwitz 1993) (Figures 6.17 and 6.18). Recent molecular analyses of human bones showed no significant differences between samples from the northern coast of the Beagle Channel, Mitre Peninsula, and modern Yahgán populations, suggesting population homogeneity (Crespo et al. 2020).

The Late Holocene is also when strong regional zonification can be found in the southwestern archipelagos, with possible habitational nodes in the Guayaneco archipelago, the Otway Sea, the central-western Strait of Magellan, the central Beagle channel, and the Mitre Peninsula. The southwestern channels are minimally explored, and we still lack a detailed chronology (Borrero et al. 2020a; San Román and Morello 2001). Archaeological visibility is extremely poor in the western channels due to the extensive vegetation cover and the virtual destruction of most shells in the extremely

Figure 6.15 View of Bahia Valentin, Tierra del Fuego, Argentina. Photo courtesy Martín Vázquez.

Figure 6.16 Excavations at site BVS42 (3), Bahia Valentin, Tierra del Fuego, Argentina. Photo courtesy Martín Vázquez.

humid habitats. Beyond rare structures like fish traps or runways, only topographical changes can be used as good site predictors (Borrero et al. 2020b). An intense program of exploratory augering was used to identify archaeological loci and to select places for excavation (San Román, pers. comm.), but

The Late Holocene Diversification

Figure 6.17 Rio Bueno, Mitre Peninsula, Atlantic coast of Tierra del Fuego. Photo courtesy Martín Vázquez.

our knowledge about the archaeology of that large region is still limited. An entire maritime way of life is manifested at all these archipelagic sites that, with some changes, continues up to historical times (Orquera and Piana 1999; Ortiz Troncoso 1972b; San Román et al. 2016; Tafuri et al. 2017; Zangrando 2003). A sophisticated bone technology – including harpoons, awls, and wedges – is associated with substantial shell middens (Christensen 2016; San Román 2013; Scheinsohn 1993–1994; Orquera and Piana 1999). The fact that the decoration of the earlier Middle Holocene harpoons was subsequently lost is noteworthy (Fiore 1999). Interestingly, there are pulses of use of lithic projectile points, presumably to hunt guanacos (Alvarez 2004; Morello et al. 2004; Zangrando 2009a), and increases in the exploitation of fishes and birds in the Late Holocene (Tivoli and Zangrando 2011). Lithic tools from these occupations are generalized, a property related to the high degree of residential mobility (Álvarez 2004, 2006). Although these sites are marked by the dominance of sea mammals, mollusks, and fish, terrestrial fauna were also a regular diet component (Morello et al. 2012a; San Román et al. 2002; Sierpe 2020; Zangrando 2009a; Zangrando et al. 2014). It must be stated that similar maritime adaptations are also present in the northwestern channels, for example, at Seno Reloncavi, Chiloé, and the Guayaneco archipelago (Gaete

Figure 6.18 Site B, Flinders 3, Isla de los Estados, Argentina. Photo courtesy Atilio F. Zangrando.

et al. 2004; Legoupil 2005; Ocampo and Rivas 2004; Reyes 2021; Reyes et al. 2015, 2018, 2019, 2020; Rivas et al. 1999), but given the distances involved, the degree of interdependence between the northern and southern adaptations is not known (Orquera et al. 2011).

These patterns of extensive use of diverse environments are almost inevitably related to changing adaptations, demographic growth, and sometimes intensification. The increasing number of sites recorded during the Late Holocene suggests a more densely populated Patagonia, a condition that significantly changed the social landscape. At any rate, as already mentioned, empty lands still existed during the Late Holocene because hunter-gatherers never saturated Patagonian environments. The appearance of territoriality with its corollary of close neighbors and competence characterized the subsequent history of Patagonian human adaptations, causing at least two effects: first, the formation of relatively closed populations, and second, the appearance of economic intensification. Indeed, this is when archaeologists began to find contrasting regional patterns, with relatively discrete populations in different regions (Franco et al. 2005; Goñi et al. 2006; Martínez et al. 2017; Mena 2013). García and Mena (2016) described what they see as a culturally closed system in the middle Ibañez basin, Aisén. Also, different populational nodes were

The Late Holocene Diversification

recognized in the south since ca. 4000 BP for both the Pali Aike Volcanic Field and a relatively narrow longitudinal band from the south of the Argentino Lake to Última Esperanza (Borrero 2015; Borrero and Charlin 2010). These populations do not represent ethnic entities but simply reflect the accumulation of relatively isolated and distinctive archaeological assemblages (Ortiz Troncoso 1973b). Recent archaeological work is slowly showing that this relative isolation was terminated around 500 BP when evidence of dispersal to the peripheries of those nodes appeared, and some cultural mix is identified (Belardi et al. 2020).

A process of intensification was proposed to explain Late Holocene adaptations in southern Cuyo. It certainly can be defended in some cases but should not be considered axiomatic (Giardina et al. 2017; Johnson et al. 2009; Neme 2007; Otaola et al. 2012, 2015). It is not always clear to what point the recorded labor-intensive food resources were really part of the human subsistence or simply were incorporated by other agents (Borrero 1994–1995, 2012). Another problem is that large mammals rarely present evidence of intensive butchering, nor are there indications of diminution of high-ranked resources until historical times. Gil and collaborators (2020) showed that changes in temperature and precipitation over approximately the last 1,000 years in southern Cuyo – without significant changes in human population size – influenced the use of domestic plants and the hunting of the highest-ranked wild animals. Indeed, intense taphonomic research will be required to evaluate the importance of these patterns (Otaola 2013; Otaola et al. 2014). Similar discussions are published for Northeast Patagonia (Stoessel and Martínez 2014). Archaeological intensification was also proposed for the southern extreme of Fuego-Patagonia (Tivoli and Zangrando 2011; Zangrando 2009b). The case for Tierra del Fuego is based on evidence of increasing efforts in fishing and bird hunting, perhaps resulting from pressure by neighbors.

Interestingly, a series of superimposed occupations starting at 3200 BP was recorded at Las Vueltas 1, in North Tierra del Fuego, where abundant guanaco remains formed an extensive bone bed ca. 560 BP. This bed was interpreted as evidence for a guanaco mass kill that produced a minimum of ca. 1,500 kg of meat, bones, and skin (Santiago 2013). Alternative interpretations suggest that averaged (mixing of different depositional episodes) fauna are represented at Las Vueltas (Borrero 2013). Unless storage is implicated, for which there is no evidence, it remains a fascinating and difficult site to interpret.

Accompanying all this Late Holocene evidence of intensification, there is an increasing diversity in the ways of disposing of the dead. Corpses were placed on caves or open-air sites, as isolated individuals or concentrated, in elaborate structures or in conditions suggesting immediate abandonment after death (Castro and Moreno 2000; Flesborg et al. 2017; Franco et al. 2011a; Goñi and Barrientos 2000; Guichón et al. 2001; Reyes 2002). In fact, with a few exceptions, most of our information about human burials comes from the Late

Holocene. This is a time during which the archaeological visibility of the dead increased. In North Patagonia, there are relatively large cemeteries, such as Aquihuecó or Caepe Malal I (Della Negra and Novellino 2005; Hajduk et al. 2000), with some burials accompanied by pottery or other goods. At the mouth of the Negro River, there were hundreds of Late Holocene human burials on dunes near lagoons and oxbows, with Laguna del Juncal as the most famous locality (Bernal et al. 2008; Bórmida 1950, 1953–1954; Fisher and Nacuzzi, 1992; Moreno 1874). Burials are found within habitational sites like shell middens on the coasts of North Patagonia and the Strait of Magellan, while generally they are deposited at special places in the interior (Carden and Prates 2015; Goñi and Barrientos 2004; Guichón et al. 2001; Prates et al. 2019; Reyes and Méndez 2010). Most of the latter are large burial mounds made with rocks, locally known as *chenques*. They were the best solution to dispose of the dead in a land where the ground remains frozen for months. This is particularly important in the mountains, as in Cerro Guido (Morano Büchner et al. 2009). The older evidence for this mode of interment was found in the Early Holocene levels of Baño Nuevo cave (Mena and Reyes 2001; Mena et al. 2003; Reyes and Méndez 2010). Another antecedent for a *chenque* was recorded at Orejas de Burro cave (L'Heureux and Barberena 2008) dated ca. 3500 BP. But the classic *chenques* are a later open-air phenomenon, perhaps marking an increase in population density. Intensive excavations at the Salitroso basin indicated three main forms of Late Holocene disposal of the bodies. Niches – natural holes on outcrops – and bodies covered with rocks located under large boulders were used during the period 2800–2200 BP. Proper *chenques* were used after that time (Barrientos et al. 2007; Bernal et al. 2004; Cassiodoro et al. 2013; García Guráieb et al. 2007, 2015; Goñi and Barrientos 2000, 2004; Goñi et al. 2000–2002, 2004; Reyes 2002). Large concentrations of *chenques* were also recorded near the coast (Zilio 2017; Zilio and Hammond 2019) (Figure 6.19).

Cerro Sota was used as a burial place for nine individuals around 3700–3400 BP (Hedges et al. 1992), more or less at the time of the five individuals buried at Orejas de Burro 1, ca. 3500 BP (L'Heureux 2008; L'Heureux and Amorosi 2010; L'Heureux and Barberena 2008). This is also the time during which multiple burials were identified at other caves in South Patagonia, such as Río Bote and Cueva Lago Sofía 1 (Franco et al. 2010b, 2017b; Prieto 1991). Beyond its use for human burials, Orejas de Burro was redundantly occupied in different seasons, particularly during fall and winter (L'Heureux and Kaufmann 2012: 164). Tools, hearths, and broken guanaco bones were recorded. Mollusks and driftwood that were transported at least 17 km from the Strait of Magellan were also recovered (Caruso Fermé et al. 2015).

Burials in North Tierra del Fuego are particularly varied, ranging from individuals deposited in dunes or shell middens (Martin 2004, 2006; Martin et al. 2004; Prieto et al. 2019; Salemme et al. 2007b; Santiago et al. 2011) to

Figure 6.19 *Chenque* at Punta Medanosa, Argentina. Photo courtesy Heidi Hammond, Leandro Zilio.

chenques (Ocampo et al. 2000). In the forests of the Beagle Channel, small shelters or shell middens were used (Alvarez et al. 2008; Aspillaga and Ocampo 1996; Piana et al. 2006, 2008), while in the western channels, funerary packages on structures made of painted sticks deposited in crevices or in rock shelters are dominant (Aspillaga et al. 1999; Legoupil and Prieto 1991; Legoupil et al. 2004; Palacios and Sierpe 2019; San Román and Morello 2001). All these studies disclosed important information on past lifeways, demography, and cultural dynamics (Gómez Otero and Dahinten 1997–1998; Gómez Otero and Novellino 2010; Gordón 2009; Gordón and Bosio 2012; Novellino et al. 2007; Prieto and Cárdenas 2007; Rizzo 2018). Interestingly, false associations between human burials and animal remains were detected (Rizzo and Fernández 2020), and relatively abundant rock structures of different forms and size, sometimes similar to *chenques* but without human bodies, were identified (Borella et al. 2015; Borrero et al. 2011; Goñi and Barrientos 2000; Goñi et al. 2004; Reyes et al. 2006). They might be associated with revisiting burial sites to perform additional rituals resulting in secondary burials, but this is not really known.

Diverse manifestations of painted and engraved images accompanied all these cultural processes. According to Fiore (2006), the first small and mobile groups of Late Pleistocene people probably were not inscribing places with rock art. Only when people settled was communication effective enough to serve its purpose. During the Early Holocene, places began to be redundantly occupied, and rock art became an effective way of communication. Beyond the evidence of Early Holocene antiquity in the Pinturas River basin (Gradin et al. 1976), the chronology of rock art is far from resolved. A radiocarbon chronology for rock paintings is slowly emerging. Rock paintings at Viuda Quenzana 1 and 2 correspond to the Late Holocene (Brook et al. 2018), while at Cueva Huenul 1 they present a Middle Holocene chronology (Romero Villanueva 2019). Growing Late Holocene population density is expressed in the abundance of sites with rock paintings or engravings, increasing the potential to integrate huge areas. Elaborate scenes were recorded at some places – especially guanaco hunting scenes, which are restricted to the older occupations (Aschero et al. 2019a) – but simpler motifs are more frequent (Bate 1971; Carden 2008; Carden and Borella 2015; Carden et al. 2009; Fiore 1999; Sepúlveda 2011). Several "styles" were defined and recognized through time and their distributions – basically in Central Patagonia – are well mapped (Aschero 1988; Bate 1970; Belardi 2004; Fiore 1999; Gradin 1987; Menghin 1952b). This panorama changes completely south of the Santa Cruz River, where an impoverished repertoire of motifs can be found (Bate 1971; Boschin 2009; Fiore 1999; Gallardo 2009; Hernández Llosas et al. 1999; Massone 1982; Sepúlveda 2011). At any rate, the recent discovery of engravings in the Gallegos Basin complicates our understanding of what was previously considered a homogeneous area (Manzi et al. 2019). The distribution of painted motifs in South Patagonia presents three geographic groupings: Pali Aike, the area south of Lago Argentino–Última Esperanza, and the western archipelagos (Charlin and Borrero 2012). This geographic patterning can be used to argue for the existence of relatively closed systems, in which some form of territoriality or circulation control was in place, a situation that can be defended on the basis of other markers like provenance of raw material or stable isotopes on human bones (Borrero 2015). The western archipelago variant is particularly interesting in that it results from the activities of maritime hunters moving along the dangerous waters of the outer channels of the Pacific (Gallardo 2007). Recent work south of the Isla Grande of Tierra del Fuego discovered other sites with rock paintings at Hoste and Picton islands, necessarily adscribed to maritime peoples (González Calderón et al. 2014; Muñoz et al. 2016). Open social systems are recognized in the homogeneity of some late rock art representations, like those of frets ("grecas"), and in the so-called ceremonial axes that are among the best evidence of information networks (Belardi 2004; Fisher 2009). However, beyond sharing a graphic vocabulary during the Late Holocene, the behavior of other markers is not concordant and points to restrictions in the intensity of interactions with neighbors, probably as part of the mentioned regionalization processes (Martinez et al. 2017; Pallo and Borrero 2015a).

The Late Holocene Diversification

Decorated objects are not abundant but significant in Patagonia, showing the use of bones, mollusks, or eggshells for decorative or transcendent reasons (Arias et al. 2012; Carden and Borges Vaz 2017; Carden and Martínez 2014; Fiore and Borella 2010; Romero Villanueva 2019; Romero Villanueva and Barberena 2017; Zubimendi and Ambrústolo 2011). Particularly abundant in Tierra del Fuego are transversal striae on bird long bones. Also, decorated stone axes were widespread in North Patagonia (Acevedo 2015; Fisher 2009).

THE CONTACT PERIOD AND THE COLONIAL TIMES

When the first Europeans arrived in the Pampas and Patagonia at the very beginning of the sixteenth century, they found a land of hunter-gatherers (Figure 6.20). There were a few exceptions, such as some Guaraní "colonies" and the Chana-Timbú ethnic complex. While the former was the apparent continuation of the Guaraní archaeological tradition, the latter was the ethnographic expression of the Goya-Malabrigo archaeological entity. The several early colonial accounts show a culturally heterogeneous panorama as well as an intense population dynamic in the Lower Paraná and Uruguay Rivers (Lothrop 1932; Madero 1902; Serrano 1950). These Indians were canoe people known as Chaná-Timbú – a generic denomination that includes several groups or subgroups such as the Chaná, Timbú, Chaná-Mbeguá, Mbeguá, and Coronda. They had a mixed economy of fishing, hunting, and gathering. Most of them developed small-scale horticulture and lived in the river islands and riverside, forming semi-permanent villages organized under a paramount chief. Evidence of some political hierarchy led Politis and Bonomo (2012) to identify a ranked society. These societies would be regionally integrated and be able to develop political alliances to confront the Spaniards. There were no marked frontiers between these groups, which supports the existence of fluid ethnic borders, but historical accounts mentioned more frequently some ethnonyms associated with certain places.

As we said, the Guaraní spread through several regions of southeastern South America, reaching the northeastern border of the Pampas about two centuries before the European arrival (Bonomo et al. 2015; Brochado 1984). In terms of sociopolitical organization and kinship, they formed several nuclear families, sometimes up to 60 or more, around a political/religious leader. The larger villages could integrate four or five extended families, given an average of 300–600 inhabitants. The subsistence of the Guaraní population was quite generalized, based on horticulture, gathering of plants and insects, hunting, and fishing. Despite the great geographical expansion and the tendency to systematically incorporate non-Guaraní people, pottery maintains a great uniformity. The typical painted and corrugated pottery is found in distant locations, thousands of kilometers apart, with minimal variation, indicating that it was

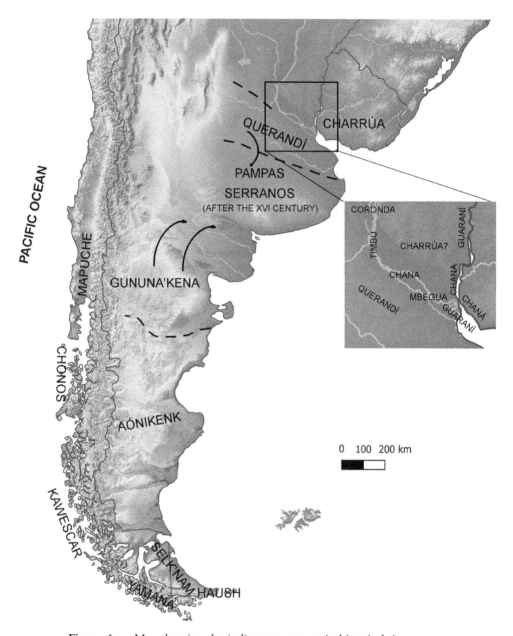

Figure 6.20 Map showing the indigenous groups in historical times.

produced in the context of a rigid stylistic, highly standardized pattern (Noelli 1999–2000). At the time of contact with Europeans there were Guaraní villages in the Lower Paraná Delta and the Lower Uruguay River.

Toward the west, the Pampean grassland was occupied by the Querandí Indians (Casamiquela 1969; Conlazo et al. 2006; Madero 1092; Roulet 2016). The first colonial documents placed them in the plains between the Lower Paraná and La Plata Rivers and the Central Hills and between the Salado River

The Late Holocene Diversification

of the Buenos Aires Province and the Carcarañá River. They were highly mobile people who built temporary and light leather shelters (*toldos*). The Querandí were originally hunters of small- and medium-sized game (basically Pampas deer and greater rhea) who quickly became horse riders and substantially changed their way of life. They promptly lost ethnic identity, were incorporated by indigenous neighboring groups, or were subject to missions or the encomienda system.

There are few archaeological sites in the Pampas that reflect the "first contact": the Sancti Spiritus fort and the San Salvador post; both were built in 1527 by the expedition of Sebastian Gaboto and lasted less than two years. The archaeological research at Sancti Spiritus shows that the fort was built over a Chaná-Timbú village (probably abandoned at that moment); pottery indicates the interaction with the Guaraní and the Chaná-Timbú people. Sherds from these two groups were found inside the fort associated with abundant European types (Columbia Gunmetal, Columbia Green Dippel, Isabela Polychrome, etc.) and majolica (Cocco et al. 2011; Fritegotto et al. 2013; Letieri et al. 2015).

The excavation in the San Salvador post at the Lower Uruguay River also recovered European material associated with Chaná and Guaraní pottery and some types that would belong to the Charrúa Indians (hunter-gatherers of the Uruguay Campos). This context suggests sporadic contact with the Chaná, whose presence in the Lower Uruguay River was less intense than in the Lower Paraná River (López Mazz et al. 2014).

In continental Patagonia, the Aónikenk and Gununa'kena hunter-gatherers (Casamiquela 1969; Martinic 1995) were the last representatives of a long tradition of guanaco hunters, combining bola stone and bow and arrow hunting. After the adoption of the horse and being attracted by the domestic and wild cattle and horse, which flourished in the Pampas since the sixteenth century, they moved north back and forth and even reached the Salado Depression. In the mid-eighteenth century, the ethnonym Tehuelche showed up in various ethnic groups such as the Aónikenk and Gununa'kena and the previously named Serranos (Nacuzzi 1998; Roulet 2016).

As soon as the Hispanic conquest advanced, several settlements were founded in the sixteenth century in the Pampas, notably Buenos Aires and Santa Fe. The former was founded in 1536 and abandoned a few years later. No archaeological remains have been recovered from this settlement; they would have been destroyed as a result of the refoundation of the city in 1580. Santa Fe was erected in 1573 on the banks of the Paraná River but was abandoned 80 years later and relocated in its current place. This abandonment allowed the colonial city, now called Santa Fe la Vieja, to remain and be available for further archaeological excavation (Carrara and De Grandis 2005; Cocco 2005; Zapata Gollan 1981). The pottery there included the typical sixteenth-century European pottery, associated with Guaraní and Goya-

Malabrigo types (Ceruti 2005). Also, many pieces of a local style, a mixture of Hispanic and Guaraní motifs and techniques, reveal the materiality of an ethnogenesis process initiated decades before in Asunción in Paraguay (Cocco 2005).

Along with the foundation of cities, in the Americas the Spanish developed an institution called encomienda, which was a strategy to acquire Indian services, or goods, by using the local indigenous system of authority and taking advantage of the already existing traditional political units (Lockhart and Schwartz 1983: 68). Many Indians were given to the first conquerors in encomiendas at the same time their land was distributed. However, given the nomadic way of life, the band fluidity, and the unstable political units of the Querandí Indians, these encomiendas never succeeded.

In the early colonial years, how the Spaniards named the Indians changed and adopted a binary geographical system. The Indians living in the flat grasslands were called Pampas, while those inhabiting (although probably never exclusively) the Tandilia and Ventania hills and the Andean Cordillera were called Serranos (Roulet 2016). Progressively, these original foragers changed toward a mixed economy that combined hunting and gathering with herding (cattle, horses, and sheep), agriculture, and raids for cattle in the colonial frontier (Mandrini 1986).

Besides the encomiendas, the other strategy for domination and territorial control was missionization, which in some way was conjoined with the former. During the seventeenth century, several Franciscan missions, also called *reducciones*, were founded in the eastern Pampa to settle the Chaná, Timbú, Mbeguá, and Guaraní, but they were not successful and were depopulated at the end of the century. The main missions were San José del Bagual (1611), San Juan Bautista (1611), Santiago de Baradero (1616), and San Bartolomé de los Chanás (1615). Some of them left archaeological remains, such as Santiago de Baradero (Debenedetti 1911; Tapia 2002; Tapia and Pinau 2011) and San Bartolomé de Los Chaná (Rochietti and De Grandis 2016), whose excavations added to the meager historical information. A mix of Hispanic and indigenous materials formed the archaeological record of both sites. These missions failed in retaining the Indian families, and many died of epidemic diseases, escaped, or were forced to return to the encomiendas (Birocco 2009; Rochietti and de Grandis 2016). By the beginning of the eighteenth century, some of these missions became Pueblos de Indios, and they had to pay tribute to the Spanish Crown under the mita service system (Birocco 2009). In the Uruguay River, the Santo Domingo Soriano Mission (1662), initially for the Chaná, quickly became multiethnic, and at the beginning of the nineteenth century, it was a Pueblo de Indios. In the Salado River Depression and in Tandilia, the Jesuits founded three missions in the eighteenth century, well inside Indian territory: Nuestra Señora de La Concepción de los Indios Pampas (1740–1753), Nuestra Señora del Pilar del Volcan

The Late Holocene Diversification

(1747–1751), and Nuestra Señora de los Desamparados (1750–1751). These missions intended to settle and Christianize the nomadic (horse-riding) Pampas, Serranos, and Tehuelches. However, they also failed, and the missions had an ephemeral life, always under the threat of hostile indigenous groups. On the border of the Salado River were the scattered remains of the former mission, but no systematic archaeological excavations could be done (Pedrotta 2013).

The pattern that emerged from the colony's first centuries is that all the attempts to settle the different Pampean and Patagonian ethnic groups, whether in *reducciones* or encomiendas, failed. However, the traditionally semi-sedentary groups with some degree of food production, such as the Guaraní and Chaná-Timbú latu sensu, eventually transformed these settlements in Pueblos de Indios with some autonomy. Most of them suffered a process of *mestizaje* and were diluted into the rural Hispanic-criollo population in the following two centuries. On the other hand, the Querandí (Pampas), Serranos, and Tehuelches maintained a nomadic style, now revolving around horses and cattle herding; developed a resistance strategy (the assault of the ranchers in the frontier, the *malón*); and forged political alliances with the Mapuche since the eighteenth century. As a result of the dynamic in the frontier, some Pampas lineages maintained close and regular contact with the Hispanic-criollo people; they settled in the vicinities of the military forts and rural stores (*pulperías*) in the advancing frontier and were known as *Indios amigos* (Indian friends). They were important mediators with those populations in the hinterland and gave military support on the frontier (de Jong et al. 2020). Once the state's military campaigns of occupation in the territories of the Pampa and Patagonia, known as the Conquista del Desierto (the Conquest of the Desert), took place, the militarization of the *Indios amigos* was stronger, extending to those hinterland Indians who were captured and became part of the army or the National Guard's civil corps (de Jong et al. 2020). The archaeological traces of one of these lineages, Catriel, have been recovered in the borders of the Arroyo Nievas, close to Azul, in lands given to these Indians by the national government (Pedrotta 2005).

On the other hand, since the middle of the sixteenth century in southern Chile, south of the Bio Bio, the Mapuche Indians strongly reacted to the occupation of their territories, called Araucanía by the Europeans (Bechis 2010 [1989]; Bello 2011; Dillehay 2007) and got involved in commercial and social links with Hispanic-criollos. The pre-Hispanic connection between the Indians on both sides of the Cordillera has been attested archaeologically (e.g., the Vergel-Valdivia pottery in the Tapera Moreira site; see above), and since the early colonial times, documents refer to the presence in the Pampas of Indians from the other side of the Andes – the letter from Juan de Garay in 1581 being the earliest account. However, commercial networks and social links deepened the precolonial connections between people from Araucanía

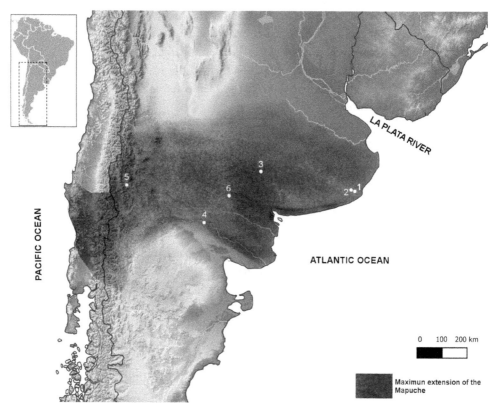

Figure 6.21 Maximum extension of the Mapuche in the nineteenth century. Some archaeological sites related to the Mapuche are marked. (1) Amalia; (2) Dos Naciones; (3) Gascón 1; (4) Chimpay; (5) Caepe Malal 1; (6) Cerro de los Viejos.

and the Pampas and North Patagonia during the eighteenth century. This complex and fluid commercial network was based mainly on the traffic of cattle and horses (partly raised by the Indians, some taken to the Hispanic-criollo in the frontier), salt, and indigenous textiles. It remained until the end of the nineteenth century and gave rise to an important Arauco-Pampean-Patagonian sociocultural unit (de Jong et al. 2020). This unit, a product of an ethnogenesis process, spoke Mapudungun as a common language.

In the eighteenth century, Pampean-Patagonia Indians developed a new political organization based on large *cacicazgos* (chiefdoms) or confederations with stable territories and mainly under the leadership of Mapuche *caciques* (Bechis 2008 [1989]; Mandrini and Ortelli 2002; Roulet 2016). Sustained on parental reciprocity, these chiefdoms' commercial and political ties connected peoples and places, from the Araucanía to the Pampas and Patagonia, forming a large political territory (Figure 6.21). The Mapuche, Pampas, Serranos, Gununa'kena (Tehuelches), Pehuenches, and others integrated into this political unit, joined by a common enemy, commercial benefits, and kinship links.

The Late Holocene Diversification 241

The relationships in the frontier alternated between diplomacy and war, depending on the political capacity of the *caciques*; when diplomatic instances failed, they organized raids against the criollos, called *malones* (Crivelli Montero 1991; de Jong 2016).

In the eastern Pampa, a few sites testified to the Mapuche presence. Notably, the archaeological locality of Amalia in the foothills of Tandilia shows residential camps with several associated stone structures (corrals, water reservoirs, enclosures, etc.) (Mazzanti 2007). Abundant lithic material, typical Mapuche pottery, glass beads, and colonial pottery (olive jars, gres, etc.) indicate a well-defined Mapuche occupation at the end of the eighteenth century (Mazzanti 2007).

This sociopolitical unit developed a road system to transport cattle and horses between the Pampas and Chile. These trails, known as *rastrilladas*, integrated a dense network of *tolderías* (e.g., the excavated sites Don Isidoro 1 y 2, Poitahue and Quillay Lauquen; Tapia 2002) and connected the cordilleran passes, the Pampean grasslands, and the strategic locations in between (Curtoni 2007; Tapia 2002, 2011, 2014). They survived until the end of the nineteenth century and were recorded by the first topographers; nowadays, some sections can still be recognized in the western Pampa as deep and wide ditches.

In Tandilia and Ventania, there is a great variety of stone structures of different dimensions and shapes, which should have had different functions (Ferrer and Pedrotta 2006; Madrid 1991a, b; Pedrotta 2005; Ramos et al. 2008). Some of them are large rectangular or circular enclosures that would serve as corrals (Ferrer and Pedrotta 2006; Ramos et al. 2008), while others are made of long walls, stone corridors to drive cattle, or smaller constructions that would be used as shelters or defensive structures (Mazzanti 2005; Pedrotta 2005). Most of these structures have been interpreted as constructions for the management and commerce of domestic animals (cattle, horses, sheep, and goats) by Indians during the eighteenth and nineteenth centuries. In Cerro de Los Viejos, in the Close Basins area (Figure 6.21), six stone dams, well connected with *rastrilladas*, were interpreted as water reservoirs for transferring cattle between the Pampas and Chile (Piana 1981). In Ventania, there are clusters of standing stones, sometimes aligned, and others forming enclosures whose age and function are still under debate (Madrid 1991a; Panizza et al. 2013; Roa and Saghessi 2004).

Throughout the nineteenth century, there was a growing centralization of the political power of the leaders of the Indian confederation (Jiménez and Alioto 2011). The empowerment of the Mapuche leadership was evident in the economic, social, and religious dimensions, including the mortuary ceremonies of the *caciques* themselves (de Jong et al. 2020; González 1979). In these ceremonies, leaders were buried along with valuable objects, food, belongings, sacrificed animals, and occasionally sacrificed women. Several sites in the

Pampa and Patagonia are the product of these burial ceremonies (Figure 6.21). In the Dos Naciones site, in Tandilia, an individual was inhumated with a horse and a quartzite stone marking the tomb (Casamiquela and Noseda 1970), and in Gascon 1, five individuals were found in association with glass beads, metal earrings and buckles, and horse paraphernalia (Oliva et al. 2007). Quarters of sheep were placed as offerings.

In Northwest Patagonia, the Mapuche cemetery of Caepe Malal 1, dating to the eighteenth century, is one of the best funerary records of this period (Varela de Fernandez and Biset de Muñoz 1987). Several individuals in at least three tombs were buried with a variety of offerings (Mapuche pottery, European clothes, metal horse paraphernalia, horse and guanaco quarters, etc.), among which leather armor with metal plates, a leather helmet, and an iron sword stand out. On the border of the Negro River in the Chimpay site, a man wearing a military uniform and a woman were buried together with a varied funerary accompaniment (Prates et al. 2016). This finding corresponds to a late nineteenth-century Mapuche burial; the man was probably a chief, and the woman appeared to have a prestigious social position. The sacrifice of women during funerary ceremonies of male leaders could have resulted from the gender asymmetry in favor of males. De Jong and collaborators (2020) suggest that this burial was produced by the practice of the suttee (a ritual sacrifice of an individual to accompany or provide service to the dead in the afterlife).

During historical times there has been an increase in the diversity of recovered evidence in Patagonia. However, there is no important increase in the number of archaeological sites, since most of this new evidence was obtained at the same known places. This could be at least in part the result of lack of interest in the historical period, selective destruction of the upper occupations of sites, or incapacity to recognize the upper layers as archaeologically significant. A combination of these three factors probably conspired to limit the list of known historical sites. Nevertheless, this increased diversity involved different kinds of weapons, like bolas, bows and arrows (with tips made of stone or glass), and horse-related paraphernalia (Belardi et al. 2013; Cirigliano and Pallo 2019; Nuevo Delaunay 2012; Nuevo Delaunay et al. 2017, 2020; Palermo 1986; Saletta and Fiore 2019; Saletta and Sacchi 2019). To make things more complicated, the small number of known historical sites testifies to important changes in social organization and settlement during short periods. Since those periods are usually less than 500 years, it becomes difficult to assess the rate of change or even accurately date the sites. This methodological problem plagues the analysis of changing repertoires of tools and bones within these short sequences (Cirigliano and Pallo 2019; Saletta and Fiore, 2019; Saletta and Sacchi 2019). Interestingly, a recent analysis of stable isotopes on samples from before and after contact showed evidence of persistence of subsistence strategies across that boundary in South Tierra del

The Late Holocene Diversification

Fuego (Tafuri et al. 2017), and there are no significant changes expected for the rest of the area. At any rate, written sources describe important changes in subsistence for natives living at the South America Missionary Society in Ushuaia, basically the incorporation of carbohydrates (Chapman 2010). This is also the situation at the Misión Nuestra Señora de la Candelaria in North Tierra del Fuego, where stable isotope studies showed "an imbalance in the diet, with a higher proportion of carbohydrates and a lower proportion of animal proteins" in comparison with pre-contact hunter-gatherers (Valenzuela et al. 2019). Beyond the noted changes in subsistence produced by foods introduced by the missionaries, there were also organizational changes. These changes were precipitated by the intensive early European contact on the coasts (Moreno 2008), particularly the foundation of European forts and other settlements (Bianchi Villelli 2007; Buscaglia 2007, 2015; Gawronski 1999; Marschoff 2007; Palombo 2007; Senatore 2007; Suby et al. 2009). These settlements – and the movement of people around them – affected in different ways the nomadic circuits of local foragers, an issue barely touched on by the archaeological literature. Effectively, important subsistence changes in continental Patagonia resulted from a combination of horses, new tactics, and weapons. For example, the emphasis on lesser rhea consumption is well recorded by most historical sources and, together with the increasing consumption of horse meat and fat, constituted a major dietary change. The use of larger huts and the location at places near good pastures were only some of the organizational changes produced by the incorporation of horses. The slow dispersal of people after 500 BP to the west of PAVF could be related.

In spite of the mentioned limitations, a growing corpus of studies is informative about those final years. Scattered evidence from the north of Patagonia offers a complex image of human distribution, ethnic attribution, and subsistence practices (Fernández 2010; Fernández et al. 2011, 2019; Hajduk et al. 2000, 2007; Leonardt et al. 2015; Nacuzzi 1998). Some of the most important historic settlements of the southern Aónikenk were located near the central Strait of Magellan and the forests (Buscaglia 2019; Fitz Roy 1839). These people were basically commuting between the Cordillera Chica, an important guanaco hunting place, and the open steppes (Childs 1936; Martinic 1995; Martinic et al. 1995; Pallo and Borrazzo 2017). Demographic growth in areas near the central Strait of Magellan was considered as a push factor for the displacement of people to Tierra del Fuego (Goñi 2013). Evidence for cohabitation between Aónikenk and what the travelers called Fuegians – not necessarily people from the island, but certainly people who adapted to the sea – was recorded in the mainland and on Elizabeth Island (Borrero et al. 2011, 2019b). Nuevo Delauney (2012) described the final phase of the Aónikenk organization. Sheep farming advanced near the end of the nineteenth century (Barbería 1995), and the surviving Aónikenk groups were concentrated at "reservations," a transformation that limited their wanderings and triggered several economic changes. Some of the most important ethnographic camps and reservations on the Lago Viedma, the Zurdo, or the Coyle Basins were archaeologically interrogated (Jackson 1991; Nuevo Delaunay et al. 2020), documenting highly distinctive architectonic features and other evidence of organizational change. Clusters of glass scrapers, sometimes accompanied by metal artifacts, guanaco, and horse bones with anthropic marks, characterize these redundantly used places.

The expansion of Euro-American sheep exploitation in North Tierra del Fuego was associated with the increasing conflict with the Selk'nam. This new economic system associated with the sheep required extensive open prairies, which were the lands inhabited by the Selk'nam. Killings of natives occurred regularly starting in the 1880s, and some workers hired by the sheep farms became famous as Selk'nam hunters (Borrero 1991; Chapman 1986). European miners searching for gold also violently interacted with the Selk'nam. The Romanian Julius Popper is one of the best known (Chapman 1986). Although there were skirmishes, the responses of the Selk'nam rarely included armed conflict. Instead, a retraction toward the forest took place (Borrero 1991; Massone 2009). Natives sometimes found work at some ranches, like Estancia San Pablo, in the island's center (Casali and Manzi 2017). All these habitat changes, basically focused on the forests of the Fagnano Lake, led to important reorganizations of their economic and social life (Gusinde 1982 [1937]; Mansur and Piqué 2012). This was also a time when several religious missions began to settle. Salesian missions were starting to function on the Atlantic coast of the island and at Isla Dawson on the Strait of Magellan. These centers of acculturation also served as places where Selk'nam people, mainly women and children, were concentrated (Salerno and Guichón 2017). These processes led to the termination of tribal life within a few decades.

The general area where some of the last Selk'nam camps were located was practically limited to the forests of the mouth of the Fuego River and the headwaters of the Fagnano Lake (Borrero 1991). The Ewan site, located in the open forest east of Fagnano Lake, includes two historical huts, one of them considered as ceremonial (Mansur and Piqué 2012). Glass was an important raw material in those and other historical sites in Tierra del Fuego (De Angelis 2015; Parmigiani et al. 2012). As already mentioned, during that time there were religious missions operating in different places of Tierra del Fuego, some of which were archaeologically investigated (Salerno and Guichón 2017; Salerno et al. 2016; Suby and Guichón 2010).

CHAPTER 7

FINAL REMARKS

The chapters presented before showed diverse historical trajectories, different adaptive patterns, and continuous human occupation of the Pampas and Patagonia since the end of the Pleistocene. Both regions were probably among the last continental lands, except Antarctica, colonized by *Homo sapiens* after their dispersal from Africa. The first outcome of this review of the archaeology of the Pampas and Patagonia is that it does not support a pre-15,000 cal BP human occupation of the Southern Cone. Putting this in the global discussion means that the Pampas-Patagonia peopling holds up a pre-13,000 cal BP (the so-called pre-Clovis Model) but post–Late Glacial Maximum human arrival at the continent, which is in agreement with current archaeological, ancient DNA, and paleoclimatic models (Llamas et al. 2016; Pitblado 2011; Posth et al. 2018; Prates et al. 2020; Sutter 2021; Waters and Stafford 2013). Moreover, most of the paleoclimatic evidence supports the hypothesis that the earliest human arrivals at the Pampas and Patagonia took place under cold climatic conditions in semiarid to arid environments (Borrero and Martin 2018; Prado et al. 2021) during the cooling period known as the Antarctic Cold Reversal (14,700–13,000 cal BP).

Summed calibrated probability density (SCPD) curves of radiocarbon dates have been suggested to be proxies for population size or population density (Williams 2012). While they do not directly reflect the density of people, they help to visualize the number of radiocarbon dates per period, which in turn are related to the rate of discard of archaeological material, which is a derivation of human occupation. Despite critics and limitations (e.g., Freeman et al. 2018; Surovell et al. 2009), they have been useful to explore and discuss the temporal frequency of prehistoric populations in the region (Barrientos 1997; Martínez et al. 2015; Perez et al. 2016), and we find that it is a helpful tool to explore changes in demography through time. Therefore, we built a Pampean radiocarbon database (Supplementary Tables 1–3), following the criteria for inclusion/

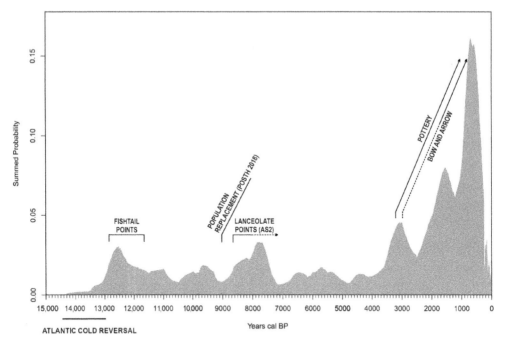

Figure 7.1 Summed calibrated probability density (SCPD) curve of radiocarbon dates from the Pampas region.

exclusion explained in Politis and Prates (2018) and Prates et al. (2020). The database was formed by 633 dates, which we used to generate an SCPD curve (Figure 7.1), the implications of which we discuss below. Patagonia is too extended and diverse, and its record is too patchy, to produce useful SCPD curves of radiocarbon dates. This problem is also evident when we try to establish connections between human occupations recorded in distant and very different places, such as the San Matías Gulf and Última Esperanza.

THE EARLY PEOPLING

It seems that the early evidence of human occupation in the Pampas and Patagonia (exploration phase; Borrero 1999) shows a generalized technology and does not register any model of lithic projectile points. However, this is not clear-cut since it is based on evidence from only a few places. Although the absence of projectile points is not unexpected from an organizational perspective because not all occupations need to present the same tools (see Chapter 4), these artifacts have not been found in the earliest sites so far. This first phase, dated between ~14,000 and 12,900 cal BP, is documented in Arroyo Seco 2 (the two lower occupations ~ 14,060 and 13,000 cal BP); the lower layers of Tigre (13,300 cal BP), Cueva Casa del Minero, and Cerro Tres Tetas (~ 12,900 cal BP). These levels show the exploitation of a few taxa: guanaco and the two

Final Remarks 247

species of American horse (*Equus* and *Hippidion*); in the Pampas, we can add giant ground sloth, and in Patagonia, *Lama gracilis*. Notably, the earlier occupations do not differ much from those that follow, and their chronological precedence is minimal. Possible causes for the lack of projectile points in these earliest levels are inadequate sampling, the use of perishable materials such as wood, or a low frequency of lithic projectile points, highly curated, which in turn generates a low rate of discard. As we will see below, evidence for the low deposition rate of Fishtail projectile points characterizes the older Patagonian occupations.

The dates of initial colonization of the Pampas and Patagonia are also in agreement with the estimated data of human entry in South America based on a quantitative analysis of screened radiocarbon databases adjusted by Marshall's method, under the assumption that the oldest documented archaeological record occurs after the actual first arrival (Prates et al. 2020). This study suggested that the earliest chronological threshold for the peopling of South America was between 16.6 and 15 kyr. It also agrees with recent mitogenomic analysis of 18 human skeletal remains from three Early to Late Holocene Pampean archaeological sites (Laguna de Los Pampas, Arroyo Seco 2, and Laguna Chica; Roca-Rada et al. 2021). Genomic studies from past and present native samples have revealed that the major founding lineages (A2, B2, C1b, C1c, C1d, D1, and D4h3a) are distributed across the Americas with temporal and spatial variation (Bisso-Machado et al. 2012; Perego et al. 2010), but there are specific clades that show a highly restricted geographic distribution, such as B2i2, C1b13, D1g, and D1j, that are found nearly exclusively in the Southern Cone (Bodner et al. 2012; de Saint Pierre et al. 2012). Roca-Rada and collaborators (2021) proposed that the coalescence time estimates for D1j, D1g, and even the subclade D4h3a were synchronous at ~ 15.6 cal BP, suggesting that the three might have emerged during the initial peopling of the Americas and diversified en route to South America or even arose in the Southern Cone. These studies would imply a rapid expansion of *Homo sapiens* from Beringia to the Pampas and Patagonia at a speed that seems difficult to model (but see Martino et al. 2007; Steele 2009).

In the Pampas, a possible change occurred at ~ 12,900 cal BP associated with Fishtail points first (Figure 7.1), and shortly after, in the Campos, with other stemmed models of projectile points such as Tigre and Pay Paso. The evidence from Patagonia associated with Fishtail points need not necessarily correspond to an occupational pulse that follows that represented at Cueva Casa del Minero and Cerro Tres Tetas. It might well be that the early occupational history of the Pampas and Patagonia was slightly decoupled, being older in the former region. Faunal exploitation continued to be restricted to several species: guanaco, *Hippidion*, *Equus*, *Megatherium*, *Doedicurus*, and *Hemiauchenia*. *Mylodon* and *Lama gracilis* are represented in layers associated with Fishtail points in Patagonia, but the most frequent species associated with humans is *Hippidion saldiasi.* Prates and Perez (2021) recently proposed a substantial spatial and temporal relationship between the Fishtail point, which was directly associated with large mammal hunting, and the density and distribution of Pleistocene megafauna. On this basis, they put forward that human predatory behavior was the main factor driving the megafaunal decline in South America at the onset of the Fishtail points expansion, after 12,900 cal BP. Other alternatives could also be considered, such as a better knowledge of the megamammals' behavior in conjunction with more efficient hunting strategies and new settlement/mobility patterns. In the neighboring Campos of Uruguay, other technological traits such as blade technology, large bifacial tools, and bifacial knives (some in a crescent/half-moon shape) have been identified by Suarez (2017), who proposed a regional social and technological reorganization. For Patagonia, Metcalf and collaborators (2016) put forward that human disruption of mega-faunal metapopulation processes, and more intense hunting pressure linked with decreased habitat range, caused local population extinctions. Megafaunal extinctions did not occur for these authors until human presence and climate warming coincided after the Antarctic Cold Reversal. However, the Patagonian archaeo-logical record does not support a major role for humans since only Fell Cave has an archaeofaunal assemblage dominated by an extinct mammal, *Hippidion saldiasi* (Martin 2021). Moreover, the association with cut-marked *Mylodon* remains at that site was explained by scavenging carnivore kills (Martin 2008). *Mylodon* remains were also recovered at other places in Patagonia, but only those at Piedra Museo were found associated with tools and hearths and presented cut-marks (Marchionni and Vázquez 2012). The association suggested for the early layers of El Trébol in North Patagonia (Hajduk et al. 2010) is still difficult to sustain because it is based on what appears to be the use of a piece of *Mylodon* skin, which easily may remain years after the death of the animal. Of course, there are many difficulties in assessing the interaction between the larger mammals like *Mylodon* or *Megatherium*, animals that we can adequately call megafauna, and humans. In the first place, it is not expected that humans who hunt or scavenge these large mammals will transport carcasses or their parts to habitation sites. More probably, they will process the carcass and transport only the meat in the way observed among recent foragers (O'Connell et al. 1990). Also, not many cut-marks are expected in a bone assemblage derived from the processing of megamammals. Given the large amounts of meat attached to the bones, the possibilities of stone tools making contact with the bone are low. Accordingly, it remains possible that the incidence of extinct megafauna in the human diet was higher than what the archaeological record shows. As a result of these considerations, and given the paucity of cave sites with megafauna in the Pampas and open-air sites in Patagonia, probably the record of none of these large regions fully conveys the relationship between foragers and prey.

There are five nodes in the Pampas (including the Campos) and Patagonia area, which suggest areas of more intense occupation during the post ~ 12,900

Final Remarks 249

cal BP phase: (1) the Lower Uruguay and Negro Rivers in Uruguay, (2) Tandilia and the Interserrana area, (3) the Somuncurá Plateau, (4) the Deseado Massif, and (5) the Pali Aike Volcanic Field–Última Esperanza Sound. Although sampling bias, geomorphological factors, taphonomic conditions, and differences in archaeological visibility would affect the archaeological coverage, the existence of areas with null or very low human signal (e.g., Rolling Pampa, CPD, Salado River Depression, the Santa Cruz River Basin) during the early stages supports a "leapfrogging" migration (Anthony 1990) into these regions. The earliest foragers would travel faster between concentrated resources, such as patches of megaherbivores and other food supplies (Anderson and Gillam 2000; Haynes 2002) or high-quality raw materials, and would slow down when reaching similarly attractive patches. Beyond sharing the Fishtail points, the first three areas have a few other common traits (discoidals, small spheres, raw materials, etc.), indicating some links between them (Flegenheimer et al. 2013c, 2015a; Nami 2017). The presence of the Queguay limestone in several Tandilia and Interserrana sites could be explained as the remnants of rocks or artifacts brought by early migrants from the Campos or as the result of back-and-forth travels between these two areas favored by social and kinship ties (see Chapter 4).

The subsequent human dispersal to South Patagonia probably proceeded at different rhythms, according to the broader distances between suitable places for long-term human installation at the end of the Pleistocene (Borrero and Martin 2021). Minimal evidence exists to judge the comparative importance of the Somuncurá Plateau in terms of early human settlement because the high visibility of projectile points in that area makes it difficult to compare with places where burial was important. All the available evidence points to the Deseado Massif as the earliest important node or staging area for Late Pleistocene foragers in South Patagonia, an area from which the later peopling of the Pali Aike Lava Field and other areas in west Patagonia probably occurred. Several sites occupied during the Early Holocene in the Deseado Massif, such as Maripé, Cerro Tres Tetas, La Gruta, El Verano, or La Martita, located on the periphery of the earlier sites, can be easily considered as stations connecting with places outside the massif. Long-distance logistical mobility, probably with a seasonal rhythm, was undoubtedly important for the successful peopling of the peri-Andean areas, where winters were extremely harsh (Pallo 2012). Well-researched places like Aisén present a relatively detailed record of short occupational pulses of the complicated topography of peri-Andean environments, showing a relatively protracted process in which time for acquisition of local geographic knowledge was required (Borrero et al. 2019a; Méndez et al. 2019). It is safe to assume that similar situations surely applied all along the eastern border of the Andes (Figures 7.2 and 7.3), with slightly different requirements. Not only are variations in topography important, but also differences in types of subsistence resources available, especially

Figure 7.2 View of an eastern valley of Baguales Range, Argentina.

Figure 7.3 Transects in the highlands, Baguales Range. Photo courtesy Karen Borrazzo.

Final Remarks 251

plants (Belmar 2019). It must also be taken into account that the distance from the Deseado Massif could also have been a factor. Incidentally, it was probably during these later stages of human dispersal, during the Early Holocene, that the obsidian source of Pampa del Asador was discovered. The few Late Pleistocene findings made at the Deseado Massif can be easily explainable due to the use of smaller sources of redeposited pebbles discovered by Nora Franco and collaborators, such as 17 de Marzo (Franco et al. 2017a).

It must be pointed out that humans did not visit all Pampean and Patagonian areas at the end of the Pleistocene. Sometimes this is the result of difficulties for human inhabitation in some places. For example, no Late Pleistocene arch-aeological evidence was found near the Cardiel Basin, which presented low water levels before 10,000 BP. Access for foragers remained difficult during the Early Holocene, and only during the Middle Holocene was that basin utilized (Goñi et al. 2014a). The same would happen in the CPD or some western Pampa areas where aridity was extreme during this period. Other areas simply were not even known to exist until the beginning of the Holocene. As far as we know, there is no evidence of Late Pleistocene human presence near the modern coasts of the Atlantic or Pacific Oceans. It may well be that any preexistent remains were destroyed, buried, or redeposited by the Middle Holocene sea transgression, but we presently have no hints suggesting their existence (Aguirre and Whatley 1995; Bujalesky 2007; Reyes et al. 2018). The analysis of the distribution of the earliest evidence of human occupation must always consider the fact that those were very small populations or subsets of the population concentrated elsewhere. Their wanderings across the Pampas and Patagonia probably were oriented toward finding the best places, but those quests were not necessarily successful.

Keeping in mind the separation of hundreds of kilometers between the earliest nodes or staging areas and differences in connectivity between them, some important characteristics of the earliest occupations of South Patagonia and North Patagonia/Pampas must be highlighted. First, it can be defended that the earliest southern occupations found in the Pali Aike Volcanic Field, Última Esperanza Sound, and Cerro de Los Onas in Tierra del Fuego were interconnected until the beginning of the Holocene when the rise of the oceans formed the Strait of Magellan, cutting off the island, and the expansion of forests and bogs in the lowlands of the Llanuras de Diana made access to Última Esperanza relatively difficult. Their chronology and contents are basic-ally the same, a condition recognized by Mauricio Massone with his concept of "Fell I Cultural Mode" of occupation (Massone 2009; Massone and Prieto 2004). Second, high concentrations of Fishtail projectile points are no longer found on hilltops, and their number in proportion to other tools markedly decreases. Except for Fell Cave, with 20 Fishtail points, the rest of the early occupations present only between one and three points. These two differences are related to the mode and intensity of occupation of the land. Perhaps one of the reasons behind some of these differences is the important changes in the available raw materials that varied from the high-quality rocks utilized in the north to relatively coarse-grained rocks in the south. It must also be recalled that there are no Fishtails made of Pampa del Asador obsidian, suggesting that this extensive source was not already incorporated during the initial exploration of Patagonia.

Another pattern that emerges from the current data is that it does not support a first peopling of both regions from the Pacific rim. First, the earliest sites in northwestern Patagonia have an Early Holocene age, suggesting later colonization (see Chapter 4). This is also the case for all the Early Holocene sites located on the eastern fringe of the Andes, from the Baguales Range to Aisén (Borrero 2004). As we just mentioned, most of these places probably were logistically explored and colonized from the earliest eastern nodes, like the Deseado Massif or the Pali Aike Volcanic Field. Moreover, beyond their strictly Holocene age, the earlier human occupations near the Andes are routinely associated only with modern fauna. When extinct fauna are present at all, it is always in layers below the oldest human evidence (Borrero 2004; Flores Coni et al. 2020), suggesting that people arrived after their extinction. Second, as we said, at least the D1g, D1j, and likely B2b haplogroups arrived in the Pampas during the initial settlement of the region as inferred from archaeological evidence (~ 14 kya), and the molecular dating (~ 15.5 kya) (Roca-Rada et al. 2021). Although the caution of ancient mitochondrial studies does not allow the detection of specific migration routes and the scarce evidence for the first phase of migration, it is unlikely that the peopling of the Pampas and Patagonia was through the Pacific coast followed by the crossing of the Southern Andes. The Patagonian Ice Sheet reached the $35°$ S parallel during the Late Glacial Maximum, and it was still in the Late Glacial phase at ~ 16–14 kya (Dickinson 2011; Rabassa et al. 2011). Even if trans-cordilleran passes were open during that time, not only were they unlikely to be suitable for human transit, but they also would have connected the eastern Patagonian steppes with fiords and channels covered by ice where no terrestrial fauna would have been available. In fact, the first recorded opening of the Patagonian Ice Sheet, separating what we now call the North and South Ice Sheets, occurred at ca. 12,500 BP (McCulloch et al. 2000), but human occupations were recorded in the channels west of the Andes only starting ca. 7000 BP (Reyes et al. 2016). Thus, an Atlantic coast (Miotti 2006b) or inland route is more probable for the peopling of the Pampas and Patagonia.

Sixteen extinct taxa were associated with humans in the Pampas, but only six of them showed evidence of human butchery: *Equus, Hippidion, Megatherium, Doedicurus, Hemiauchenia,* and *Eutatus* (Gutiérrez and Martínez 2008: 61). However, all the others would also be exploited, not only for food but for fuel or perhaps for leather, but no clear traces were left, as happens with megamammal exploitation in other parts of the world. In Patagonia, the

Final Remarks

number of available extinct species associated with archaeological sites decreases, and evidence for human exploitation is concentrated on *Hippidion* and camelids. Minimal evidence of exploitation of *Mylodon* or *Lama gracilis* also exists. Other species without any trace of human manipulation were recovered at paleontological layers on the same or other sites, some of them relatively synchronic with the human peopling of Patagonia. The list includes *Macrauchenia patachonica*, *Arctotherium*, and *Smilodon*. Data summarized by Gutiérrez and Martínez (2008) suggest a generalized regional economy based on a wide-ranging diet during the Late Pleistocene and Early Holocene periods. Álvarez et al. (2013), who noted that this model covered an extensive period and did not capture the variability in the critical stage of the Pleistocene to Holocene transition, adjusted it, suggesting that for the earliest time (before 9500 BP), the subsistence was still generalist, and the emphasis on artiodactyls is not clear (Martínez at al. 2016). While the role of guanaco and Pampas deer for early Pampean hunter-gatherer groups needs evaluation, the importance of guanaco is clear for the earlier Patagonian occupations – with the proviso that in some cases, it is an extinct clade of guanaco (Metcalf et al. 2016). There is absolutely no evidence of huemul or pudu exploitation at the earlier layers of the nearby Andean sites. We must assume that it probably took some time for the first foragers inhabiting the fringes of the Andes to systematically incorporate those animals characterized by behaviors differing drastically from that of guanacos.

In Tandilia, most Late Pleistocene sites are caves or rock shelters that generate a sampling bias: these places attract ancient peoples and archaeologists. This potential bias has been widely discussed worldwide (among many others, Arrizabalga et al. 2015; Bergsvikand Skeates 2012; Galanidou 2000). No open-air campsites were detected in this area, and therefore a part of the settlement system is missing unless open-air residential camps were only in the Interserrana area. In any case, it seems clear that during the Late Pleistocene in the latter area, extinct megamammals were part of the diet, while in central-eastern Tandilia, they were absent. These differences would be explained by the fusion-fission of the bands (Politis and Madrid 2001), a property that seems to be very frequent among hunter-gatherers (Marlowe 2005), even almost universal according to some authors (Lee 1999). Mazzanti (2003) has proposed that easily accessible caves or shelters at lower elevations (e.g., Cueva Tixi, Los Pinos, and El Abra rock shelters) were preferred as domestic settings, while those at higher locations in the hills were ephemerally occupied or used for specific tasks. All sites in Tandilia would have been generated by small bands in a pulse of band fission. During this period, only two medium-sized prey, *Eutatus* and guanaco, were hunted as well as smaller fauna (plains viscacha, Patagonian hare, smaller rodents, etc.), although as we discuss in Chapter 4, the bone remains in the area are restricted to only a few sites. No megafauna were recorded, suggesting that they were scarce in the Tandilia hills or were not hunted due to foragers' behavior. The low number of hunters and potential consumers would be criteria for avoiding the risk and the effort to hunt megamammals. It might be the case that Late Pleistocene Pampean hunter-gatherers in Tandilia used individual or collective hunting (Driver 1989) strategies. On the contrary, the sites in the plains are more extensive and were the product of field-processing camps of some prey (AS2 and PO5) or kill/scavenging sites for only one megamammal (Campo Laborde and La Moderna). Both situations implied larger bands and a cooperative or communal hunting strategy (Haynes 2002). To optimize the meat yield, more hunters would be needed to kill and butcher the prey and more consumers to benefit from them. Although not matching perfectly in the time frame (AS2 is older than the Tandilia sites, and we do not yet know the age of La Moderna), the Interserrana sites would be the product of band fusion. Therefore, these mobility/settlement/economic patterns would be seen as positioning tactics (in the sense of Binford 1982) across the landscape, probably in a seasonal rhythm.

The already mentioned contrast between the Pampas and Patagonia is striking, since there is not a single Late Pleistocene open-air site in the latter. Efforts to find open-air locations were scattered and only partially successful. This difficulty in finding open-air sites is probably related to a combination of sampling and geomorphological reasons. Beyond the concentration of Fishtail points recovered in the Somuncurá plateau (Miotti et al. 2010), the work of Martin and San Román (2010) in the alluvial plains in front of Fell Cave and other locations of the Chico River, and the exploration by Méndez and collaborators in Aisén (2010), there is not much discussion in the literature. These efforts are among the few that pursue a systematic search for open-air evidence. The research of Miotti and collaborators took advantage of the high visibility of Fishtail projectile points on the surface of low-altitude hills. This visibility probably was the result of people using the summits of the hills, where sedimentation was low. Martin and San Román systematically sampled the alluvial plain with a borer, and dated peat bogs and tephra layers, which were easily recognized in borer samples. Their chronological results showed the difficulties involved in finding open-air stratigraphic locations, since the Late Pleistocene landscape at the Chico Valley is buried by meters of sediment. Expanding some of their drilling places, they were able to localize a probable Early Holocene open-air concentration of flakes, as well as naturally deposited fox bones (Martin and San Román 2010). Méndez and collaborators selected surficial sites where abrasion was relatively higher than in the rest of the locality and sites where tools characteristically associated with the earlier periods – such as a discoidal stone – were recorded. Substantial surfaces were thus selected for future intensive operations (Méndez et al. 2010). All these are promising avenues for the eventual integration of open-air locations within our discussions of past human adaptations in Patagonia. This integration is needed in order to analyze in depth the mobility systems used at the end of the Pleistocene.

Final Remarks 255

Although other variables would define mobility among hunter-gatherers (Politis 1996; Wiessner 1982), resource structure is significant (Kelly 1995). Toolstone procurement strategies have a prime effect on planning mobility and subsistence (Andrefsky 2009; Brantingham 2003; Kuhn 1991). In this sense, the "gravity model" indicates that hunter-gatherer settlement sites will tend to be closer to the less mobile resources (Jochim 1976), which would primarily be the rock outcrops in the eastern Pampa and, second, the forests. Both are located, although not exclusively, in Tandilia, which had high-quality raw material and scattered forests of *tala* (*Celtis tala*) and *criollo* willow (*Salix humboldtiana*) and bushlands of *chilca* (*Baccharis* sp.), *Senecio* sp., and eventually *currumamuel* (*Colletia* sp.) (Brea et al. 2014). Also, permanent springs would be available during the frequent drought periods that occurred during the Late Pleistocene and Early Holocene times. In line with these ideas, a model integrating resource structures, mobility patterns, and economic strategies can be outlined. Caves and shelters in lower elevations were occupied for longer periods by small coresident groups as residential camps. Some shelters and locations in higher elevations were used only for specific purposes or were occupied only ephemerally (e.g., hunting stops, overnight camps). During this time, people hunted guanaco, *Eutatus*, plains viscacha, and smaller prey (armadillos and rodents), obtaining SBG and Balcarce Formation orthoquartzites, phtanite, silicified dolomite, and a few other toolstones, and exploiting wood from the local trees and bushes. They might be quarrying the high-quality SBG orthoquartzites from Barker-La Numancia (Colombo and Flegenheimer 2013), which would be a node in spatial and social itineraries (Mazzia 2010/2011). The phtanite, silicified dolomite, and orthoquartzite quarries from the northwestern sector of Tandilia might be another node. On the scale of the annual round, bands got together and moved toward the grassland plains where megafauna was probably more dense and diverse. During the annual rounds, bands would reach the western border of the Interserrana area, the Ventania hills, obtaining raw material (metaquartzite, rhyolite, etc.) and other resources (e.g., wood). Also, they visited the Interserrana coastal seashore, where rounded cobbles (a lower-quality raw material) were collected and transported throughout the plains. While on the coast, they might exploit some marine food resources. Fishtail points and the associated hunting strategies would become popular and efficient. The distribution of these projectile points reached the far south of Patagonia, particularly Fell Cave, the place where they were first discovered in the 1930s (Bird 1946), and some variants even arrived at Tierra del Fuego before the flooding of the Strait of Magellan (Jackson 2002; Massone 2004). These projectile points, so popular in the Campos of Uruguay, the Pampas, and other areas, are South America's most characteristic early tools. They are well recorded in places like Central Chile, the coast of Peru, or the highlands of Ecuador, always with a Late Pleistocene chronology.

However, some questions appear if we consider areas where Fishtails are not abundant or where they are not even present. A critical discussion about the definition of the earlier archaeological manifestations of Northwest Patagonia is not focused on projectile points. For example, it has been suggested that some early occupations in Northwest Patagonia were representative of an Early Holocene unifacial lithic tradition (Crivelli et al. 1993), a concept that is difficult to defend. First, it is necessary to accept that the samples used in these discussions are small and that circumstantial or functional requirements within the context of initial colonization may explain the limited importance of bifacial work. Several records show that bifacial reduction, blades, and other relatively complex technologies were always available for the initial explorers of Fuego-Patagonia and that their absence on small samples should not be considered significant (Aguerre 1997b; Borrero 2011; Nami 1993–1994; Orquera 1987; Paunero 1993–1994; Yacobaccio and Guraieb 1994). More importantly, several sites have indirect evidence of bifacial flaking, even when no bifacial tools were recovered or when they were not abundant (Cuneo 1993; Hajduk et al. 2007; Nami 1993–1994; among others). On this basis and the small size of the samples, the concept of an Early Holocene unifacial tradition for this sector of Patagonia appears to be poorly substantiated.

During the early period of human adaptation to the various Fuego-Patagonian habitats, lithic artifacts were routinely and expediently made of rocks available in the immediate vicinity, accompanied by the transport of a few finished bifacial artifacts and/or preforms (Borrero and Franco 1997). It was recently observed that the low depositional rates of curated tools are the expected result of low-intensity, ephemeral occupations (Prates 2008: 257), which is an important consideration that needs to be taken into account. As just mentioned, high-quality and heavily curated exotic rocks are sometimes present at very low frequencies, pointing to the existence of logistical mobility, as in Cueva Epullán Grande (Crivelli et al. 1996) or Cueva del Medio (Huidobro 2016). This is the kind of evidence to be expected at places that are beginning to be integrated within human circuits (Franco 2002b) and certainly made sense when recovered at the start of most early archaeological sequences in Fuego-Patagonia. More recently, Cueto and collaborators analyzed tools from the earliest occupations at Cerro Tres Tetas and Casa del Minero 1 at the Deseado Massif and failed to find evidence of versatility, as predicted by Borrero and Franco (1997), suggesting that the tool kits were designed for specific functions (Cueto et al. 2017). There are two ways to interpret this interesting information, either as proof of the lack of importance of versatility during the early colonization or as evidence that those sites do not represent the earliest occupations of the area. Instead, those sites can now be seen as representing an already colonized region (Franco et al. 2019). If we remember that the archaeological record of Patagonia presents at least four well-separated nodes tightly dated between 10,880 and 9500 cal BP, it is not a stretch to suggest that previous occupations are waiting to be discovered.

DEMOGRAPHIC DYNAMICS ALONG THE HOLOCENE

During the Early Holocene times, environmental conditions changed in the Pampas and Patagonia. All megamammals became extinct – as we saw, the Holocene survival of *Doedicurus* is under debate (Chapter 4) – while only a few smaller Pleistocene species, *Eutatus seguini* and *Dusicyon avus*, survived until the Holocene. The situation in Patagonia was similar. After Saxon's work at Cueva del Milodón in 1976, it was maintained for years that *Mylodon* survived until Middle Holocene times. Subsequent work showed the depositional problems that led to that interpretation (Borrero et al. 1991; Saxon 1976). Removing megafauna from the Late Pleistocene Pampean and Patagonian ecosystems changes vegetation and small mammal communities over ecological time scales (Barnosky et al. 2015). These environmental changes precipitated by the disappearance of the Pleistocene fauna were sometimes closely accompanied by other drastic changes, like the dispersal of the *Nothofagus* forests in South Patagonia (McCulloch et al. 2021; Moreno et al. 2012). The new environmental conditions generated a novel scenario for human adaptation. The reduction of animal body size and the decrease in prey diversity should have caused a significant impact on the Pampean and Patagonian foragers. The population declined, as suggested in the archaeological record during the Early Holocene (see the SCPD curve of Figure 7.1), but a few areas, such as the CPD and the western Pampa, show a human signal for the first time. Fishtail points were no longer in use, and, after some time, triangular projectile points showed up although they are not yet well dated. It is unclear if these new models were derived from the Fishtail or a different technological tradition. Similar changes were occurring in Patagonia, including the widespread presence of triangular points, consistently dated to the Early Holocene, with the potential exception of Última Esperanza Sound, where they might be older (Martin et al. 2019). The main distribution of these triangular points includes the area between the Deseado River Basin and the Strait of Magellan (Aguerre 1997b; Gradin et al. 1979). There are also relatively isolated clusters in Northwest Patagonia (Crivelli et al. 1993). Schobinger (1969) was tempted to unify all these findings with others beyond Patagonia within a single tradition, but at this moment, there are too many distributional, technological, and chronological issues to maintain that concept.

Although still based on a small sample, recent ancient nuclear DNA studies would add a new source of variation at the Early Holocene (Posth et al. 2018). These studies suggested a new gene flow in the Southern Cone and showed that the earliest AS2 skeletons were an admixed population containing two main genetic ancestries, including the Early Holocene Lapa do Santo (Brazil) and the Middle to Late Holocene ancestry predominating in present-day South Americans. Posth et al. (2018) postulated a partial population replacement in South America at ~ 9000 BP based on these data. However, the Laguna de Los

Pampas skeleton carrying the D1j haplogroup predates such a putative replacement event (Roca-Rada et al. 2021). Since AS2 harbors both genetic ancestries, the proposed replacement event could not have been complete as some mitochondrial lineages persisted from the Early Holocene until the Late Holocene (Roca-Rada et al. 2021). The SCPD curve (Figure 7.1) showed a valley at the end of the Early Holocene, and at ~ 9000 cal BP, the onset of the curve might be related to the proposed arrival of new people. Shortly after, at 8700 cal BP, a new type of projectile point, medium to large unstemmed lanceolate or long triangular, appeared (Chapter 5, Figure 5.3). This type was found nailed in the five older human burials of AS2 and marked an unprecedented violence situation in the whole region. Although it is tempting to correlate the new gene flow with the lanceolate/long triangular projectile point type and the novel mayhem, limited evidence still prevents it.

Based on archaeological data, Heider and Rivero (2018) reached similar conclusions and proposed at least a second process of exploration and colonization of central Argentina different from the one in the Late Pleistocene. They suggest this process would have happened in the late Early Holocene and been integrated into a macro-regional context that included the Argentine midwest and central Chile. Additional discussions of repopulation were presented for Última Esperanza Sound during the Early Holocene and the Upper Santa Cruz River Basin during the Late Holocene (Borrero and Martin 2018; Franco et al. 2004). In both cases, a number of convergent markers supported models of a complex interaction between land and people. It appears clear that the human peopling of South Patagonia never was a linear process and that some zones were successively occupied, abandoned, and reoccupied. Both environmental and social factors are behind these occupational pulses. Whole regions like the longitudinal band that goes from the south of Lago Argentino to Cerro Benitez in Última Esperanza and the Pali Aike Volcanic Field were basically separated during millennia, with an extensive portion of empty land in between that was populated only near the end of the Holocene (Belardi et al. 2020; Borrero 2015; Franco et al. 2019). We already mentioned that evidence exists for relatively early processes of exploration of western Patagonia, such as in Aisén or western Santa Cruz (Borrero et al. 2019a; Méndez et al. 2019). Molecular analyses show the Early Holocene presence of haplotype B at Baño Nuevo in Aisén (Reyes et al. 2012) and slightly later in the Madre de Dios Archipelago and the Patagonian steppes, at Río Bote and Orejas de Burro (Moraga et al. 2009). This limited molecular information clearly complicates the human dispersal panorama in the south of the continent. Given all this evidence of the complex interdigitation of peoples and cultures, it appears wise to assume that we are still a long way from having a full grasp of the whole populational history of Patagonia.

Climatic and environmental oscillations are necessary for analyzing human occupational histories in the Pampas and Patagonia. For the Middle Holocene,

Final Remarks 259

there is a consensus that prevailing conditions for most of the period in eastern Pampa (Hypsithermal) were warmer than today's climate, probably with alternating wetter/drier periods for this interval (Kruck et al. 2011). This environmental frame generates a new scenario for human adaptations in the region. If guanacos were sensitive to increases in humidity as proposed (Politis et al. 2011b; Tonni and Politis 1980), warmer and wetter conditions in eastern Pampa would have affected the density of this prey. In this sense, it has been suggested that during these periods, the potential retraction of guanaco to the south and the west or the decrease in population density would impact Pampean hunter-gatherers, generating lower population density (Politis 1984). This Middle Holocene guanaco depletion, and its putative impact on Pampean foragers, is still under debate and has not been identified in subsequent research (Barrientos and Masse 2012: 192–193; Barrientos and Perez 2005; Politis et al. 2011a), although Álvarez (2014) proposed a generalized economy in the first half of the Middle Holocene and a specialization in guanaco only after 4500 BP.

Barrientos (2009; Barrientos and Perez 2005) proposed that a population replacement took place in the southeastern Pampa and that a new biological population probably entered these areas sometime between 6000 and 5000 BP, after the "emigration or local extinction" of the early Middle Holocene local population. A roughly synchronic hiatus in the human signal was also proposed for the western Pampa (Berón 2004) and southern Cuyo (Neme and Gil 2009). Later, Barrientos (2009: 205) recognized the cultural continuity – concerning technology and economic patterns – during the Middle Holocene (as has been proposed by Martínez 1999, 2002; Politis 1984; Politis and Madrid 2001) but maintained the biological discontinuity, holding that the hiatus in the sequence of radiocarbon dates is indicative of a population discontinuity. In line with this model, Barrientos and Masse (2014) enlarged the geographical scale of analysis. They identified a low archaeological signal in the Middle Holocene and especially a very low signal between 7.5 and 4.4 kyr cal BP in the calibrated data sequence from Central Argentina (in which they included southern Pampa). These authors also saw a null signal between 4.9 and 4.4 kyr cal BP and suggest a link between this gap – as expressed in a sequence of ^{14}C dates – and the potential effect on the human population and biomass that the Rio Cuarto cosmic event would have generated. Although some of these hypotheses are provocative, the cluster of archaeological and ancient DNA evidence from the Middle Holocene in the Pampas summarized and discussed in Chapter 5 (see also Figure 7.1 and Supplementary Table 1) does not support a population replacement in southeastern Pampa. In fact, there is a concentration of ^{14}C dates in these areas within and close to the 6000–5000 BP (6.8–5.7 kyr cal BP) interval, where the putative gap in the radiocarbon date was placed. As shown in Figure 7.1 (see also Supplementary Table 2), there is not a depression in the SCPD curve in this interval, and there are now at least

20 radiocarbon dates, from 13 different sites from the Tandilia, Interserrana, South Pampa, and CPD which fall within it (Paso Mayor, Abrigo Los Pinos, Lobería 1, Alero El Mirador, Abrigo La Grieta, La Cautiva S2, La Esperanza, Laguna de Los Pampas, Laguna Chica, El Puente, Alfar, Tres Bonetes, and La Modesta). Beyond the hiatus in the radiocarbon dates sequence, Barrientos' model was based on changes in craniofacial morphology and temporal variation in cranial vault deformation. However, the morphological studies were based exclusively on analyses of the facial regions of seven Middle Holocene individuals of AS2, compared with several Late Holocene samples from different sites and collections (Barrientos and Perez 2005). For Barrientos and Masse (2014: 194), these differences "are too significant to be explained in terms of microevolutionary mechanisms operating on a single lineage in so short of a time period." Although there are some craniofacial differences between the Middle and the Late Holocene samples, it has not been proven why these differences should be the result of only two different populations. The small sample from the Middle Holocene does not allow robust conclusions, and Perez and Monteiro (2009) have shown that a large divergence in craniofacial features can arise in a short time interval and can be related to modifications derived from changes in diet and climate. Barrientos and Masse (2014) did not fully explore other alternative explanations, such as micro-evolutionary processes or changes in the original population due to genetic flux with neighboring populations.

Finally, ancient mitochondrial DNA analysis data from Early to Late Holocene human samples indicates biological continuity at a regional level (Postillone et al. 2020; Roca-Rada et al. 2021). Beyond mtDNA results, nuclear genome data from Posth and collaborators (2018) demonstrated that the ancient individuals from AS2 have the highest affinity with present-day populations of the Southern Cone. Also, the data from Burial 4, from Laguna Chica, dated to 1750 BP, support a strong gene continuity in the region as well as gene flow between the Pampas and the Central Andes (Nakatsuka et al. 2020). These authors identify this individual as a mixture of 80% ± 12% ancestry related to Burial 1 from Laguna Chica dated to ~ 6000 BP and 20% ± 12% ancestry associated with a representative Andes group (Nakatsuka et al. 2020: figure S6C and table S7D).

Demography and mobility during the Middle Holocene in the Interserrana area were also discussed by Martínez (1999, 2002, 2006), who proposed a possibly lower population density product of the increased residential mobility due to unstable and fluctuating ecological situations. More recently, Martínez and collaborators (2015), based on an SCPD curve, detected a low frequency in this period but a continuous human signal. Our SCPD curve (Figure 7.1) also shows a relatively low density between ~ 7 and 4 kyr cal BP, with a continuous track and moderate ups and downs. On the other hand, some authors have also suggested that low archaeological records in eastern Pampa during the Middle Holocene may be related to geological biases and geomorphological factors, where erosive agents may have erased archaeological records close to riverbeds or areas affected by wind and/or marine erosion (Favier Dubois et al. 2017; Martínez et al. 2015).

Donadei Corada (2020; see also Mazzanti et al. 2015), based on a detailed analysis of several sites in the eastern sector of Tandilia, proposes that occupations of the Middle Holocene were generated by small bands that made specialized trips in search of natural resources as well as for social reasons. They obtained the immediately available raw materials through low mobility displacements within a radius <10 km (daily foraging trips), which, together with short-term occupations, would reflect a radius of logistical mobility around residential camps, possibly in open and wide locations near watercourses within the hill valleys (Donadei Corada 2020).

Middle Holocene sites in the CPD area occurred in the framework of the Thermal Maximum under climate conditions warmer and mostly drier than the present subhumid to humid ones (Messineo et al. 2019a). These environmental conditions created regional eolian sedimentation in partially vegetated dunes and brackish water bodies in the lowlands. During drought periods, the salinity of the water increased, and numerous shallow lakes disappeared (Quiroz et al. 2003). Together with drought, warm and dry climate conditions would reduce the population densities of artiodactyls (Broughton and Bayham 2003), which in the CPD included the two principal resources: guanaco and Pampas deer. The size and density of the guanaco groups are conditioned by the heterogeneity of grasses and shrubs and the presence of competitors and predators (Nugent et al. 2006). The environment's carrying capacity determines the number of guanacos that can be supported without deteriorating the pasture. Therefore, aridity reduces biomass (pastures) and lowers prey density (Álvarez 2014).

During the Middle Holocene, human occupation in the CPD would have revolved around the main lake systems such as the Encadenadas or the Hinojo-Las Tunas complex (Scheifler et al. 2017), which would function as an oasis. Smaller or temporary lakes were probably visited only during humid cycles and occupied for a short term (Messineo et al. 2019a, b). The area would not have been inhabited on a long-term basis due to the shortage of water (intermittent or salty lakes, no rivers or creeks), the absolute lack of lithic toolstone, and the low prey density resulting from the reduction of biomass. In contrast, the neighboring areas to the south (Close Basins, Transversal Valleys, Salado-Chadileuvú-Curacó, Interserrana, Tandilia, and Ventania) had better conditions (raw material, permanent water bodies, xerophytic forests, etc.). Therefore, the CPD would have been temporarily occupied during humid cycles, when fresh water was available and prey were more abundant during the Middle Holocene.

The burial practices in the CPD are different from the surrounding areas during the Middle Holocene and support this model: no secondary burials denote a more profound sense of territorial ancestry.

The lithic raw material sources also suggest different vectors in the CPD but with a clear one, in the eastern sector, from Tandilia (Messineo et al. 2019b). Most artifacts are in the later stages of the reduction sequence, flakes with cortex are rare, and small exhausted cores are frequent. It indicates an intense use of raw material expected in areas far from outcrops or secondary deposits (Torrence 1986). However, there is a good record of bone tools, probably the highest in the Pampas after the Lower Paraná and Uruguay Rivers (Álvarez 2014, 2020; Cornaglia Fernández and Buc 2013). Bone is easy to obtain and light for transportation, minimizing the dependency on the lithic quarries.

In sum, we interpret the human presence in the CPD during the Middle Holocene as a logistical occupation during humid cycles, from bands with more permanent settlements that occupied the neighboring areas. The CPD would function as a lax and open territory, with a low degree of exclusivity and exploited by different bands from other areas. In any case, one strategy to cope with droughts was also implemented by creating caches of greater rhea egg canteens, recovered exclusively in this area in five sites (see Chapter 5). The occupation of the CPD would match what Binford (1983) called *extended range*, places sporadically visited for specific purposes through long-distance mobility.

Although arid climatic conditions continued in the CPD until the Early to Late Holocene, several long-term, multi-activity camps were recorded, such as Cabeza de Buey (Messineo and Scheifler 2016) and Huencú Nazar (Scheifler 2019). The abundance of hearths and site furniture (grinding stones) suggests well-structured camps at ~ 3100 cal BP in the latter site, which have not been documented in previous periods. Also, new sites in the northwestern area started to be used for funerary activities at ~ 3800 cal BP (Tapia et al. 2020). For example, in Chadilauquen, humans were inhumated when more humid and warm conditions occurred, which in turn increased the lake's resources. New results support the hypotheses by Aguerre (1996), who proposed the occupation of northwestern area lakes by Late Holocene hunter-gatherers who arrived from different directions (Tapia et al. 2020).

One important innovation that emerged in the Middle Holocene is persistent, liminal places in the landscape. It is associated with some kind of sacrality in specific spots. The primary evidence of this are the human burials of AS2, which open avenues for many interpretations. First, the inhumation of 50 human skeletons in 39 graves in a restricted space, dated between ~ 7800 and 4500 BP (8.7–5.1 kyr cal BP), implies the continuity of a burial place for about 3.6 kyr. This is usually associated with territorial behavior and redundancy in the use of specific spaces (Littletone and Allen 2007). It also means continuity in a sacred practice, loaded with strong symbolic connotations reflected in rich funerary goods and the frequent presence of red ochre around the bodies. However, the marked difference in the burial paraphernalia also indicates the existence of personal status, individual hierarchy, or spiritual

Final Remarks

263

power. Other burials with funerary goods in the region (CDLV2, Necochea, and Arroyo del Moro) support this hypothesis. Finally, the early presence of secondary burials would result from affirming ancestry in the territory, which seems to have originated in this period. At the onset of the Middle Holocene, Pampean hunter-gatherers exploited marine resources and occupied the Atlantic coast. This adaptive pattern would have occurred earlier in the Holocene, but the rise in sea level might have destroyed this archaeological evidence, as we discussed before.

The Middle Holocene in Patagonia also was a very complex period, during which the increasing influence of the southern westerlies (Mayr et al. 2007) and volcanic activity (Stern 2008) probably prompted several locational changes. The selection of both rock shelters and open-air locations appears to have depended on the strong winds blowing from the west. Also, volcanic activity, particularly that of the Hudson volcano, affected the ecology of extensive areas for years or decades at most. Several areas began to be peopled at this time. We know that around 6000–7000 BP the late human colonization of the important endorheic Cardiel Basin began. This process was immediately followed by the reconnaissance and intermittent utilization of the Strobel plateau (Goñi et al. 2014a). Previously used cave sites continue to be occupied in most Patagonian regions, and open-air sites began to appear in a variety of locations, but especially near lakes and lagoons (Goñi et al. 2014a; Massone 1989–1990) or the Atlantic and Pacific coasts (Ambrústolo et al. 2011; Castro et al. 2007; Emperaire and Laming 1961; Legoupil 1997; Ortiz Troncoso 1975; San Román 2013) (Figures 7.4 and 7.5). The coast's occupation process appears to have been swift since sites dated around 6000 BP dotted the whole Atlantic coast. Indeed, the coastal sites from both oceans present a notable contrast. Those on the Atlantic side attest to the complementary use of maritime resources, a process that started during the Middle Holocene and was well recorded at several places along the long coast, including Tierra del Fuego. In contrast, open-air sites near the Pacific Ocean on the broken western archipelagos, where caves are almost nonexistent, indicate a process of full adaptation to maritime resources (see Chapter 5). The Middle Holocene is manifested at caves in the Deseado Massif and Upper Pinturas River Basin as reiterated visits to the sites of Maripé, Piedra Museo, Cerro Tres Tetas, La Gruta, El Verano, La Martita, Cueva de las Manos, or Arroyo Feo, among others. There are differences in the activities and length of occupation, but it is clear that the human presence is firmly established everywhere. The same patterns are seen at Los Antiguos (Fernández 2015; Mengoni Goñalons et al. 2009) or the Pali Aike Lava Field (Bird 1988; Massone 1981). The Middle Holocene can be considered a time of technological experimentation and the discovery of new Patagonian habitats. In terms of technology, one of the most important issues was the widespread presence of blade technology. Another issue was the supposed replacement of projectile points by bolas

Figure 7.4 View of Andean lakes, south of Argentino Lake.

Figure 7.5 Dunes on the North Atlantic Patagonian coast, Las Grutas. Photo courtesy Florencia Borella.

Final Remarks

presumably associated with those blades. The peopling of coastal habitats also implied the appearance of the different bone and lithic tool kits related to the exploitation of maritime resources. Bone tools required dependable raw materials, which were mainly provided by sea mammals on the coasts (Scheinsohn 2014).

THE LATE HOLOCENE: INNOVATIONS, DIVERSIFICATION, AND INTENSIFICATION

During the Late Holocene, Pampean foragers experienced significant reconfigurations in economic, social, and demographic structures. In this period, the archaeological visibility of the Pampas and Patagonia increased significantly, a fact that also suggests a rise in the regional population density (Figure 7.1). Of course, the longer a site is in existence, the more taphonomic processes such as erosion and weathering have chances to reduce and destroy the archaeological record, generating, in consequence, an overrepresentation of recent events relative to older events (Dubois et al. 2017; Surovell et al. 2009). However, this process is not exclusive to later periods, since, as has been discussed, there was a lack or scarcity of the archaeological signal during earlier periods in the western areas (Berón 2015) and the South (Catella 2014: 170; Martínez and Martínez 2011; Martínez et al. 2013). It is also true that younger components are located in higher stratigraphic units, and, therefore, they have more chances to be exposed, by both natural processes and human activity. However, even taking into account this preservation bias, the number of sites and their wider distribution, including areas previously unoccupied or poorly inhabited, suggest that during the Late Holocene, there was a demographic increase in the Pampas after ~ 3.5 kyr cal BP (Figure 7.1). Moreover, some ecosystems, such as the Paraná River delta and the lower section of the Salado River Depression, show a human signal for the first time.

Some technological innovations also took place in the region, producing economic and social advantages: the bow and arrow weapon system and pottery. It is not clear when Pampean hunter-gatherers adopted the bow and arrow, but the earliest dated appearance of small triangular projectile points, interpreted as arrowheads, are in the Calera site, associated with an age of 3000 BP (3.1 kyr cal BP). However, as we said, this date is the only one that suggests such an early chronology and therefore should be taken with caution. Roughly at the same time, pottery was recorded for the first time in the region at Zanjón Seco 2 (Politis et al. 2001). Both innovations coincide with a peak in the SCPD curve, which would suggest that they might bring some adaptive benefits that resulted in a population increase. The bow and arrow system was such a technological step ahead that it could have increased meat consumption and population growth rates. It may also have caused a change from communal/collective hunting to smaller groups or individual hunting (Marlowe 2005). Pottery is a means of food processing and displaying social symbols. Ceramic vessels created unprecedented cooking and storage techniques and facilities, generating regional cooking practices. Storage facilities allowed supply accumulation, delayed consumption, increased predictability, and provision of food reserves. Stored plant or animal foodstuffs could also offer opportunities to set aside supplementary resources for rituals or feasts. Since its first appearance Pampean pottery was decorated by different varieties of incisions (mostly drag and jab and linear incisions), providing a medium for symbolic expressions and identity at different levels (social, ethnic, individual, etc.). In this context, the design element defined as "small flags" (see Chapter 6) is ubiquitous in the region and would have functioned as a diacritic for social interaction on a broad spatial scale (Di Prado 2018).

These innovations, along with other social behaviors (territorial circumscription, changes in mortuary practices, wide exchange networks, etc.), as well as higher population densities, resulted in the process of economic intensification along with an increase in complexity in the Pampean region in the Late Holocene (Barrientos 2001; Berón and Politis 1997; Loponte et al. 2006; Madrid et al. 2002; Martínez 2006; Mazzanti 2006; Politis and Madrid, 2001; Quintana and Mazzantti, 2001; Scheifler 2019, among others). However, this process was not homogenous and generated diversification in social forms and adaptive patterns. For example, in the Interserrana area, changes in social organization and the incorporation of new technologies were not accompanied by increased animal resource procurement. On the contrary, subsistence strategies maintained a continuity with the previous periods, not leading to resource depletion (Álvarez 2014). In the CPD, it was a specialization toward guanaco exploitation, complemented by an increment in the processing and consumption of vegetables, and bola stones seem to have been the primary hunting weapon (Scheifler 2019). In other areas, such the Salado-Chadileuvú-Curacó and the South, mortuary practices and subsistence patterns indicate significant changes in mobility and territoriality (Berón 2018; Martínez 2017). For the latter area, it was proposed for the Final to Late Holocene (~ 1000–250 BP) an increase in relatively closed social networks as well as spatial circumscription, changes in population dynamics, social differentiation, and more intense and competitive social interactions, all of which resulted in regionalization (Martínez et al. 2017).

In the littoral zones of the Salado River Depression, the Rolling Pampa, and the Northeast, the economic intensification process was associated with a burst in the human population, probably related to the strong exploitation of aquatic resources, which includes not only fish but also the aquatic rodent coypu and in some cases freshwater shells. Concomitantly, this new economic pattern was possible thanks to well-developed bone hunting and fishing tools, a deep knowledge of making pottery, the use of canoes, and probably nets. In this

Final Remarks

period, it seems that hunter-gatherers concentrated in the littoral zones, leaving the inland Rolling Pampa with low population density.

In addition, in Goya-Malabrigo, in the northeastern area, the horticulture of maize, beans, and squash, as well as the occurrence of more stable settlement in anthropogenic mounds after ~ 2000 BP and the development of a low-level social hierarchy, completely changed the cultural scenario of the area and probably impacted the neighboring hunter-gatherers (such as in Tandilia; Mazzanti 2006). These significant changes do not seem to be the exclusive outcome of the local hunter-gatherers' evolutionary – monophyletic – process as proposed by Loponte and Acosta (2016). On the contrary, it seems to be the product of a complex ethnogenetic process probably derived from the migration and expansion of the Arawak people along the main South American rivers (Eriksen 2011; Heckneberger 2002; Hornborg and Hill 2011). However, there are still gaps in our understanding of how these demic processes impacted the local population, when ethnogenesis occurred, and how it gave rise to a new cultural form as the Goya-Malabrigo archaeological entity (Politis and Bonomo 2012, 2018). Although the linguistic and archaeological Arawak record in the continent shows a patchy pattern (Eriksen 2011), by no means does this pattern neglect the contribution of the Arawak in the genesis of Goya-Malabrigo. First, this is because a continuous record is unlikely in any given migration or expansion process since people do not move in a population void nor in a homogenous environment; second, because the Arawak expansion (Heckenberger 2002) would be better described as an "enclave colonization" (in the sense of Zilhão 2000). Arawak migrants would move long distances to colonize or integrate selected locations that met specific ecological and social criteria. The Middle and Lower Paraná River floodplains would bring together these criteria: high biomass with a great variety of resources within a fluvial ecosystem and unpopulated or sparsely populated thousands of islands. This process would have occurred in a scenario of low competition and greater possibilities for integration. The expansion and the successful occupation of the wide floodplains of this area would be favored by a pre-adaptation (Steele and Rockman 2003) to the fluvial ecosystems. The contribution of the local Late Holocene hunter-gatherers from the adjacent plains to the generation of a new cultural form is still unknown. Hopefully, the ongoing regional paleogenomic studies will provide some clues to approach this subject.

The construction of earth mounds is one of the outstanding traits of Goya-Malabrigo as well as of other related people in the Lower Paraná and Uruguay Rivers. These mounds are related to a supra-regional phenomenon that includes the Paraguay River as well as the Campos: eastern Uruguay and southeastern Brazil (see review in Iriarte et al. 2016). They have been interpreted as a specific adaptive strategy used by different South American indigenous populations to occupy fluvial plains that are periodically flooded and have high biodiversity (Bonomo and Politis 2018; Gianotti and Bonomo 2013). However, despite some common characteristics (most are in flood zones and were built in the Late Holocene), the earth mounds have specific regional traits and belong to different cultural contexts. The earth mounds of the Lower Paraná and Uruguay Rivers are the most visible archaeological features in the landscape of the area and are the result of a significant investment of human labor, which has marked the cultural topography for two millennia. These mounds had primarily residential and funeral functions and were major settlements within the hierarchy of settlements in the region (Apolinaire and Bastourre 2016). The most important ones were probably village loci, while others would have been also used for house-garden horticulture. The characteristics and sociocultural context of these mounds are different from those of nearby areas such as eastern Uruguay and southeastern Brazil, associated with the Vieira tradition. The great complexity with which the dead were treated in the Lower Paraná and Uruguay River areas indicates a significant investment of time and effort in treating the remains of the ancestors and shows the central role of ancestry in social reproduction. In this sense, the mounds were signified and resignified over time and probably constituted places of memory and ancestry. They had the adaptive advantage of occupying floodplains but at the same time became spaces of high social and symbolic value (Bonomo and Politis 2018).

The picture of mainland Patagonia during the Late Holocene reflects a period of multiplication of evidence. More sites are represented across Patagonia and Tierra del Fuego. These clearly can be the effect, at least in part, of better archaeological visibility. However, the increased deposition of artifacts and bones at many sites with long Holocene occupational histories suggests that the trend has validity. Larger sites, sometimes suggesting multiple activities, are recorded in different habitats. They are usually located near drinking water, which, in contrast to the case of the Pampas or Tierra del Fuego, is the critical locational factor. Low frequencies of heavily broken pottery containers are found on the North Patagonian coast, usually with decorated borders (Bellelli 1980). Pottery is less abundant in the interior, to the point that it was considered the result of unsuccessful dispersal (Borrero 1994–1995). However, decorated and relatively complex ceramics can be found near the end of the Holocene, particularly associated with burials (Hajduk 1978; Hajduk et al. 2007) but also in other contexts (Aldazabal and Eugenio 2009; Vitores 2012). Influences from independent sources located west of the Andes can be seen in many decorated vases. Containers in North Patagonia and southern Pampa were not restricted to ceramic vases but also probably included scarcely represented rhea egg canteens – represented by decorated fragments (Carden and Martínez 2014; Fiore and Borella 2010) – and skin containers.

At any rate, not all these sites – especially those on dune fields – present good stratigraphic resolution (Borrazzo 2016), and some could result from

Final Remarks

269

short-term reoccupations probably within a logistically organized mobility system. This appears to be especially the case for coastal sites, both on the mainland and in North Tierra del Fuego. There is also important occupational redundancy at sites in the Beagle Channel, an area where higher levels of place fidelity result from the prevalence of coastal forager lifeways (Orquera and Piana 1999; Zangrando 2009a). As a norm, it is clear that reoccupied sites have better archaeological visibility than smaller sites that are difficult to find unless special search efforts are implemented.

Even when it is clear that people were using all the available Patagonian habitats, this does not translate into a picture of successful colonization of those habitats. More than once, the successful occupation of one area must have been correlated with the gradual abandonment of another. Many cases of highly discontinuous stratigraphies make it apparent that short- and large-term gaps exist at the site and at regional scales. If we look carefully at the distribution of sites, it is not unusual to find places that began to be occupied only during the Late Holocene. This is coherent with a picture of different pulses of occupation of extensive areas of Patagonia, sometimes with seasonal rhythms. The evidence indicates that discontinuity character-ized many systems of land occupation as a response to environmental and social conditions. One result is that many places in Patagonia remained uninhabited even near the end of the Late Holocene. It is clear that only in limited areas do human densities sufficiently grow to require strict territorial markers. A good example of the relatively open use of large areas can be seen at the Strobel plateau, a place where people from different locations probably converged to hunt guanacos (Belardi and Goñi 2006). The attractiveness of different basins during drought times was variable, with places like the Salitroso Basin, which concentrated people (Goñi et al. 2014a), and others like the Argentino Lake, which apparently was aban-doned (Borrero and Franco 2000).

Another interesting pattern is the recovery of multiple burials at sites such as Cerro Sota, Río Bote, Orejas de Burro, and Cueva Lago Sofía 1. This trend started at the beginning of the Late Holocene. Interestingly, these South Patagonian sites are not confined to any particular habitat but are found almost everywhere, from the Pali Aike Volcanic Field to the Santa Cruz Basin or the coasts of the Almirante Montt Gulf. Some Late Holocene open-air locations – *chenques* – are found in the south, but the really large concentrations of *chenques* are found along central Patagonia (Goñi et al. 2004; Zilio 2017). Burials in North Patagonia also varied from true cemeteries in the northwest extreme (Hajduk 1981–1982) to groups of individuals buried in neatly ordered positions (Flensborg et al. 2017) or concentrated in the lowlands of the Negro River Basin (Bernal et al. 2004; Bórmida 1950). All these different burial modes characterizing different zones across Patagonia can be seen as the varied selection of forms of multigenerational interment places.

LITHIC RESOURCES, TERRITORY, AND MOBILITY

As we saw, lithic material in the Pampas is almost restricted to the south and west, leaving an extensive area without toolstones (see Chapter 3, Figure 3.5). The essential SBG orthoquartzite quarries are located in the Barker-La Numancia area, where intensive exploitation of high-quality rock has been recorded. The SBG orthoquartzite has been the most used raw material in the eastern Pampa and has reached the western Pampa, although in lower frequencies (Berón et al. 2015; Carrera Aizpitarte 2014; Curtoni 2007; Heider 2016). It is clear that the hunter-gatherers from the eastern Pampa had a great dependence on these quarries, and probably residential and logistical mobilities were deeply influenced by the need of obtaining toolstones from these sources. However, Ventania, the El Fresco Plateau, smaller quarries (El Carancho-Valle de Daza), the secondary deposits from the Colorado River, the Patagonian Shingle Mantle, and the Atlantic seashore cobbles were also important and locally significant sources. They were certainly considered when planning residential and logistical mobility. In the Late Holocene, two strategies were operating to reduce the spatial incongruence of the lithic availability in the southeastern Pampa and the CPD: (1) lithification (stockpiling large cores and blanks in strategic locations; Flegenheimer and Bayón 2004; Martínez and Mackie 2003–2004) and (2) derived from the former, the deposit of lithic reservoirs or caches, which is a more sophisticated way to equip places. Usually, these caches are purposely buried in compacted assemblages of cores (in early reduction stages), blanks, and finished artifacts.

A key issue discussed in the archaeology of the region was direct versus indirect lithic procurement. The maximum distance that hunter-gatherers will travel to obtain raw material has been calculated at about 175 km (Kelly 2013), although some authors pose that Upper Paleolithic hunter-gatherers directly procured material up to a maximum distance of 200 km (Picin and Cascalheira 2019). Indirect provisioning or exchange implies the attainment of goods through social networks (Ericson 1984) and is understood as the process by which some goods change hands based on some type of barter or reciprocity (Marlowe 2005; Torrence 1986). The distinction between direct or indirect (exchange) access is difficult to determine due to the lack of unambiguous indicators (Meltzer 1989). The high-quality rocks were heavily exploited and are widely distributed in great quantities along the Pampas region. This would initially favor a direct procurement strategy, since it is unlikely that any hunter-gatherer society would depend entirely on exchanging one of the most critical resources, which in this case are the rocks for making artifacts. In this sense, the threshold of 200 km for direct procurement would not work in the region, and a longer distance has to be considered (Messineo and Barros 2021)

The other alternative is the quarries being exploited by a few bands that had exclusive control of the territory with the toolstone outcrops, and they

Final Remarks 271

exchanged the raw material with the other bands, a hypothesis raised by Bayón and Flegenheimer (2004). They proposed a social control of the Tandilia quarries, although they did not specify if this control meant the exclusive procurement of raw material by the controlling bands. It would mean that local groups would claim exclusive use rights over resource locations. Or, on the contrary, the outcrops may have been in open territories available to different groups to obtain the toolstone by direct procurement, perhaps with some permission from the local bands. This would imply that no ownership is claimed, but associations with a territory may be recognized (Binford 2001; Freeman and Anderies 2015). Among these options, the former seems to be less probable since it would produce great inequality in favor of a few bands, which is against the hunter-gatherers' social system based on egalitarianism (Lee 1999). It also would suggest a complex exchange network of massive amounts of rocks along and across the eastern Pampa, in which a few bands from Tandilia would strongly dominate. Moreover, few hammerstones were found in the quarries (Colombo 2011, 2013), which supports the direct procurement hypothesis. Hammerstones are part of personal gear, highly curated items used in the quarries and then carried back with the knappers when they left. If only a few bands were exploiting the quarries, a site provisioning strategy would be expected. It means that they would generate site furniture and leave hammerstones for future (personal) use in the quarries. If many groups exploited the quarries, there would be fewer hammerstones remaining. Therefore, we propose that the quarries of Tandilia were of open access, with lax territorial behavior. This does not imply the absence of territorial conduct by Pampean foragers but suggests that boundaries were permeable and the rights of transit and resource exploitation were permissive (see also Martínez et al. 2017). In the Pampas, during historical times, many different indigenous groups from distant locations exploited the salt from the Salinas Grandes, which was considered common property (Roulet 2016: 333–336). A relevant ethnographic analogy is the case of the Nukak, who obtained high-quality reeds for blowpipes in the eastern hills of their land. Although the territories of only two bands border these hills, all bands have free access to them, traveling along paths between territorial boundaries, which allow passage and the occasional exploitation of resources (Politis 2007). The free access of distant bands to the stranded whales on the coast among the Selk'nam (Bridges 1951) is another ethnographic example of permissive territorial behavior, as well the Eastern Shoshoni, who "all denied any form of family, village, or band ownership of seed lands ... anyone was privileged to utilize territory ordinarily visited by other people" (Steward 1938: 73).

In the northwestern sector of Tandilia, the Calera site also suggests that territories with quarries were open and with no or low restrictions. Calera was defined as a Late Holocene site of aggregation and feasting, operating for about 1700 years (Álvarez 2014; Politis et al. 2007). Band reunions helped hunter-gatherers maintain social links and form new couples; aggregation makes information flow more fluid and allows the exchange of objects (Conkey et al. 1980; Hamilton et al. 2007; Kelly 1995). Calera is the only site in the region with these characteristics, and it is located in the Sierras Bayas, precisely where several quarries of high-quality toolstones and minerals occurred.

The main SBG quarries from Barker-La Numancia show evidence of intense exploitation, which for Colombo (2013) shows that quarrying was not embedded in other activities as has been previously suggested for the Tandilia toolstones (Politis 1984). Messineo (2002) raised the hypothesis of a combined strategy: bands with territories near hills could have exploited the rocks while doing other activities, while groups that moved further away from the hills acquired rocks through trips with specific purposes. More recently, Donadei Corada (2020) proposed that in southeastern Tandilia, lithic procurement during the Middle Holocene was embedded in other tasks and defined the mobility pattern. These options are difficult to test due to the lack of clear evidence to favor any of them, and also, both strategies can operate at the same time (Close 1996). The main problem is the lack of chronological control and the very low resolution of the deposits, which opens the possibility to many extraction strategies: a few knappers extracting rocks over a long time per event or many knappers quarrying for short periods during each visit. Countless events (including both strategies) were repeated during millennia since the Late Pleistocene all through the Holocene, producing a dense palimpsest that makes it impossible to dissect.

In the southeastern sector of Tandilia, rhyolite and metaquartzite artifacts have been recorded. Both rocks, originating from the Ventania hills, were detected in very low percentages in archaeological levels assigned to the Middle Holocene. The great distance that separates the procurement area from the sites, besides the fact that only a small quantity of materials was recorded, was interpreted by Donadei Corada (2020) as possible evidence of exchange between the groups that occupied these two hill systems. However, it is difficult to explain why lower-quality rocks from Ventania would be exchanged when high-quality toolstones were locally available in abundance. The Ventania rocks found in Tandilia could be interpreted as the consequence of very large band mobility circuits with lax territorial behaviors, at least during the Middle Holocene, as has been previously suggested.

Beyond the few cases of lithic caches known in Patagonia (Franco et al. 2011b), there are abundant sectors with places equipped for future use, mainly with relatively large and heavy items like mortars. Also, less obstrusive items, such as polishers made of Miraflores rocks, conform to the furniture of coastal sites in Tierra del Fuego (Borrazzo et al. 2018). Toolstones recovered at focal sources were distributed in varied proportions according to complex systems of human interaction. The shape of their distribution as well as peculiarities related to their changing abundances away from the sources are

Final Remarks 273

highly informative about human adaptations and suggest the existence of varied ways of organizing the use of space.

Whatever the situation, the study of these rocks illustrates how the recorded patterns of their acquisition and distribution affect our understanding of the social organization of Patagonian hunter-gatherers. A limited number of localities constituted central bases from which large numbers of people operated, on both short- and long-term logistical expeditions. These expeditions do not appear to have been exclusively for the acquisition of toolstones. Indeed, extensive social networks related to toolstones are sometimes invoked in archaeology, including regular references to the existence of exchange webs. That particular interpretation is confronted with the problem of the small frequency of involved goods (Méndez et al. 2019; Pallo and Borrero 2015a). Some additional associated methodological problems also exist; for example, Neme and Gil (2012: 267) wondered to what degree reclamation of old obsidian cores transformed them into large numbers of flakes. This could explain some changes in the rate of obsidian deposition through time without invoking extensive exchange. Studies of obsidian hydration were made with the goal of tackling that issue, but they still need precision and control (Garvey 2012, 2021; Neme and Gil 2012). The problem of the number of items involved is not fully recognized when using surface averaged samples, a situation that sometimes leads to postulating vast networks in excess of 200 km. Indeed, networks of this size are ethnographically recorded, and archaeological support can also be found in our recent discussion of the Pampas. They generally imply *hxaro*-like systems, which serve many different social purposes, such as strengthening social ties (Kelly 1995; Wiessner 2002). However, more evidence beyond the wide distribution of tools made of any given rock is certainly required to support their archaeological existence. To start with, large amounts of the presumably involved exotic items should be present far away from their sources. It is certainly possible that exchange systems existed where food, spouses, or knowledge circulated. Of course, these are alternatives difficult to identify in the archaeological record, and their potential existence is largely dependent on an understanding of the circulation of items that do have archaeological visibility. The problem increases when we learn that the classically held position of wide social networks serving as buffers against ecological risk (i.e., Gould 1980) was not recently supported (Smith 2013: 273). This opens a vast area of research that requires not only better-quality field evidence but also relevant middle-range theory.

Exchange is basically a two-sided process in which we should expect to find evidence of exchanged goods being transported in both directions. This is the concept of trade as "a one-for-one exchange of items" (Heizer 1978: 690), and its archaeological detection presents the problem that the exchanged goods need not be exotic. Pallo and Borrero (2015a) explored the distribution of obsidians with known provenance and maritime items (see Zubimendi and

Ambrústolo 2011) because they possess both archaeological visibility and precise provenance. Certainly, many goods that cannot be easily traced back to the point of origin or that are archaeologically invisible could have been involved in wide circulation circuits, limiting our discussions. Sometimes, stable isotope studies on human bones can be used to discuss the consumption of maritime resources in the interior (Borrero and Barberena 2006), or molecular studies on human bones may serve discussions of circulation of individuals (de la Fuente et al. 2018; Moraga et al. 2010), but it is almost a truism to accept that more sophisticated models relying on social organization will be required to deal with those issues in the future.

Fall-off curves do not provide a clear measure of exchange systems as originally conceived (Renfrew 1977). Ian Hodder's (1982) analysis demonstrated problems of equifinality for their interpretation, which suggests that it is better to use them simply as devices to measure the distribution of raw materials (Méndez et al. 2019; Pallo and Borrero 2015a). Nevertheless, it is interesting to consider what was behind some of Renfrew's models. This is particularly the case for "down-the-line exchange," in which raw materials are moving through a network of related groups, with a process of progressive reduction taking place along the line (Renfrew 1977: 77–79), or what Binford (1979) treats as a staged manner of stone tool production. If present, down-the-line exchange probably was a process embedded within a more complicated net of social interactions.

As already mentioned, visiting is one important process among these alternative ways of interaction and one that certainly deposited foreign items away from their sources. There is abundant ethnographic support for the importance of visits as a predominant mode of interaction in Tierra del Fuego (Borrazzo et al. 2018; Borrero et al. 2020b; Gusinde 1991 [1974]). However, this process only rarely will explain concentrations of items at specific places. Visiting is a recorded behavior among hunter-gatherers worldwide that results from either economic or social requirements (Chapman 1986; Gusinde 1982 [1937]; Lee 1979). Sometimes visiting is the result of seasonal or other cyclic schedules dependent on a variety of environmental and social variables (Lee 1979; Williams and Wobst 1974). For example, all kinds of ceremonial gatherings implicate different forms of visiting with various durations and purposes. Feasting is only one of many gatherings that attract intense archaeological scrutiny, simply because archaeological outcomes of feasts can be identified (Hayden 1995; Yellen 1977). Other alternatives need more work to transform them from vague possibilities into archaeological certainties. Kin-related obligations or neighbor courtesies also played a part, many times conforming to stated rules of visiting (Gusinde 1982 [1937]; Hitchcock and Babchuk 2007; Williams and Wobst 1974). The result is that a constantly changing membership characterizes so-called hunter-gatherer bands, and one of the consequences is the very large area where individuals interact (Binford 2006; Borrero et al. 2011; Politis 2007; Yellen 1977).

Final Remarks 275

Fuego-Patagonian ethnography presents cases of visiting between terrestrial and maritime hunter-gatherers (Coan 2007; De Agostini 2005 [1956]: 346; Gusinde (1991 [1974]): 130–134), and in some cases, there is even some archaeological support for their prehistoric existence (Borrero et al. 2011, 2019a; Borrero et al. 2020b). The concept of long-distance logistical movement (Lovis et al. 2005) is relevant for discussing some of these visiting schemes, especially those involving crossing geographic barriers. Visiting goals are not necessarily focused on the exchange of goods but sometimes indirectly result in the deposition of exotic materials. However, as it was recently pointed out, "the association of abundant exotic material from faraway sources need not automatically translate into evidence for exchange" (Borrazzo et al. 2018: 225). The main alternative to these models of the wide circulation of goods is offered by mobility and direct acquisition of raw materials, for which there is good ethnographic and archaeological support (Belardi et al. 2006; Borrazzo 2008; Bridges 1951; Espinosa and Goñi 1999; Lothrop 2002 [1928]). Combined models including mobility and exchange are rare but realistic when dealing with faraway sources (Ambrústolo et al. 2015). Sometimes continuous spatial models are used to organize archaeological research (Barrientos et al. 2018), a method that works with the mentioned fall-off principles. However, the location of the source of the rocks is inferred from the distribution of tools made of that rock. Archaeological patterns recorded away from sources are sometimes difficult to interpret. At least six types of obsidian were recognized on the northeastern Atlantic coastal sites (west coast of Gulf San Matías), some obtained at nearby sources, like the eastern border of the Somuncurá plateau (<100–250 km), and some as far as 300–400 km away at Sacanana, or 500 km at Lago Lolog, perhaps transported as nodules, cores, preforms, or finished tools (Favier Dubois et al. 2009a; Gómez Otero and Stern 2005; Stern et al. 2000, 2007, 2013). Many similar cases of convergence of toolstones from different origins exist in other areas of Patagonia. They are difficult to explain as the result of a single process, and the use of varied kinds of tactics is required to understand the formation of the deposits.

Analysis of recently published evidence shows that the general distribution of Pampa Del Asador (PDA) obsidian during the Late Holocene conforms to the scheme proposed by Borrero (2012), in which the dispersion of regularly interacting individuals is characterized as a ring or semi-ring of variable width surrounding a core. Bands with variable percentages of obsidian are located near the source, resulting from particular and probably asymmetric forms of use of space. A marked fall-off threshold for obsidian is beyond 140 km, after which values below 15% are found, and beyond 400 km, obsidian falls to values around 1%. An interesting exception to the general pattern is provided by sites at the San Martín lake, which are outliers with 35–48% obsidian, exceeding what was expected from its distance over 164 km from the source (Belardi et al. 2009; Pallo 2009; Pallo and Borrero 2015a: 290). Belardi and collaborators (2009) believe that a system of direct acquisition was in place using a low-cost route connecting with PDA. While this is a reasonable explanation for the obsidians found at the San Martin-Tar, the discovery of the 17 de Marzo obsidian source no longer makes acceptable similar explanations for the few findings at the Deseado Massif, where minimal presence during the final Pleistocene and small frequencies during the Early and Late Holocene were recorded (Cueto et al. 2018, 2020; Skarbun 2011).

A neat fall-off is observed in other regions, with some thresholds worth mentioning. For example, spatial analyses made by Borrazzo and collaborators indicated that ca. 125 km from the source probably represents the threshold of direct acquisition for the Miraflores rocks in Tierra del Fuego, which is approximately the same threshold known for the distribution of obsidian in sectors of Cuyo, and for the distribution of malacological remains in mainland Patagonia (Borrazzo et al. 2018; Cortegoso et al. 2012; Méndez et al. 2019; Pallo and Borrero 2015a; Zubimendi and Ambrústolo 2011). The contrast with the distribution of the Chaitén obsidian west of the Andes, with high frequencies found more than 300 km from the source (Reyes 2021), highlights a significant difference between terrestrial and maritime mobility.

ETHNICITY AND TERRITORY

The concept of ethnicity has always been challenging to deal with for archaeology (Jones 1997; Shennan 1989), and on occasion, it was heavily politically loaded (e.g., Kossina 1921). However, archaeologists have always tried to approach ethnic identities in the past based mainly, although not exclusively, on the properties of the archaeological record (Veit 1989), since there is *some* correlation between identity and material culture (Gosselain 2000). Archaeologists are still looking for the sharing of material culture as indicators of mutual practices or identity because it is almost all they have to approach this subject (Bauer and Agbe-Davis 2016). Needless to say, ethnic groups and ethnic territories are not fixed; they are dynamic, change through time, and operate in multiple dimensions.

In the Pampas, the historical accounts and the ethnographic information provide clues to approach ethnic territories in late pre-Hispanic times. The Europeans identified three ethnic group groups in the sixteenth century in the Lower Paraná and La Plata Rivers: Guaraní, Chaná-Timbú (latu sensu, see Chapter 6), and Querandí. The former two can be traced back to several centuries before the Spanish conquest and are the ethnographic expression of the Guaraní and Goya-Malabrigo archaeological entities (Ceruti 2003; González 1977; Politis and Bonomo 2012). The latter has not had a distinctive technology, and the adaptive pattern seems to be broadly related to the Late Holocene hunter-gatherers, making it challenging to trace them back.

Final Remarks

Moreover, the territory of the Querandí, as defined by early colonial accounts, encompasses several different Late Holocene archaeological configurations and subsistence strategies (Chapter 6). Toward the south and west, ethnic adscriptions to historically defined groups were more diffuse and vague; they were made in the following centuries when transformation produced by European colonization was notable (Nacuzzi 1998; Roulet 2016).

In Patagonia, archaeologists like Vignati (1927) believed that some archaeological deposits could be easily related to ethnographic groups like the Selk'nam or the Haush, a claim that was even repeated by some ethnographers (Chapman 1986). Similar associations were made between the content of the upper layers of sites and the general ethnic category Tehuelche, in itself a general name that minimally includes the Gununa'kena and the Aónikenk (Menghin 1952). All these initial exercises in identifying historical ethnicities failed for a lack of good chronological support and generality of the apparent diacritical elements. In other words, it was never clear which traits could be used to substantiate these interpretations. In a few cases, the association of parts of the record to ethnographic entities is better sustained, as exemplified by Mauricio Massone in his identification of Selk'nam-related layers in North Tierra del Fuego (Massone 2009). In this case, Massone used his deep knowledge of Selk'nam ethnographic sources, together with an archaeological record tightly restricted to the end of the Late Holocene that overlaps with the time of European contact. Alternatively, a strict focus on the search of very late sites in historically known open-air places, usually with the guide of oral traditions and/or recent ethnohistorical information, produced important results concerning the Tehuelche/Aónikenk-Mapuche (Nuevo Delaunay 2012; Nuevo Delaunay et al. 2017, 2020).

In spite of the difficulties with the concept of ethnic identity, several authors have approached ethnic borders for the Late Holocene based on different cultural markers (Curtoni 1999b, 2006; Heider 2016; Mazzanti 2006; Messineo and Barros 2021). In this sense, some conspicuous instruments were considered diacritical of ethnic identity. Given the highly standardized condition of the amygdaloid double-sided scraper made of SBG orthoquartzite (Chapter 6), it has been considered a diacritical element of the Pampean hunter-gatherers of the Tandilia, Interserrana, and CPD areas during Middle and Late Holocene times. Heider (2016) proposed an ethnic boundary in the Late Holocene in the northwestern sector of the northwestern area, based on the fall-off curve of the SBG orthoquartzite in the lithic contexts. Northwest of this frontier, he also detected an increase in obsidian, and there are some artifacts, such as the pottery statuettes, which suggest a vector from the west and northwest (see also Aguerre 1996). Messineo and Barros (2021) made a similar proposition based on the percentages of Tandilia toolstones (SBG orthoquartzite and phtanite), and determined a line between 350 and 400 km from the outcrops that could be interpreted as a flexible territorial

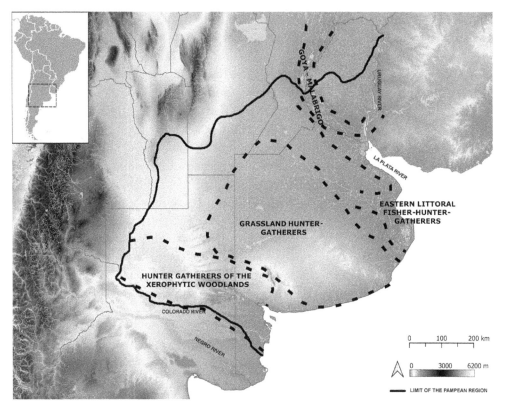

Figure 7.6 Possible ethnic borders in the very Late Holocene in the Pampas.

boundary. Alternatively, the rock recovered more than 350 km from the outcrops could have been traded. Beyond this radius, in the Salado-Chadileuvú-Curacó and the western fringe of the Northwest area, the predominant lithic material is the silicified chert from the Fresco Plateau, basalt and silex from the river cuts, and quartz, chalcedony, and rhyolites from the Central Hills (Messineo and Barros 2021).

Other elements were taken into account to discuss ethnic identities, such as the style of rock art and engraved artifacts (Curtoni 2006), pottery decoration (Di Prado 2015), and the presence of exotic items (Salazar Siciliano and Berón 2013). Although all these traits do not co-occur in all areas, they form some archaeological configurations that allow exploring the very Late Holocene period from an ethnic perspective (Figure 7.6). Of course, these social forms did not have fixed boundaries; objects, information, symbols, ideas, and people circulated widely among them, forming macro-regional sociopolitical networks. The construction of alterities is a complex and multidimensional process that includes prestige items, pottery designs, consumption patterns, technological practices, hunting strategies, and so on. These sociocultural units are related to generic archaeological configurations, which can be characterized as follows. These characterizations are not bounded and have the purpose

Final Remarks 279

of providing a model against which current and future data can be contrasted. It is also pertinent to reintroduce the discussion about ethnicity, from a contemporary anthropological perspective, in the Pampean archaeology. Except for Goya-Malabrigo, none of the others can be ascribed to any of the ethnic groups defined in the early colonial accounts. All that said, regional analyses like this one always require some allowances for the piecemeal nature of the archaeological record.

1. The southern fringe of the expansion of Goya-Malabrigo was characterized by hydrocentrality and a mixed economy that included fishing, hunting, gathering, and small-scale horticulture (house gardens). Bell-shaped pottery with zoomorphic appendages is a diacritical element, and pottery designs are incised decoration including the drag and jab technique. Bone technology is fully developed. Semi-permanent settlements in anthropogenic mounds are frequent. The main exotic element (metal) is of Andean origin. The ethnographic expression of Goya-Malabrigo is the Chaná-Timbú complex (Chapter 6).

2. Eastern littoral fisher-hunter-gatherers, whose territory includes the lower sector of the Salado River Depression and the floodplain of the Lower Paraná and La Plata Rivers (including the western littoral strip), are characterized by a mixed economy of fishing, hunting of coypu and the Pampas and marsh deer, as well as the gathering of fruits from the *tala* forest. Pottery is abundant and includes a variety of incised decorated designs by drag and jab, linear incised, and punctuated. Lithic technology is formed by small and heavily reduced instruments, mainly on SBG orthoquartzite and phtanite, including small triangular arrow points. Tandilia seems to be the almost exclusive source for toolstone. Exotic materials include chrysocolla and amazonite. The site material density suggests extended periods of occupation.

3. The grassland hunter-gatherers, whose territory included Tandilia, Interserrana, the upper sector of the Salado Depression, the CPD, the Transversal Valleys, the eastern sector of the Northwest area, and probably the eastern ranges of Ventania, are basically guanaco hunters, who also exploited Pampas deer and various smaller fauna (armadillos, greater rhea, rodents, and lizards, with areal variations). The gathering is restricted to fruits from a few isolated xerophytic forests and some unidentified grassland products. Basic tools include various types of bola stones (probably the most conspicuous weapon), scrapers such as the amygdaloid double-sided scraper of GSB orthoquartzite, phtanite micro-scrapers, small-sized triangular arrow points, and *piéce esquillée* on seashore rounded cobbles. Tandilia is the primary source of toolstone, while Ventania is secondary. Lithic caching and stockpiling were strategies to cope with the heterogeneous raw material distribution. Pottery,

both plain and decorated by incision (drag and jab, lineal, etc.), has a moderate to low frequency and was a favored means for symbolic communication. Marine mollusks (*Adelomedon* sp.) are widespread. Rock art is almost exclusive to Tandilia and is dominated by abstract motifs in red (geometric, rectilinear). Obsidian, in extremely low quantities, is the main extra-regional material.

4. The hunter-gatherers of the xerophytic woodlands, whose territory encompassed the Salado-Chadileuvú-Curacó, Close Basins, South areas, and the western ranges of Ventania, had a mixed economy of guanaco as the main prey, followed by Pampas deer, greater rhea, and a variety of small mammals (armadillos and rodents), integrated with the exploitation of the fruits of the xerophytic forest from the Spinal area (*caldén, algarrobo, chañar*, etc.). In the Lower Colorado River, marine and freshwater fish became part of the diet. The main sources of lithic raw material are the Fresco Plateau, the Patagonian Shingle Mantle (including the reworked pebble from the Colorado River), and Ventania. The use of pottery is relatively scarce, and a design of incised crossing diagonal lines seems to be idiosyncratic in these groups. Decorative designs, both in rock art (in Ventania) and in engravings on different materials, are dominated by abstract motifs with a high proportion of geometric-rectilinear patterning. Funerary modalities incorporate intense body manipulation in multiple packed secondary burials where reassembling of body parts is frequent. Obsidian from the Andes is the primary exotic material. In the last 1,000 years, some rocks from North Patagonia (translucent chalcedony) have been used more intensively. At the same time, in the western sector, the Vergel-Valdivia pottery from Chile indicates trans-cordilleran contacts.

Patagonia's situation is slightly more complicated, given the limited spatial coverage of archaeological research and the fragmented and partial ethnographic record. If we exclusively attend to the archaeological items recovered in excavations, some patterns suggest the existence of idiosyncratic cultural configurations. These configurations are difficult to frame in ethnic identities since their temporality is long enough – usually longer than 2,000 years – to hide significant cultural changes. Multiple evidence, mainly the distribution of selected toolstones, isotope values on human bones, rock art, and maritime resources in South Patagonia, confirms a certain degree of territoriality in which a piece of land 100 km wide, starting near the ocean, is occupied by people that interacted with coastal resources, while beyond that 100-km threshold diets become fully terrestrial, maritime items are not found, different sources of rocks are exploited, and differences in rock art are observed (Barberena 2002; Borrero 2015; Charlin and Borrero 2012). But it is not only the lack of chronological precision that is affecting our interpretations. The

Final Remarks 281

problem of identifying ethnic entities remains important even in places where the oldest archaeological remains are about 500 years old or even less.

Regardless of the already mentioned archaeological difficulties with the concept of ethnicity, Patagonia presents the added difficulty of uneven ethnographic evidence, mostly derived from contacts along the coastline (Moreno 2008). Excepting the northern part of Patagonia, only near the end of the nineteenth century, some information begin to be collected in the interior. Entries into the interior, such as those of Antonio Viedma in the eighteenth century or Robert Fitz Roy at the beginning of the nineteenth century, were exceptions that did not result in any detailed ethnographic information (Fitz Roy 1839; Viedma 1980 [1783]). This concentration of contact with Europeans on the coast, at least in part, had an enduring affect on Patagonian societies. Effectively, the main contrast between maritime and terrestrial foragers was already mentioned, a contrast that is in desperate need of recognizing its greater complexity. In the first place, we need to know the age of the southern historic ethnographic groups that came to be known as Gununa'kena, Aónikenk, Selk'nam, Kawésqar, Haush, and Yámana/ Yahgán. It is becoming clear that this list is incomplete and that it will be very difficult to finish it using only a few available ethnographic reports and observations by travelers (Borrero 1997). If we also include the groups inhabiting North Patagonia in our questioning, where even older ethnohistoric information for the interior exists, the answer is even more discouraging (Nacuzzi 1988).

Returning to the south, the existence of so-called mixed cultural configurations – those with important maritime and terrestrial protein components in their subsistence, a complementary coastal and interior settlement pattern, and so on – is well recognized. What is not clear is the historical depth of those cases. A recent review of archaeological and ethnographical evidence for the area between the central Strait of Magellan and the middle Gallegos River Basin shows the existence of similarly mixed adaptations going back at least a few hundred years into the prehistoric past (Borrero et al. 2011). This was based on several markers beyond those based on subsistence. Certainly, we should not trust any evaluation of ethnicity made exclusively on the basis of subsistence resources. These markers help us understand that there is much more variability in Patagonian subsistence than what was classically accepted, but not necessarily associated with ethnicity (Buscaglia 2017; Castro Esnal 2014; Nacuzzi 1998).

Our ethnographic and archaeological pictures of the Patagonian hinterland are terribly unbalanced. Not only is the level of archaeological variation observed near the end of the Late Holocene at odds with the classic ethnographic divisions recorded during historical times, but the variation suggests that cultural configurations were changing fast (Borrero 1997; Nacuzzi 1998). Ethnic assignations were sometimes made on the basis of geographic locations, which is a dangerous procedure (Constantinescu 1999; Morano Büchner 2013). The main problem is that our knowledge about the past distribution of individuals challenges any determination of strict correspondence between geography and ethnicity. Sometimes ethnic assignations were made on the basis of the convergence of geographic, molecular, and stable isotope studies (i.e., de la Fuente et al. 2018), but it always remains true that the speed at which cultures change is fast enough to make those assignations unacceptable (Perreault 2012). Of course, human populations' occupational continuity or discontinuity needs to be carefully distinguished from changes in cultural content, making the attribution of ethnographic names to prehistoric cultures a dangerous game. It is more than possible that subtle material differences among human groups went unrecognized during contact times, a fact highlighted by the abundance of discrepancies between the late archaeological record and ethnographic sources. For example, the distribution of bone wedges and the importance of rodents or birds in the human diet discovered in archaeological work in North Tierra del Fuego differ substantially from the observations made by voyagers and ethnographers (Borrero 1997). This is not surprising since it is in full accordance with the dynamic cultural times characterizing the European contact and with the odds of any particular behavior being recorded by voyagers. We must recall that the introduction of new raw materials, such as glass and metal, led to innovations and technological diversification. It was also a time of massive displacement of human groups by force or indirect pressure, creating situations during which drastic social and demographic changes occurred (Buscaglia 2019). It becomes clear that the virulence of introduced illnesses was only part of the reason behind decreasing population density after intensive contact with European visitors occurred (Casali and Manzi 2017).

If we focus our analysis exclusively on the mainland, the introduction of the horse produced a quantum change in the material culture, social organization, and home range of local foragers (Palermo 1986). These changes spurred, among other things, a reformulation of hunting tactics, in which the use of bolas was favored over that of the bow and arrow. At this time, there was also a push toward semi-sedentary lifeways, related to the increasing home range that the use of horses made possible. Large camps located close to good pastures for the horses become the norm. Well-defined routes and rest places were routinely used by mounted hunters, who sometimes traveled hundreds of kilometers for various social and economic reasons (Castro Esnal 2014; Nacuzzi and Pérez de Micou 1994). Not unexpectedly, we know very little of the archaeology associated with these routes despite highly detailed narratives and precise geographical references for some of the most important areas (Musters 1964 [1871]). Only recently have serious efforts been made to acquire pertinent chronological information for these routes (Castro Esnal 2014; Leonardt et al. 2015).

FINAL REMARKS

Beyond commonalities and differences, the archaeology of the Pampas and Patagonia is a unique chapter in the long-term history of the New World hunter-gatherers. This history started in the Southern Cone at the end of the Pleistocene and lasted until a couple of centuries ago, indicating successful adaptive strategies and suitable social forms. This basic adaptive pattern revolved around the exploitation of the guanaco, the distant mobility ranges (which in many instances include the seashore), and a flexible technology in which bola stones, a few types of projectile points, and double-sided amygdaloid scrapers stand out. While land hunting and gathering were the critical economic components in the Middle Holocene, the adaptation to littoral maritime environments, especially in the far south, created new adaptive patterns and gave origin to new ethnic groups. In the Late Holocene, horticulture was also practiced in the main rivers' floodplains in the Northeast area and changed the conceptual relationship between humans and nature. These changes impacted not only the economy but also the social and spiritual life of these people.

When the Spaniards arrived, the brutality of the conquest, plus the diseases brought by them, significantly altered the long-term ways of life, and all Indian groups had to adapt to the new situation. The adoption of the horse, the use of metal tools, and the increasing incorporation into trade networks with the Mapuche Indians and the Spaniards changed their daily life and generated dynamic ethnogenesis processes. Horses, cows, and sheep replaced the hunting of guanaco and deer, and some hunters became herders or traders. Gradually, metal tools superseded lithic technology, although the bola stone remains longer. Of course, these transformations did not have the same rhythm in all areas. Around Buenos Aires, the impact was strong early in the Spanish conquest, in the sixteenth century, while in Tierra del Fuego, the Selk'nam and the Yahgán maintained their traditional life – with minor changes – until the end of the nineteenth century.

When we compare the mounted grassland cultures of the Southern Cone with those of the Great Plains and the Asian steppes, we note some important commonalities, like the role of horses in ritual life, their generation of social hierarchies, and their use for transport of people and their belongings – as mentioned, promoting long-distance caravans. The horse was adopted very early in the Pampas, and chronicles mentioned that the Querandí were already horseback Indians in the mid-sixteenth century. Also decisive is their role in hunting, which in Patagonia led to increased burning of pastures and the use of circle tactics, sometimes producing results close to mass killings. Finally, the use of horses as food, with a particular interest in the fat of mares, needs to be mentioned. Pampean and Patagonian ethnohistoric sources are full of references to the use of mare fat to make the lean meat of guanacos more attractive.

In the Pampas, some indigenous people preferred horse meat over cow, until very recent times (the mid-twentieth century). As in the North American Plains, the horses were effectively used for war against the Europeans first and later against the Hispanic-criollo people. Indigenous people from the Pampas and Patagonia developed well-planned battle strategies in which the horses were extremely useful.

But there are also contrasts. Among the differences, it is notable that while on the North American Plains, the use of horses led to increasing hunts of bison with bows and arrows, in the Pampas and Patagonia it led to the disappearance of this weapon, to be replaced by bolas (Mitchell 2015: 344). The use of the bola frees one arm, which can be used to steer the horse more precisely, leading to the abandonment of the bow and arrow system. Also, especially for war, spears with metal or lithic tips and long shafts were used. Since the topography is mostly flat in the Pampas, and the guanaco is lighter, more agile, and clustered in much smaller herds than bison, hunting strategies differed from the Northern Plains. Basically, no drive lanes or jump sites were recorded in the Pampas.

The profound economic and technological transformations and the incorporation of the Pampas and Patagonia lands during the nineteenth century into the states of Argentina and Chile and the global market left little room for the continuation of traditional indigenous lives. The result was a dramatic reduction in the Indian population and the violent expulsion from their ancestral territories. By the beginning of the twentieth century, only scattered and isolated communities survived in the Pampas and Patagonia, usually confined to small plots of land.

However, recent genetic studies in these regions show significant – and unexpected – components of Native American genes in contemporary people. At the same time, the current emergence of reethnicity processes and new political reorganizations, in both the Pampas and Patagonia, are empowering and giving new visibility to the indigenous people in the Southern Cone. Ultimately, the new scenario shows the vitality of the Native Americans in both regions. Although they do not maintain a traditional hunter-gatherer way of life, they still struggle to keep their identities, beliefs, rights, and languages in a global world.

SELECT BIBLIOGRAPHY

Full bibliography available at www.cambridge.org/politisborrerofullbibliography.

Abraham de Vazquez, Elena M., Karsten Garleff, Helga Liebricht, Alberto C. Regairaz, Frank Schäbitz, Francisco Squeo, Helmut Stingl, Heinz Veitz, and Carolina Villagrán 2000 Geomorphology and Paleoecology of the Arid Diagonal in Southern South America. *Zeitschrift fur Angewandte Geologie* 1:55–61.

Acosta, Alejandro 2005 Zooarqueología de cazadores-recolectores del extremo nororiental de la provincia de Buenos Aires (humedal del río Paraná inferior, región pampeana, Argentina). PhD dissertation. Facultad de Ciencias Naturales y Museo-UNLP, La Plata.

Acosta, Alejandro, Natacha Buc, and Daniel Loponte 2020 Tecnología ósea de los grupos cazadores-recolectores de la Pampa Ondulada (provincia de Buenos Aires). *Revista del Museo de Antropología* 13(2):79–92.

Acosta, Alejandro, Daniel Loponte, and Pablo Tchilinguirian 2013 Nuevos aportes para la arqueología del Humedal del Paraná Inferior: el sitio Médanos de Escobar. *Relaciones de la Sociedad Argentina de Antropología* 37(1):19–35.

Adán, Leonor, Rodrigo Mera, María Becerra, and Marcelo Godoy 2004 Ocupación arcaica en territorios boscosos y lacustres de la región pericordillerana (IX y X Regiones): el sitio Marifilo 1 de la localidad de Pucura. *Chungara* 11:1121–1136.

Aguerre, Ana M. 1996 Arqueología en la Laguna Chadilaufquen, Embajador Martini, Provincia de La Pampa. In *El pasado en la Laguna Chadilaufquen, Departamento Realicó, Provincia de la Pampa, República Argentina*, compiled by Ana Maria Aguerre, pp. 21–43. Santa Rosa: Instituto de Antropología Rural.

———1997a Nuevos sitios con arte rupestre en la Meseta Basáltica del Oeste de la Provincia de La Pampa-Rep. Argentina. In *Documentos del Congreso Internacional de Arte Rupestre*, edited by Matias Strecker, p. 59. Cochabamba: Sociedad de Investigación del Arte Rupestre de Bolivia.

———1997b Replanteo de la industria Toldense. Arqueología de Patagonia Centro Meridional. PhD dissertation, Universidad de Buenos Aires.

Alcaráz, Ana 2017 La fauna menor de sitios arqueológicos del curso inferior del río Colorado (Provincia de Buenos Aires): aspectos tafonómicos y subsistencia de cazadores-recolectores durante el Holoceno medio y tardío. PhD dissertation, Universidad Nacional del Centro de la Provincia de Buenos Aires.

Aldazabal, Verónica 2002 La ocupación humana en el sector centro-oriental de la pampa deprimida. PhD dissertation, Facultad de Filosofia y Letras-UBA, Buenos Aires.

Aldazabal, Verónica, and Emilio Eugenio 2009 Entre el fuego y el juego. La cerámica del sitio Rincón Chico 2/87. In *Arqueología de rescate en Rincón Chico, provincia del Neuquén*, edited by Eduardo Crivelli Montero, Mabel Fernández, and Mariano Ramos, pp. 163–186. Buenos Aires: Dunken.

———2013 La cerámica unguicular y corrugada en la Pampa Deprimida. Contextos y discusión. *Cuadernos del Instituto Nacional de Antropología y Pensamiento Latinoamericano* 1(4):95–107.

Álvarez, Maria C. 2008 Zooarqueología y Tafonomía del sitio Calera (partido de Olavarría, provincia de Buenos Aires). PhD dissertation. Universidad Nacional del Centro de la Provincia de Buenos Aires.

———2014a Tecnología ósea en el oeste de la región pampeana: identificación de las técnicas de manufactura a partir de las evidencias arqueológicas y experimentales. *Chungara Revista de Arqueología Chilena* 46(2):93–210.

———2014b Subsistence Patterns during the Holocene in the Interserrana Area (Pampean region, Argentina): Evaluating Intensification in Resource Exploitation. *Journal of Anthropological Archaeology* 34:54–65.

Álvarez, Maria C., Ana P. Alcaráz, Maria A. Gutiérrez, and Gustavo Martínez 2013 Análisis zooarqueológico del sitio Paso Otero 4 (partido de Necochea). Aportes a la discusión de modelos de subsistencia de la región pampeana. *Intersecciones en Antropología* 14:383–398.

Ambrosetti, Juan B. 1894 Los paraderos precolombianos de Goya. *Boletín del Instituto Geográfico Argentino* 14:242–265.

Ambrústolo, Pablo, and Miguel Ángel Zubimendi 2019 Explotación de sílex rojo en Bahía del Oso Marino (Patagonia Argentina). *Intersecciones en Antropología* 20(1):39–54.

Ambrústolo, Pablo, Miguel Angel Zubimendi, María Laura Ciampagna, and Verónica Trola 2011 Alero el Oriental: evidencias de las primeras ocupaciones de la Costa Norte de Santa Cruz (Patagonia, Argentina). *Revista Werkén* 14:9–22.

Ameghino, Florentino 1880–1881 *La Antigüedad del Hombre en el Plata*, edited by G. Masson e Igon hermanos. Paris: G. Masson; Buenos Aires: Igor hermanos.

———1898 Premiére notice sur le *Neomylodon Listai* un représentant vivant des anciens Edentés Gravigrades fossiless de l'Argentine. An existing ground-sloth in Patagonia. *Natural Science* 13:324–326.

———1910c La industria de la piedra quebrada en el Mioceno superior de Monte Hermoso. In *Separata del XVII Congreso Científico Internacional Americano*, pp. 1–5. Buenos Aires: Museo Nacional de Buenos Aires.

———1910d Une nouvelle industrie lithique: l'industrie de la pierre fendeu dans le tertiaire de la region littorale au sud de Mar del Plata. *Anales del Museo Nacional de Buenos Aires* 13(3):189–204.

Andrefsky, J. William 2009 The Analysis of Stone Tool Procurement, Production, and Maintenance. *Journal of Archaeological Research* 17(1):65–103.

Aparicio, Francisco de 1948 The Archaeology of the Paraná River. In *Handbook of South American Indians 3*, edited by J. Steward, pp. 57–68. Washington, DC: Smithsonian Institution.

Apolinaire, Eduardo, Carola Castiñeira, and Mariano Bonomo 2019 Nuevos aportes para la delimitación de la base regional de recursos líticos de la provincia de Entre Ríos: relevamiento de afloramientos primarios y caracterización microscópica de rocas siliciclásticas. *Arqueología* 25(2):71–22.

Armentano, Gabriela 2012 Arqueología del curso inferior del río Colorado. Estudio tecnológico de las colecciones líticas de Norpatagonia oriental durante el Holoceno Tardío. Departamentos de Villarino y Patagones, Provincia de Buenos Aires, Argentina. PhD dissertation, Universidad Nacional del Centro de la Provincia de Buenos Aires.

Aschero, Carlos, Mariana De Nigris, María J. Figuerero Torres, Gabriela Guráieb, Guillermo Mengoni Goñalons, and Hugo Yacobaccio 1999 Excavaciones recientes en Cerro de los Indios 1, Lago Posadas (Santa Cruz): nuevas perspectivas. In *Soplando en el viento . . . Actas de las III Jornadas de Arqueología de Patagonia*, pp. 269–286. Neuquén-Buenos Aires: INAPL-UNCO.

Austral, Antonio 1965 Investigaciones prehistóricas en el curso inferior del río Sauce Grande. *Trabajos de Prehistoria* 19:7–123.

———1971 El yacimiento arqueológico Vallejo en el NO de la provincia de La Pampa. Contribución a la sistematización de la prehistoria y arqueología de la región pampeana. *Relaciones de la Sociedad Argentina de Antropología* 5(2):49–70.

Avigliano, Esteban, Gustavo Martínez, Luciana Stoessel, Ana Mendez, Nerea Bordel, Jorge Pisonero, and Alejandra Volpedo 2020 Otoliths as Indicators for Fish Behaviour and Procurement Strategies of Hunter-Gatherers in North Patagonia. *Heliyon* 6(3):e03438.

Ávila, J. David 2011 Resultados de los fechados radiocarbónicos del sitio LED, Departamento General López, Provincia de Santa Fe. *Relaciones de la Sociedad Argentina de Antropología* 36:337–343.

Barberena, Ramiro 2008 *Arqueología y biogeografía humana en Patagonia meridional*. Buenos Aires: Sociedad Argentina de Antropología.

Barberena, Ramiro, Mónica Berón, and Leandro Luna 2018 Isótopos estables en el sitio Chenque I: paleodieta y procedencia geográfica. In *El sitio Chenque I. Un cementerio prehispánico en la Pampa Occidental. Estilo de vida e interacciones culturales de cazadores-recolectores del Cono Sur Americano*, edited by Mónica Berón, pp. 367–395. Buenos Aires: Sociedad Argentina de Antropología.

Barberena, Ramiro, Karen Borrazzo, Agustina A. Rughini, Guadalupe Romero, María P. Pompei, Carina Llano, Maria E. De Porras, Victor Durán, Charles R. Stern, Anahí Re, Diego Estrella, Analía Forasiepi, Fernando Fernández, Manuel Chidiak, Luis Acuña, Alejandra Gasco, and Marianela N. Quiroga 2015 Perspectivas arqueológicas para Patagonia septentrional: sitio cueva Huenul 1 (provincia del Neuquén, Argentina). *Magallania* 43(1):137–163.

Barnosky, Anthony, and Emily Lindsey 2010 Timing of Quaternary Megafaunal Extinction in South America in Relation to Human Arrival and Climate Change. *Quaternary International* 217, 10–29.

Barrientos, Gustavo 1997 Nutrición y dieta de las poblaciones aborígenes prehispánicas del sudeste de la región pampeana. PhD dissertation, Universidad Nacional de La Plata. La Plata.

Barrientos, Gustavo, Luciana Catella, and Fernando Oliva 2014 The Spatial Structure of Lithic Landscapes: The Late Holocene Record of East-Central Argentina as a Case Study. *Journal of Archaeological Method and Theory*, 22:1151–1192.

Barrientos, Gustavo, and W. Bruce Masse 2014 The Archaeology of Cosmic Impact: Lessons from Two Mid-Holocene Argentine Case Studies. *Journal of Archaeological Method and Theory* 21:134–211.

Barrientos, Gustavo, and Sergio I. Perez 2005 Was There a Population Replacement during the Late Mid-Holocene in the Southeastern Pampas of Argentina? Archaeological Evidence and Paleoecological Basis. *Quaternary International* 132:95–105.

Barros, Maria P. 2009 Analyses des stratégies d'acquisition et de production lithique dans la région pampeana, province de Buenos Aires, Argentine. PhD dissertation, Université Paris Ouest Nanterre-La Défense.

Barros, Maria P., Guillermo Heider, María C. Álvarez, Cristian Kaufmann, and Jonathan Bellinzoni 2018 First Results of the Hunter-Gatherer Weapon System Studies in the Middle Basin of the Salado Creek (Pampas Region, Argentina). *Journal of Lithic Studies* 5:1–23.

Barros, María P., and Pablo Messineo 2006 Modos de abastecimiento y explotación de materias primas líticas en la cuenca del Arroyo Tapalqué (Olavarría, Provincia de Buenos Aires, (Argentina). *Habitus* 4(2):711.

Bastourre, Maria L. 2014 Estudios arqueofaunísticos en el Delta Superior del Paraná: el sitio Los Tres Cerros 1 (Provincia de Entre Ríos, Argentina). *Revista Chilena de Antropología* 30: 109–115.

Bastourre, Maria L. and María M. Azpelicueta 2020 Del registro ictioarqueológico a las prácticas alimentarias: el caso de Los Tres Cerros 1 (Delta Superior del Paraná, Entre Ríos). *Relaciones de la Sociedad Argentina de Antropología* 45(1):13–57.

Bate, Luis F. 1982 *Orígenes de la comunidad primitiva en Patagonia*. Mexico, D.F.: Cuicuilco.

Bayón, Cristina, Nora Flegenheimer, and Alejandra Pupio 2006 Planes sociales en el abastecimiento y traslado de roca en la pampa bonaerense en el Holoceno temprano y tardío. *Relaciones de la Sociedad Argentina de Antropología* 31:19–45.

Bayón, Cristina, Nora Flegenheimer, Miguel Valente, and Alejandra Pupio 1999 Dime cómo eres y te diré de dónde vienes: la procedencia de rocas cuarcíticas en la región pampeana. *Relaciones de la Sociedad Argentina de Antropología* 24:187–235.

Bayón, Cristina, and Gustavo Politis 1996 Estado actual de las investigaciones en el Sitio Monte Hermoso 1 (prov. de Buenos Aires). *Arqueología* 6:83–115.

———2014 The Inter-Tidal Zone Site of La Olla: Early-Middle Holocene Human Adaptation on the Pampean Coast of Argentina. In *Prehistoric Archaeology on the Continental Shelf*, edited by A. Evans, J. Flatman, and N. Flemming, pp. 115–130. New York: Springer.

Bayón, Cristina, and Carlos Zavala 1997 Coastal Sites in South Buenos Aires: A Review of Piedras Quebradas. In *Quaternary of South America and Antarctic Peninsula*, edited by J. Rabassa and M. Salemme, Vol. 10, pp. 229–253. Ushuaia: Centro Austral de Investigaciones Científicas and Universidad de la Patagonia.

Bechis, Martha A. 2010 (1989) Redefiniendo la etnohistoria y un estudio de caso: el área pampeana. In *Piezas de etnohistoria y de antropología histórica*, edited by M. Bechis, pp. 47–65. Buenos Aires: Sociedad Argentina de Antropología.

Belardi, Juan B., Flavia Carballo Marina, and Silvana Espinosa (editors) 2006 *La cuenca del río Coyle*. Río Gallegos: Universidad Nacional de la Patagonia Austral.

Belardi, Juan B., Silvana Espinosa, Flavia Carballo Marina, Gustavo Barrientos, Rafael A. Goñi, Alejandro Súnico, Tirso Bourlot, Cecilia Pallo, Augusto Tessone, Solana García Guráieb, Anahí Re, and Patricia Campan 2010 Las cuencas de los lagos Tar y San Martín (Santa Cruz, Argentina) y la dinámica del poblamiento humano del sur de Patagonia: integración de los primeros resultados. *Magallania* 38(2):137–159.

Bellelli, Cristina, and Ana G. Guráieb 2019 Re-evaluación cronológica de la secuencia arqueológica del curso medio del río Chubut (Área Piedra Parada). In *Arqueología de la Patagonia: el pasado en las arenas*, edited by Julieta Gómez Otero, Ariadna Svoboda, and Anahí Banegas, pp. 259–269. Puerto Madryn: Instituto de Diversidad y Evolución Austral.

Bello, Álvaro 2011 *Nampülkafe: el viaje de los mapuches de la Araucanía a las pampas argentinas: territorio, política y cultura en los siglos XIX y XX.* Temuco, Chile: Universidad Católica de Temuco.

Belmar, Carolina 2019 *Los cazadores-recolectores y las Plantas en Patagonia. Perspectivas desde el sitio cueva Baño Nuevo 1, Aisén.* Santiago: Social-Ediciones.

Bernardi, Lila, Mario Alberto Arrieta, and Ignacio Lynch Ianniello 2020 Preliminary study of the age-at-death profile in a prehistoric skeletal sample from Médano Petroquímica Site, Argentina. *Journal of Archaeological Science: Reports* 4(A):1–9.

Berón, Mónica 2004 Dinámica poblacional y estrategias de subsistencia de poblaciones prehispánicas de la cuenca Atuel-Salado-Chadileuvú-Curacó, provincia de La Pampa. PhD dissertation, Universidad de Buenos Aires.

———2006 Base regional de recursos minerales en el occidente pampeano. Procedencia y estrategias de aprovisionamiento. *Relaciones de la Sociedad Argentina de Antropología* 31:47–88.

———2018 *El sitio Chenque I. Un cementerio prehispánico en la Pampa Occidental. Estilo de vida e interacciones culturales de cazadores-recolectores del Cono Sur Americano.* Edited by Mónica Berón. Buenos Aires: Sociedad Argentina de Antropología.

Berón, Mónica, and Manuel Carrera Aizpitarte 2019 Materias primas y circuitos de movilidad en el Noroeste de Patagonia. Una aproximación al estudio de los conflictos sociales a partir de la evidencia arqueológica. *Revista del Museo de Antropología* 12(1):7–22.

Berón, Mónica, Manuel Carrera Aizpitarte, and Florencia Páez 2015 Arqueología en el área de Valles Transversales (provincia de La Pampa, Argentina). Caracterización y tendencia de los conjuntos arqueológicos. Implicancias sociales en la construcción del paisaje. *Relaciones de la Sociedad Argentina de Antropología* 40(2):549–587.

Berón, Mónica, Leandro Luna, and Ramiro Barberena 2009 Isotopic Archaeology in the Western Pampas (Argentina): Preliminary Results and Perspectives. *International Journal of Osteoarchaeology* 19:250–265.

Binford, Lewis R. 1980 Willow Smoke and Dogs' Tails: Hunter-Gatherer Settlement Systems and Archaeological Site Formation. *American Antiquity* 45:4–20.

———1982 The Archaeology of Place. *Journal of Anthropological Archaeology* 1:5–31.

———1983 *Working at Archaeology.* New York: Academic Press.

Bird, Junius 1988 *Travel and Archaeology in South Chile.* Iowa City: University of Iowa.

Blasi, Adriana, Gustavo Politis, and Maria Cristina Bayón 2013 Palaeo-Environmental Reconstruction of La Olla, a Holocene Archaeological Site in the Pampean Coast. *Journal of Archaeological Science* 40(3):1554–1567.

Bodner, Martin, Ugo A. Perego, Gaabriela Huber, Liane Fendt, Alexander W. Rock, Betina Zimmermann, Anna Olivieri, Alberto Gomez-Carballa, Hovirag Lancioni, Norman Angerhofer, Maria C. Bobillo, Daniel Corach, Scott R. Woodward, Antonio Salas, Alessandro Achilli, Antonio Torroni, Hans-Jürgen Bandelt, and Walther Parson 2012 Rapid Coastal Spread of First Americans: Novel Insights from South America's Southern Cone Mitochondrial Genomes. *Genome Research* 22(5):811–820.

Bonnat, Gustavo F. 2016 Análisis de la organización de la Tecnología Lítica de Grupos Cazadores-recolectores tempranos del área de Tandilia Oriental (Buenos Aires).

PhD dissertation, Universidad Nacional del Centro de la Provincia de Buenos Aires.

Bonnat, Gustavo, and Diana Mazzanti 2015 Análisis de la tecnología lítica de las ocupaciones humanas efímeras durante la transición Pleistoceno-Holoceno: el caso de Cueva La Brava (Buenos Aires, Argentina). *Intersecciones en Antropología* 16:287–300.

Bonomo, Mariano 2005 *Costeando las llanuras: Arqueología del litoral marítimo pampeano.* Buenos Aires: Sociedad Argentina de Antropología.

Bonomo, Mariano, Francisco J. Aceituno Bocangera, Gustavo Politis, and María L. Pochettino 2011b Pre-Hispanic Horticulture in the Paraná Delta (Argentina): Archaeological and Historical Evidence. *World Archaeology* 43(4):557–579.

Bonomo, Mariano, and Adrina M. Blasi 2010 Base regional de recursos líticos del Delta del Paraná. Estudio petrográfico de artefactos y afloramientos en el sur de Entre Ríos. *Cazadores-Recolectores del Cono Sur, Revista de Arqueología* 4(1):17–41.

Bonomo, Mariano, Edgardo D. Cabanillas, and Ricardo Montero 2017 Archaeometallurgy in the Paraná Delta (Argentina): Composition, Manufacture, and Indigenous Routes. *Journal of Anthropological Archaeology* 47:1–11.

Bonomo, Mariano, Rodrigo Costa Angrizani, Eduardo Apolinaire, and Francisco S. Noelli 2015 A Model for the Guaraní Expansion in the La Plata Basin and Littoral Zone of Southern Brazil. *Quaternary International* 356:54–73.

Bonomo, Mariano, and Gustavo Politis. 2018 Mound Building, Social Complexity and Horticulture in the Lower Paraná River. In *Encyclopedia of Global Archaeology*, edited by Claire Smith, pp. 1–22. New York: Springer International. https://doi.org/10.1007/978-3-319-51726-1_3035-1.

Bonomo, Mariano, Gustavo Politis, Laura Bastourre, and Germán Moreira 2021 Humanized Nature: Symbolic Representation of Fauna in Pottery from the Paraná River of South America. In *South American Contributions to World Archaeology*, edited by Sonia Archila and Mariano Bonomo, pp. 411–446. Cham: Springer Nature.

Bonomo, Mariano, Gustavo Politis, and Camila Gianotti 2011a. Montículos, jerarquía social y horticultura en las sociedades indígenas del Delta del Delta del río Paraná (Argentina). *Latin American Antiquity* 22(3):297–333.

Borella, Florencia 2004 *Tafonomía regional y estudios arqueofaunísticos de cetáceos en el norte de Tierra del Fuego y Patagonia Meridional.* BAR International Series No. 1257. Oxford: Archaeopress.

Borges Vaz, Erika 2017 Arqueología de Cazadores-Recolectores del curso inferior del río Colorado (Provincia de Buenos Aires, Argentina): Aportes al conocimiento de las ocupaciones humanas Pampeano-Patagónicas. PhD dissertation, Universidad Nacional del Centro de la Provincia de Buenos Aires.

Bórmida, Marcelo 1960 Investigaciones paleontológicas en la región de Bolívar (Provincia de Buenos Aires). *Anales de la Comisión de Investigación Científica de la Provincia de Buenos Aires* 1:190–283.

———1962 El Jabaliense. Una industria de guijarros de la península de San Blas, Provincia de Buenos Aires (República Argentina). *Trabajos de Prehistoria* 6:7–55.

Borrazzo, Karen 2008 Distribuciones artefactuales en la periferia sudeste de la sierra Baguales (Santa Cruz, Argentina). *Magallania* 36(1):103–116.

———2016 Lithic Taphonomy in Desert Environments: Contributions from Fuego-Patagonia (Southern South America). *Quaternary International* 422:19–28.

Borrazzo, Karen, G. Lorena L'Heureux, Natalia Cirigliano, M. Cecilia Pallo, Ivana Ozán, Liliana Manzi, and Judith Charlin 2019 Prospecciones en el interfluvio Gallegos-Chico (Santa Cruz, Argentina): nuevos datos arqueológicos. In *Arqueología de la Patagonia: el pasado en las arenas,* edited by Julieta Gómez Otero, Ariadana Svodova and Anahía Banegas, pp. 271–282. Puerto Madryn: Instituto de Diversidad y Evolución Austral.

Borrazzo, Karen, María C. Pallo, and Luis A. Borrero 2018 Exploring Lithic Transport in Tierra del Fuego (Southern South America). *Journal of Archaeological Science: Reports* 24:220–230.

Borrero, Luis A. 1989 Replanteo de la arqueología patagónica. *Interciencia* 14(3):127–135.

———1994-1995 Arqueología de la Patagonia. *Palimpsesto* 4:9–69.

———1997 The Origin of Ethnographic Subsistence Patterns in Fuego-Patagonia. In *Patagonia: Natural History, Prehistory and Ethnography at the Uttermost End of the Earth,* edited by Colin McEwan, Luis A. Borrero, and Alfredo Prieto, pp. 60–81. London: British Museum Press.

———1999 The Prehistoric Exploration and Colonization of Fuego-Patagonia. *Journal of World Prehistory* 13(3):321–355.

———2004 The Archaeozoology of Andean "Dead Ends" in Patagonia: Living Near the Continental Ice Cap. In *Colonisation, Migration, and Marginal Areas: A Zooarchaeological Approach*, edited by Mariana Mondini, Sebastián Muñoz, and Stephen Wickler, pp. 55–61. Oxford: Oxbow Books.

———2008 Early Occupation in the Southern Cone. In *Handbook of South American Archaeology*, edited by Helaine Silverman and William H. Isbell, pp. 59–77. New York: Springer.

Borrero, Luis A., and Fabiana M. Martin 2018 Archaeological Discontinuity in Ultima Esperanza: A Supra-Regional Overview. *Quaternary International* 473B:290–305.

———2021 Pioneer Population Nodes in Southern Patagonian Lands. In *South American Contributions to World Archaeology*, edited by Mariano Bonomo and Sonia Archila, pp. 159–183. Cham: Springer.

Borrero, Luis A., Fabiana Martin, and Ramiro Barberena 2011 Visits, "Fuegians," and Information Networks. In *Information and Its Role in Hunter-Gatherer Bands*, edited by Robert Whallon, William Lovis, and Robert Hitchcock, pp. 249–269. Los Angeles: University of California Press.

Borrero, Luis A., Flavia Morello, and Manuel San Román 2020a Geografía cultural de los archipiélagos de Fuego-Patagonia en tiempos recientes: movilidad y planificación. *Magallania* 48(2):45–70.

———2020b Circulación de bienes, uso del espacio interior y espacios programados en los archipiélagos de Fuego-Patagonia en tiempos recientes. *Magallania* 48(2):71–98.

Borrero, Luis A., Amalia Nuevo Delaunay, and César Méndez 2019a Ethnographical and Ethnohistorical Accounts for Understanding the Exploration of New Lands: The Case of Central Western Patagonia, Southernmost South America. *Journal of Anthropological Archaeology* 54:1–16.

Brochado, Jose P. 1984 An Ecological Model of the Spread of Pottery and Agriculture into Eastern South America. PhD dissertation, University of Illinois at Urbana-Champaign.

Broughton, Jack, and Frank Bayham 2003 Showing Off, Foraging Models, and the Ascendance of Large-Game Hunting in the California Middle Archaic. *American Antiquity* 68(4):783–789.

Buc, Natacha 2012 Tecnología ósea de cazadores-recolectores del humedal del Paraná inferior. Bajíos ribereños meridionales. Arqueología de la cuenca del Plata. Series Monográfica 3. Instituto Nacional de Antropología y Pensamiento Latinoamericano, Buenos Aires.

Buscaglia, Silvana 2019 El origen de la cacica María y su familia. Una aproximación genealógica. (Patagonia, siglos XVIII–XIX). *Corpus* (Online) 9(1). http://journals .openedition.org/corpusarchivos/2915.

Caggiano, Maria A. 1977 Contribución a la arqueología del Delta del Paraná. *Obra del Centenario del Museo de la Plata* 2:301–324.

———1984 Prehistoria del N.E. argentino sus vinculaciones con la República Oriental del Uruguay y sur de Brasil. *Pesquisas* 38:5–109.

Capdepont Caffa, Irina 2012 Arqueología de sociedades indígenas del litoral del río Uruguay. PhD dissertation, Universidad Nacional del Centro de la Provincia de Buenos Aires.

———2018 Distribución de sitios arqueológicos con representaciones plásticas en el litoral oriental del río Uruguay. In *Goya-Malabrigo: arqueología de una sociedad indígena del noreste argentino*, edited by Gustavo Politis and Mariano Bonomo, pp. 247–268. Tandil: Editorial UNICEN.

Carballo Marina, Flavia 2007 La cuenca superior del río Santa Cruz: las poblaciones humanas y el uso del espacio. PhD dissertation, Universidad Nacional de La Plata.

Carballo Marina, Flavia, and Bettina Ercolano 2003 La ocupación humana en la margen sur del lago Argentino, Santa Cruz, Argentina. *Intersecciones en Antropología* 4:45–58.

Carden, Natalia 2008 *Imágenes a través del tiempo: arte rupestre y construcción social del paisaje en la Meseta Central de Santa Cruz*. SAA: Buenos Aires.

Carden, Natalia, and Florencia Borella 2015 Symbols by the Sea: The First Recording of Atlantic Coastal Rock Art in Patagonia (Punta Odriozola, Río Negro, Argentina). *Rock Art Research* 32(2):146–162.

Cardich, Augusto 1987 Arqueología de Los Toldos y El Ceibo (Provincia de Santa Cruz, Argentina). *Estudios Atacameños* 8:98–117.

Cardich, Augusto, Lucio Cardich, and Adan Hajduk 1973 Secuencia arqueológica y cronología radiocarbónica de la Cueva 3 de Los Toldos. *Relaciones de la Sociedad Argentina de Antropología* 7:85–123.

Carrara, Maria T., and Nelly de Grandis (editors) 2005 *Santa Fe La Vieja: arqueología de los siglos XVI y XVII. Programa de Arqueología Histórica de Santa Fe La Vieja.* Rosario: Escuela de Antropología de la Universidad Nacional de Rosario.

Carrera Aizpitarte, Manuel 2014 Estudio de las estrategias de aprovisionamiento lítico en las áreas Curacó, Bajos sin Salida, Valles Transversales y Centro-este (provincia de La Pampa, Argentina). PhD dissertation, Universidad Nacional del Centro de la Provincia de Buenos Aires.

Carrera Aizpitarte, Manuel, and Mónica A. Berón 2021 Explotación de recursos líticos en dos canteras prehispánicas de la provincia de La Pampa (Argentina): Meseta del Fresco y Manto Tehuelche. *Estudios Atacameños* 66:7–34.

Casamiquela, Rodolfo 1969 *Un nuevo panorama etnológico del área pan-pampeana y patagónica adyacente: pruebas etnohistóricas de la filiación tehuelche septentrional de los querandíes.* Santiago de Chile: Museo Nacional de Historia Natural, Dirección de Bibliotecas, Archivos y Museos.

Casamiquela, Rodolfo, and Gesué Noseda 1970 Diagnosis de restos humanos exhumados de una sepultura indígena bonaerense. *Etnía* 11:16–23.

Cassiodoro, Gisela, Alejandra Aragone, and Anahí Re 2004 Más allá de los chenques ... Registro arqueológico de sitios a cielo abierto en la cuenca de los lagos Salitroso-Posadas-Pueyrredón. In *Contra viento y marea. Arqueología de Patagonia*, edited by M. Teresa Civalero, Pablo Fernandez, and Gabriela Guráieb, pp. 325–338. Buenos Aires: INAPL-SAA.

Cassiodoro, Gisela, Silvana Espinosa, Josefina Flores Coni, and Rafael Goñi 2015 Disponibilidad de recursos líticos y movilidad durante el Holoceno Tardío en el centro-oeste de la provincia de Santa Cruz. *Intersecciones en Antropología* 16(1):75–86.

Castiñeira, Carola, Adriana Blasi, Mariano Bonomo, Gustavo Politis, and E. Apolinaire 2014 Modificación antrópica del paisaje durante el Holoceno Tardío: las construcciones monticulares en el delta Superior del río Paraná. *Revista de la Asociación Geológica Argentina* 71(1):33–47.

Castiñeira, Carola, Adrina Blasi, Gustavo Politis, Mariano Bonomo, Laura del Puerto, Roberto A. Huarte, Jorge E. Carbonari, Florencia Mari, and Felipe García-Rodríguez 2013 The Origin and Construction of Pre-Hispanic Mounds in the Upper Delta of the Paraná River (Argentina). *Archaeological and Anthropological Sciences* 5:37–57.

Castiñeira, Carola, Judith Charlin, Marcelo Cardillo, and Jorge Baeza 2011 Análisis de morfometría geométrica en Puntas Cola de Pescado del Uruguay. *Latin American Antiquity* 22(3):335–358.

Castro, Alicia, and Eduardo Moreno 2000 Noticias sobre enterratorios humanos en la costa norte de Santa Cruz – Patagonia – Argentina. *Anales del Instituto de la Patagonia* 28:225–232.

Castro, Juan C. 2017 Investigaciones arqueológicas en la cuenca media e inferior del río Uruguay (provincia de Entre Ríos). PhD dissertation, Universidad Nacional de La Plata.

————2018 La entidad arqueológica Goya-Malabrigo en el río Uruguay. In *Goya-Malabrigo: arqueología de una sociedad indígena del noreste argentino.* Edited by Gustavo Politis and Mariano Bonomo, pp. 217–246. Tandil: Editorial UNICEN.

Castro Esnal, Analía 2014 *Camino y piedra: rutas indígenas y arqueología en la Provincia del Chubut.* Buenos Aires: Fundación de Historia Natural Félix de Azara.

Castro Esnal, Analía, Cecilia Pérez de Micou, and María Laura Casanueva 2017 Early Holocene Occupation of the Forest-Steppe Ecotone of Southern South America: Evidence from Casa de Piedra de Roselló Cave (Chubut, Patagonia Argentina). *PaleoAmerica* 3(3):276–282.

Catella, Luciana 2014 Movilidad y utilización del ambiente en poblaciones cazadoras-recolectoras del sur de la región pampeana: la cuenca del arroyo Chasicó como caso de estudio. PhD dissertation, Universidad Nacional de La Plata.

Catella, Luciana, Marcelo Manassero, Jorge Moirano, and Fernando Oliva 2013 Nuevos aportes al estudio del aprovisionamiento de cuarcita en la región pampeana, Argentina. *Cuadernos del Instituto Nacional de Antropología y Pensamiento Latinoamericano – Series Especiales* 1(2):200–215.

Cattáneo, Roxana. 2005 *Tecnología lítica del Pleistoceno Final/Holoceno Medio: un estudio de los Cazadores-Recolectores de la Patagonia Austral (Argentina)*. Oxford: BAR International Series.

Ceruti, Carlos N. 2003 Entidades culturales presentes en la cuenca del Paraná Medio (margen entrerriana). *Mundo de Antes* 3:111–135.

———2005 La cerámica de Santa Fe La Vieja: hacia una revaloración del componente indígena. In *Santa Fe La Vieja: arqueología de los siglos XVI y XVII. Programa de Arqueología Histórica de Santa Fe La Vieja*, edited by María T. Carrara and Nelly de Grandis. Rosario: Escuela de Antropología de la Universidad Nacional de Rosario.

Charlin, Judith 2009a Aprovisionamiento, explotación y circulación de obsidianas durante el Holoceno Tardío en Pali Aike (Provincia de Santa Cruz). *Relaciones de la Sociedad Argentina de Antropología* 34:53–73.

———2009b *Estrategias de aprovisionamiento y utilización de las materias primas líticas en el campo volcánico Pali Aike (Prov. Santa Cruz, Argentina)*. British Archaeological Reports, International Series 1901. Oxford: Archaeopress.

Charlin, Judith, and Cecilia Pallo 2015 Disponibilidad de rocas y costos de aprovisionamiento en el extremo austral de Patagonia meridional: integración de resultados en una escala regional. *Intersecciones en Antropología* 16 (1):125–138.

Ciampagna, María Laura, Marcelo Cardillo, and Jimena Alberti 2020 Estudio arqueobotánico de artefactos de molienda provenientes de la localidad arqueológica Punta Odriozola (golfo San Matías, Río Negro). *Revista del Museo de Antropología* 13(2):37–44.

Cigliano, Eduardo, Pedro I. Schmitz, and María A. Caggiano 1971 Sitios cerámicos prehispánicos en la costa septentrional de la provincia de Buenos Aires y de Salto Grande, Entre Ríos. Esquema tentativo de su desarrollo. *Anales de la Comisión de Investigaciones Científicas de la provincia de Buenos Aires* 192 (2–3):131–191.

Civalero, María T., and Carlos A. Aschero 2003 Early Occupations at Cerro Casa de Piedra 7, Santa Cruz Province, Patagonia Argentina. In *Where the South Winds Blow: Ancient Evidences of Paleo South Americans*, edited by Robson Bonnichsen, Laura Miotti, Mónica Salemme, and Nora Flegenheimer, pp. 141–147. College Station: Center for the Study of the First Americans (CSFA), Texas A&M University Press.

Civalero, María T., and Nora Franco 2003 Early Human Occupations in Western Santa Cruz Province, Southernmost South America. *Quaternary International* 109–110:77–86.

Cocco, Gabriel 2005 Investigaciones arqueológicas en Santa Fé La Vieja. *América* 17:45–56.

Cocco, Gabriel, Fabian Letieri, and Guillermo Frittegotto 2011 El descubrimiento y estudio del fuerte Sancti Spiritus. *América* 20:69–85.

Colobig, María M., Jorge Sánchez, and Alejandro Zucol 2015 Análisis de macrorrestos vegetales en el sitio arqueológico Los Tres Cerros 1 (isla Las Moras, Victoria, Entre Ríos). *Revista del Museo de Antropología* 8 (1):115–124.

Colombo, Mariano 2011 El área de abastecimiento de las ortocuarcitas del grupo Sierras Bayas y las posibles técnicas. *Intersecciones en Antropología* 12:155–166.

———2013 Los cazadores recolectores pampeanos y sus rocas. La obtención de materias primas líticas vista desde las canteras arqueológicas del centro de Tandilia. PhD dissertation, Universidad Nacional de La Plata.

Conlazo, Daniel, María Marta Lucero, and Teresa Authié 2006 *Los Querandíes*. Buenos Aires: Galerna.

Cornaglia Fernández, Jimena, and Natasha Buc 2013 Evidence of Bone Technology on the Santa Fe's Pampa Lagoons: The Laguna El Doce Site (Sante Fe Province, Argentina). In *From These Bare Bones: Raw Material and the Study of Worked Osseus Objects*, edited by A. Choyke and S. O'Connor, pp. 109–115. Oxford: Oxbow Books.

Cornero, Silvia 2021 El camino de llamas en la arqueología del río Paraná. *Anti* 2(4):7–41.

Cornero, Silvia, and Lucía Rangone 2013 Análisis de microrrestos en sitios arqueológicos del Holoceno Tardío ubicados en el Paraná medio, centro Norte de Santa Fe. Paper presented at the Encuentro de Discusión de Arqueología del Nordeste, Goya, Argentina.

Crivelli, Eduardo, Mabel Fernández, and Mariano S. Ramos 2009 *Arqueología de rescate en Rincón Chico, provincia del Neuquén*. Buenos Aires: Editorial Dunken.

Crivelli Montero, Eduardo 1991 Malones ¿saqueo o estrategia? El objetivo de las invasiones de 1780 y 1783 a la frontera de Buenos Aires. *Todo es Historia* 323:9–32.

———1994 Estructuras en sitios arqueológicos de la pampa interserrana bonaerense: casos e implicancias. *Relaciones de la Sociedad Argentina de Antropología* 19:257–283.

Crivelli Montero, Eduardo, Mario Silveira, Emilio Eugenio, P. Escala, M. Femández, and Nora Franco 1987/1988. El sitio fortín Necochea (partido de General La Madrid, provincia de Buenos Aires): estado actual de los trabajos. *Paleoetnológica* 4:39–48.

Cruz, Isabel 2000 Líneas tafonómicas y ecológicas para evaluar la explotación prehistórica de aves acuáticas en la zona cordillerana (Santa Cruz, Argentina). In *Desde el país de los gigantes: perspectivas arqueológicas en Patagonia*, Vol. 1, pp. 202–217. Río Gallegos: Universidad de la Patagonia Austral.

Cueto, Manuel, Ariel D. Frank, and Alicia Castro 2017 A Technomorphological and Functional Study of Late Pleistocene and Middle Holocene Lithic Assemblages from Patagonia Argentina. *Quaternary International* 442:67–79.

Curtoni, Rafael 2006 Expresiones simbólicas, cosmovisión y territorialidad en los cazadores-recolectores pampeanos. *Relaciones de la Sociedad Argentina de Antropología* 31:133–160.

———2007 Arqueología y paisaje en el área centro-este de la provincia de La Pampa: la espacialidad humana y la formación de territorios. PhD dissertation, Universidad Nacional de La Plata.

Day Pilaria, Fernanda. 2018 Gestión de los recursos faunísticos en sociedades cazadoras, recolectoras y pescadoras. Análisis arqueozoológico en sitios del litoral del Río de la Plata (partidos de Magdalena y Punta Indio, provincia de Buenos Aires). PhD dissertation, Universidad Nacional de La Plata.

de Jong, Ingrid 2016 Prácticas de la diplomacia fronteriza pampeana, siglo XIX. *Habitus* 14:175–197.

de Jong, Ingrid, Alejandro Serna, Emiliano Mange, and Luciano Prates. 2020 Mortuary Rituals and the Suttee among Mapuche Chiefdoms of Pampa-Patagonia: The Double Human Burial of Chimpay (Argentina). *Latin American Antiquity* 31(4):838–852.

Dillehay, Tom 2007 *Monuments, Empires and Resistance: The Araucanian Polity and Ritual Narratives*. Cambridge: Cambridge University Press.

Di Prado, Violeta 2015 Estudio comparativo de las prácticas de elaboración y uso de la alfarería prehispánica del centro-este de Argentina desde una perspectiva macrorregional. PhD thesis, Universidad Nacional de La Plata.

———2018 Prácticas alfareras prehispánicas y procesos de interacción social en el centro-este de Argentina durante el Holoceno Tardío. *Latin American Antiquity* 29 (3):552–531.

Donadei Corada, Juan P. 2019 Local and Nonlocal Rocks: Technological Strategies and Raw Material Management. Hunter-Gatherer Mobility for Mid-Holocene Groups of Eastern Tandilia Range (Argentina). *Journal of Archaeological Science: Reports* 24:264–275.

———2020 Cazadores: recolectores del Holoceno medio en las sierras de Tandilia Oriental (Argentina). Tecnología lítica, gestión de materias primas y movilidad en el territorio. PhD dissertation, Universidad de Buenos Aires.

———2021 Logistical mobility in the Eastern Tandilia Mountain Range (Argentina): Technological analysis for Mid-Holocene Hunter-Gatherer Occupations. *Quaternary International* 610:65–79.

Eriksen, Love 2011 Nature and Culture in Prehistoric Amazonia: Using G.I.S. to Reconstruct Ancient Ethnogenetic Processes from Archaeology, Linguistics, Geography, and Ethnohistory. PhD dissertation, Lund University.

Escosteguy, Paula, Mónica Salemme, and María I. González 2012 *Myocastor coypus* ("coipo," Rodentia, Mammalia) como recurso en los humedales de la Pampa bonaerense: patrones de explotación. *Revista del Museo de Antropología* 5:13–30.

Espinosa, Silvana, Juan Bautista Belardi, Gustavo Barrientos, and Flavia Carballo Marina 2013 Poblamiento e intensidad de uso del espacio en la cuenca del lago San Martin (Patagonia Argentina): nuevos datos desde la margen norte. Comechingonia. *Revista de Arqueología* 17:105–121.

Espinosa, Silvana, Pedro Tiberi, Charles Stern, Gisela Cassiodoro, Josefina Flores Coni and Agustín Agnolin 2019 Elementos traza en basaltos de la cordillera y precordillera de

Santa Cruz (Argentina). Su aplicación en localización de canteras arqueológicas. In *Arqueología de la Patagonia: el pasado en las arenas*, edited by Julieta Gómez Otero, Ariadna Svoboda, and Anahí Banegas, pp. 609–619. Puerto Madryn: Instituto de Diversidad y Evolución Austral.

Eugenio, Emilo, and Verónica Aldazabal 1988 El sitio arqueológico Laguna Sotelo, partido de Mar Chiquita, provincia de Buenos Aires. *Paleoetnologica* 4:79–86.

Falkner, Tomás 1974 [1774] *Descripción de la Patagonia y de las partes contiguas de la América del Sur*. Buenos Aires: Librería Hachette S.A.

Favier Dubois, Cristian, Liliana Manzi, Marcelo Cardillo, Sonia Lanzellotti, Federico Scartascini, Mariano Carolina, and Erika Borges Vaz 2008 Aproximación regional al registro arqueológico de la costa rionegrina. In *Arqueología de la costa patagónica: perspectivas para la conservación*, edited by Isabel Cruz and Soledad Caracotche, pp. 51–69. Río Gallegos: Universidad Nacional de la Patagonia Austral.

Favier Dubois, Cristian M., Agustina Massigoge, and Pablo G. Messineo 2017 El Holoceno Medio en valles fluviales del sudeste pampeano: ¿Escasez de sitios o de unidades portadoras? Una perspectiva geoarqueológica. *Revista del Museo de Antropología* 10(2):19–34.

Fernández, Jorge 1982 *Historia de la Arqueología Argentina*. Mendoza: Asociación Cuyana de Antropología.

———1983 Cronología y posición estratigráfica del llamado "Hombre fósil" de Mata Molle. *Historia Natural* 3:57–72.

Fernández, Pablo M. 2010 *Cazadores y presas: 3500 años de interacción entre seres humanos y animales en el Noroeste de Chubut*. Buenos Aires: Fundación de Historia Natural Félix de Azara.

Ferrer, Eduardo A., and Victoria Pedrotta 2006 *Los corrales de piedra: comercio y asentamientos aborígenes en las sierras de Tandil, Azul y Olavarría*. Tandil: Crecer Ediciones.

Fidalgo, Francisco, and Juan C. Riggi 1970 Consideraciones geomórficas y sedimentológicas sobre los rodados patagónicos. *Revista de la Asociación Geológica Argentina* 25:430–443.

Fiore, Dánae 1999 Diseños y técnicas en la decoración de artefactos: el caso de los sitios del Canal Beagle, Tierra del Fuego. *Actas del XIII Congreso Nacional de Arqueología Argentina* 2:75–89.

Flegenheimer, Nora 2003 Cerro El Sombrero: A Locality with a View. In *Where the South Winds Blow: Ancient Evidences of Paleo South Americans*, edited by Robson Bonnichsen, Laura Miotti, Mónica Salemme, and Nora Flegenheimer, pp. 51–56. College Station: Center for the Study of the First Americans, Texas A&M University.

Flegenheimer, Nora, and Cristina Bayón 1999 Abastecimiento temprano de rocas en sitios pampeanos tempranos: recolectando colores. In *Los tres reinos: prácticas de recolección en el Cono Sur de América*, edited by Carlos Aschero, María A. Korstanje, and Patricia M. Vuoto, pp. 95–107. Tucumán: Instituto de Arqueología y Museo, Facultad de Ciencias Naturales e Instituto Miguel Lillo.

Flegenheimer, Nora, Cristina Bayón, Miguel Valente, Jorge Baeza, and Jorge Femenías 2003 Long Distance Tool Stone Transport in the Argentine Pampas. *Quaternary International* 109–110:49–64.

Flegenheimer, Nora, Natalia Mazzia, and Celeste Weitzel 2015 Landscape and Rocks in the East-Central Portion of the Tandilia Range (Buenos Aires Province, Argentina). *PaleoAmerica* 1(2):163–180.

Flegenheimer, Nora, and Celeste Weitzel 2017 Fishtail Points from the Pampas of South America: Their Variability and Life Histories. *Journal of Anthropological Archaeology* 45:142–156.

Flegenheimer, Nora, Celeste Weitzel, and Natalia Mazzia 2015b Miniature Points in an Exceptional Early South American Context. *World Archaeology* 47(1):1–20.

Flensborg, Gustavo, Gustavo Martínez, and Augusto Tessone 2018 First Approach to the Paleodiet of Hunter-Gatherers through Stable Isotopes ($\delta^{13}C$ and $\delta^{15}N$) in the Eastern Pampa-Patagonia Transition during the Middle Holocene. *Journal of Archaeological Science: Reports* 17:571–580.

Franco, Nora V. 1994 Maximización en el aprovechamiento de los Recursos Líticos: un caso analizado en el Área Interserrana Bonaerense. *Arqueología Contemporánea* 5:75-88.

Franco, Nora V., Pablo Ambrústolo, and Lucas Vetrisano 2015 Materias primas líticas y su utilización en las cuencas de los ríos Chico y Santa Cruz (provincia de Santa Cruz, Patagonia argentina). *Intersecciones en Antropología – Volumen especial* 2:113–123.

Select Bibliography

Freeman, Jacob, and John M. Anderies. 2015 The Socioecology of Hunter–Gatherer Territory Size. *Journal of Anthropological Archaeology* 39:110–123.

Frenguelli, Joaquín, and Francisco de Aparicio 1923 Los paraderos de la margen derecha del río Malabrigo (departamento de Reconquista, Prov. de Santa Fe). *Anales de la Facultad de Ciencias de la Educación* 1:7–112.

Frère, María M. 2015 Tecnología cerámica de los cazadores-recolectores pescadores de la microrregión del río Salado, provincia de Buenos Aires. PhD dissertation, Facultad de Filosofía y Letras, Universidad de Buenos Aires, Buenos Aires.

Frère, Maria M., Maria I. González, and Catriel Greco 2016 Continuity in the Use of Shallow Sites of the Salado River Basin in the Pampean Region, Argentina. *Radiocarbon* 58:921–933.

Frontini, Romina 2008 Análisis faunístico del sitio 2 de la localidad arqueológica El Guanaco. In *Libro de resúmenes del V Congreso de Arqueología de la Región Pampeana*, pp. 84–85. Santa Rosa: V Congreso de Artqueología de la Región Pampeana.

———2012 El aprovechamiento de animales en valles fluviales y lagunas del sur bonaerense durante el Holoceno. PhD dissertation, Universidad de Buenos Aires.

García, Christian, and Francisco Mena 2016 ¿Funcionó un sistema sociocultural discreto en el Ibáñez medio? Evaluando fronteras mediante prospecciones en los andes centropatagónicos (Aisén, Chile). *Magallania* 44(2):187–207.

Ghiani Echenique, Naiquen, and María C. Paleo 2018 Los Tres Ombúes, un sitio arqueológico de cazadores-recolectores en Punta Piedras (partido de Punta Indio, provincia de Buenos Aires). *Revista de Antropología del Museo de Entre Ríos* 4(1):68–86.

Ghiani Echenique, Naiquen, Angélica R. Uvietta, and Rocio Gambaro 2013 Alfarerías tubulares en el noreste de la provincia de Buenos Aires: caracterización y distribución. *Revista del Museo de La Plata, Sección Antropología* 13(87):299–314.

Giesso, Martín, Mónica Berón, and Michael D. Glascock 2008 Obsidian in Western Pampas, Argentina: Source Characterization and Provisioning Strategies. *IAOS Bulletin* 38:15–18.

Gómez Otero, Julieta 1991 Discusión sobre el límite occidental del territorio de los Proto-Tehuelches y Tehuelches meridionales en el extremo Sud de Patagonia (cuenca del río Gallegos). *Waxen* 6(3):3–22.

Gómez Otero, Julieta, Juan B. Belardi, Alejandro Súnico, and Robert Taylor 1999 Arqueología de cazadores recolectores en Península Valdés (Provincia del Chubut). In *Soplando en el viento: Actas de las III Jornadas de Arqueología de la Patagonia*, pp. 393–417. Neuquén/Buenos Aires: Instituto Nacional de Antropología y Pensamiento Latinoamericano-Universidad Nacional del Comahue.

Goñi, Rafael, Juan B. Belardi, Gisela Cassiodoro, and Anahi Re (editors) 2014a *Arqueología de las cuencas de los lagos Cardiel y Strobel: poblamiento humano y paleoambientes en Patagonia*. Buenos Aires: Aspha.

Goñi, Rafael A., Anahí Re, Juan B. Belardi, Josefina Flores Coni, and Francisco Guichón 2014b Un lugar muy particular. Caza, convergencia de poblaciones y circulación de información en la meseta del Strobel. In *Arqueología de las cuencas de los lagos Cardiel y Strobel: poblamiento humano y paleoambientes en Patagonia*, edited by Rafael A. Goñi, Juan B. Belardi, Gisela Cassiodoro, and Anahí Re, pp. 155–185. Buenos Aires: Aspha.

González, Alberto Rex 1947 *Investigaciones arqueológicas en las nacientes del Paraná Pavón*. Córdoba: Universidad Nacional de Córdoba.

———1960 La estratigrafía de la gruta de Intihuasi (Prov. de San Luis, R.A.) y sus relaciones con otros sitios precerámicos de Sudamérica. *Revista del Instituto de Antropología* 1:5–296.

———1977 *Arte Precolombino en Argentina*. Buenos Aires: Filmediciones Valero.

———1979 Las exequias de Painé Güor: el suttee entre los araucanos de la llanura. *Relaciones de la Sociedad Argentina de Antropología* 13:137–161.

González, Maria I. 2005 *Arqueología de alfareros-cazadores y pescadores pampeanos*. Buenos Aires: Sociedad Argentina de Antropología.

González, Maria I., and María M. Frère 2009 Talares y paisaje fluvial bonaerense: arqueología del río Salado. *Intersecciones en Antropología* 10:249–265.

González, María I., María M. Frère, and Danae Fiore 2007 Redes de interacción en el curso inferior y medio del Salado. In *Arqueología en las Pampas II*, edited by Cristina Bayón, Alejandra Pupio, María I. González, Nora Flehenheimer, and María Frère, pp. 365–384. Buenos Aires: Sociedad Argentina de Antropología.

Gradin, Carlos J. 1975 *Contribución a la arqueología de La Pampa*. Panzini Hnos. SAIC. Santa Rosa: Dirección Provincial de Cultura.

———1984 *Investigaciones arqueológicas en Casa de Piedra*. Santa Rosa: Ministerio de Educación y Cultura. Dirección General de Cultura.

———1987 Tendencias estilísticas del arte rupestre de Patagonia central y meridional. In *Comunicaciones de las Primeras Jornadas de Arqueología de la Patagonia*, pp. 139–144. Rawson: Dirección de Cultura de la Provincia del Chubut.

Gradin, Carlos J., Carlos Aschero, and Ana M. Aguerre 1976 Investigaciones arqueológicas en la Cueva de las Manos, Estancia Alto Río Pinturas. *Relaciones de la Sociedad Argentina de Antropología* 10:201–251.

Greslebin, Hector 1931 La estructura de los túmulos indígenas prehispánicos del Departamento de Gualeguaychú (provincia de Entre Ríos, R. Argentina). *Revista Sociedad Amigos de la Arqueología* 5:5–51.

Gutiérrez, María A., and Gustavo A. Martínez 2008 Trends in the Faunal Human Exploitation during the Late Pleistocene and Early Holocene in the Pampean Region (Argentina). *Quaternary International* 191(1):53–68.

Gutiérrez, María A., Gustavo Martínez, Heidi Luchsinger, Silvia Grill, Alejandro F. Zucol, Gabriela S. Hassan, María P. Barros, Cristian A. Kaufmann, and María C. Álvarez 2011 Paleoenvironments in the Paso Otero Locality during Late Pleistocene-Holocene (Pampean Region, Argentina): An Interdisciplinary Approach. *Quaternary International* 245:37–47.

Hajduk, Adam, Estela M. Cúneo, Ana M. Albornóz, Claudia Della Negra, and Paula S. Novellino 2000 Nuevas investigaciones desarrolladas en el sitio Caepe Malal I (cuenca del Curi Leuvú, departamento Chos Malal, provincia del Neuquén). In *Desde el País de los Gigantes: perspectivas arqueológicas en Patagonia*, Vol. 1, pp. 297–313. Río Gallegos: Universidad Nacional de la Patagonia Austral.

Hajduk, Adán, Ana M. Albornóz, Maximiliano J. Lezcano, and Pablo Arias 2012 The First Occupations of the El Trébol site during the Pleistocene-Holocene Transition (Nahuel Huapi Lake, Patagonia Argentina). In *Southbound: Late Pleistocene Peopling of Latin America*, edited by Laura Miotti, Mónica Salemme, Nora Flegenheimer, and Ted Goebel, pp. 117–120. Special Edition of Current Research in the Pleistocene, Center for the Study of the First Americans, Department of Anthropology, Texas A&M University, College Station.

Hamilton, Marcus J., Bruce T. Milne, Robert S. Walker, Oskar Burger, and James H. Brown 2007 The Complex Structure of Hunter-Gatherer Social Networks. *Proceedings of the Royal Society B* 274:2195–2202.

Hammond, Heidi, Leandro Zilio, and Alicia Castro 2019 Tecnología lítica de cazadores recolectores en ocupaciones costeras: el caso del conchero UNPA (Puerto Deseado, Patagonia Argentina). *Cuadernos del Instituto Nacional de Antropología y Pensamiento Latinoamericano* 28(1):36–57.

Heckenberger, Michael. 2002 Rethinking the Arawakan Diaspora: Hierarchy, Regionality, and the Amazonian Formative. In *Comparative Arawakan Histories: Rethinking Language and Culture Area in Amazonia*, edited by Jonathan Hill and Fernando Santos Granero, pp. 99–122. Urbana: University of Illinois Press.

Heider, Guillermo 2015 Los pueblos originarios del norte de Pampa Seca: una mirada arqueológica a los cazadores recolectores del sur de las provincias de Córdoba y San Luis, Argentina. PhD dissertation, Universidad Nacional de Córdoba.

———2016 Un aporte a la discusión sobre las ortocuarcitas del grupo Sierras Bayas: ¿El sur de Córdoba como una frontera? *Intersecciones en Antropología* 17:303–313.

Heider, Guillermo, and Diego Rivero 2018 Estudios morfométricos aplicados a puntas de proyectil lanceoladas del holoceno temprano-medio en sierras y llanuras pampeanas de Argentina. *Latin American Antiquity* 29(03):1–19.

Hermo, Darío, and Virginia Lynch 2015 Core Technology from Maripe Cave Site (Santa Cruz, Argentina): Implications for Rocks Provisioning Processes and Lithic Production. *Quaternary International* 375:135–144.

Hermo, Darío, and Lucía Magnin 2012 Blade and Bifacial Technology in Mid-Holocene Occupations at Deseado Massif, Santa Cruz Province, Argentina. *Quaternary International* 256:71–77.

Select Bibliography

Holmberg, Eduardo L. 1884 *La sierra de Curá-Malal*. Buenos Aires: Imprenta de Pablo E. Goñi.

Holmes, William H. 1912 Stone Implements of the Argentine Littoral. In *Early Man in South America*, edited by Aleš Hrdlička, pp. 125–151. Washington, DC: Smithsonian Institution, Bureau of American Ethnology.

Hornborg, Alf, and Jonathan D. Hill 2011 Introduction: Ethnicity in Ancient Amazonia. In *Ethnicity in Ancient Amazonia: Reconstructing Past Identities from Archaeology, Linguistics, and Ethnohistory*, edited by Alf Hornborg and Jonathan D. Hill, pp. 1–27. Boulder: University Press of Colorado.

Howard, George, and Gordon Willey 1948 *Lowlands Argentine Archaeology*. New Haven, CT: Yale University Press.

Hrdlička, Aleš 1912 *Early Man in South America*. Bulletin 52. Washington, DC: Smithsonian Institution, Bureau of American Ethnology.

Imbelloni, José 1928 La industria de la piedra en Monte Hermoso. *Anales de la Facultad de Ciencias de la Educación* 2:147–168.

———1936 *Epítome de culturología*. Buenos Aires: Editorial Humanior.

———1937–1938. Tabla clasificatoria de los indios: regiones biológicas y grupos humanos de América. *Physis* 12:229–249.

Iriarte, José, Irene Holst, Oscar Marozzi, Claudia Listopad, Eduardo Alonso, Andrés Rinderknecht, and Juan Montaña 2004 Evidence for Cultivar Adoption and Emerging Complexity during the Mid-Holocene in the La Plata Basin. *Nature* 432:561–562.

Jackson, Donald 2002 *Los instrumentos líticos de los primeros cazadores de Tierra del Fuego*. Santiago: Dirección de Bibliotecas, Archivos y Museos.

Jiménez, Juan F., and Sebastián Alioto 2011 El sistema judicial indígena como expresión de complejidad política (Pampas y Patagonia norte, mediados del siglo XIX). *Journal de la Société des Américanistes* 97:45–74.

Johnson, Eileen, Gustavo Politis, and Maria Gutiérrez 2000 Early Holocene Bone Technology at the Coastal La Olla 1 Site along the Pampas Seashore of Argentina. *Journal of Archaeological Science* 27:463–477.

Joly, Delphine, Ramiro J. March, and Gustavo Martínez 2005 Les os brûlés de Paso Otero 5: un témoignage possible de l'utilisation de l'os comme combustible par des chasseurs-cueilleurs de la fin du Pléistocène en Argentine. *ArchéoSciences Revue d'Archéométrie* 29:83–93.

Jones, Sian 1997 *The Archaeology of Ethnicity Constructing Identities in the Past and Present*. London: Routledge.

Joyce, Thomas 1913 *South American Archaeology: An Introduction to the Archeology of the South American Continent with Special Reference to the Early History of Peru*. London: Macmillan and Philip Lee Warner.

Kaufmann, Cristian, and Maria A. Guitérrez 2004 Dispersión potencial de huesos de guanaco en medios fluviales y lacustres. In *Aproximaciones contemporáneas a la arqueología pampeana: perspectivas teóricas, metodológicas, analíticas y casos de estudio*, edited by Gustavo Martínez, María A. Gutiérrez, Rafael Curtoni, Mónica Berón, and Patricia Madrid, pp. 129–146. Olavarría: INCUAPA-UNICEN.

Kohl, Philip L., and José Pérez Gollán 2002 Mixing Religion, Politics, and Prehistory: The Life and Writings of O. Menghin. *Current Anthropology* 43:561–586.

Kossina, Gustav 1921 Die deutsche Vorgeschischste: eine hervorragend nationale Wissenschaft. *Mannus Bibliothek* 9.

Kuhn, Steven L. 1991 "Unpacking" Reduction: Lithic Raw Material Economy in the Mousterian of West-Central Italy. *Journal of Anthropological Archaeology* 10:76–106.

Lafon, Ciro R. 1971 Introducción a la arqueología del nordeste argentino. *Relaciones de la Sociedad Argentina de Antropología* 5 (2):119–152.

———1972 El replanteo para la arqueología del nordeste argentino. *Antiquitas* 14:1–16.

Legoupil, Dominique 1989 *Ethno-archéologie dans les Archipels de Patagonie: les Nomades Marins de Punta Baja*. Paris: CNRS.

———1997 *Bahía Colorada (île d'Englefield): les premiers chasseurs de mammifères marins de Patagonie australe*. Mémoires de l'A.D.P.F., Recherches sur les Civilisations. Paris: CNRS.

———2000 El sistema socioeconómico de los nómades del mar de Skyring (Archipiélago de Patagonia). *Anales del Instituto Patagonia* 28:81–119.

Lehmann-Nitsche, Robert 1907a Nouvelles reserches sur la formation pampéenne et l'homme fossile de la République Argentine. *Revista del Museo de La Plata* 14(1):143–479.

———1910 El hombre fósil pampeano. *Boletín Oficina Nacional Estadística* 6:363–366.

Leipus, Marcela 2006 Análisis de los modos de uso prehispánicos de las materias primas líticas en el sudeste de la región pampeana. PhD dissertation, Universidad Nacional de La Plata.

———2016 Variabilidad tecnológica y funcional en las raederas de la región pampeana. *Revista de Antropología del Museo de Entre Ríos* 2(2):47–67.

Leipus, Marcela, and Cecilia Landini 2014 Materias primas y tecnología: un estudio comparativo del material lítico. In *Estado actual de las investigaciones en el sitio arqueológico Arroyo Seco 2 (Partido de Tres Arroyos, Provincia de Buenos Aires, Argentina)*, edited by Gustavo G. Politis, María A. Gutiérrez, and Clara Scabuzzo, pp. 179–228. Buenos Aires: INCUAPA-CONICET-UNICEN.

León, Catriel, María A. Gutiérrez, Gustavo Politis, and María C. Bayón 2017 Análisis faunístico del sitio arqueológico La Olla (Sectores 3 y 4), Costa Sudeste del Litoral Atlántico Bonaerense. *Relaciones de la Sociedad Argentina de Antropología* 42(1):107–131.

Letieri, Fabián, Sergio Escribano Ruiz, Cristina Pascualli, Agustín Azkarate Garai-Olaun, Gabriel Cocco, Iban Sánchez Pinto, and Guillermo A. de la Fuente 2015 Approaching the Cultural Complexity of Pottery from Sancti Spiritus Village and Fort (Puerto Gaboto, Argentina). In *Global Pottery 1: Historical Archaeology and Archaeometry for Societies in Contact*, pp. 241–252. Oxford: Archaeopress.

Lewis-Williams, David, and Thomas A. Dowson 1988 The Signs of All Times: Entoptic Phenomena in Upper Palaeolithic Art. *Current Anthropology* 29(2):201–245.

Linares, Enrique, Eduardo Llambías, and Carlos Latorre 1980 Geología de la provincia de La Pampa, República Argentina y geocronología de sus rocas metamórficas y eruptivas. *Revista de la Asociación Geológica Argentina* 35(1):87–146.

Littleton, Judith, and Harry Allen 2007 Hunter-Gatherer Burials and the Creation of Persistent Places in Southeastern Australia. *Journal of Anthropological Archaeology* 26:283–298.

Llamazares, Ana 2004 Arte chamánico: visiones del universo. In *El lenguaje de los dioses: arte, chammanismo y cosmovisión indígena en Sudamérica*, edited by Ana Llamazares and Carlos Martínez Sarasola, pp. 67–125. Buenos Aires: Editorial Biblos.

López Mazz, José M. 2001 Las estructuras tumulares (cerritos) del Litoral Atlántico uruguayo. *Latin American Antiquity* 12:1–25.

———2013 Early Human Occupation of Uruguay: Radiocarbon Database and Archaeological Implications. *Quaternary International* 301:94–103.

López Mazz, José M., and Rocío López Cabral 2020 The Presence of Guaraní Groups in the Current Uruguayan Territory. *Journal of Anthropological Archaeology* 59:1–10.

Loponte, Daniel 2008 *Arqueología del Humedal del Paraná Inferior (Bajíos Ribereños Meridionales)*. Buenos Aires: Asociación Amigos del Instituto Nacional de Antropología y Pensamiento Latinoamericano.

Loponte, Daniel, Alejandro Acosta, Isabel Capparelli, and Maricel Pérez 2011 La arqueología guaraní en el extremo meridional de la cuenca del Plata. In *Arqueología Tupi guaraní*, edited by Alejandro Acosta and Daniel Loponte, pp. 111–157. Buenos Aires: Instituto Nacional de Antropología y Pensamiento Latinoamericano.

Loponte, Daniel, Alejandro Acosta, and Leonardo Mucciolo 2012 Contribución a la arqueología del Delta del Paraná: el nivel acerámico del sitio Isla Lechiguanas 1. *Comechingonia* 16(1):207–246.

Loponte, Daniel, Alejandro Acosta, and Javier Musali 2006 Complexity among Hunter-Gatherers from Pampean Region, South America. In *Beyond Affluent Forager: Rethinking Hunter-Gatherers Complexity*, edited by Colin Grier, Jangsuk Kimn, and Junzo Uchiyama, pp. 106–125. Oxford: Oxbow Books.

Loponte, Daniel, Alejandro Acosta, and Pablo Tchilinguirián 2010 Avances en la arqueología de la Pampa Ondulada: sitios Hunter y Meguay. In *XVII Congreso Nacional del Arqueología Argentina*, vol. 5, edited by J. Roberto Bárcena and Horacio Chiavazza, pp. 1811–1816. Mendoza: Universidad Nacional de Cuyo.

Luna, Leandro H. 2008 *Estructura demográfica, estilo de vida y relaciones biológicas de cazadores recolectores en un ambiente de desierto. Sitio Chenque 1 (Parque Nacional Lihué Calel, provincia de la Pampa, Argentina)*. BAR International Series 1886. Oxford: Archaeopress.

Madrazo, Guillermo B. 1968 Hacia una revisión de la prehistoria de la Pampa Bonaerense. *Etnia* 7:1–12.

———1973 Síntesis de arqueología pampeana. *Etnia* 17:13–25.

———1979 Los cazadores a la larga distancia de la región pampeana. *Prehistoria Bonaerense* 11–67. Olavarría: Municipalidad de Olavarría.

———1985 Determinantes y orientaciones de la antropología Argentina. *Boletín del Instituto Interdisciplinario de Tilcara* 1:13–56.

Madrid, Patricia 1991a Estudio arqueológico de los sitios con estructuras de piedra en las sierras de Pillahuincó, provincia de Buenos Aires. *Revista del Museo de Historia Natural de San Rafael, Mendoza* 11(3):129–155.

Madrid, Patricia, and Gustavo Politis 1991 Estudios paleoambientales en la región pampeana: un enfoque multidisciplinario del sitio La Toma. *Actas del XI Congreso Nacional de Arqueología Chilena* 1:131–152.

Madrid, Patricia, Gustavo Politis, Ramiro March, and Mariano Bonomo 2002 Arqueología microregional en el sudeste de la región pampeana argentina: el curso del río Quequén Salado. *Relaciones de la Sociedad Argentina de Antropología* 27:327–355.

Madrid, Patricia, Gustavo Politis, and Daniel Poiré 2000 Pinturas rupestres y estructuras de piedra en las Sierras de Curicó (extremo noroccidental de Tandilia, región pampeana). *Intersecciones en Antropología* 3:57–78.

Mandrini, Raúl 1986 La agricultura indígena en la región pampeana y sus adyacencias (Siglos XVIII y XIX). *Anuario del IHES* 1:11–43.

Mandrini, Raúl, and Sara Ortelli 2002 Los araucanos en las Pampas (c. 1700–1850). In *Colonización, resistencia y las américas (S. XVI–XX)*, edited by Guillaume Boccara, pp 237–258. Quito: Ediciones Abya-Yala.

Martin, Fabiana M. 2013 *Tafonomía de la transición Pleistoceno-Holoceno en Fuego-Patagonia: interacción entre humanos y carnívoros y su importancia como agentes en la formación del registro fósil*. Punta Arenas: Ediciones de la Universidad de Magallanes.

———2021 Fell Cave Reinterpreted. *Chungara Revista de Antropología Chilena* 54(3):535–556.

Martin, Fabiana M., and Luis A. Borrero 2017 Climate Change, Availability of Territory, and Late Pleistocene Human Exploration of Ultima Esperanza, South Chile. *Quaternary International* 428:86–95.

Martin, Fabiana M., Dominique Todisco, Joel Rodet, Manuel San Román, Flavia Morello, Francisco Prevosti, Charles Stern, and Luis A. Borrero 2015 Nuevas excavaciones en cueva del Medio: procesos de formación de la cueva y avances en los estudios de interacción entre cazadores recolectores y fauna extinta (Pleistoceno Final, Patagonia Meridional). *Magallania* 43(1):165–189.

Martínez, Gustavo 1999 Tecnología, subsistencia y asentamiento en el curso medio del Río Quequén Grande: un enfoque arqueológico. PhD dissertation, Universidad Nacional de La Plata.

———2002 Organización y cambio en las estrategias tecnológicas: un caso arqueológico e implicaciones comportamentales para la evolución de las sociedades cazadoras-recolectoras pampeanas. In *Perspectivas integradoras entre arqueología y evolución: teoría, método y casos de aplicación*, edited by Gustavo Martínez and José L. Lanata, pp. 121–156. Olavarría: INCUAPA-UNC.

———2006 Arqueología del curso medio del río Quequén Grande: estado actual y aportes a la arqueología de la región pampeana. *Relaciones de la Sociedad Argentina de Antropología* 31:249–275.

———2010 Entierros humanos en lugares sagrados y domésticos durante el Holoceno Tardío: el registro bioarqueológico del curso inferior del río Colorado (provincia de Buenos Aires, Argentina). *Revista Werkén* 13:145–160.

———(editor) 2017 *Arqueología de cazadores-recolectores del curso inferior del río Colorado (provincia de Buenos Aires, Argentina): aportes al conocimiento de las ocupaciones humanas pampeano-patagónicas*. Olavarría: INCUAPA-FACSO-UNICEN.

Martínez, Gustavo, and María Gutiérrez 2004 *Tendencias en la explotación humana de la fauna durante el Pleistoceno final y Holoceno en la región pampeana (Argentina)*. In *Zooarchaeology of South America*, edited by Guillermo Mengoni Goñalons, pp. 81–98. Oxford: Archaeopress.

———2011 Paso Otero 5: A Summary of the Interdisciplinary Lines of Evidence for Reconstructing Early Human Occupation and Paleoenvironment in the Pampean Region, Argentina. In *Peuplements et préhistoire en Amèriques, collection documents préhistoriques*, edited by Denis Vialou, Vol. 28, pp. 271–284. Paris: CTHS.

———2018 Early Holocene Water Well in the Pampas of Argentina: Human Responses to Water Shortage Events. *The Holocene* 29:145–157.

Martínez, Gustavo, María A. Gutiérrez, Pablo G. Messineo, Cristian A. Kaufmann, and Daniel J. Rafuse 2016 Subsistence Strategies in Argentina during the Late Pleistocene and Early Holocene. *Quaternary Science Reviews* 144:51–65.

Martínez, Gustavo, Luciano Prates, Gustavo Flensborg, Luciana Stoessel, Ana Alcaraz, and Pablo Bayala 2015 Radiocarbon Trends in the Pampean Region (Argentina): Biases and Demographic Patterns during the Final Late Pleistocene and Holocene. *Quaternary International* 356:89–110.

Massigoge, Agustina 2009 Arqueología de los cazadores-recolectores del sudeste de la región pampeana: una perspectiva tafonómica. PhD dissertation, Universidad Nacional de La Plata.

———2012 Las Brusquillas 1 (partido de San Cayetano, provincia de Buenos Aires): un nuevo sitio del Holoceno Tardío del Área Interserrana de la región pampeana. *Intersecciones en Antropología* 13:377–392.

Massigoge, Agustina, Daniel J. Rafuse, Juan M. Rodriguez, Rocío F. Torino, and Cristian M. Favier Dubois 2021 Technology, Subsistence, and Mobility of Middle to Late Holocene Hunter-Gatherers in the Southern Pampas: New Archaeological Data from Las Toscas Shallow Lake (Argentina). *Archaeological and Anthropological Sciences* 13 (4):1–27.

Massone, Mauricio 2004 *Los cazadores después del hielo*. Santiago de Chile: Centro Diego Barros Arana.

Matarrese, Alejandra 2015 Tecnología lítica entre los cazadores-recolectores pampeanos: los artefactos formatizados por picado y abrasión y modificados por uso en el área Interserrana Bonaerense. PhD dissertation, Universidad Nacional de La Plata.

Matarrese, Alejandra, and Daniel Poiré 2009 Rocas para moler: análisis de procedencia de materias primas líticas para artefactos de molienda (Área Interserrana Bonaerense). *Intersecciones en Antropología* 10:121–140.

Mazzanti, Diana 1993 El período tardío en la arqueología Bonaerense. In *Huellas en la tierra: Indios, agricultores y hacendados en la Pampa Bonaerense*, edited by Raul Mandrini and Andrea Reguera, pp. 31–44. Tandil: IEHS.

———1997 Excavaciones arqueológicas en el sitio Cueva Tixi, Buenos Aires, Argentina. *Latin American Antiquity* 8:55–62.

———2003 Human Settlements in Caves and Rockshelters during the Pleistocene-Holocene Transition in the Eastern Tandilia Range, Pampean Region, Argentina. In *Where the South Winds Blow: Ancient Evidences for Paleo South Americans*, edited by Mónica Salemme, Nora Flegenheimer, and Laura Miotti, pp. 57–61. College Station: Texas A&M University Press.

———2006 La constitución de territorios sociales durante el Holoceno Tardío: El caso de las Sierras de Tandilia, Argentina. *Relaciones de la Sociedad Argentina de Antropología* 31:277–300.

———2007 Arqueología de las relaciones interétnicas en las sierras de Tandilia. PhD dissertation, Universidad de Buenos Aires.

Mazzanti, Diana L., and Gustavo F. Bonnat 2013 Paisajes arqueológicos y cazadores-recolectores de la transición pleistoceno-holoceno: análisis de las cuencas de ocupación en Tandilia Oriental, provincia de Buenos Aires, Argentina. *Relaciones de la Sociedad Argentina de Antropología* 38 (2):521–541.

Mazzanti, Diana L., Gustavo A. Martínez, and Carlos Quintana 2012 Early Settlements in Eastern Tandilia, Buenos Aires Province, Argentina: Archaeological Contexts and Site-Formation Processes. In *Late Pleistocene Peopling of Latin America Special Edition, Southbound*, special publication of *Current Research in the Pleistocene*, edited by Laura Miotti, Mónica Salemme, Nora Flegenheimer, and Ted Goebel, pp. 99–103. College Station: Texas A&M University Press.

Mazzanti, Diana, and Carlos A. Quintana (editors) 2001 *Cueva Tixi: cazadores y recolectores de las Sierras de Tandilia Oriental*. Publicación Especial 1. Mar del Plata: Universidad Nacional de Mar del Plata.

Mazzanti, Diana, and Federico Valverde 2003 Representaciones rupestres en cazadores-recolectores en las Sierras de Tandilia: una aproximación arqueológica del paisaje. *Actas del XIII Congreso Nacional de Arqueología Argentina* 3:311–316.

Mazzia, Natalia 2010–2011 Lugares y paisajes de cazadores-recolectores en la pampa bonaerense: cambios y continuidades durante el Pleistoceno final-Holoceno, PhD dissertation, Universidad Nacional de La Plata.

——2013 Cueva Zoro: nuevas evidencias sobre pobladores tempranos en el sector centro oriental de Tandilia. *Intersecciones en Antropología* 14:93–106.

Mazzia, Natalia, Clara Scabuzzo, and Ricardo Guichón 2006 Sobre cráneos, pelvis y otros huesos: entierros humanos en el sitio El Guanaco. In *Aproximaciones arqueológicas pampeanas: teorías, métodos y casos de aplicación contemporáneos*, pp. 293–304. Olavarría: Editorial Facultad de Ciencias Sociales-UNCPBA.

Mederos Martin, Alfredo 2014 El espejismo nacional-socialista: la relación entre dos catedráticos de Prehistoria, Oswald Menghin y Julio Martínez Santa-Olalla (1935–1952). *Trabajos de Prehistoria* 71(2):199–220.

Méndez, César, M. Eugenia de Porras, Antonio Maldonado, Omar Reyes, Amalia Nuevo Delaunay, and Juan Luis García 2016 Human Effects in Holocene Fire Dynamics of Central Western Patagonia (∼44° S, Chile). *Frontiers in Ecology and Evolution* 4:100.

Méndez, César, Amalia Nuevo Delaunay, Omar Reyes, Ivana Ozán, Carolina Belmar, and Patricio López 2019 The Initial Peopling of Central Western Patagonia (Southernmost South America): Late Pleistocene through Holocene Site Context and Archaeological Assemblages from Cueva de la Vieja Site. *Quaternary International* 473:261–277.

Méndez, César, and Omar Reyes 2008 Late Holocene Human Occupation of the Patagonian Forests: A Case Study in the Cisnes River Basin. *Antiquity* 82 (317):560–570.

Mendonça, Osvaldo, Ana Aguerre, Mario Arrieta, and Lía Pera 2013 Investigaciones bioarqueológicas en la laguna Chadilauquen, Embajador Martini, departamento Realicó, Provincia de La Pampa. Segunda etapa. *Revista del Museo de La Plata, Sección Antropología* 13(87):137–152.

Menghín, Osvaldo, and Marcelo Bórmida 1950 Investigaciones prehistóricas en Cuevas de Tandilia (Pcia. de Buenos Aires). *Runa. Archivos para la Ciencia del Hombre* 3:1–36.

Mengoni Goñalons, Guillermo L. 1999 *Cazadores de Guanaco de la Estepa Patagónica.* Buenos Aires: Sociedad Argentina de Antropología.

Mengoni Goñalons, Guillermo L., María J. Figuerero Torres, María V. Fernandez, Mercedes Rocco, and Wendy Dekmak 2019 Persistencia y hiatos en el área de Los Antiguos, Monte Zeballos y Paso Roballos: nuevas dataciones para la cronología regional. In *Arqueología de la Patagonia: el pasado en las arenas*, edited by Julieta Gómez Otero, Ariadna Svoboda, and Anahí Banegas, pp. 327–338. Puerto Madryn: Instituto de Diversidad y Evolución Austral.

Messineo, Pablo 2008 Investigaciones arqueológicas en la cuenca superior del Arroyo Tapalqué (partidos de Olavarría y Benito Juárez, provincia de Buenos Aires). PhD dissertation, Universidad Nacional de La Plata.

Messineo, Pablo G., and Maria P. Barros 2021 Hunter-Gatherer Mobility and Territories in the Dunefields of Center Argentina. *Journal of Lithic Studies* 8(1):1–19.

Messineo, Pablo G., María P. Barros, Nélida Pal, and Nahuel A. Scheifler 2019b Transporting Rocks to an Empty Environment of Lithic Raw Materials: The Case of the Central Pampean Dunefield (Argentina). *Journal of Archaeological Science Report* 25:433–446.

Messineo, Pablo G., Mariela E. González, María C. Álvarez, and Nélida Pal 2018 Las ocupaciones humanas en la localidad arqueológica Laguna de los Pampas (Campo de Dunas del Centro Pampeano, Argentina) durante el Holoceno. *Latin American Antiquity* 29 (4):736–753.

Messineo, Pablo G., Nahuel Scheifler, María C. Álvarez, Mariela González, Nélida Pal, María P. Barros, and Gustavo G. Politis 2019d Was the Central Pampean Dunefields of Argentina Occupied during the Late Pleistocene? A Reappraisal of the Evidence. *PaleoAmerica: A Journal of Early Human Migration and Dispersal* 5(4):378–391.

Messineo, Pablo G., Nahuel A. Scheifler, Mariela E. González, Alfonsina Tripaldi, Ivana L. Ozán, and Jazmín Paonessa 2019c Estado actual de las investigaciones en la localidad arqueológica Laguna Chica (Sistema Lagunar Hinojo-Las Tunas, Trenque Lauquen). In *XX Congreso Nacional de Arqueología Argentina: 50 Años de Arqueologías*, edited by Andrés Laguens, Mirta Bonnin, and

Bernarda Marconetto, pp. 217–218. Córdoba: Universidad Nacional de Córdoba.

Miotti, Laura 1998 *Zooarqueología de la meseta central y la costa de la provincia de Santa Cruz: un enfoque de las estrategias adaptativas y los paleoambientes*. Mendoza: Museo de Historia Natural de San Rafael.

——2006b La fachada atlántica, como puerta de ingreso alternativa de la colonización humana de América del Sur durante la transición Pleistoceno/Holoceno. In *2° Simposio Internacional el Hombre Temprano en América*, pp. 155–188.

——2012 El uso de los recursos faunísticos entre los cazadores-recolectores de Patagonia: tendencias espacio/temporales de las estrategias durante el Holoceno. La Potenciación de los recursos entre los cazadores-recolectores de Patagonia. Factores, procesos e implicancias arqueológicas. *Archaeofauna* 21:137–160.

Miotti, Laura, and Enrique Terranova 2015 A Hill Full of Points in Terra Incognita from Patagonia: Notes and Reflections for Discussing the Way and Tempo of Initial Peopling. *PaleoAmerica* 1(2):181–196.

Miotti, Laura, Eduardo Tonni, and Laura Marchionni 2018 What Happened When the Pleistocene Megafauna Became Extinct? *Quaternary International* 473:173–189.

Morello, Flavia, Charles R. Stern, and Manuel San Román 2015 Obsidiana verde en Tierra del Fuego y Patagonia: caracterización, distribución y problemáticas culturales a lo largo del Holoceno. *Intersecciones en Antropología* 15(3):139–153.

Moreno, Eduardo 2008 *Arqueología y etnohistoria de la Costa Patagónica Central en el Holoceno Tardío*. Rawson: Fondo Editorial Provincial. Secretaría de Cultura del Chubut.

Nami, Hugo G. 2013 Archaeology, Paleoindian Research and Lithic Technology in the Middle Negro River, Central Uruguay. *Archaeological Discovery* 1(1):1–22.

——2017 Silcrete as a Valuable Resource for Stone Tool Manufacture and Its Use by Paleo-American Hunter-Gatherers in Southeastern South America. *Journal of Archaeological Science: Reports* 15:539–560.

——2021 Fishtailed Projectile Points in the Americas: Remarks and Hypotheses on the Peopling of Northern South America and Beyond. *Quaternary International* 548:47–72.

Nami, Hugo G., and Adriana Menegaz 1991 Cueva del Medio: aportes para el conocimiento de la diversidad faunística hacia el Pleistoceno-Holoceno en la Patagonia austral. *Anales del Instituto de la Patagonia* 20:117–132.

Neme, Gustavo, and Adolfo F. Gil 2008 Biogeografía humana en los Andes meridionales: tendencias arqueológicas en el sur de Mendoza. *Chungara, Revista de Antropología Chilena* 40(1):5–18.

Noelli, Francisco 1998 The Tupi: Explaining Origin and Expansion in Terms of Archaeology and Historical Linguistics. *Antiquity* 72(277):648–663.

——1999–2000 A ocupação humana na região sul do Brasil: arqueologia, debates e perspectivas – 1872–2000. *Revista USP* 44:218–269.

——2004 La distribución geográfica de las evidencias arqueológicas Guaraní. *Revista de Indias* 64(230):17–34.

Nordenskjöld, Erland 1930 *Ars Americana I: l'archélogie du Bassin de l'Amazone*. Paris: Les ëditions G. Van Oest.

Nuevo Delaunay, Amalia 2012 Disarticulation of Aónikenk Hunter-Gatherer Lifeways during the Late Nineteenth and Early Twentieth Centuries: Two Case Studies from Argentinean Patagonia. *Historical Archaeology* 46(3):149–164.

Oliva, Fernando 2000 Análisis de las localizaciones de los sitios con representaciones rupestres en el sistema de Ventania, Provincia de Buenos Aires. In *Arte en las Rocas*, edited by María M. Podestá and María de Hoyos, pp. 143–158. Buenos Aires: Sociedad Argentina de Antropología.

——2006 Uso y contexto de producción de elementos "simbólicos" del sur y oeste de la provincia de Buenos Aires, República Argentina (Área Ecotonal Húmeda Seca Pampeana). *Revista de la Escuela de Antropología* 12:101–116.

Oliva, Fernando, and Mariana Algrain 2004 Una aproximación cognitiva al estudio de las representaciones rupestres del Cashuati (Sistema Serrano de Ventania y Llanura Adyacente). In *La región pampeana su pasado arqueológico*, edited by Carlos Gradín and Fernando Oliva, pp. 49–60. Rosario: Laborde Editor.

Oliva, Fernando, Gabriela L'Heureux, Hernán De Angelis, Vanesa Parmigiani, and Florencia

Select Bibliography 303

Reyes 2007 Poblaciones indígenas de momentos post-contacto en el borde occidental de la Pampa Húmeda: Gascón 1, un sitio de entierros humanos. In *Arqueología argentina en los inicios de un nuevo siglo*, edited by Fernando Oliva, Nélida de Grandis, and Jorge Rodríguez, pp. 265–274. Rosario: Laborde Libros.

Oliva, Fernando, María C. Panizza, and Mariana Algrain 2010a Diferentes enfoques en la investigación del Arte Rupestre del Sistema Serrano de Ventania. *Comechingonia* 13:89–107.

Oría, Jimena, Mónica C. Salemme, and Fernando C. Santiago 2010 Obsidiana verde en la estepa fueguina: un hallazgo en Amalia 4. *Magallania* 38(2):231–237.

Orquera, Luis A. 1971 Paleoantropología de la Pampa Húmeda. Monografía correspondiente al Cursillo de Especialización en Arqueología, Buenos Aires. Facultad de Filosofía y Letras, Universidad de Buenos Aires.

Orquera, Luis A., and Ernesto L. Piana 1999 *Arqueología de la región del canal Beagle (Tierra del Fuego, República Argentina)*. Buenos Aires: Sociedad Argentina de Antropología.

———2009 Sea Nomads of the Beagle Channel in Southernmost South America: Over Six Thousand Years of Coastal Adaptation and Stability. *Journal of Island & Coastal Archaeology* 4:61–81.

Orquera, Luis A., Ernesto L. Piana, Arturo Sala, and Alicia Tapia 1977 *Lancha Packewaia: arqueología de los canales fueguinos*. Buenos Aires: Editorial Huemul.

Ortiz Troncoso, Omar 1979 Punta Santa Ana et Bahía Buena: deux gisements sur une ancienne ligne de rivage dans le Détroit de Magellan. *Journal de la Société des Américanistes* 66:133–204.

Otaola, Clara, Miguel Giardina, Mercedes Corbat, and Fernando J. Fernández 2012 Zooarqueología en el Sur de Mendoza: integrando perspectivas zooarqueológicas en un marco biogeográfico. In *Paleobiogeografía en el Sur de Mendoza*, edited by Adolfo Gil and Gustavo Neme, pp. 85–115. Buenos Aires: Sociedad Argentina de Antropología.

Ottalagano, Flavia V. 2009 Aproximaciones al simbolismo de los grupos cazadores-recolectores de las Tierras Bajas del Paraná Medio: un abordaje contextual del arte mobiliar cerámico. PhD dissertation, Universidad Nacional de Rosario.

Outes, Felix, and Carlos Bruch 1910 *Los aborígenes argentinos*. Buenos Aires: Estrada.

Paleo, María C., Marta Páez, and Mercedes Pérez Meroni 2002 Condiciones ambientales y ocupación humana durante el Holoceno Tardío en el litoral fluvial bonaerense. In *Del mar a los salitrales: diez mil años de historia pampeana en el umbral del tercer milenio*, edited by Diana Mazzanti, Mónica A. Berón, and Fernando Oliva, pp. 365–376. Mar del Plata: Universidad Nacional de Mar del Plata.

Paleo, María C., and Mercedes Pérez Meroni 2007 Primeros resultados del sitio Las Marías, partido de Magdalena, provincia de Buenos Aires. In *Actas del XIV Congreso Nacional de Arqueología Argentina*, Vol. 1, pp. 275–283. Rosario: Laborde Editor.

Paunero, Rafael S. 2009 *El arte rupestre milenario de Estancia La María, Meseta Central de Santa Cruz*. La Plata: Ediciones Estudio Denis.

Paunero, Rafael, Ariel Frank, Fabiana Skarbun, Manuel Cueto, Catalina Valiza Davis, and Raul González Dubox 2020 Arqueología del área La María en la Meseta Central. In *Actualización de las investigaciones en patrimonio cultural realizadas en Santa Cruz*, edited by Carla García Almazán, pp. 1–35. Río Gallegos: Dirección de Cultura Santa Cruz.

Paunero, Rafael, Catalina Valiza Davis, Diego Rindel, and Augusto Tessone 2017 La fauna pleistocénica: evidencias zooarqueológicas en la meseta central de Santa Cruz, los sitios de La María. *Magallania* 45(2):181–198.

Pedrotta, Victoria 2005 Las sociedades indígenas de la provincia de Buenos Aires entre los siglos XVI y XIX. PhD dissertation, Universidad Nacional de La Plata.

Pedrotta, Victoria, Patricia Madrid, and Gustavo G. Politis 2009 Pinturas, pircas y aleros en las sierras de Curicó (pdo. de Olavarría). In *Patrimonio, Ciencia y Comunidad*, edited by María L. Endere and José Prado, pp. 187–206. Olavarría: Ediciones INCUAPA.

Pérez, Alberto E., Augusto Tessone, and José L. Lanata 2019 Paleodietas en restos humanos del bosque meridional de Neuquén, *Patagonia Argentina*. *Magallania* 47(2):183–191.

Pérez, Sergio I., and Leandro Monteiro 2009 Nonrandom Factors in Modern Human Morphological Diversification: A Study of Craniofacial Variation in Southern South American Populations. *Evolution* 63(4):978–993.

Piana, Ernesto 1981 *Toponimia y arqueología del siglo XIX*. Buenos Aires: Eudeba.

Podgorny, Irina 1997 De la santidad laica del científico: Florentino Ameghino y el espectáculo de la ciencia en la Argentina moderna. *Entrepasados* 1997:37–61.

———2009 *El sendero del tiempo y de las causas accidentales: los espacios de la prehistoria en la Argentina, 1850–1911*. Rosario: Prohistoria.

———2021 *Florentino Ameghino y Hermanos: empresa argentina de paleontología ilimitada*. Buenos Aires: Edhasa.

Podgorny, Irina, and Maria M. Lópes 2008 *El desierto en una vitrina: museos e historia natural en la Argentina, 1810–1890*. Mexico D.F.: Limusa.

Politis, Gustavo 1984 Investigaciones arqueológicas en el Área Interserrana Bonaerense. *Etnia* 32:3–52.

———1988 Paradigmas, modelos y métodos en la arqueología de la Pampa Bonaerense. In *Arqueología Argentina Contemporánea*, edited by Hugo Yacobaccio, pp. 59–107. Buenos Aires: Búsqueda.

———1991 Fishtail Projectile Points in the Southern Cone of South America. In *Clovis: Origins and Adaptations*, edited by Robson Bonnichsen and Karen Turnmine, pp. 287–303. Orono: Center for the Study of First Americans.

———1995 The Socio Politics of the Development of the Archaeology in Hispanic South America. In *Theory in Archaeology: A World Perspective*, edited by Peter Ucko, pp. 197–235. London: Routledge.

———1999 La actividad infantil en la producción del registro arqueológico de cazadores recolectores. *Revista do Museu de Arqueología e Etnología* 3:263–283.

———2007 *Nukak: Ethnoarchaeology of an Amazon People*. Walnut Creek, CA: Left Coast Press.

———2008 The Pampas and the Campos. In *Handbook of South American Archaeology*, edited by Helaine Silvermann and William Isbell, pp. 235–262. New York: Springer.

Politis, Gustavo, Gustavo Barrientos, and Tom Stafford 2011a Revisiting Ameghino: New 14c Dates from Ancient Human Skeletons from the Argentine Pampas. In *Pouplements et Préhistoire en Amérique*, edited by Denis Vialou, pp. 43–45. Paris: Éditions du Comité des travaux historiques et scientifiques.

Politis, Gustavo, and Mariano Bonomo 2011 Nuevos datos sobre el "hombre fósil" de Ameghino. In *Vida y obra de Florentino Ameghino*, Publicación Especial 12, edited by Juan C. Fernicola, Alejandro Prieto, and D. Lazo, pp. 101–119. Buenos Aires: Asociación Paleontológica Argentina.

———2012 La entidad arqueológica Goya-Malabrigo (ríos Paraná y Uruguay) y su filiación arawak. *Revista de Arqueología Sociedade de Arqueologia Brasileira* 25(1):10–46.

———2015 Una revisión del Túmulo de Campana. *Relaciones de la Sociedad Argentina de Antropología* 40(1):149–181.

Politis, Gustavo, and María A. Gutiérrez 1998 Gliptodontes y cazadores-recolectores de la región pampeana (Argentina). *Latin American Antiquity* 9(2):111–134.

Politis, Gustavo, María A. Gutiérrez, Daniel Rafuse, and Adriana Blasi 2016 The Arrival of *Homo sapiens* into the Southern Cone at 14,000 Years Ago. *PLoS ONE* 11(9):1–27.

Politis, Gustavo, María A. Gutiérrez, and Clara Scabuzzo (editors) 2014 *Estado actual de las investigaciones en el sitio arqueológico Arroyo Seco 2 (pcia. de Buenos Aires, Argentina)*. Serie Monográfica INCUAPA, Vol. 5. Olavarría: INCUAPA.

Politis, Gustavo, Gustavo Martínez, and Mariano Bonomo 2001 Alfarería temprana en sitios de cazadores-recolectores de la región pampeana (Argentina). *Latin American Antiquity* 12(2):167–181.

Politis, Gustavo, Pablo Messineo, Cristian Kaufmann, María P. Barros, María C. Álvarez, Violeta Di Prado, and Rocío Scalise 2007 Persistencia ritual entre cazadores-recolectores de la llanura pampeana. *Boletín de Arqueología PUCP* 9:67–90.

Politis, Gustavo, Pablo G. Messineo, Thomas W. Stafford Jr., and Emily L. Lindsey 2019 Campo Laborde: A Late Pleistocene Giant Ground Sloth Kill and Butchering Site in the Pampas. *Science Advances* 5 (3):1185–1197.

Politis, Gustavo, and Victoria Pedrotta 2006 Recursos faunísticos y estrategias de subsistencia en el este de la región pampeana durante el Holoceno Tardío: el caso del guanaco (*Lama guanicoe*). *Relaciones de la Sociedad Argentina de Antropología* 31:301–336.

Politis, Gustavo, Clara Scabuzzo, and Robert Tykot 2009 An Approach to Prehispanic Diets in the Pampas during Early/Middle

Holocene. *International Journal of Osteoarchaeology* 19:266–208.

Politis, Gustavo G., Pablo G. Messineo, Mariela E. González, María C. Álvarez, and Cristian Favier Dubois. 2012 Primeros resultados de las investigaciones en el sitio Laguna de los Pampas (Partido de Lincoln, Provincia de Buenos Aires). *Relaciones de la Sociedad Argentina de Antropología* 37(2):463–472.

Posth, Cósimo, Nathan Nakatsuka, Iosif Lazaridis, Pontus Skoglund, Swapan Mallick, Thiseas C. Lamnidis, et al. 2018 Reconstructing the Deep Population History of Central and South America. *Cell* 175 (5):1185–1197.

Postillone, María B., Gustavo Martínez, Gustavo Flensborg, and Cristina B. Dejean 2020b First Analysis of Mitochondrial Lineages from the Eastern Pampa – Patagonia Transition during the Final Late Holocene. *American Journal of Physical Anthropology* 171:659–670.

Prado, José L., María T. Alberdi, and Jonathan Bellinzoni 2021 Pleistocene Mammals from Pampean Region (Argentina): Biostratigraphic, Biogeographic, and Environmental Implications. *Quaternary* 4(2):15.

Prates, Luciano 2008 *Los indígenas del río Negro: un enfoque arqueológico*. Buenos Aires: Sociedad Argentina de Antropología.

Prates, Luciano, and Emiliano Mange 2016 Paisajes de tránsito y estaciones en las planicies y bajos del centro-este de Norpatagonia. *Relaciones de la Sociedad Argentina de Antropología* 41(1):217–236.

Prates, Luciano, and S. Iván Pérez 2021 Late Pleistocene South American Megafaunal Extinctions Associated with Rise of Fishtail Points and Human Population. *Nature Communications* 12(1):2175.

Prates, Luciano, Gustavo G. Politis, and S. Iván Perez 2020 Rapid Radiation of Humans in South America after the Last Glacial Maximum: A Radiocarbon-Based Study. *PLoS ONE* 15(7):e0236023.

Prieto, Alfredo 1991 Cazadores tempranos y tardíos en Cueva Lago Sofía 1. *Anales del Instituto de la Patagonia* 20:75–99.

Quintana, Carlos, Federico Valverde, and Diana Mazzanti 2002 Roedores y lagartos como emergentes de la diversificación de la subsistencia durante el Holoceno Tardío en las Sierras de la región pampeana Argentina. *Latin American Antiquity* 13(4):455–473.

Rafuse, Daniel J. 2017 Early to Middle Holocene Subsistence Strategies in the Pampas Region: Evidence from the Arroyo Seco 2 Site. *Journal of Archaeological Science: Reports* 12:673–683.

Re, Anahí, Rafael Goñi, Josefina Flores Coni, Francisco Guichón, Juan Dellepiane, and Milva Umaño 2017 Arqueología de la meseta del Strobel (Patagonia meridional): 15 años después. *Relaciones de la Sociedad Argentina de Antropología* 42(1):133–158.

Reyes, Omar 2021 *The Settlement of the Chonos Archipelago, Western Patagonia, Chile*. Cham: Springer.

Reyes, Omar, César Méndez, Manuel San Román and Jean Francois 2018 Earthquakes and Coastal Archaeology: Assessing Shoreline Shifts on the Southernmost Pacific Coast (Chonos Archipelago 43°50′–46°50′ S, Chile, South America). *Quaternary International* 463:161–175.

Reyes, Omar, Mauricio Moraga, César Méndez, and Alexander Cherkinsky 2015 Maritime Hunter-Gatherers in the Chonos Archipelago (43°50′–46°50′ S), Western Patagonian Channels. *The Journal of Island and Coastal Archaeology* 10(2):207–231.

Rindel, Diego D., Carla C. Martínez, and Juan M. Dellepiane 2011 Evidencias de procesamiento de guanacos en sitios a cielo abierto y aleros estratificados del noroeste de la provincia de Santa Cruz. In *Temas de Arqueología: Estudios Tafonómicos y Zooarqueológicos (II)*, edited by Alejandro Acosta, Daniel Loponte, and Leonardo Mucciolo, pp. 107–136. Luján: Universidad de Luján.

Roca-Rada, Xavier, Gustavo Politis, Pablo G. Messineo, Nahuel Scheifler, Clara Scabuzzo, Mariela González, et al. 2021 Ancient mitochondrial genomes from the Argentinian Pampas inform the early peopling of the Southern Cone of South America. *IScience* 24(6):102553.

Rodríguez, Jorge 1992 Arqueología del sudeste de Sudamérica. In *Prehistoria Sudamericana: nuevas perspectivas*, edited by Betty Meggers, pp. 177–209. Washington, DC: Taraxacum.

———2001 Nordeste Prehispánico. En *Historia Argentina Prehispánica*, edited by Eduardo Berberián and Axel Nielsen. Córdoba: Editorial Brujas.

Romero Villanueva, Guadalupe 2019 Biogeografía humana y circulación de información en el norte de Neuquén: un análisis arqueológico sobre la comunicación visual en grupos cazadores-recolectores del noroeste de Patagonia. PhD dissertation, Universidad de Buenos Aires.

Romero Villanueva, Guadalupe, and Ramiro Barberena 2017 Los huesos de guanaco pintados de Cueva Huenul 1 (norte del Neuquén, Patagonia septentrional). *Relaciones de la Sociedad Argentina de Antropología* 42 (2):369–377.

Roulet, Florencia 2016 *Huincas en tierras de indios: mediaciones e identidades en los relatos de viajeros tardocoloniales*. Buenos Aires: Eudeba.

Salemme, Mónica C. 1987 Paleoetnozoología del sector Bonaerense de la región pampeana, con especial atención a los mamíferos. PhD dissertation, Universidad Nacional de La Plata.

———2014 Zooarqueología y paleoambientes. In *Estado actual de las investigaciones en el sitio arqueológico Arroyo Seco 2 (Partido de Tres Arroyos, entative de Buenos Aires, Argentina)*, edited by Gustavo Politis, María A. Gutiérrez, and Clara Scabuzzo, pp. 67–96. Olavarría: Facultad de Ciencias Sociales (UNCPBA).

Salemme, Mónica, Paula Escosteguy, and Romina Frontini 2012 La fauna de porte menor en sitios arqueológicos de la región pampeana, Argentina. Agente disturbador vs. recurso económico. *Archaeofauna* 21:151–173.

Salemme, Mónica, and Laura Miotti 2008 Archaeological Hunter-Gatherer Landscapes since the Latest Pleistocene in Fuego-Patagonia. In *The Late Cenozoic of Patagonia and Tierra del Fuego*, edited by Jorge Rabassa, pp. 437–483. New York: Elsevier.

San Román, Manuel 2014 Sea-Level Changes and Coastal Peopling in Southernmost Pacific South America: Marine Hunters from Patagonia. In *Encyclopedia of Global Archaeology*, edited by C. Smith, pp. 6515–6525. New York: Springer-Verlag.

San Román, Manuel, Omar Reyes, Jimena Torres, and Flavia Morello 2016 Archaeology of Maritime Hunter-Gatherers from Southernmost Patagonia, South America: Discussing Timing, Changes and Cultural Traditions during the Holocene. In *Marine Ventures: Archaeological Perspectives on Human-Sea Relations*, edited by Hein B. Bjerck, Heidi M. Breivik, Slije E. Fretheim,

Ernesto L. Piana, Birgitte Skar, Angélica M. Tivoli, and Atilio F. J. Zangrando, pp. 157–174. Sheffield: Equinox Publishing.

Santiago, Fernando 2013 *La ocupación humana en el norte de Tierra del Fuego durante el Holoceno medio y tardío. Su vinculación con el paisaje*, Ushuaia: Aguafuerte.

Santos Valero, Florencia 2020 Gestión del volumen de rocas durante el Holoceno medio y tardío en el curso inferior del río Colorado (pcia. de Buenos Aires). *Revista del Museo de Antropología* 13(1):243–248.

Sartori, Julieta, and María B. Colasurdo 2011 El análisis arqueofaunístico del sitio Playa Mansa: nuevas perspectivas. In *Avances y Perspectivas en la Arqueología del Nordeste*, edited by María R. Feuillet Terzaghi, María B. Colasurdo, Julieta Sartori, and Sandra Escudero, pp. 25–41. Buenos Aires: El Talar.

Scabuzzo, Clara, and Agustina Ramos Van Rapp 2017 Nuevos resultados de estudios osteológicos del sitio Los Tres Cerros 1 (Delta Superior del río Paraná). *Comechingonia: Revista de Arqueología* 21 (2):201–228.

Scabuzzo, Clara, Agustina Ramos Van Rapp, Mariano Bonomo, and Gustavo Politis 2015 Estudios bioarqueológicos en el sitio Los Tres Cerros 1 (Delta Superior del Río Paraná, Entre Ríos, Argentina). *Boletim del Museu do Pará Emilio Goeldi: Ciencias Humanas* 10 (2):509–535.

Scheifler, Nahuel 2019 *Ecología y subsistencia de los cazadores-recolectores pampeanos en el Campo de Duna del centro pampeano*. Buenos Aires: Sociedad Argentina de Antropología.

———2020 Fogones, combustible óseo y procesamiento faunístico en el sitio de Huencú Nazar (Sistema Lagunar Hinojo-Las Tunas, entat pampeana, Argentina): implicancias para el uso del espacio por cazadores-recolectores. *Latin American Antiquity* 31(3):517–537.

Scheifler, Nahuel, Pablo Messineo, and Ailén Antiñir 2017 Cazadores-recolectores en el entati lagunar Hinojo-Las Tunas (región pampeana – Área Oeste) durante el Holoceno temprano/medio y tardío. Primeros resultados de las investigaciones arqueológicas. *Comechingonia: Revista de Arqueología* 21 (1):287–314.

Scheinsohn, Vivian 2010 *Hearts and Bones: Bone Raw Material Exploitation in Tierra del Fuego*. Oxford: Archaeopress.

Schmitz, Pedro 1991 Migrantes da Amazonia: a tradição Tupiguarani. In *Arqueología prehistorica do Rio Grande do Sul*, edited by Arno Kern, pp. 295–330. Porto Alegre: Mercado Aberto.

Serrano, Antonio 1950 *Los primitivos habitantes de Entre Ríos*. Entre Ríos: Biblioteca Entrerriana "General Perón," Ministerio de Educación.

———1955 *Los pueblos y culturas indígenas del Litoral*. Santa Fé: El Litoral.

———1972 *Líneas entativels de la arqueología del litoral (una entative de periodización)*. Córdoba: Instituto de Antropología, Universidad Nacional de Córdoba.

Silveira, Mario, and Eduardo Crivelli Montero 1982 El sitio Fortín María II: informe preliminar. In *Actas del VII Congreso Nacional de Arqueología de Uruguay*, pp. 128–135.

Soriano, Alberto, Rolando J. C. León, O. E. Sala, V. Alejandro Deregibus, M. A. Cauhépé, O. A. Scaglia, C. A. Velázquez, and J. H. Lemcoff 1992 Río de La Plata Grasslands. In *Natural Grasslands: Introduction and Western Hemisphere*, edited by R. Coupland, pp. 367–407. Amsterdam: Elsevier.

Steele, James 2009 Human Dispersals: Mathematical Models and the Archaeological Record. *Human Biology* 8(2–3):121–140.

Steele, James, and Gustavo Politis 2009 AMS ^{14}C Dating of Early Human Occupation of Southern South America. *Journal of Archaeological Science* 36(2):419–429.

Stern, Charles R. 2018 Obsidian Sources and Distribution in Patagonia, Southernmost South America. *Quaternary International* 468(A):190–205.

Stoessel, Luciana 2015 Tendencias preliminares sobre el consumo de peces durante el Holoceno medio en el área de transición pampeano-patagónica oriental (Pcia. de Buenos Aires). *Archaeofauna: International Journal of Archaeozoology* 24:103–117.

Stoessel, Luciana, and Ana P. Alcaráz 2017 Los conjuntos faunísticos. Subsistencia y tafonomía. Arqueología de cazadores-recolectores del curso inferior del río Colorado (provincia de Buenos Aires, Argentina). In *Aportes al conocimiento de las ocupaciones humanas pampeano-patagónicas*, edited by Gustavo Martínez, pp. 100–120. Olavarría: INCUAPA-FACSO-UNICEN.

Stoessel, Luciana, and Gustavo Martínez 2014 El proceso de intensificación en la transición pampeano-patagónica oriental: discusión y perspectivas comparativas con regiones aledañas. *Comechingonia: Revista de Arqueología* 18:65–94.

Suárez, Rafael 2014 Pre-Fishtail Settlement in the Southern Cone ca. 15,000–13,100 yr cal. BP: Synthesis, Evaluation, and Discussion of the Evidence. In *Pre Clovis in Americas: International Science Conference Proceedings*, edited by Dennis Stanford and Alison Stanger, pp. 153–191. Washington, DC: Smithsonian Institution.

———2017 The Human Colonization of the Southeast Plains of South America: Climatic Conditions, Technological Innovations and the Peopling of Uruguay and South of Brazil. *Quaternary International* 431:181–193.

Suárez, Rafael, Gustavo Piñeiro, and Flavia Barceló 2018 Living on the River Edge: The Tigre Site (K-87) New Data and Implications for the Initial Colonization of the Uruguay River Basin. *Quaternary International* 473:242–260.

Surovell, Todd, Judson Byrd Finley, Geoffrey M. Smith, P. Jeffrey Brantingham, and Robert Kelly 2009 Correcting Temporal Frequency Distributions for Taphonomic Bias. *Journal of Archaeological Science* 36:1715–1724.

Tapia, Alicia 2011 El patrón de asentamiento ranculche y la construcción social del paisaje, la memoria y la identidad (Siglos XVIII y XIX). In *VIII Jornadas de Investigadores en Arqueología y Etnohistoria del Centro-Oeste del país*, pp. 161–175.

———2014 Fusión y fisión de tolderías ranquelinas como respuesta a las tácticas militares de la conquista del desierto. *Cuadernos de Antropología* 11:97–110.

Tapia, Alicia, Adriana Salvino, and Ana M. Aguerre 2020 Chadilauquen y Neicorehue, dos asentamientos lagunares con cerámica en el nordeste de la Pampa Seca. *Relaciones de la Sociedad Argentina de Antropología* 45(2):323–353.

Tivoli, Angelica M. 2010 Las aves en la organización socioeconómica de cazadores-recolectores-pescadores del extremo sur sudamericano. PhD dissertation, Universidad de Buenos Aires.

Todisco, Dominique, Joel Rodet, Carol Nehme, Fabiana Martin, and Luis A. Borrero 2018 Les cavités du Cerro Benitez (Patagonie, Chili) Hypothèses génétiques glacio-karstiques. *Karstologia* 67:31–42.

Toledo, Marcelo J. 2011 Geoarchaeology of the Pleistocene-Holocene Transition in NE Pampas: Evidence of Human Presence Prior to 13,000 BP, Buenos Aires, Argentina. In *IV Simposio Internacional El Hombre Temprano en América*, edited by José C. Jiménez López, Carlos Serrano Sánchez, Arturo González, and F. Aguilar Arellano, pp. 259–296. Mexico D.F.: Instituto Internacional de Investigaciones.

———2016 Ameghino en contexto: nuevos datos históricos y revisión geoarqueológica del sitio Arroyo Frías (1870–1874). Mercedes, provincia de Buenos Aires, Argentina. *Revista del Museo Argentino de Ciencias Natáturales, Nueva Serie* 18 (2):147–187.

Tonni, Eduardo, and Gustavo Politis 1980 La distribución del guanaco (Mammalia, Camelidae) en la Provincia de Buenos Aires durante el Pleistoceno Tardío y Holoceno: los factores climáticos como causa de su retracción. *Ameghiniana* 17(1):53–66.

Torino, Rocío 2020 Tecnología lítica en el sitio Las Toscas 3 (llanura Interserrana, región pampeana, Argentina): uso de materias primas líticas y manufactura de artefactos. *Intersecciones en Antropología* 21:29–42.

Torres, Luis M. 1911 *Los primitivos habitantes del Delta del Paraná.* Buenos Aires: Biblioteca Centenaria 4, Universidad Nacional de La Plata,

———1917 Los tiempos prehistóricos y protohistóricos. In *Manual de la historia de la civilización argentina*, edited by R. Carbía. Buenos Aires: Biblioteca de la Asociación Nacional del Profesorado.

Torres, Luis M., and Carlos Ameghino 1913 Informe preliminar sobre las investigaciones geológicas y antropológicas en el litoral marítimo sur de la provincia de Buenos Aires. *Revista del Museo de La Plata* 20 (7):153–167.

Valverde, Federico 2003 Análisis de desechos líticos de la ocupación inicial del sitio Cueva Tixi (provincia de Buenos Aires): cadena operativa de producción y técnicas de talla tempranas. *Relaciones de la Sociedad Argentina de Antropología* 28:185–202.

Vázquez, Martin 2019 Distribución del registro arqueológico en la costa Norte de península Mitre. In *Arqueología de la Patagonia: el pasado en las arenas*, edited by Julieta Gómez Otero, Ariadna Svoboda, and Anahí Banegas, pp. 181–192. Puerto Madryn: Instituto de Diversidad y Evolución Austral.

Vázquez, Martin, Atilio F. Zangrando, Augusto Tessone, and Antonio Ceraso 2011 Arqueología de la costa meridional de Península Mitre. In *Los cazadores-recolectores del extremo oriental fueguino: arqueología de península Mitre e Isla de los Estados*, edited by Atilio F. Zangrando, Martin Vázquez, and Augusto Tessone, pp. 203–229. Buenos Aires: Sociedad Argentina de Antropología.

Vecchi, Rodrigo 2011a Bolas de boleadora en los grupos cazadores-recolectores de la pampa bonaerense. PhD dissertation, Universidad de Buenos Aires.

———2011b Bolas de boleadora del curso inferior del río Salado: materias primas y redes de intercambio. In *Armas prehispánicas: múltiples enfoques para su estudio en Sudamérica*, edited by Jorge G. Martínez and Damián L. Bozzuto, pp. 195–213. Buenos Aires: Fundación Azara.

Vignati, Milcíades A. 1948 Nuevos elementos de la industria lítica de Monte Hermoso. *Notas del Museo de La Plata* 12:173–201.

———1960 El indigenado de la Provincia de Buenos Aires. *Anales de la Comisión de Investigaciones Científicas de la Provincia de Buenos Aires* 1:95–182.

Walker, Mike, Martin J. Head, Max Berkelhammer, Svante Björck, Hai Cheng, Les Cwynar, et al. 2018 Formal Ratification of the Subdivision of the Holocene Series/Epoch (Quaternary System/Period): Two New Global Boundary Stratotype Sections and Points (GSSPs) and Three New Stages/Subseries. Episodes. *Journal of International Geoscience* 41(4):213–223.

Weitzel, Celeste, Natalia Mazzia, and Nora Flegenheimer 2018 Assessing Fishtail Points Distribution in the Southern Cone. *Quaternary International* 473:161–172.

Willey, Gordon 1946 The Archaeology of the Greater Pampa. In *Handbook of South American Indians*, edited by Julian H. Steward, Vol. 1, pp. 25–46. Washington, DC: Smithsonian Institution.

Zangrando, Atilio F. 2003 *Ictioarqueología del canal Beagle: explotación de peces y su implicación en la subsistencia humana.* Buenos Aires: Sociedad Argentina de Antropología.

———2009a *Historia evolutiva y subsistencia de cazadores-recolectores marítimos de Tierra del*

Fuego. Buenos Aires: Sociedad Argentina de Antropología.

————2009b Is Fishing Intensification a Direct Route to Hunter–Gatherer Complexity? A Case Study from the Beagle Channel Region (Tierra del Fuego, Southern South America). *World Archaeology* 41(4):589–608.

Zangrando, Atilio F., Karen B. Borrazzo, Angélica M. Tivoli, Daniela V. Alunni, and Marìa P. Martinoli 2014 El sitio Heshkaia 35: nuevos datos sobre la arqueología de Moat (Tierra del Fuego, Argentina). *Revista del Museo de Antropología* 7(1):11–24.

Zapata Gollán, Antonio 1981 *La urbanización hispanoamericana en el Río de la Plata*. Santa Fe: Ministerio de Educación y Cultura, Departamento de Estudios Etnográficos y Coloniales.

Zárate, Marcelo, and Nora Flegenheimer 1991 Geochronology of the Cerro La China Locality (Buenos Aires, Argentina): Site 2 and 3. *Geoarchaeology* 6(3):273–294.

Zeballos, Estanislao, and Pedro Pico 1878 Informe sobre el túmulo prehistórico de Campana. *Anales de la Sociedad Científica Argentina* 6:244–260.

Zilio, Leandro, and Heidi Hammond 2019 El registro arqueológico superficial en la margen sur de la ría Deseado (Santa Cruz, Patagonia): estructuras de rocas y concheros. *Revista de Antropología del Museo de Entre Ríos* 5 (1):88–92.

INDEX

Adelomedon, 159, 169, 175, 280
Aisén, 20, 97, 100, 138, 140, 185, 187, 189, 195, 222, 230, 249, 252, 254, 258
Alero Dásovich, 140, 185
Alero del Diablo, 191
Alero Entrada Baker, 186
Alero Fontana, 187
Alero del Paisano Desconocido, 189
Alero Pedro Cárdenas, 191
Alero Quemado, 191
algarrobo, 68, 196, 212, 280
Altos del Varela I, 110
Ameghino, Carlos, 35, 37, 42, 45
Ameghino, Florentino, 10, 24, 27–35, 37, 39, 41, 42, 43, 44, 45, 46, 59, 208
American Museum of Natural History, 50
ancient DNA, 140, 155, 245, 258, 259, 260
Andes, 4, 6, 7, 8, 9, 19, 20, 75, 76, 80, 93, 96, 98, 99, 102, 104, 109, 113, 114, 133, 137, 140, 146, 147, 155, 158, 188, 189, 191, 193, 195, 210, 215, 217, 219, 220, 222, 239, 249, 252, 253, 260, 268, 276, 279, 280
annual range, 111, 127, 152, 153, 219, 255
Antarctic Cold Reversal, 8, 155, 245, 248
Antarctica, 13, 77, 245
Aónikenk, 3, 208, 237, 243, 277, 281
Aptenodytes patagonico, 77
Aquihuecó, 232
Araucaria araucana, 218
Araucarian forest, 75
Arawak, 31, 43, 213, 267
Arctocephalus australis, 76, 165, 226. *See also* southern fur seal
Arctotherium, 78, 149, 253
armadillos, 70, 112, 125, 130, 159, 167, 169, 174, 175, 176, 192, 196, 204, 255, 279, 280
Arroyo Feo, 145, 186
Arroyo de Frías site, 32, 33, 128
Arroyo Seco 2, 117, 118, 121, 152, 156, 159, 167, 170, 173, 176, 192, 246, 247, 254, 257, 260, 262

Atlantic seashore, 14, 15, 39, 44, 121, 126, 127, 169, 206
attractor, 20, 21, 184
Austro-German cultural history, 53, 56, 59
averaged faunas, 231
averaged materials, 149, 155, 224, 273

Baguales Range, 101, 106, 189, 195, 217
Bahía Colorada, 179
Bahía Inútil, 22, 75, 224
Bahía Lomas, 77
Bahía del Oso Marino, 103
Bahía San Sebastián, 22, 77, 224
Bahía Solano, 47
Bajo Caracoles, 104
Baker River, 21
Balcarce Formation, 83, 84, 86, 88, 168
band aggregation, 121, 205, 271
banded gray obsidian, 224
banded gray-green obsidian, 101
Baño Nuevo 1, 97, 138, 139, 140, 185, 186, 232, 258
barrier, 25, 158
basalt, 44, 90, 91, 93, 94, 102, 103, 105, 106, 108, 132, 138, 166, 169, 171, 173, 278
Basaltic Plateau, 3, 11, 16, 18
base camps, 159, 222, 253, 255, 261
Beagle Channel, 20, 22, 47, 51, 64, 110, 112, 151, 158, 177, 178, 179, 181, 225, 226, 233, 269
Belardi, Juan Bautista, 218, 220, 275
bifacial artifact, 135, 201, 256
Binushmuka, 179
bipolar, 90, 163, 167, 207
bipolar technique, 39
Bird, Junius, 19, 24, 46, 49, 50, 51, 56, 61, 64, 65, 116, 147, 149, 190, 255, 263
black obsidian, 114, 223
Blastoceros dichotomus. See marsh deer
Bloque Oquedad, 145, 158
bone collagen, 118, 120, 128, 156
bone tools, 31, 48, 51, 55, 115, 165, 170, 172, 184, 192, 198, 209, 229, 262, 265, 279

Bórmida, Marcelo, 11, 53, 56, 57, 58, 81, 90, 149, 174, 175, 190, 206, 232, 269
Borrazzo, Karen, 108, 111, 276
Brazo Sur, 106
British Museum, 29, 31, 37
brocket deer, 70, 72
broken stone industry, 39, 41, 45
Brunswick Peninsula, 179
Burmeister, Germán, 42

C3 plants, 176
Cabo Monmouth, 183
Cabo Vírgenes, 101, 219
caches, 174, 204, 262, 270, 272, 279
Cactaceae, 218
Caepe Malal 1, 232, 242
caldén, 17, 68, 196, 280
Caldén District, 5
Caldenar, 11, 17
Campos, 3, 4, 68, 72, 91, 112, 124, 128, 129, 151, 153, 156, 158, 191, 207, 237, 247, 248, 249, 255, 267
Cancha Carrera, 101
Canis avus, 125
canoe people, 29, 47, 111, 235
Cañada Rocha site, 30, 31, 208
Cañadón Cóndor, 222
Cañadón Leona, 51, 149
Cape Horn, 6, 18
Cardiel, Joseph, 28
Cardiel Lake, 8, 103, 104, 188, 196, 251, 263
Casa del Minero, 142, 246, 247, 256
Casa de Piedra 7, 140, 188
Casa de Piedra de Roselló, 98, 140, 185, 186
Casapedrense, 56, 188, 189
Celtis tala. See tala
Central Hills, 3, 175, 208, 236, 278
Central Pampas Dunefield, 13, 15, 59, 72, 132, 157, 159, 171, 174, 192, 199, 200, 204, 208, 249, 251, 257, 260, 261, 262, 266, 270, 277, 279
Central Patagonia, 20
Central Western Patagonia, 132, 140
ceremonial sites, 88
cerritos, 4, 212, 213
Cerro Amigo Oeste, 124, 137, 153, 154
Cerro Bandurrias, 183
Cerro Benitez, 150
Cerro Casa de Piedra 7, 187
Cerro Castillo, 189, 219
Cerro La China, 121
Cerro Guido, 232
Cerro de los Indios, 219
Cerro León 3, 158, 189, 191
Cerro de los Onas, 151, 224
Cerro Pampa, 215
Cerro El Sombrero, 24, 59, 121, 123, 124, 125, 153, 154

Cerro Sota site, 46, 51, 149, 232, 269
Cerro Tres Tetas site, 98, 105, 141, 142, 188, 189, 246, 247, 249, 256, 263
Cerro de Los Viejos site, 17, 170, 177, 199, 241, 263
Chaco-Santiagueña Plains, 3, 13
Chaitén, 276
Chaitén volcano, 97
chalcedony, 18, 81, 91, 96, 102, 105, 106, 109, 191, 224, 278, 280
Challenger, HMS, 29
Chaná, 1, 28, 235, 237, 238, 239, 276, 279
chañar, 68, 170, 196, 280
chenques, 140, 232, 233, 269
chert, 17, 81, 85, 91, 94, 95, 103, 113, 120, 132, 199, 205, 278
Chico River, 14, 21, 47, 48, 98, 107, 108, 147, 148, 183, 222, 254
children, 123, 124, 125, 161, 165, 176, 244
Chiloé, 18, 22, 50, 74, 226, 229
Chimpay site, 242
Chloephaga picta, 77
Chonos Archipelago, 74
Chorrillo Malo 2, 145, 158, 189, 191
Chorrillo Miraflores, 111
Chubut basin, 20
circular skull artificial deformation, 35
Close Basins, 11, 14, 16, 17, 95, 170, 177, 200, 241, 261, 280
Clovis, 24, 25, 245
coirón, 75
Colletia paradoxa. See currumamuel
colonization, 24, 26, 28, 144, 146, 152, 178, 217, 247, 252, 256, 258, 263, 267, 269
Colorado River, 3, 14, 16, 18, 20, 82, 83, 86, 90, 91, 93, 95, 97, 112, 113, 132, 137, 159, 169, 170, 192, 196, 199, 205, 208, 210, 220, 270, 280
connectivity, 181, 195, 217, 221, 251, 276
Consejo Nacional de Investigaciones Científicas y Técnicas (CONICET), 66
Cordillera. *See Andes*
Cordillera Chica, 243
coronillo, 13, 16, 69
Coyle Basin, 21, 244
coypu, 70, 125, 132, 167, 169, 205, 209, 211, 215, 266, 279
Cueva La Carlota 1, 190
Cueva Chica, 150
Cueva de los Chingues, 149, 190
Cueva Huenul site, 97, 102, 133, 234
Cueva Lago Sofía 1, 150, 151, 177, 269
Cueva de las Manos, 21, 48, 64, 98, 145, 186, 263
Cueva del Medio, 149, 151, 177, 256
Cueva del Milodón, 28, 35, 38, 51, 55, 61, 115, 150, 156, 257
Cueva del Paisano Desconocido, 189
Cueva Tixi site, 121, 125, 127, 167, 253
Cueva de La Vieja, 138

Index

cultural geography, 112, 179, 221
cultural history, 50, 52, 57, 60
currumamuel, 13, 127, 154, 255
Cuyo, 18, 20, 75, 96, 133, 231, 259, 276
CVPA, 101, 107

Darwin, Charles, 41, 42, 93
de Mendoza, Pedro, 28
de la Vaulx, Henry, 42
demography, 9, 20, 26, 78, 233, 245, 260
Deseado Basin, 20, 21, 145, 257
Deseado Massif, 21, 99, 100, 104, 105, 132, 140, 141, 142, 144, 145, 152, 188, 189, 249, 252, 256, 263, 276
Deseado River, 20, 21, 102
diffusionism, 53, 56, 57, 58, 59
Diprothomo, 35
direct acquisition, 79, 81, 101, 107, 114, 160, 209, 270, 275, 276
discoidal stone, 123, 137, 147, 151, 153, 154, 249, 254
diversification, 157, 194, 282
dog, 65, 67
dolomite, 83, 85, 86, 87, 132, 159, 168, 173, 255
double-side amygdaloid scraper, 192, 199, 205, 279, 281, 283
Dry Pampa subregion, 11
Dusicyon avus, 65, 74, 78, 136, 186, 257

early peopling, 140, 147, 149, 246
earth mounds, 28, 43, 48, 49, 52, 212, 214, 267
eastern Pampa subregion, 4, 73, 74, 115, 121, 128, 193, 198, 199, 206, 207, 209, 238, 241, 255, 259, 260, 270, 271
Eberhard Cave. *See* Cueva del Milodón
economic intensification, 157, 194, 200, 205, 218, 230, 266
El Ceibo 7 Cave, 141
El Chueco 1, 97, 138
El Peceño, 97
El Trébol rock shelter, 133, 136, 137, 141, 185, 248
El Verano, 143, 249, 263
Elizabeth Island, 29, 37, 243
embedded strategy, 81, 101, 272
encomiendas, 1, 237, 238, 239
Englefield, 62, 179
ephemeral occupations, 125, 126, 132, 133, 136, 145, 151, 183, 185, 189, 191, 217, 224, 255, 256
Epullán Grande Cave, 133, 135, 137, 185, 218, 256
Equus, 74, 117, 118, 129, 130, 247, 252
Equus (A.) neogeus, 74
ethnic frontiers, 159
Eubalaena australis, 73, 77
Eutatus, 74, 117, 122, 125, 130, 252, 253, 255, 257
Ewan site, 244
exchange, 79, 101, 112, 153, 160, 169, 174, 175, 209, 214, 266, 270, 271, 272, 273, 274

exploration phase, 114, 128, 144, 146, 195, 215, 246, 251
extinct fauna, 25, 41, 46, 50, 130, 136, 145, 146, 147, 252
extinct mammals, 33, 125, 136, 141, 151, 155, 184

Fagnano Lake, 110, 225, 244
Falkner, Thomas, 28
fall-off curve, 79, 100, 207, 274, 275, 277
Felis onca, 38
Fell Cave, 50, 51, 61, 62, 65, 99, 116, 141, 147, 151, 177, 190, 222, 223, 248, 251, 254, 255
Festuca gracillima. See coirón
Fitz Roy, Robert, 29, 41, 243, 281
food taboos, 176
foraging trips, 124, 168, 261
French Patagonian Mission, 62, 191
Fresco Plateau, 3, 4, 17, 81, 82, 91, 113, 173, 199, 270, 278, 280
Fuego River, 244

Gaboto, Sebastián, 1, 28, 237
Gallegos basin, 56. *See also* Gallegos River
Gallegos River, 7, 21, 78, 107, 158, 219, 222, 281
Geoffroea decorticans, 68. *See also chañar*
Geschichte der Schöpfung (History of Creation), 42
giant ground sloth, 115, 117, 118, 247
Glossotherium. See ground sloth
Glyptodon, 35, 74
glyptodont, 35, 74, 120, 154
González, Alberto Rex, 11, 48, 52, 57, 175, 210, 241, 276
Goya-Malabrigo, 31, 51, 52, 195, 210, 211, 212, 214, 235, 238, 267, 276, 279
Gradin, Carlos, 19, 60, 61, 132, 137, 145, 170, 196, 202, 234
Grande River, 15, 17, 20, 108, 168, 210
Grandi, 179
granite, 14, 17, 18, 83, 88, 93, 95, 173, 175
gravity model, 255
Great Plains, 24, 25, 283, 284
greater rhea, 72, 76, 125, 130, 159, 162, 167, 174, 192, 196, 201, 202, 204, 237, 262, 279, 280
green dacite, 106
green obsidian, 61, 80, 100, 114, 179, 223, 224
Gregory Bay, 29
gray dacite, 106
grinding stones. *See* ground stones
ground sloth, 37, 39, 61, 74, 117, 118, 136, 140, 150, 151, 154
ground stones, 83, 96, 113, 159, 192, 199, 205, 207, 262
guanaco, 1, 41, 48, 51, 58, 60, 62, 73, 74, 75, 77, 78, 112, 125, 130, 132, 133, 135, 136, 137, 139, 141, 142, 145, 149, 154, 159, 162, 165, 167, 169, 171, 172, 175, 176, 183, 184, 185, 186, 188, 189, 191, 192, 193, 196, 198, 202, 203,

204, 207, 208, 215, 217, 218, 219, 222, 224, 229, 231, 232, 234, 237, 242, 243, 244, 246, 247, 253, 255, 259, 261, 266, 269, 279, 280, 283, 284
guanaco, extinct clade, 150, 253
Guaraní, 1, 4, 28, 31, 48, 49, 60, 195, 212, 213, 214, 235, 237, 238, 239, 276
Guayaneco archipelago, 227, 229
Gulf of Corcovado, 74
Gununa'kena Indians, 237, 240, 277, 281

hand negatives, 145
Handbook of South American Indians, 19, 62
harpoon heads, 51
Haush, 48, 277, 281
Hauthal, Rodolfo, 37, 38
hematite, 88, 102
Hemiauchenia paradoxa, 142
Hippidion, 74, 117, 141, 150, 151, 156, 247, 248, 252. *See also* horses, American horse
Hippidion principale. See horses, American horse
Hippidion saldiasi, 78
Hippocamelus bisulcus. See huemul
Holocene survival, 39, 78, 120, 156, 257
Homo pampaeus, 33, 39
Homo sinemento, 33
Homunculus patagonicus, 33
horses
    adoption of, 25
    American horse, 37, 78, 117, 129, 141, 142, 149, 150, 151, 154, 156, 247
    European horse, 21, 237, 238, 239, 240, 241, 242, 243, 244, 282, 283, 284
horticulture, 3, 194, 212, 213, 214, 235, 267, 268, 279, 283
Hrdlička, Ales, 24, 28, 33, 35, 39, 43, 44, 46, 90, 206
Hudson volcano, 181, 188
huemul, 24, 37, 76, 78, 112, 136, 186, 187, 191, 217, 253
Huenul Cave, 184
human footprints, 163, 165
human land use, 25
Humid Pampa subregion, 3, 17
hunting blinds, 60, 75, 215
hunting rituals, 217
hunting sites, 26, 47, 71, 74, 120
hunting strategies, 121, 155, 183, 248, 254, 255, 266, 278, 284
hunting weapons
    arrow, 25, 29, 194, 205, 237, 242, 265, 282, 284
    atlatl, 25, 140, 175, 192
    bola stones, 25, 26, 47, 81, 83, 88, 90, 96, 109, 113, 142, 159, 183, 184, 188, 192, 193, 196, 204, 205, 217, 237, 242, 263, 267, 279, 282, 283, 284
    Fishtail projectile point, 24, 25, 59, 84, 99, 116, 118, 121, 122, 123, 124, 125, 128, 129, 137,

141, 147, 149, 151, 152, 153, 154, 155, 171, 247, 248, 249, 251, 254, 255, 257
    lanceolate projectile point, 118, 175, 258
    Pay Paso projectile point, 129, 247
    projectile points, 25, 51, 59, 109, 113, 118, 130, 145, 162, 171, 177, 186, 188, 189, 190, 191, 193, 198, 199, 204, 205, 215, 229, 246, 249, 255, 256, 263, 283
    small projectile point, 198, 209
    small triangular projectile point, 101, 220, 265, 279
    spear, 25, 284
    Tigre projectile point, 128, 129, 247
    triangular projectile point, 135, 141, 142, 143, 145, 155, 159, 161, 168, 169, 185, 186, 189, 192, 198, 257
hypercarnivores, 150
Hypsitermal, 157, 169
Hyslop, John, 51

ice fields, 6, 21, 146, 177, 221, 252
ideational dimension, 67, 125, 153, 193
Imbelloni, José, 46, 52
Imiwaia I, 179, 181, 182
interaction mechanisms, 79
Interserrana, 11, 15, 28, 44, 56, 90, 113, 117, 118, 121, 127, 130, 152, 153, 159, 162, 163, 170, 176, 191, 192, 199, 200, 204, 249, 253, 254, 255, 260, 261, 266, 277, 279
Isla Dawson, 244
Isla de los Estados, 227
Isla Grande, 75
Isla Riesco, 222

jarilla, 17

Kawésqar, 281
kill site, 25, 117, 118, 121, 152, 231, 254
kulturkreise, 53, 56, 57, 58, 60, 64, 175. *See also* Austro-German cultural history

La Arcillosa 2, 183
La Gruta, 98, 105, 142, 144, 249, 263
La Gruta sinters, 105
La María locality, 98, 142
La Martita, 99, 143, 249, 263
La Plata River, 3, 12, 13, 16, 28, 31, 48, 58, 68, 69, 73, 112, 113, 208, 209, 236, 276, 279
Lago Argentino, 42, 101, 106, 145, 196, 219, 234, 258
Lago Buenos Aires-General Carrera, 21
Lago Cardiel, 219
Lago Lolog, 97
Lago Roca, 106
Lago Salitroso, 232
Lago Viedma, 196, 219, 244
Laguna Blanca, 50
Laguna Cóndor, 108, 222
Laguna del Juncal, 232
Laguna del Maule, 96

Index

Laguna Tom Gould, 190
Lake Salitroso, 222
Lama gracilis, 78, 141, 142, 150, 247, 253
Lancha Packewaia, 51
large mammal hunting, 26, 248
Las Buitreras Cave, 149, 190
Las Cargas, 97
Las Escobas Formation, 13
Las Vueltas 1, 231
Last Glacial Maximum, 7, 136, 245, 252
leapfrogging, 249
Least Cost Paths, 111
Legoupil, Dominique, 61, 100, 146, 182
Lehmann-Nitsche, Robert, 33, 35, 37, 38, 41
lesser rhea, 76, 112
Level 11 industry, 56, 141, 145
Libby, Willard, 50
Lihué Calel, 3, 57, 83, 95, 113
Limay River, 20, 48, 77, 133, 137, 185, 218
Lista, Ramón, 42, 43
lithic transport, 111
lithic workshop, 44, 67, 81, 84, 85, 86, 87, 88, 89,
    90, 91, 94, 95, 110, 168, 207
Little Ice Age, 8
Llanuras de Diana, 147, 251
locality 17 de Marzo, 98, 100, 276
Loma de Los Pedernales, 18, 95, 96, 113
long-distance interaction, 152, 171, 217, 223
Los Toldos site, 56, 65, 140, 141, 145, 188
Lothrop, Samuel, 10, 43, 47, 49, 52, 65, 111, 235,
    275
Lower Paraná, 1, 4, 11, 18, 60, 68, 69, 72, 194, 210,
    212, 214, 236, 237, 262, 267, 268, 276, 279
Lower Paran Delta, 4, 10, 12, 28, 30, 43, 48, 49, 51,
    60, 67, 68, 71, 91, 157, 159, 210, 213, 214, 236,
    265
Luján River, 31
Lycalopex culpaeus, 76, 135
Lycalopex griseus, 76, 135

Macrauchenia patachonica, 74, 128, 253
Madre de Dios Archipelago, 24, 258
Magallanes, Hernando de, 28
Magellanic tundra, 6
Mahuidas hills, 4
Maipú peninsula, 220
maize, 195, 212, 267
Mala Cueva, 100
Manto Tehuelche. *See* Patagonian Shingle Mantle
Mapuche Indians, 205, 239, 240, 241, 242, 277, 283
Marazzi, 62, 183, 224
Marifilo, 137, 139, 187
marine diets, 176
marine mammals, 24, 29, 51, 77, 127, 177
marine resources, 62, 112, 127, 167, 169, 176, 177,
    182, 184, 191, 225, 263
Maripé Cave, 105, 143, 144, 189, 249, 263
maritime hunter-gatherers, 50, 62, 77, 97, 100, 275

marsh deer, 70, 74, 209, 211, 215, 266
Massone, Mauricio, 251, 263, 277
Mata-Molle, 46
Mazama gouazoubira. *See* crocket deer
Mbeguá, 28, 235, 238
Medieval Climatic Anomaly, 8
megafauna, 8, 25, 64, 118, 130, 133, 136, 137, 145,
    155, 156, 184, 248, 253, 255, 257
megamammals, 74, 118, 120, 121, 126, 129, 150,
    152, 154, 156, 248, 252, 253, 257
Megatherium, 74, 117, 120, 128, 247, 248, 252. *See
    also* giant ground sloth
Méndez, César, 254
Menghin, Oswald, 11, 51, 53, 55, 56, 57, 58, 61, 62,
    64, 140, 188, 206, 234, 277
Meseta Latorre, 75
metapopulation processes, 248
metaquartzite, 39, 89, 90, 152, 163, 164, 173, 200,
    255, 272
Metraux, Alfred, 52
Milodón Norte 1, 187
Miocene, 33, 41
Miraflores rocks, 111, 114, 272
Misión Nuestra Señora de la Candelaria, 243
Missionary Society, 47
Mitre Peninsula, 178, 227
mobility models, 79
molle, 13, 16, 69
mollusks, 1, 24, 29, 31, 51, 72, 77, 112, 114, 136,
    177, 183, 184, 191, 211, 217, 218, 229, 232,
    235, 280
Monte Hermoso cliff, 39, 113
Monte León, 97
Monte phytogeographic province, 5, 17
Moreno, Francisco P., 35, 37, 42
Morro Chico, 100
mound builders. *See* earth mounds
Murray Channel, 46, 51
Museo Argentino de Ciencias Naturales
    "Bernardino Rivadavia," 28, 42
Museo de La Plata, 28, 31
Mylodon, 35, 37, 78, 136, 141, 147, 247, 248, 253,
    257
Mylodon darwini. *See* ground sloth
Mylodontidae, 136
Myocastor coypus. *See* coypu
Mytilus valves, 37

Navarino Island, 110, 179
navigational technology, 111, 178, 183
Negro River, 20, 77, 91, 93, 96, 97, 102, 218, 219,
    225, 232, 242, 249, 269
neo-Darwinian approaches, 66
Neoglacial, 10
Neuquén, 20, 96, 97, 133, 198, 199
node, 21, 22, 111, 144, 196, 219, 227, 230, 248, 249,
    251, 252, 255, 256
Nordenskjöld, Erland, 28, 31, 35, 37, 61

North Patagonia, 18
Northeast Argentina, 11, 51, 52, 60, 214
Northeast Pampa, 12, 60, 70, 72, 82, 112, 129, 192, 204, 266, 283
Northeast Patagonia, 20, 97, 137, 194, 206, 267
northern archipelagos, 24
Northwest Pampa, 16, 17, 83, 95, 96, 113, 175, 262, 277, 279
Northwest Patagonia, 19, 20, 132, 137, 184, 195, 218, 242, 252, 256, 257
Nothofagus, 6, 75, 78, 136, 150, 158, 257

obsidian, 79, 80, 96, 97, 98, 99, 100, 101, 102, 103, 104, 105, 113, 133, 145, 173, 179, 186, 198, 210, 223, 251, 252, 273, 275, 276, 277, 280
open social formations, 80
Orejas de Burro, 232, 258, 269
organizational changes, 21
Orquera, Luis A., 11, 20, 24, 32, 33, 35, 41, 48, 54, 62, 64, 179, 182, 256
orthoquartzite, 70, 80, 83, 84, 86, 89, 95, 113, 118, 120, 126, 132, 153, 159, 163, 164, 167, 168, 173, 175, 192, 198, 199, 200, 204, 207, 208, 209, 255, 270, 277, 279
Ortiz Troncoso, Omar, 60, 61, 62, 182, 231
Oso Marino Bay, 224
Otaria flavescens, 76, 165, 169. *See also* southern sea lion
Otway Sea, 9, 61, 100, 101, 114, 158, 179, 182, 223, 227
Outes, Felix, 10, 39, 41, 43, 45, 46, 48
Oxalis, 218
Ozotoceros bezoraticus. *See* Pampas deer

Pali Aike Cave, 50, 51, 97, 99, 101, 149, 151, 190, 222
Pali Aike Volcanic Field (PAVF), 21, 50, 106, 132, 147, 152, 190, 222, 231, 234, 249, 251, 252, 258, 269
palms, 212, 214
  caranday (Trithrinax campestris), 68
  pindó (*Syagrus romanzoffiana*), 68
  yatay (*Butia yatay*), 68
Pampa del Asador (PDA), 97, 98, 100, 114, 145, 186, 223, 251, 252, 275
Pampas deer, 1, 58, 70, 74, 112, 125, 130, 132, 154, 159, 162, 167, 170, 175, 176, 192, 196, 204, 208, 209, 237, 253, 261, 279, 280
Panthera onca, 172
Panthera onca mesembrina, 78, 150
Paramo spit, 109
Patagon, 3, 29
Patagonian Shingle Formation, 89, 94, 98, 113
Patagonian Shingle Mantle, 17, 91, 93, 95, 102, 132, 173, 270, 280
Patagoniense, 56
PAVF. *See* Pali Aike Volcanic Field
PDA. *See* Pampa del Asador

Pehuén forest, 112
Península Mitre, 77, 227
Peninsula Valdés, 99
Penitentes Basin, 21, 222
peopling, 115
  of the Americas, 24, 44, 46, 247
Perito Moreno National Park, 140, 145, 187, 195, 219
Phalacrocorax sp., 77, 226
phenomenology, 124, 154
phtanite, 81, 84, 86, 87, 113, 118, 132, 159, 163, 173, 175, 192, 199, 205, 207, 208, 209, 255, 277, 279
Piedra Museo site, 105, 141, 147, 188, 189, 248, 263
Piedra Parada valley, 219
Pilgerodendron uviferus, 6
Pinturas River, 21, 61, 64, 142, 145, 234, 263
Piptochaetium, 15
Pizzulic, 179
plains viscacha, 118, 125, 126, 130, 132, 159, 167, 253, 255, *see* Lagostomus maximus
plant resources, 26, 112, 183, 185, 186, 218
Pleistocene fauna, 24, 58, 130, 140, 149, 257
  extinction, 39
Pleistocene glaciers. *See* Last Glacial Maximum
Pleistocene mammals. *See* megamammals
Pleistocene refugia, 8, 158
Pliocene, 33, 35, 41
Poa, 15
polishers, 111
Ponsonby, 62, 100, 146, 181, 183, 191, 222
population replacement, 56, 155, 179, 181, 257, 259
populational discontinuity, 101
post-processualism, 66
Potrok Aike Lake, 8
pottery, 28, 31, 42, 43, 46, 48, 59, 60, 194, 205, 208, 213, 214, 215, 232, 235, 237, 265, 266, 268, 278
  with basket imprints, 208
  brushed, 214
  corrugated, 28, 48, 49, 214, 235
  drag and jab, 206, 209, 211, 266, 279
  European, 237, 241
  geometric motifs, 203
  incised, 48, 49, 200, 203, 205, 209, 210, 211, 266, 279, 280
  Mapuche, 241, 242
  modeled. *See* pottery, zoomorphic appendages
  painted, 48, 49, 52, 88, 235
  plain, 205, 209
  polychrome, 28, 48
  statuettes, 277
  Vergel–Valdivia, 171, 198, 210, 239, 280
  zoomorphic appendages, 31, 43, 48, 49, 51, 209, 211, 279
process of deglaciation, 8
processual archaeology, 27, 63, 65
processualism. *See* processual archaeology
Prosopis sp., 133, 218. *See also algarrobo*

Index

Pseudalopex griseus, 187
pseudocircular deformation, 33
pudú, 24, 76, 78, 217, 226, 253
Pudu puda. See pudú
Puerto Yeruá Formation. *See* Queguay Formation
pulses of occupation, 185, 269
Punta Bustamante, 219
Punta Gualicho, 42
Punta Pórfido, 81
Punta Santa Ana, 101, 182

quarry, 67, 79, 80, 81, 83, 84, 86, 87, 88, 89, 91, 92, 94, 100, 105, 109, 113, 124, 168, 193, 200, 255, 262, 270, 271, 272
quartz, 85, 88, 90, 93, 95, 105, 110, 113, 120, 163, 175, 224, 278
quartzite, 14, 17, 39, 44, 81, 82, 84, 88, 89, 90, 93, 95, 130, 166, 205, 242
Queguay Formation, 91, 113, 118, 126, 152, 153, 249
Quequén Grande River, 15, 118, 130, 203, 204, 207
Querandí, 28, 50, 74, 236, 238, 239, 276, 283

Reclus volcano, 148, 150
Recuerdos del Río Pinturas, 61
red ochre, 52, 88, 122, 123, 125, 136, 162, 170, 262
residential camps/settlements. *See* base camps
Reyes, Omar, 24, 50, 230
RGFO, 102, 106
    Potrok Aike type, 107
Rhea americana, 141. *See also* greater rhea
Rhea pennata. See lesser rhea
Rheidae, 151, 185
rhyolite, 14, 81, 88, 89, 90, 93, 102, 108, 109, 110, 113, 173, 200, 255, 272, 278
rhyolitic tuff, 103
Riesco Island, 100
Río Bote 1, 190, 258
Río Pinturas Basin, 61
rock art, 61, 64, 88, 145, 196, 201, 202, 216, 221, 222, 234, 278, 280
Rolling Pampa, 13, 31, 73, 112, 128, 159, 192, 208, 249, 266, 267
rounded cobbles, 17, 39, 44, 67, 81, 89, 90, 91, 94, 95, 97, 113, 126, 127, 163, 164, 167, 206, 207, 255, 279. *See also* seashore cobbles

Sacanana, 97, 275
Salado-Chadileuvú-Curacó, 11, 17, 57, 91, 95, 159, 170, 192, 198, 200, 261, 266, 278, 280
Salado River, 11, 13, 16, 28
Salado River Depression, 11, 13, 70, 205
Salesian missions, 244
Salitroso Basin, 269
San Gregorio, 77, 222
San Martin Lake Basin, 103, 145, 189, 196, 219, 220, 276
San Matías Gulf, 102, 224, 246, 275

San Sebastian Bay, 108, 109
Santa Cruz basin, 20, 21
Santa Cruz River, 18, 29, 41, 78, 100, 101, 105, 145, 189, 234, 249, 258
Sauce Grande River, 14, 15, 89, 90
scavenging, 193, 248
sea lions, 166, 167
sea mammals, 1, 111, 112, 165, 167, 183, 193, 229, 265
Sea of Otway, 61, 62, 226
seashore cobbles, 118, 163, 164, 167, 169, 193, 207, 270
secondary burial, 167, 170
secondary deposits, 14, 82, 88, 89, 91, 97, 102, 103, 105, 109, 110, 113, 153, 200, 262, 270
Selk'nam, 1, 47, 48, 244, 271, 277, 281
Seno Reloncavi, 229
shell beads, 161, 170, 205
shell middens, 29, 46, 47, 179, 182, 183, 207, 226, 229, 232
short-term residential camps, 126
short-time occupations, 224
shrub-steppe, 5
Sierras Bayas Group, 83, 86, 87, 89, 113, 118, 126, 132, 153, 159, 163, 164, 167, 168, 173, 192, 193, 207, 208, 209, 255, 270, 272, 277, 279
siliceous rocks, 114
silicified tuff, 103, 111
silicified wood, 105, 106, 109
Site BVS1, 226
Skyring Sea, 9
Smilodon, 78, 150, 253
social complexity, 157, 194, 266
social dimension, 67, 125, 129, 153, 157, 174, 179, 189, 199, 210, 212, 220, 230, 234, 241, 242, 248, 249, 255, 258, 261, 265, 266, 268, 269, 270, 271, 273, 274, 278, 282, 283
social interaction, 80, 153, 206, 266
Somuncurá plateau, 98, 137, 215, 218, 224, 249, 254, 275
South, 11, 14, 15, 90, 168, 204, 265, 266, 280
South America Missionary Society, 243
southeastern archipelagos, 182
southern fur seal, 73
southern sea lion, 73
southwestern archipelagos, 18, 19, 20, 24, 177, 178, 227
southwestern channels, 178
Spanish Conquest, 25, 276
spearthrowers. *See* hunting weapons, atlatl
Sphagnum magellanicum, 6
Spheniscus magellanicus, 77
Spinal District, 3, 13, 14, 17, 68, 113, 169, 170, 280
split stone industry, 39, 45
staging area, 144, 249, 251
Stern, Charles, 98, 148, 263
Stipa, 15, 16, 75

stone axes, 48, 214

Strait of Magellan, 7, 8, 9, 18, 20, 22, 29, 50, 61, 64, 77, 99, 101, 107, 111, 151, 158, 177, 178, 179, 181, 182, 222, 225, 226, 227, 232, 243, 244, 251, 255, 257, 281

Strobel plateau, 195, 263

subtropical gallery forest, 5, 113

tala, 13, 16, 68, 69, 113, 209, 255, 279

Tandilia, 11, 13, 28, 54, 82, 83, 113, 118, 122, 125, 126, 127, 128, 132, 152, 153, 154, 159, 163, 164, 167, 168, 191, 199, 200, 201, 202, 204, 205, 209, 238, 241, 242, 249, 253, 254, 255, 260, 261, 262, 267, 271, 272, 277, 279

Tandilia hills, 3, 4, 15, 68, 80, 81, 83, 84, 86, 87, 88, 89, 113, 121, 123, 132, 163, 173, 175, 200, 205, 238, 241, 253, 271

Tapera Moreira Locality, 94, 97, 128, 170, 196, 198, 210, 239

taphonomy, 25, 27, 37, 39, 42, 72, 149, 155, 167, 231, 249, 265

Tar Lake Basin, 103, 276

Tehuelche Indians, 237, 239, 277

Tertiary outcrops, 224

Tetraprothomo, 41

Tierra del Fuego, 1, 3, 5, 7, 9, 19, 20, 22, 28, 47, 50, 51, 61, 62, 64, 73, 75, 77, 93, 99, 101, 111, 112, 114, 132, 147, 151, 177, 178, 181, 182, 183, 221, 223, 224, 225, 231, 232, 234, 235, 243, 244, 251, 255, 263, 268, 269, 272, 274, 276, 277, 282, 283

Timbú, 1, 28, 235, 237, 238, 239, 276, 279

Torres, Luis M., 10, 31, 43, 45, 48, 49, 52, 68, 214

Tournouër, Andrés, 38

Traful Cave, 133, 139, 185

trampling marks, 37

Transversal Valleys, 16, 17, 43, 199, 202, 261, 279

Tres Arroyos 1, 22, 151, 177, 221, 224

tuff, 21, 90, 93, 110, 111, 121

Túmulo de Campana, 30, 51

Túnel, 51, 179, 181, 182

Túnel Cave, 142

Última Esperanza, 8, 21, 22, 132, 146, 149, 150, 158, 191, 195, 217, 231, 234, 246, 249, 251, 257, 258

Uruguay River, 1, 3, 4, 5, 10, 11, 12, 58, 60, 68, 69, 71, 72, 91, 112, 113, 128, 129, 159, 194, 210, 212, 214, 235, 236, 237, 238, 249, 262, 267, 268

Valdivian evergreen forest, 75

Ventania, 11, 13, 39, 41, 59, 168, 173, 201, 202, 204, 241, 261, 270, 279, 280

Ventania hills, 3, 4, 15, 68, 73, 81, 82, 83, 88, 89, 90, 113, 121, 132, 152, 163, 164, 168, 175, 200, 238, 255, 272

visits, 79, 215, 274, 275

Viuda Quenzana locality, 105, 234

Volcán Payún Matrú, 96

Weinmannia, 6

Wellington, 24

Weltgeschichte der Steinzeit, 53

western archipelagos, 5, 18, 22, 24, 74, 138, 218, 234, 263

western Pampa subregion, 4, 43, 68, 81, 82, 95, 117, 128, 132, 169, 170, 175, 177, 194, 199, 200, 202, 204, 241, 251, 257, 259, 270, 280

Western Pampean Dunefield, 17

Western Patagonia, 97, 99, 103, 140

wide-spectrum diet, 25

winter stress model, 195

Wissler, Clark, 50

wooden artifacts, 164, 192

Wulaia, 46, 47

xerophytic forest, 3, 13, 17, 68, 195, 196, 280

Yahgán, 47, 227, 281, 283

Yámana, 1. *See also* Yahgán

Younger Dryas, 7

Zea mays. See maize

Zeballos, Estanislao, 27, 28, 29, 30, 31

Zone of Morros, 107

Zurdo Basin, 244

www.ingramcontent.com/pod-product-compliance
Lightning Source LLC
Chambersburg PA
CBHW080206271224
19492CB00008B/233